VOLUME 3

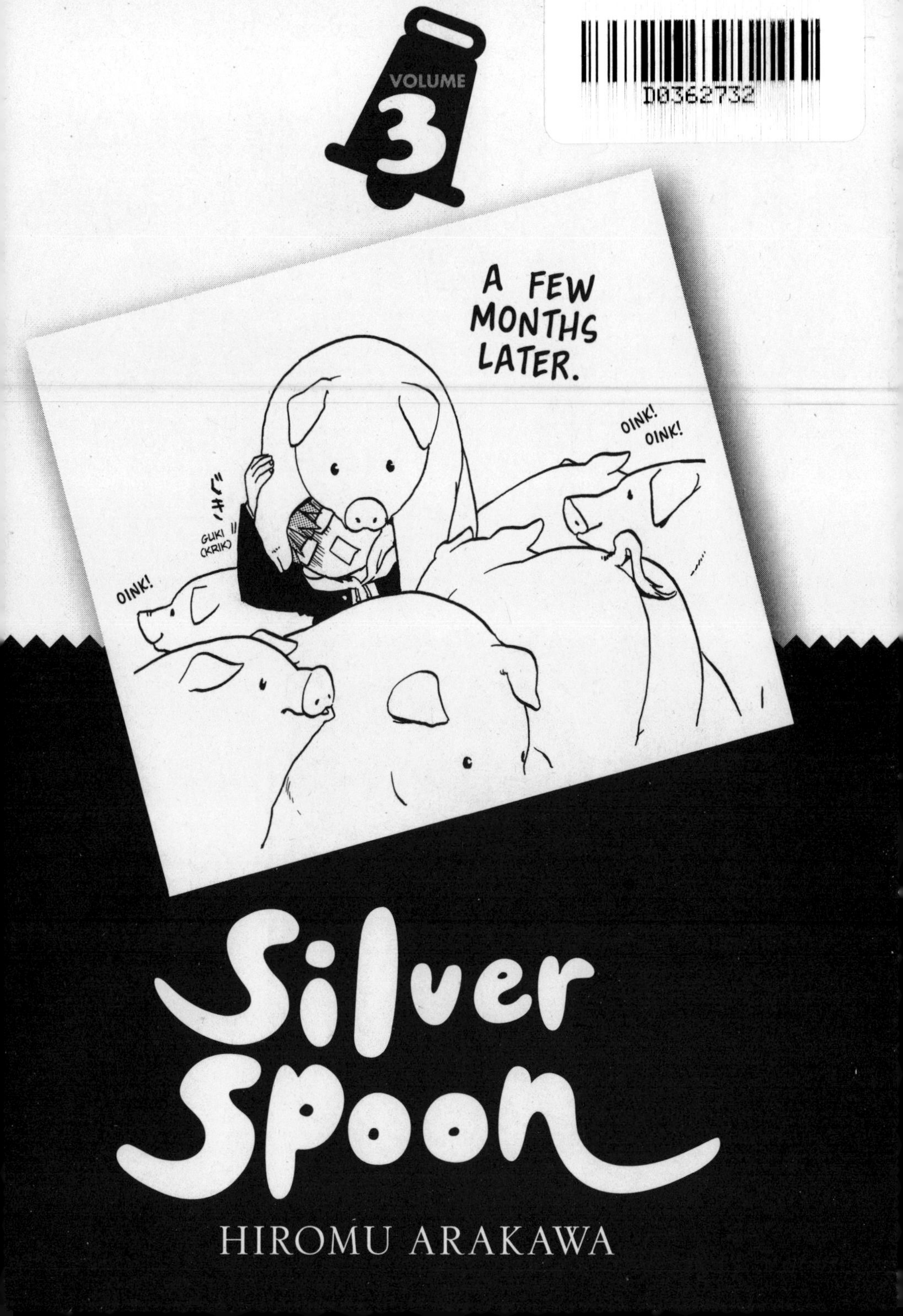
A FEW MONTHS LATER.
OINK! OINK!
GUKI (KRIK)
OINK!

Silver Spoon

HIROMU ARAKAWA

STORY & CHARACTERS

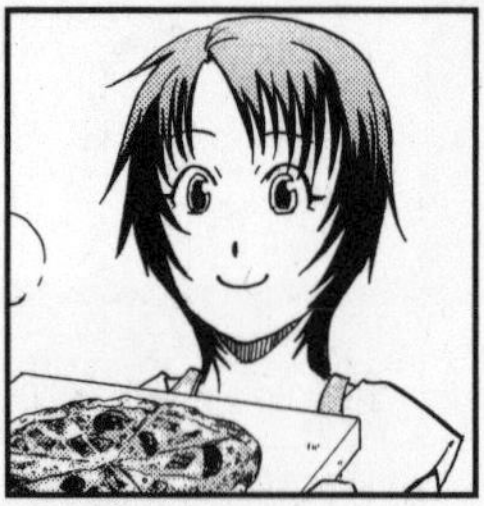

AKI MIKAGE

A first-year student at Ooezo Agricultural High School, enrolled in the Dairy Science Program. Her family keeps cows and horses. Applied to Ezo AG because she's thinking about carrying on the family business.

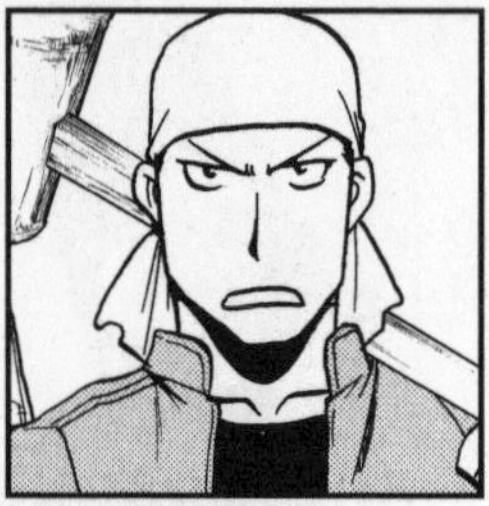

ICHIROU KOMABA

A first-year student at Ooezo Agricultural High School, enrolled in the Dairy Science Program. Plans on taking over the family farm after graduation. Member of the baseball team.

YUUGO HACHIKEN

A first-year student at Ooezo Agricultural High School, enrolled in the Dairy Science Program. A city kid from Sapporo who got in through the general entrance exam. His reason for applying? Because there's a dorm...

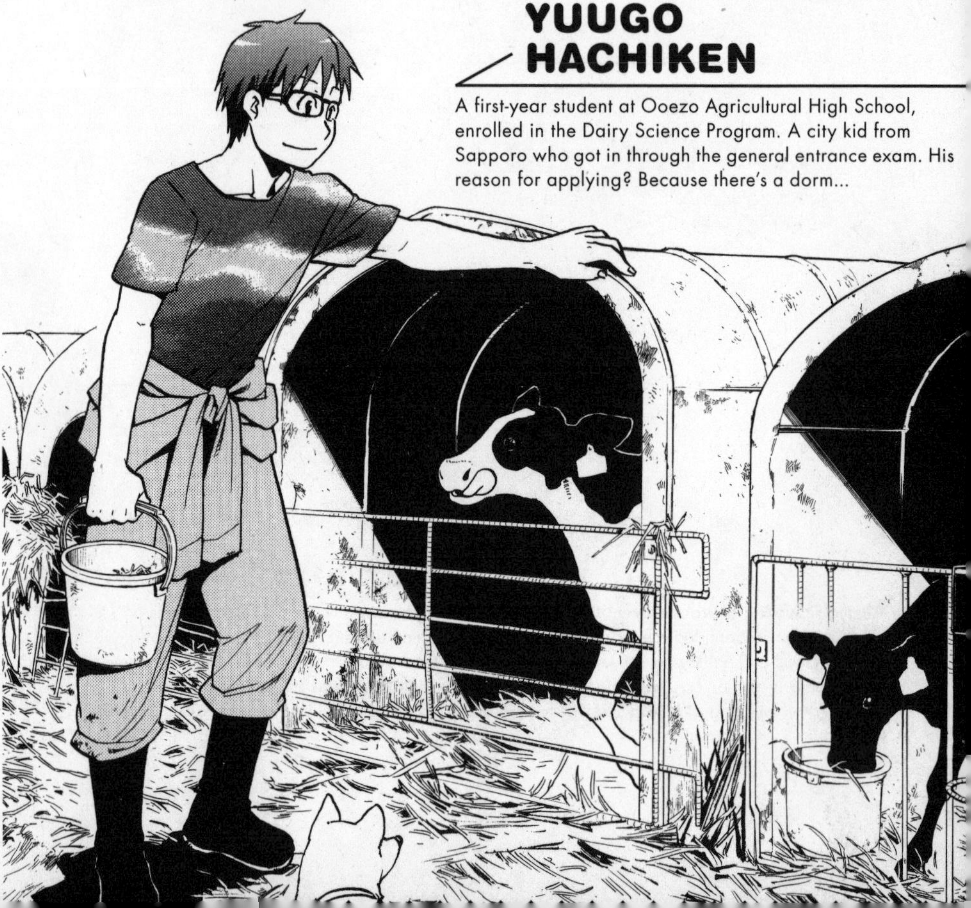

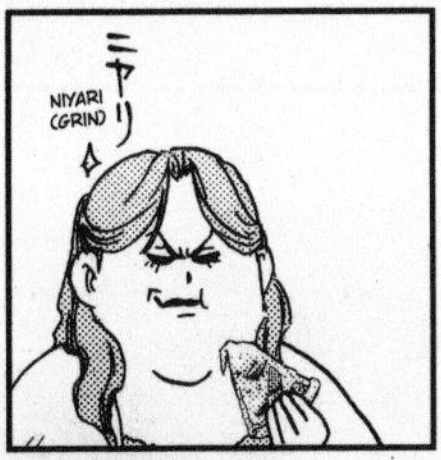
ニヤリ
NIYARI (GRIN)

TAMAKO INADA

A first-year student at Ooezo Agricultural High School, enrolled in the Dairy Science Program. A complete enigma.

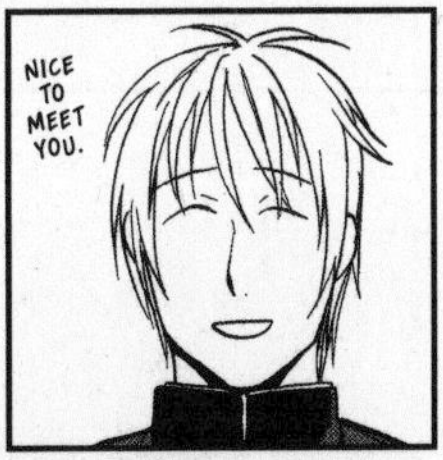
NICE TO MEET YOU.

SHINNOSUKE AIKAWA

A first-year student at Ooezo Agricultural High School, enrolled in the Dairy Science Program. His dream is to become a veterinarian.

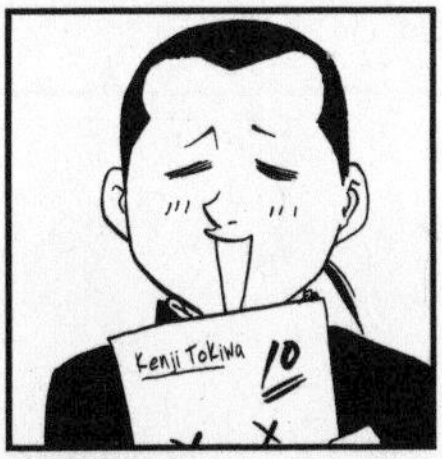

KEIJI TOKIWA

A first-year student at Ooezo Agricultural High School, enrolled in the Dairy Science Program. Son of chicken farmers. Awful at academics.

THE MIKAGE FAMILY

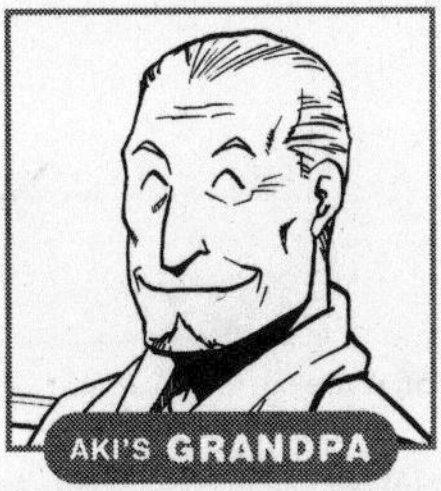
AKI'S GRANDPA

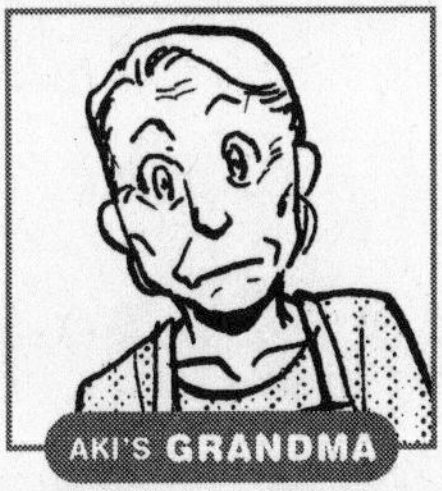
AKI'S GRANDMA

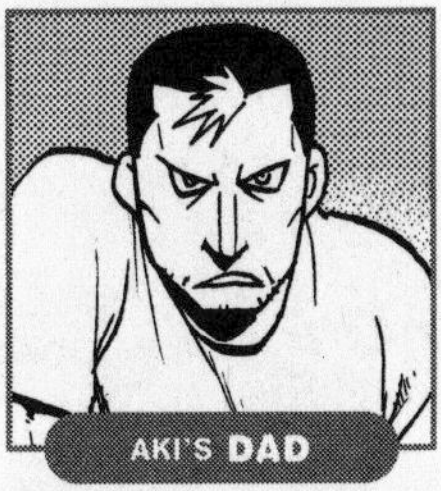
AKI'S DAD

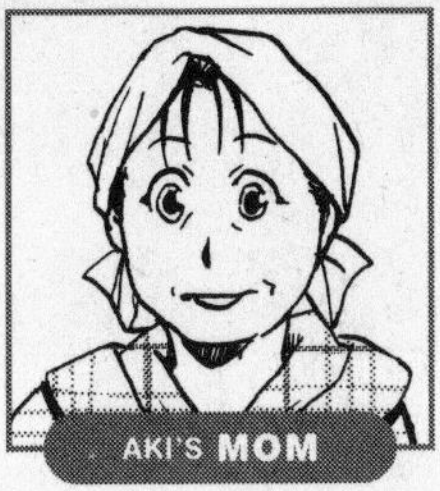
AKI'S MOM

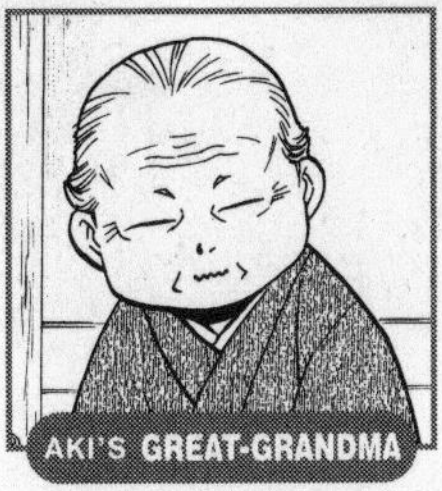
AKI'S GREAT-GRANDMA

The Story Thus Far:

After discovering a strange oven, the task of organizing a school-wide pizza party falls on Hachiken's shoulders. With everyone's (sometimes overenthusiastic) help, the pizza experiment is a delicious and satisfying success. And so the first term of the school year comes to an end, and summer vacation begins! Reluctant to go home, Hachiken jumps at Aki's invitation and finds himself working at Mikage Ranch for the break. But of course, city kid Hachiken is in for more than he bargained for!!!

CONTENTS

Chapter 18: Tale of Summer ⑧ 5

Chapter 19: Tale of Summer ⑨ 25

Chapter 20: Tale of Summer ⑩ 44

Chapter 21: Tale of Summer ⑪ 67

Chapter 22: Tale of Summer ⑫ 87

Chapter 23: Tale of Summer ⑬ 107

Chapter 24: Tale of Summer ⑭ 127

Chapter 25: Tale of Summer ⑮ 145

Chapter 26: Tale of Summer ⑯ 165

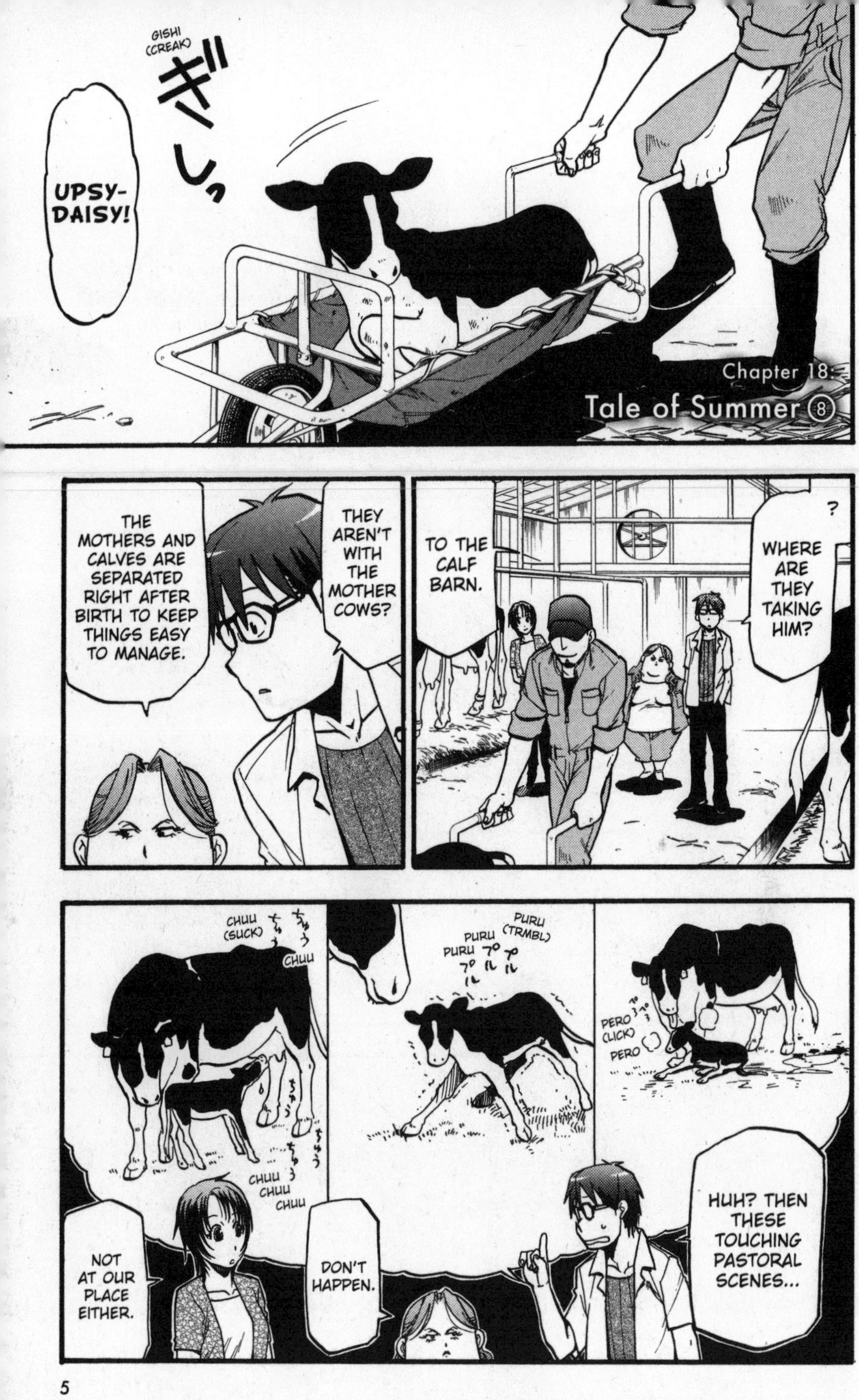
GISHI (CREAK)
ぎしっ
UPSY-DAISY!
Chapter 18:
Tale of Summer ⑧
?
WHERE ARE THEY TAKING HIM?
TO THE CALF BARN.
THEY AREN'T WITH THE MOTHER COWS?
THE MOTHERS AND CALVES ARE SEPARATED RIGHT AFTER BIRTH TO KEEP THINGS EASY TO MANAGE.
PERO (LICK)
PERO
PURU (TRMBL)
PURU
PURU
CHUU (SUCK)
CHUU
CHUU CHUU CHUU
HUH? THEN THESE TOUCHING PASTORAL SCENES...
DON'T HAPPEN.
NOT AT OUR PLACE EITHER.

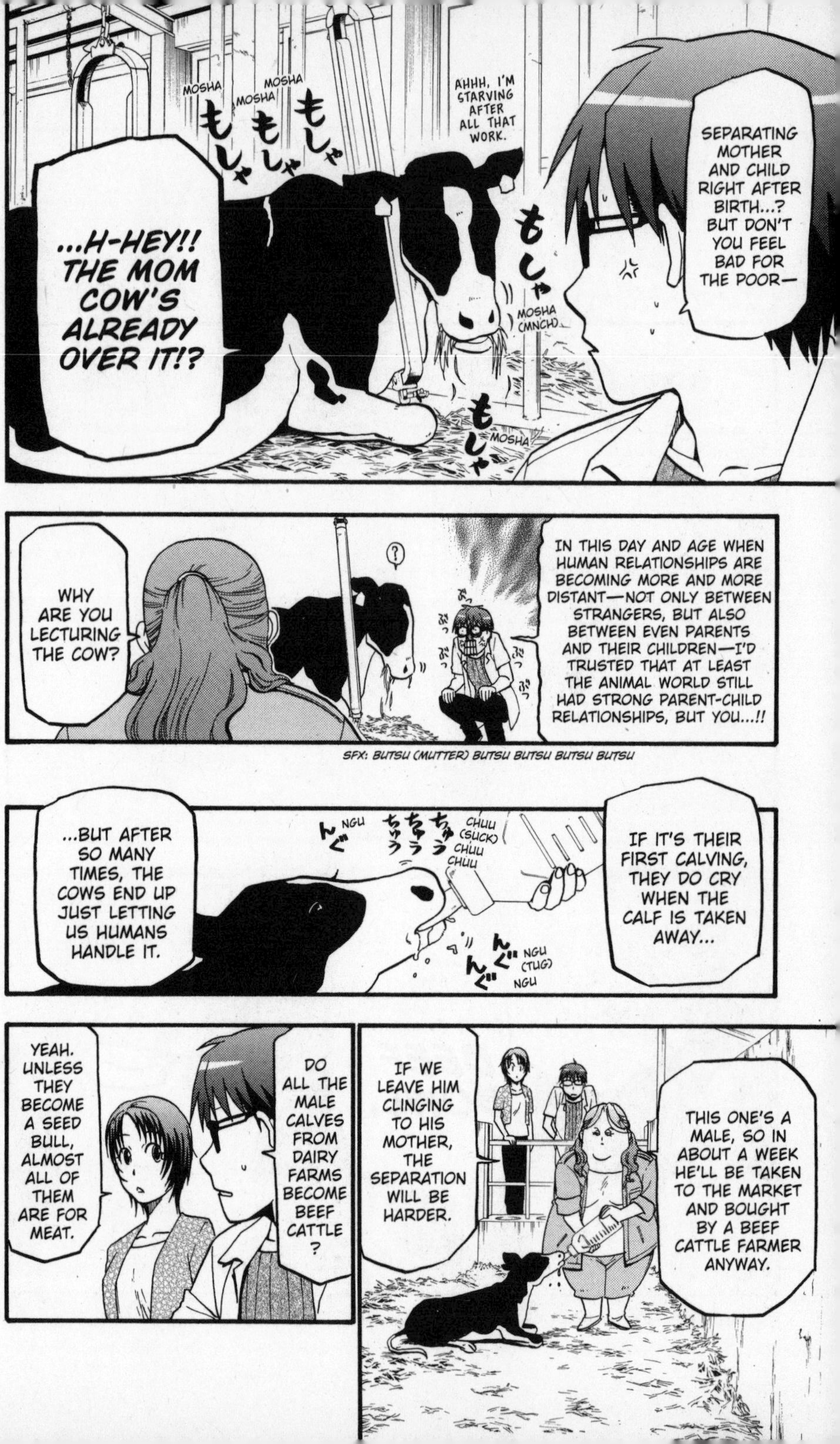
SEPARATING MOTHER AND CHILD RIGHT AFTER BIRTH...? BUT DON'T YOU FEEL BAD FOR THE POOR—
AHHH, I'M STARVING AFTER ALL THAT WORK.
もしゃ MOSHA (MNCH)
もしゃ MOSHA
もしゃ MOSHA
もしゃ MOSHA
もしゃ MOSHA
...H-HEY!! THE MOM COW'S ALREADY OVER IT!?
IN THIS DAY AND AGE WHEN HUMAN RELATIONSHIPS ARE BECOMING MORE AND MORE DISTANT—NOT ONLY BETWEEN STRANGERS, BUT ALSO BETWEEN EVEN PARENTS AND THEIR CHILDREN—I'D TRUSTED THAT AT LEAST THE ANIMAL WORLD STILL HAD STRONG PARENT-CHILD RELATIONSHIPS, BUT YOU...!!
?
WHY ARE YOU LECTURING THE COW?
SFX: BUTSU (MUTTER) BUTSU BUTSU BUTSU BUTSU
IF IT'S THEIR FIRST CALVING, THEY DO CRY WHEN THE CALF IS TAKEN AWAY...
ちゅう CHUU (SUCK) ちゅう CHUU ちゅう CHUU
んぐ NGU (TUG) んぐ NGU
んぐ NGU
...BUT AFTER SO MANY TIMES, THE COWS END UP JUST LETTING US HUMANS HANDLE IT.
THIS ONE'S A MALE, SO IN ABOUT A WEEK HE'LL BE TAKEN TO THE MARKET AND BOUGHT BY A BEEF CATTLE FARMER ANYWAY.
IF WE LEAVE HIM CLINGING TO HIS MOTHER, THE SEPARATION WILL BE HARDER.
DO ALL THE MALE CALVES FROM DAIRY FARMS BECOME BEEF CATTLE?
YEAH. UNLESS THEY BECOME A SEED BULL, ALMOST ALL OF THEM ARE FOR MEAT.

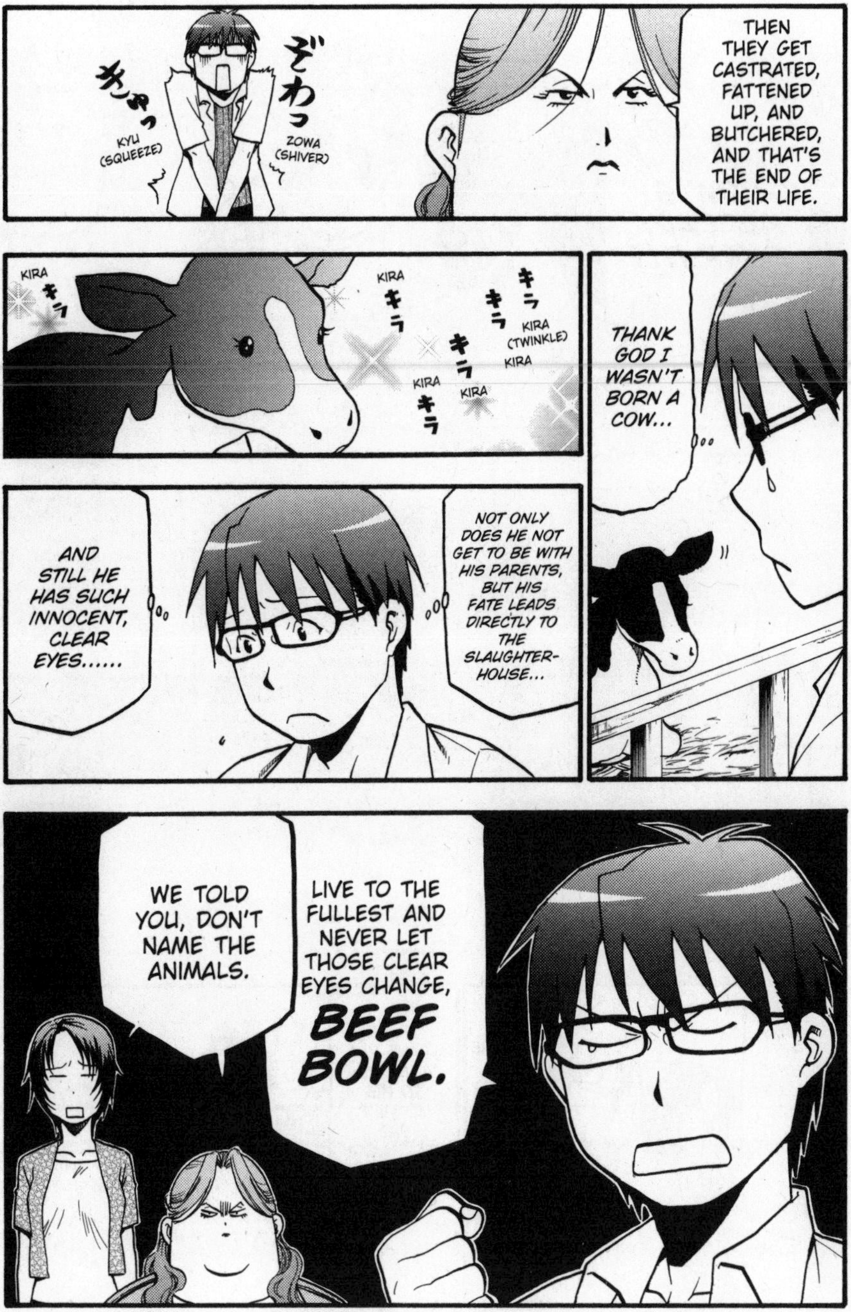

THEN THEY GET CASTRATED, FATTENED UP, AND BUTCHERED, AND THAT'S THE END OF THEIR LIFE.
ぞわっ
ZOWA (SHIVER)
きゅっ
KYU (SQUEEZE)
THANK GOD I WASN'T BORN A COW...
キラ
KIRA (TWINKLE)
キラ
KIRA
キラ
KIRA
キラ
KIRA
キラ
KIRA
NOT ONLY DOES HE NOT GET TO BE WITH HIS PARENTS, BUT HIS FATE LEADS DIRECTLY TO THE SLAUGHTER-HOUSE...
AND STILL HE HAS SUCH INNOCENT, CLEAR EYES......
LIVE TO THE FULLEST AND NEVER LET THOSE CLEAR EYES CHANGE, BEEF BOWL.
WE TOLD YOU, DON'T NAME THE ANIMALS.

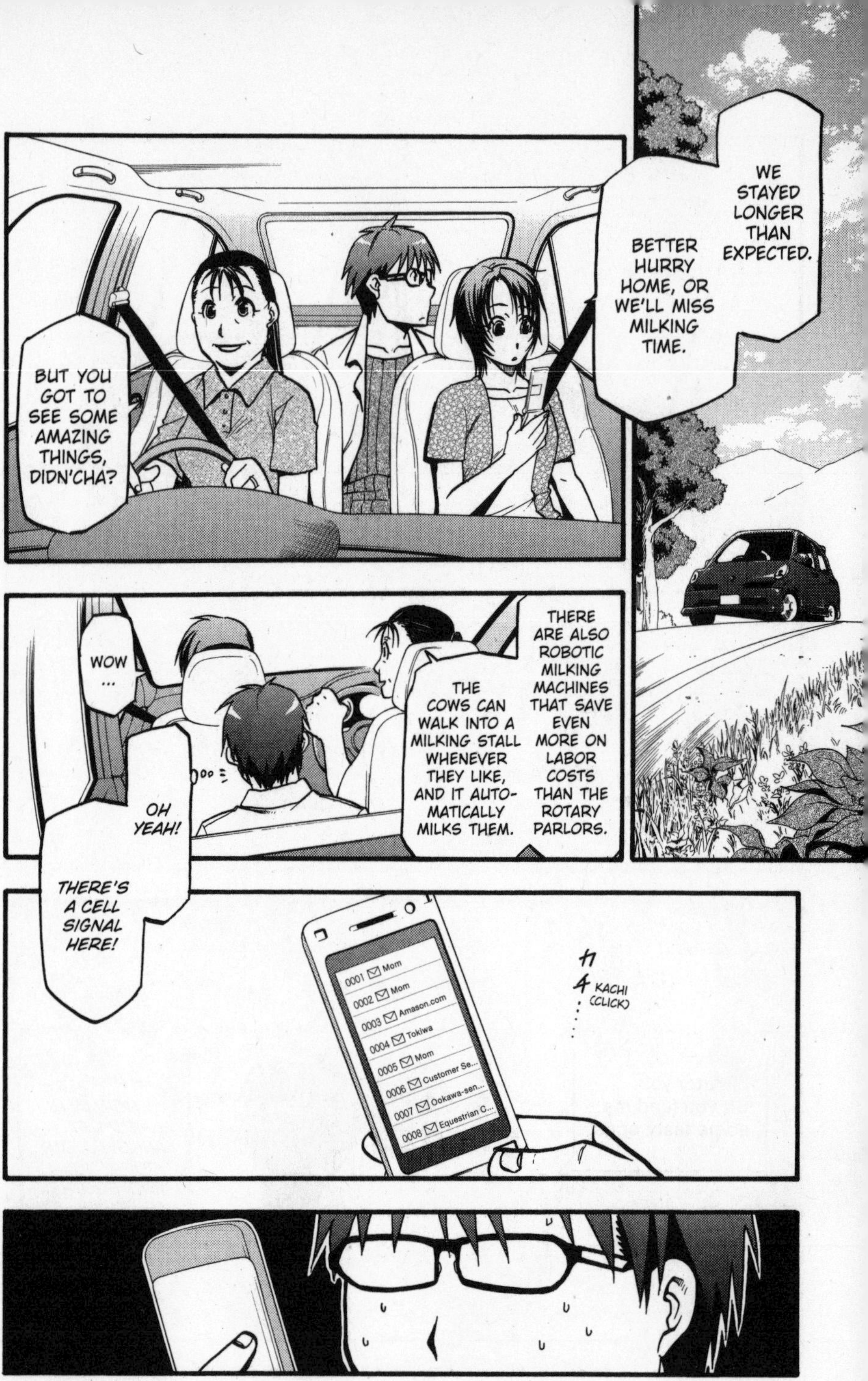
WE STAYED LONGER THAN EXPECTED.
BETTER HURRY HOME, OR WE'LL MISS MILKING TIME.
BUT YOU GOT TO SEE SOME AMAZING THINGS, DIDN'CHA?
THERE ARE ALSO ROBOTIC MILKING MACHINES THAT SAVE EVEN MORE ON LABOR COSTS THAN THE ROTARY PARLORS.
THE COWS CAN WALK INTO A MILKING STALL WHENEVER THEY LIKE, AND IT AUTO-MATICALLY MILKS THEM.
WOW ...
OH YEAH!
THERE'S A CELL SIGNAL HERE!
カチ
KACHI (CLICK)
0001 Mom
0002 Mom
0003 Amason.com
0004 Tokiwa
0005 Mom
0006 Customer Se...
0007 Ookawa-sen...
0008 Equestrian C...

From Mom
Sub
You're working at a friend's home? Is it at a farmhouse?
KACHI
カチ
KACHI
カチ…
From Mom
Sub
If they're going to be looking after you, I'd like to give them a call.
KACHI
カチ……
YOU DON'T NEED TO!!
SEND
SFX: KACHI KACHI KACHI KACHI
WHAT GIVES…? ONE REPLY FROM ME, AND YOU SUDDENLY PUT ON YOUR "MOM" FACE…?
HAAAH…
SFX: KACHI KACHI KACHI
From Tokiwa
Sub
I totes don't get the math homework <(^o^)>
Teach it to me when school starts!!
Tokiwa
KACHI
カチ……
…NORMALLY I'D GET ANNOYED, BUT TODAY YOUR TEXT SOOTHES ME, TOKIWA…!!
I'll tutor you. So you feed me some tasty eggs.
KACHI
KACHI
KACHI
AND… SENT.

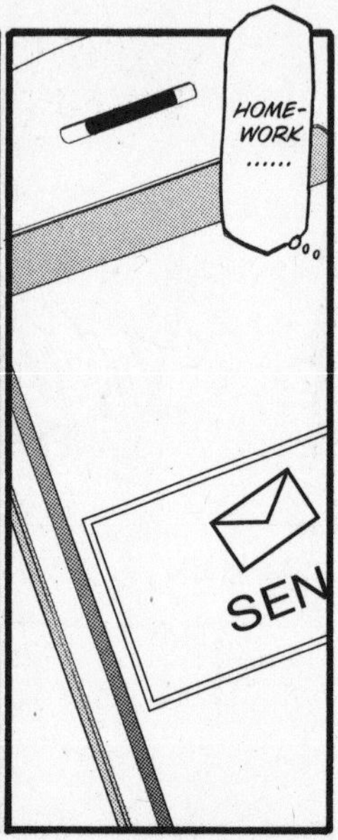
HOME-WORK ......
SEN

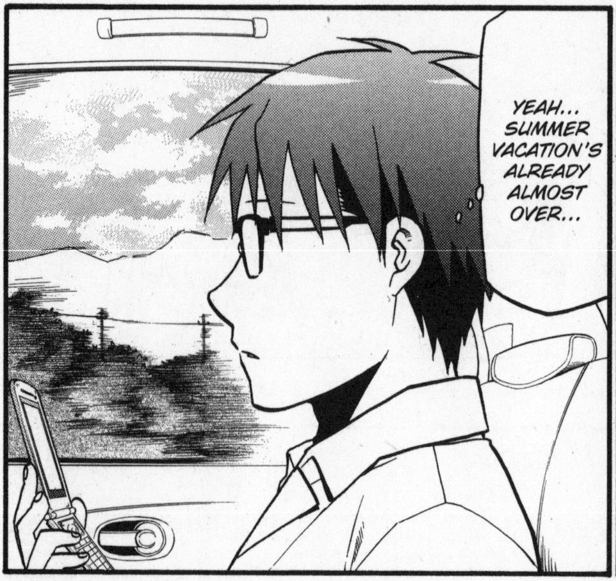
YEAH... SUMMER VACATION'S ALREADY ALMOST OVER...

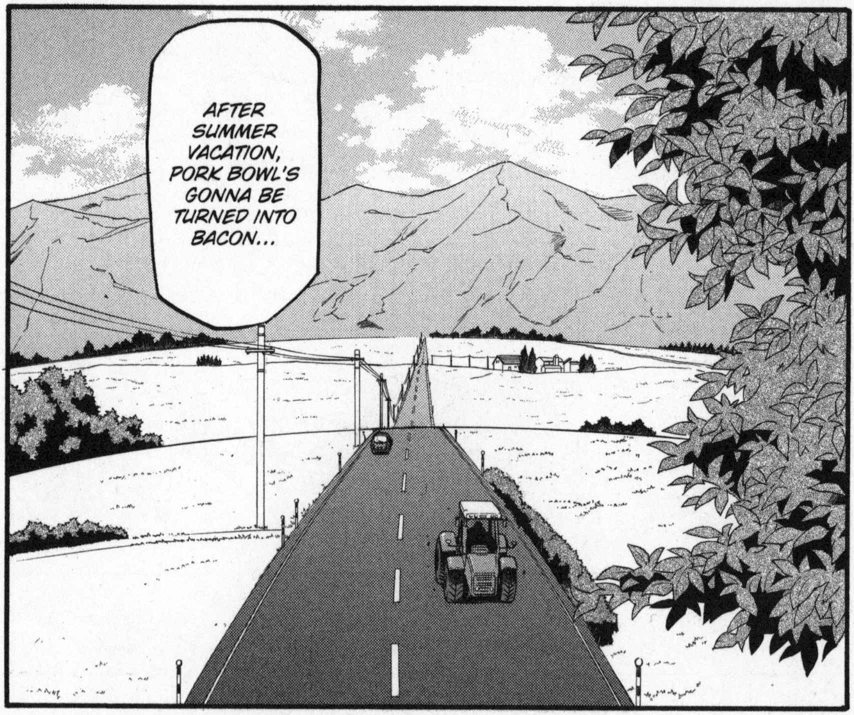
AFTER SUMMER VACATION, PORK BOWL'S GONNA BE TURNED INTO BACON...

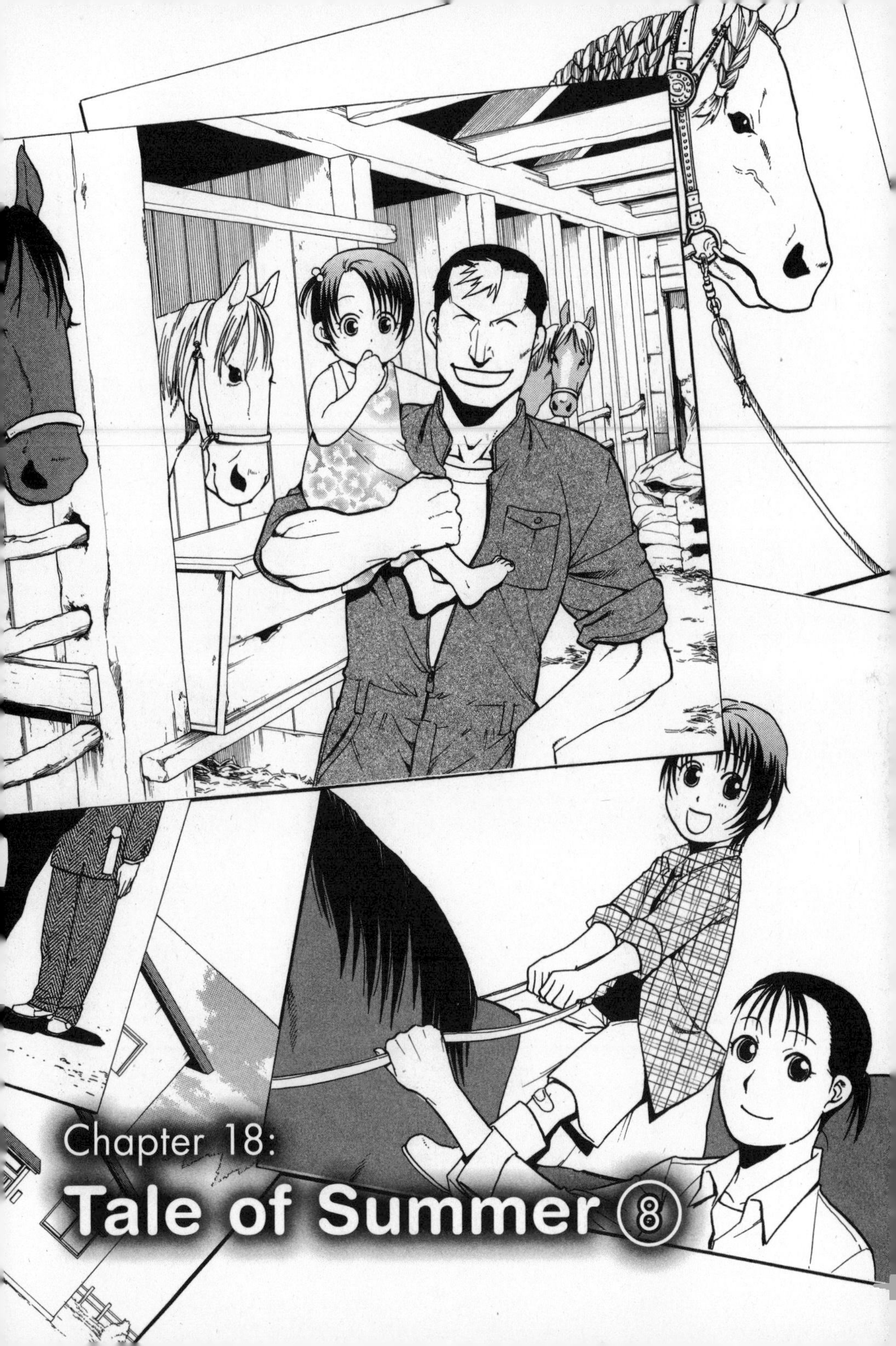
Chapter 18:
Tale of Summer ⑧

DO WE NAME OUR LIVESTOCK WITH LOVE, YOU SAY?
WELL, EACH DAIRY COW HAS A PEDIGREE DOCUMENT AND AN INDIVIDUAL NAME, BUT THE NAMES ARE PRETTY UNEMOTIONAL.
Certificate of Pedigree
0126 1
THIS IS THE CERTIFI-CATE.
Miss Sunday Shogakuk
Sire: Weekly Sunday
13501681 100%
Sunday Super Kanda Ji 100%
YOU TAKE ONE WORD FROM THE SIRE'S NAME...
...AND ANOTHER WORD FROM THE DAM'S NAME, AND ADD ONE WORD OF YOUR OWN, THAT'S ALL. THAT'S A COMMON WAY TO DO IT.
14612530C
Dam: Miss Big
141865708A
Original BW
2507097A

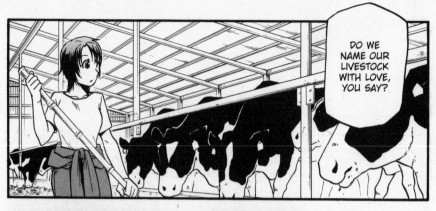

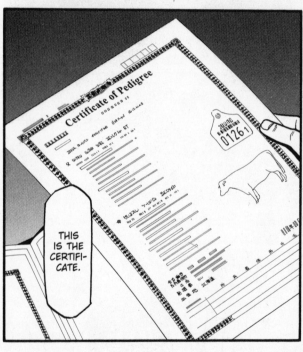

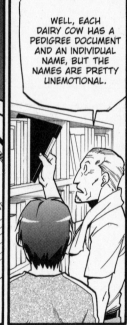

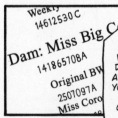

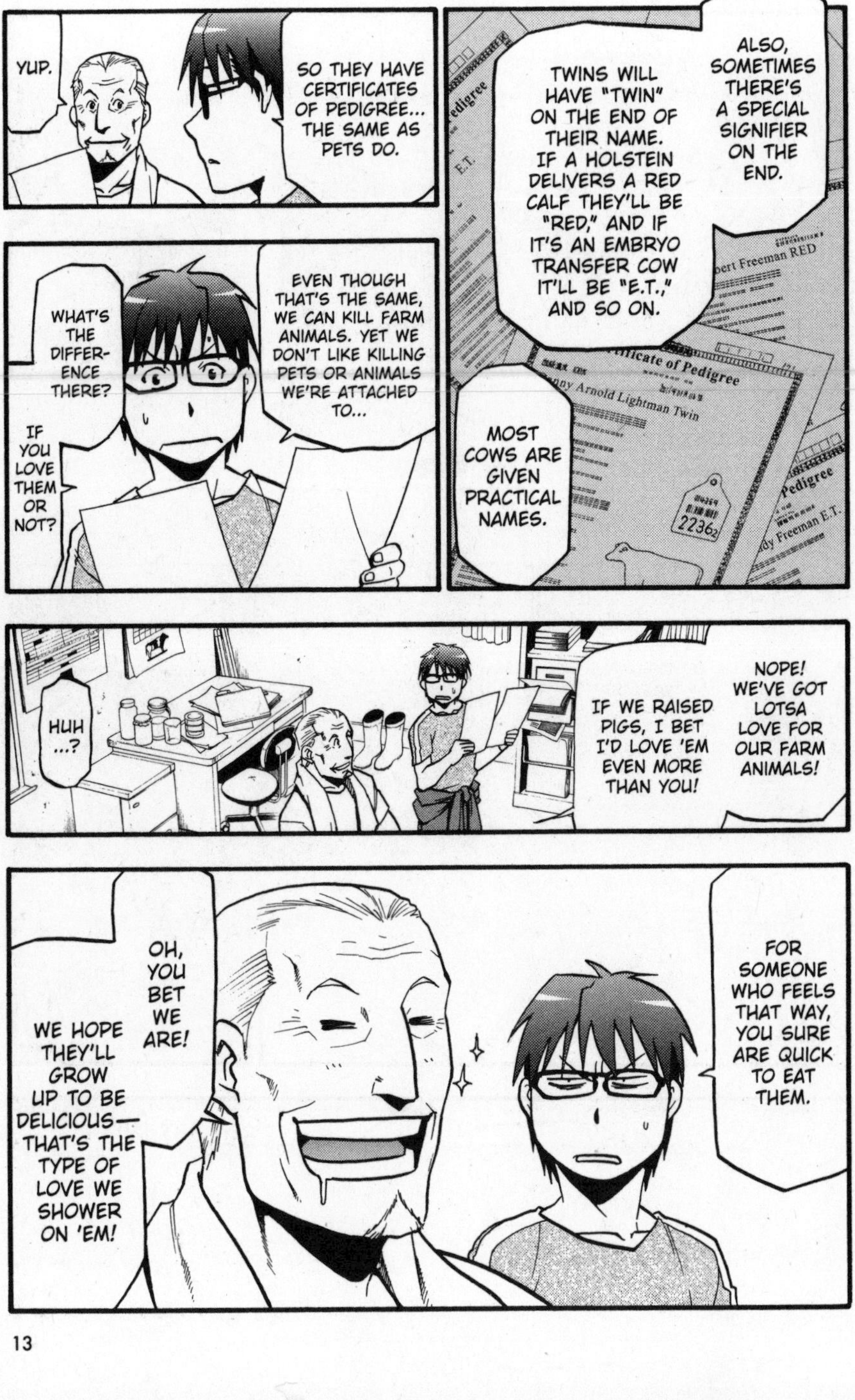
ALSO, SOMETIMES THERE'S A SPECIAL SIGNIFIER ON THE END.
TWINS WILL HAVE "TWIN" ON THE END OF THEIR NAME. IF A HOLSTEIN DELIVERS A RED CALF THEY'LL BE "RED," AND IF IT'S AN EMBRYO TRANSFER COW IT'LL BE "E.T.," AND SO ON.
MOST COWS ARE GIVEN PRACTICAL NAMES.
SO THEY HAVE CERTIFICATES OF PEDIGREE... THE SAME AS PETS DO.
YUP.
EVEN THOUGH THAT'S THE SAME, WE CAN KILL FARM ANIMALS. YET WE DON'T LIKE KILLING PETS OR ANIMALS WE'RE ATTACHED TO...
WHAT'S THE DIFFERENCE THERE?
IF YOU LOVE THEM OR NOT?
NOPE! WE'VE GOT LOTSA LOVE FOR OUR FARM ANIMALS!
IF WE RAISED PIGS, I BET I'D LOVE 'EM EVEN MORE THAN YOU!
HUH ...?
FOR SOMEONE WHO FEELS THAT WAY, YOU SURE ARE QUICK TO EAT THEM.
OH, YOU BET WE ARE!
WE HOPE THEY'LL GROW UP TO BE DELICIOUS—THAT'S THE TYPE OF LOVE WE SHOWER ON 'EM!

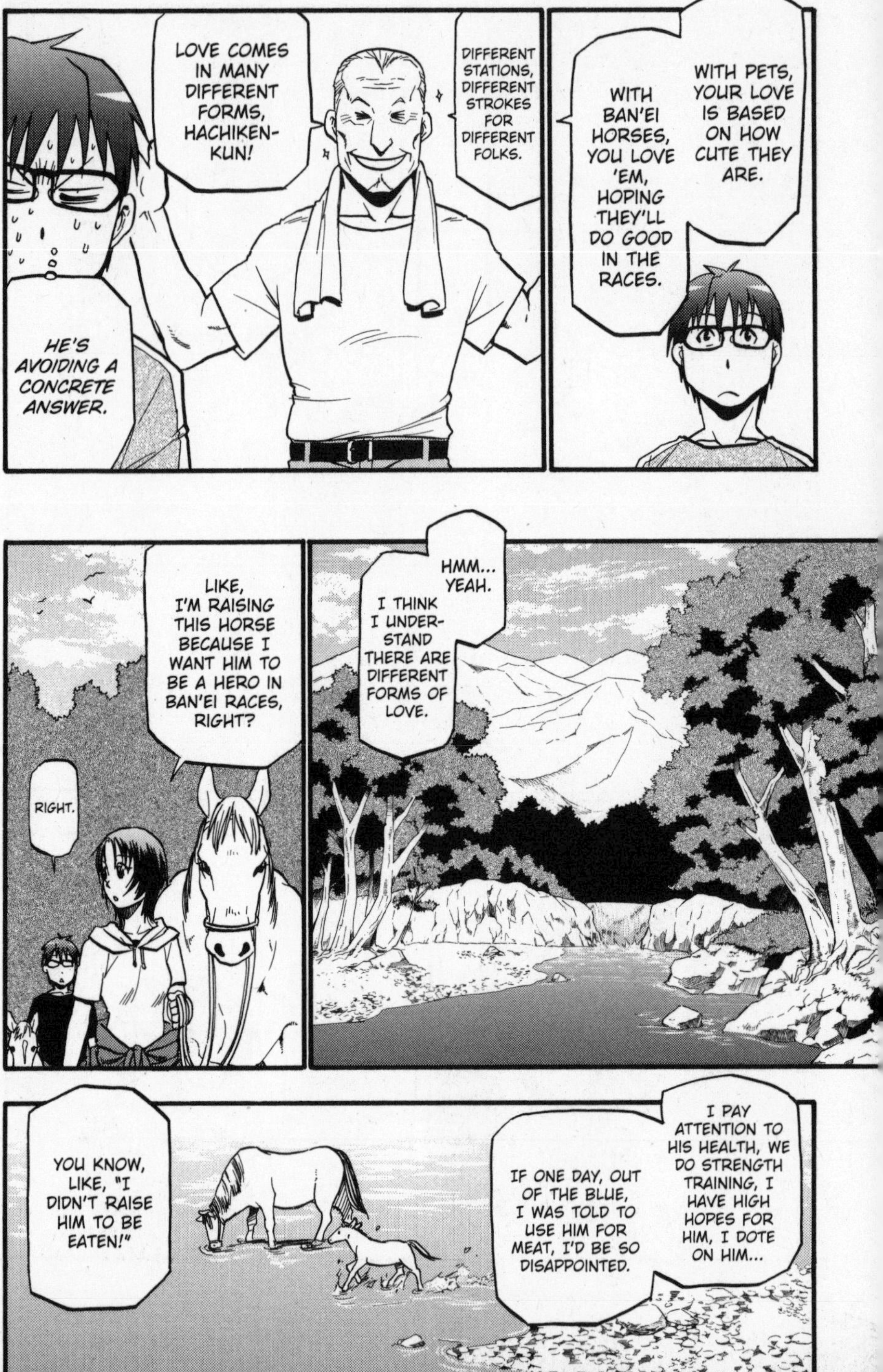
WITH PETS, YOUR LOVE IS BASED ON HOW CUTE THEY ARE.
WITH BAN'EI HORSES, YOU LOVE 'EM, HOPING THEY'LL DO GOOD IN THE RACES.
DIFFERENT STATIONS, DIFFERENT STROKES FOR DIFFERENT FOLKS.
LOVE COMES IN MANY DIFFERENT FORMS, HACHIKEN-KUN!
HE'S AVOIDING A CONCRETE ANSWER.
HMM... YEAH.
I THINK I UNDER-STAND THERE ARE DIFFERENT FORMS OF LOVE.
LIKE, I'M RAISING THIS HORSE BECAUSE I WANT HIM TO BE A HERO IN BAN'EI RACES, RIGHT?
RIGHT.
I PAY ATTENTION TO HIS HEALTH, WE DO STRENGTH TRAINING, I HAVE HIGH HOPES FOR HIM, I DOTE ON HIM...
IF ONE DAY, OUT OF THE BLUE, I WAS TOLD TO USE HIM FOR MEAT, I'D BE SO DISAPPOINTED.
YOU KNOW, LIKE, "I DIDN'T RAISE HIM TO BE EATEN!"

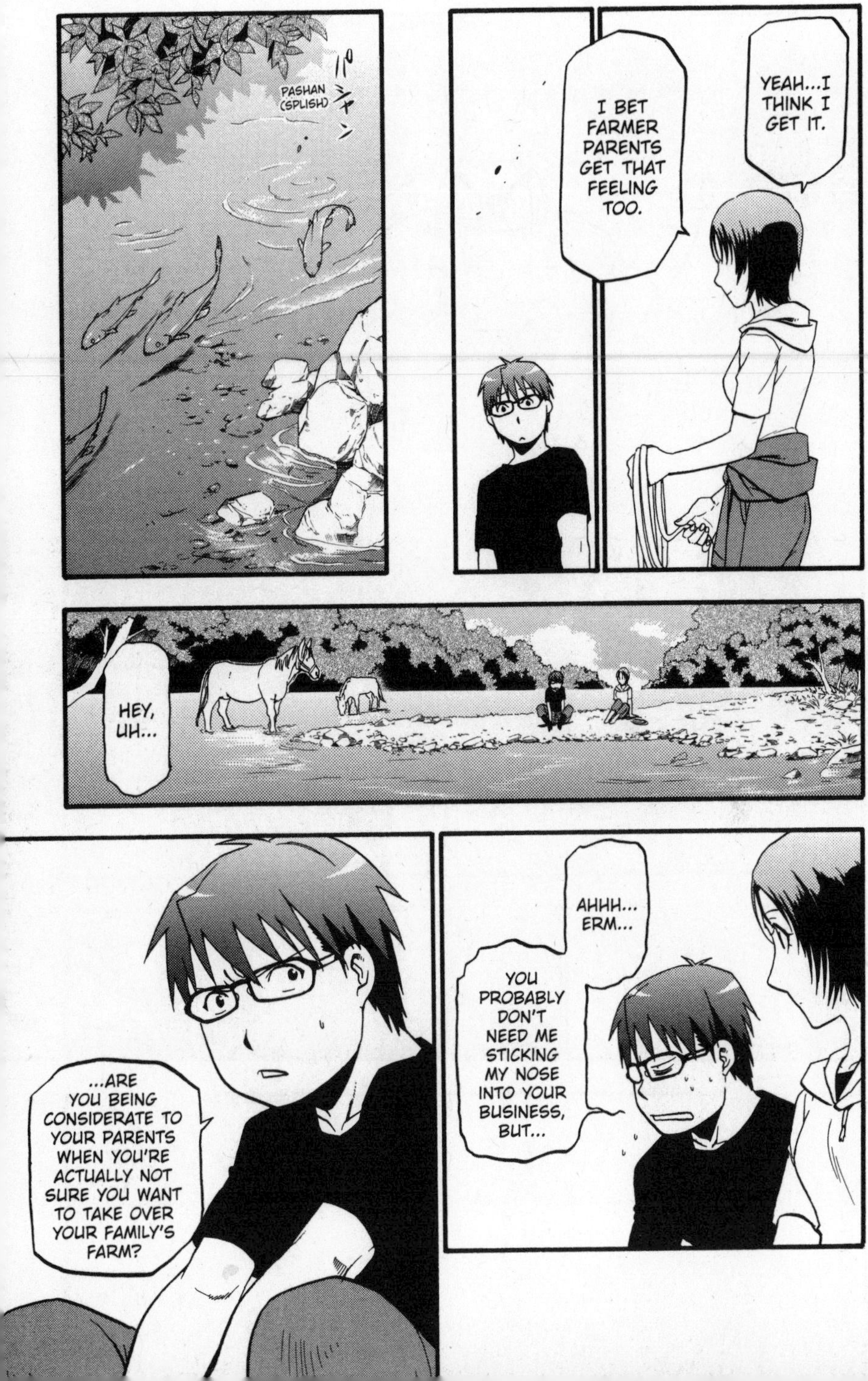
YEAH...I THINK I GET IT.
I BET FARMER PARENTS GET THAT FEELING TOO.
パシャン
PASHAN (SPLISH)
HEY, UH...
AHHH... ERM...
YOU PROBABLY DON'T NEED ME STICKING MY NOSE INTO YOUR BUSINESS, BUT...
...ARE YOU BEING CONSIDERATE TO YOUR PARENTS WHEN YOU'RE ACTUALLY NOT SURE YOU WANT TO TAKE OVER YOUR FAMILY'S FARM?

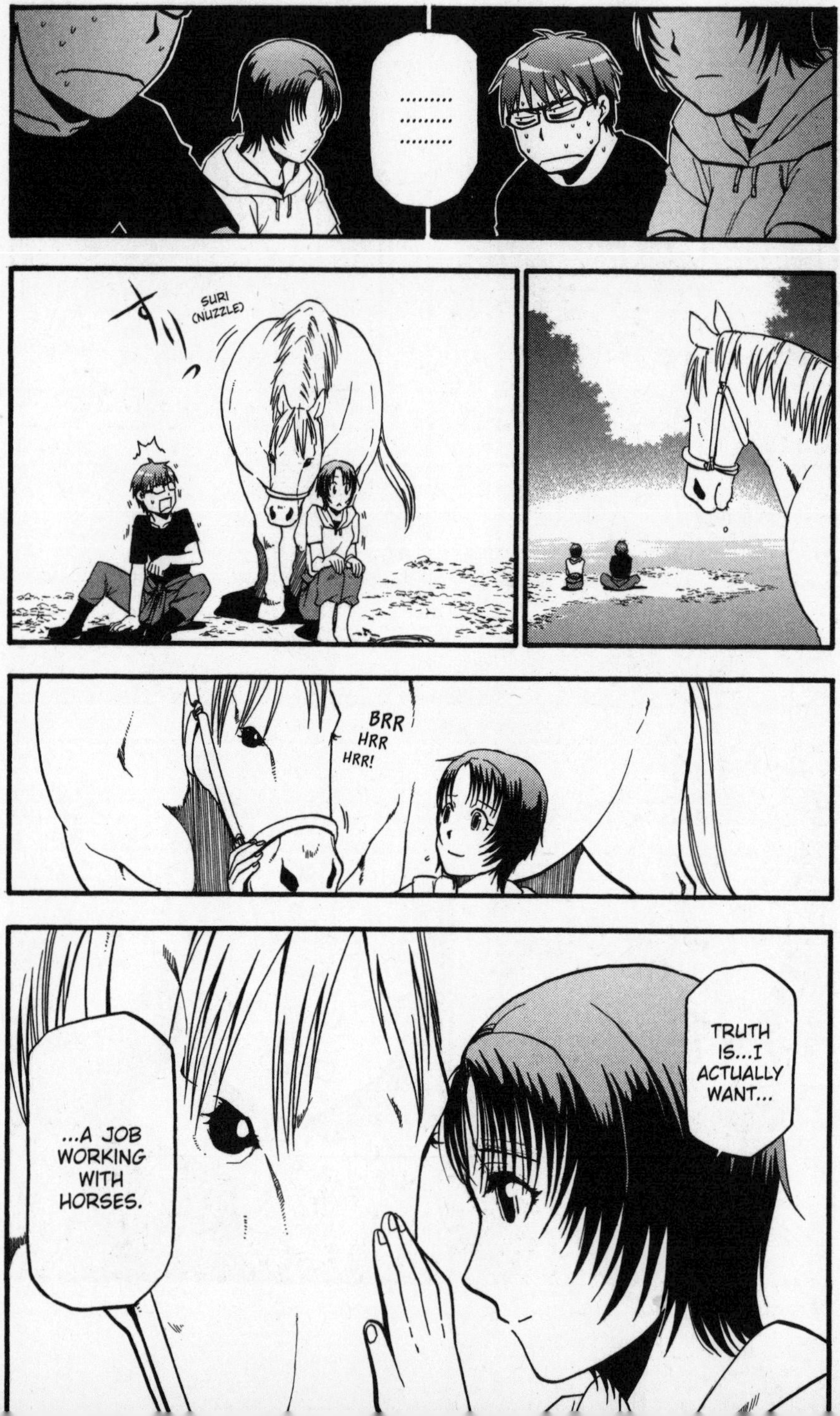
....
....
....
SURI (NUZZLE)
BRR HRR HRR!
TRUTH IS...I ACTUALLY WANT...
...A JOB WORKING WITH HORSES.

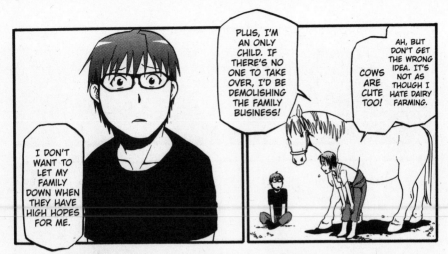

AH, BUT DON'T GET THE WRONG IDEA. IT'S NOT AS THOUGH I HATE DAIRY FARMING.
COWS ARE CUTE TOO!
PLUS, I'M AN ONLY CHILD. IF THERE'S NO ONE TO TAKE OVER, I'D BE DEMOLISHING THE FAMILY BUSINESS!
I DON'T WANT TO LET MY FAMILY DOWN WHEN THEY HAVE HIGH HOPES FOR ME.
I GUESS WHEN IT COMES TO WANTING TO MEET YOUR FAMILY'S EXPECTATIONS, I'M IN THE SAME BOAT AS YOU.
...IT'S NOT THE SAME.
MIKAGE, YOU TOLD ME THAT I HAD TO COMMUNICATE WITH MY PARENTS PROPERLY, REMEMBER?
BUT YOU HAVEN'T TOLD YOUR PARENTS HOW YOU REALLY FEEL EITHER, HAVE YOU?

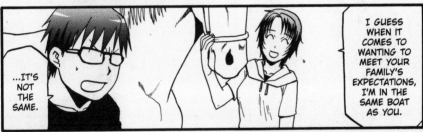

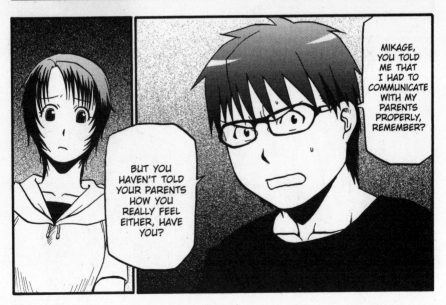

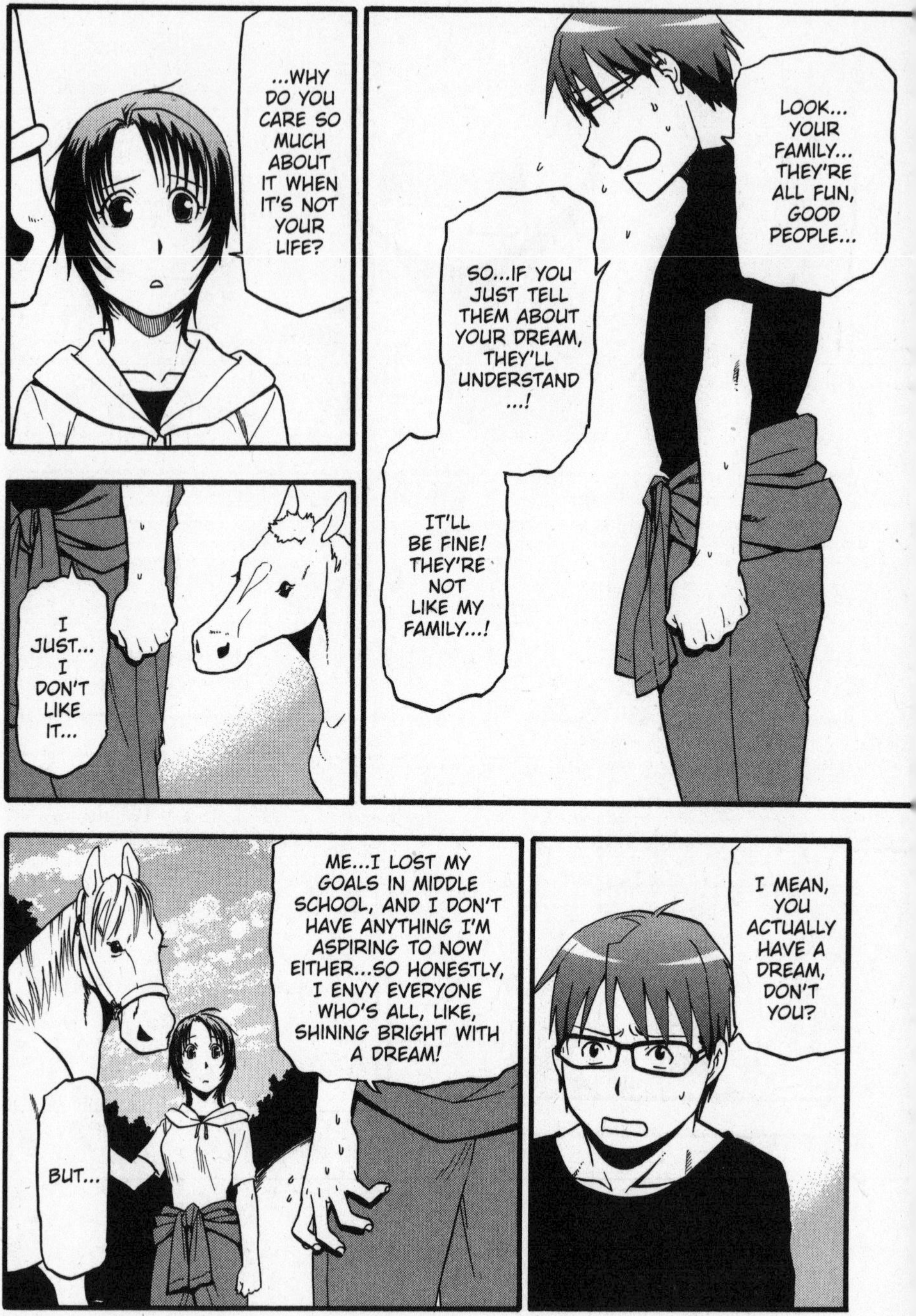
LOOK... YOUR FAMILY... THEY'RE ALL FUN, GOOD PEOPLE...
SO...IF YOU JUST TELL THEM ABOUT YOUR DREAM, THEY'LL UNDERSTAND ...!
IT'LL BE FINE! THEY'RE NOT LIKE MY FAMILY...!
...WHY DO YOU CARE SO MUCH ABOUT IT WHEN IT'S NOT YOUR LIFE?
I JUST... I DON'T LIKE IT...
I MEAN, YOU ACTUALLY HAVE A DREAM, DON'T YOU?
ME...I LOST MY GOALS IN MIDDLE SCHOOL, AND I DON'T HAVE ANYTHING I'M ASPIRING TO NOW EITHER...SO HONESTLY, I ENVY EVERYONE WHO'S ALL, LIKE, SHINING BRIGHT WITH A DREAM!
BUT...

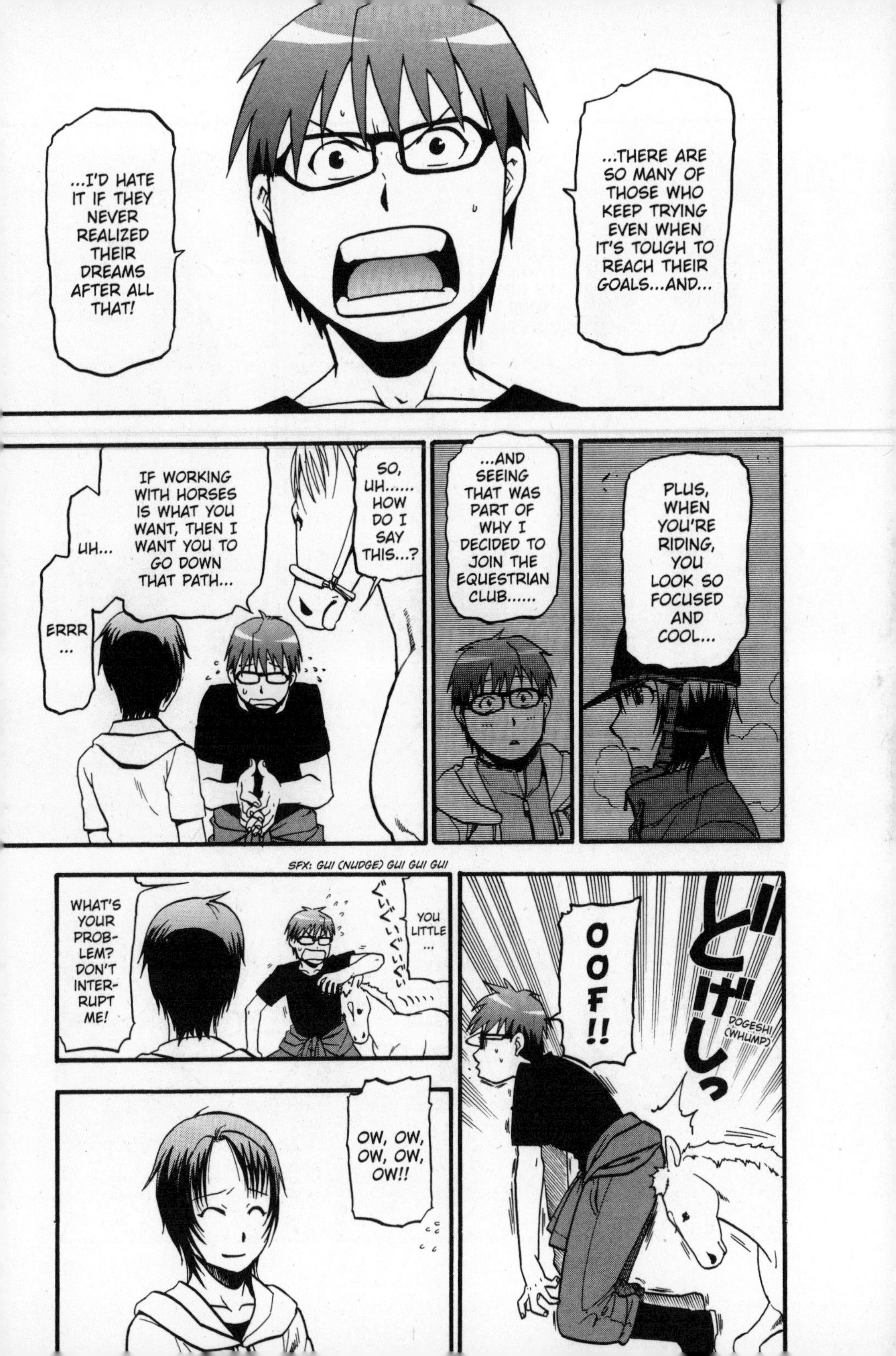
...THERE ARE SO MANY OF THOSE WHO KEEP TRYING EVEN WHEN IT'S TOUGH TO REACH THEIR GOALS...AND...
...I'D HATE IT IF THEY NEVER REALIZED THEIR DREAMS AFTER ALL THAT!
PLUS, WHEN YOU'RE RIDING, YOU LOOK SO FOCUSED AND COOL...
...AND SEEING THAT WAS PART OF WHY I DECIDED TO JOIN THE EQUESTRIAN CLUB......
SO, UH...... HOW DO I SAY THIS...?
IF WORKING WITH HORSES IS WHAT YOU WANT, THEN I WANT YOU TO GO DOWN THAT PATH...
UH...
ERRR ...
OOF!!
どげしっ
DOGESHI (WHUMP)
SFX: GUI (NUDGE) GUI GUI GUI
YOU LITTLE ...
WHAT'S YOUR PROB-LEM? DON'T INTER-RUPT ME!
OW, OW, OW, OW, OW!!

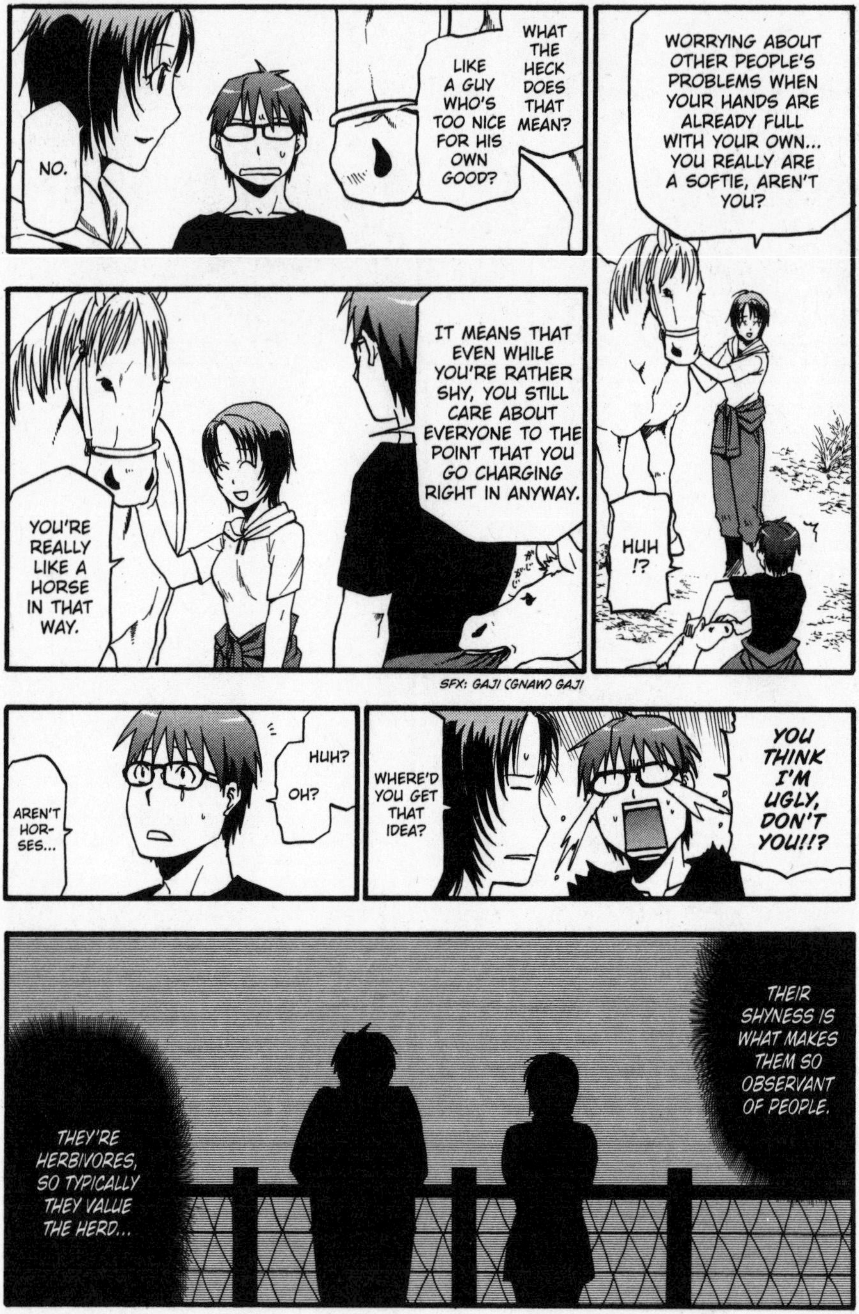
WORRYING ABOUT OTHER PEOPLE'S PROBLEMS WHEN YOUR HANDS ARE ALREADY FULL WITH YOUR OWN... YOU REALLY ARE A SOFTIE, AREN'T YOU?
HUH !?
WHAT THE HECK DOES THAT MEAN?
LIKE A GUY WHO'S TOO NICE FOR HIS OWN GOOD?
NO.
IT MEANS THAT EVEN WHILE YOU'RE RATHER SHY, YOU STILL CARE ABOUT EVERYONE TO THE POINT THAT YOU GO CHARGING RIGHT IN ANYWAY.
YOU'RE REALLY LIKE A HORSE IN THAT WAY.
SFX: GAJI (GNAW) GAJI
YOU THINK I'M UGLY, DON'T YOU!!?
WHERE'D YOU GET THAT IDEA?
HUH?
OH?
AREN'T HORSES...
THEIR SHYNESS IS WHAT MAKES THEM SO OBSERVANT OF PEOPLE.
THEY'RE HERBIVORES, SO TYPICALLY THEY VALUE THE HERD...

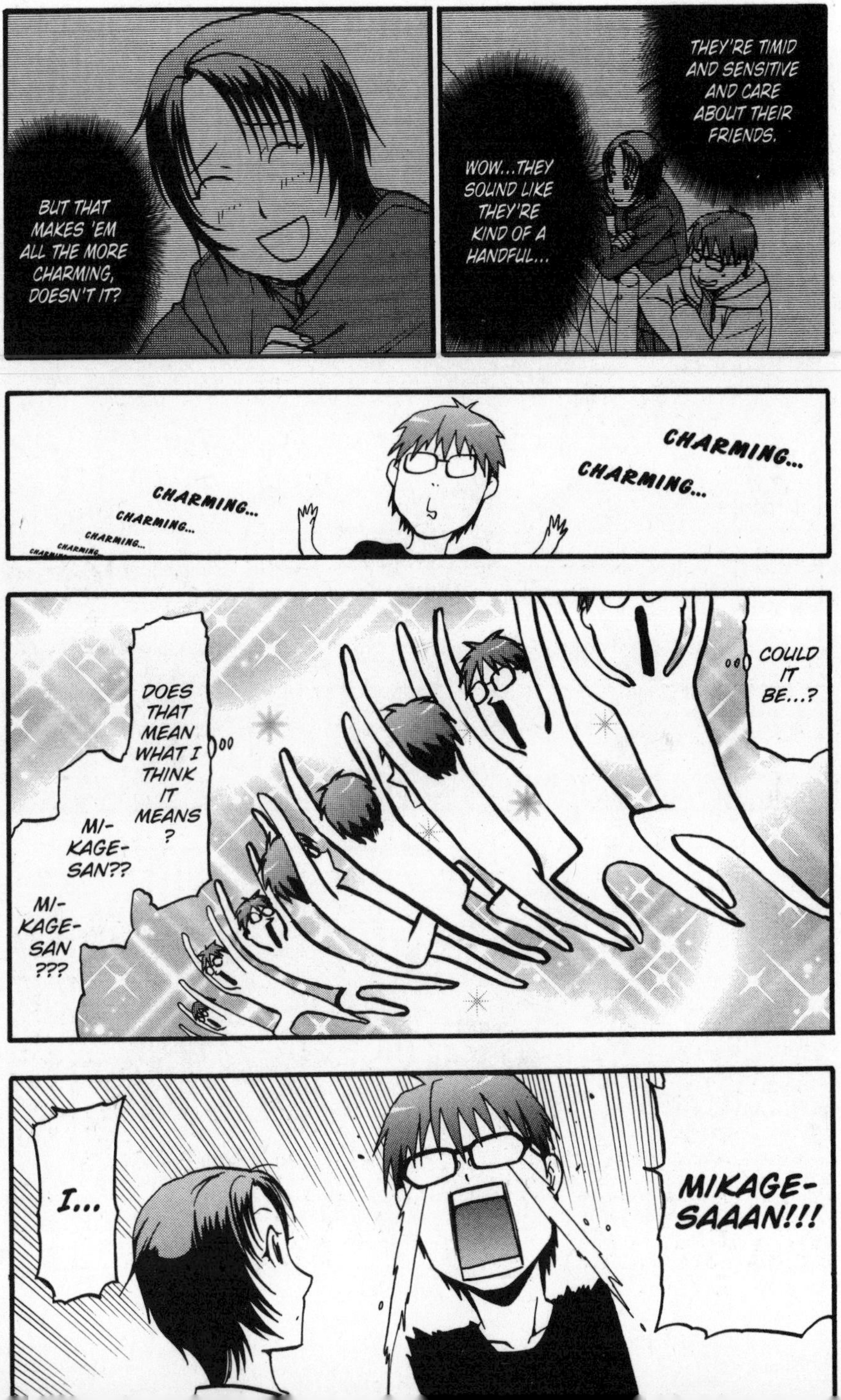
THEY'RE TIMID AND SENSITIVE AND CARE ABOUT THEIR FRIENDS.
WOW...THEY SOUND LIKE THEY'RE KIND OF A HANDFUL...
BUT THAT MAKES 'EM ALL THE MORE CHARMING, DOESN'T IT?
CHARMING...
CHARMING...
CHARMING...
CHARMING...
CHARMING...
CHARMING...
COULD IT BE...?
DOES THAT MEAN WHAT I THINK IT MEANS?
MI-KAGE-SAN??
MI-KAGE-SAN???
MIKAGE-SAAAN!!!
I...

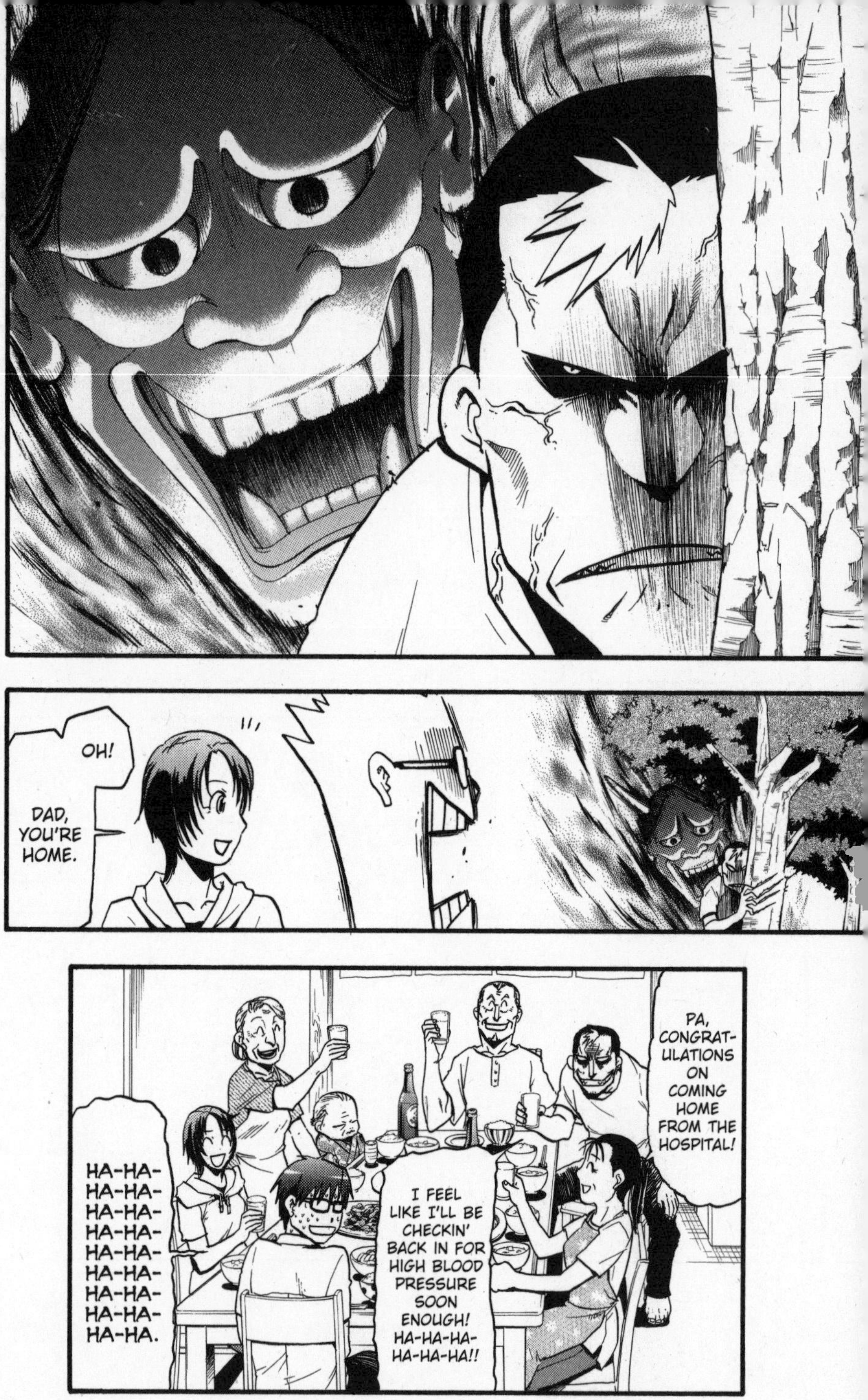
OH!
DAD, YOU'RE HOME.
PA, CONGRATULATIONS ON COMING HOME FROM THE HOSPITAL!
I FEEL LIKE I'LL BE CHECKIN' BACK IN FOR HIGH BLOOD PRESSURE SOON ENOUGH! HA-HA-HA-HA-HA-HA!!
HA-HA-HA-HA-HA-HA-HA-HA-HA-HA-HA-HA-HA-HA-HA-HA-HA-HA.

Silver Spoon

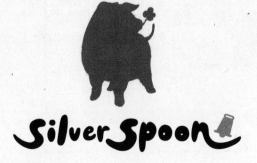

SHINJI
SAKANOUE

MEMURO EAST
MIDDLE SCHOOL

TRACK & FIELD

Chapter 19:
Tale of Summer ⑨

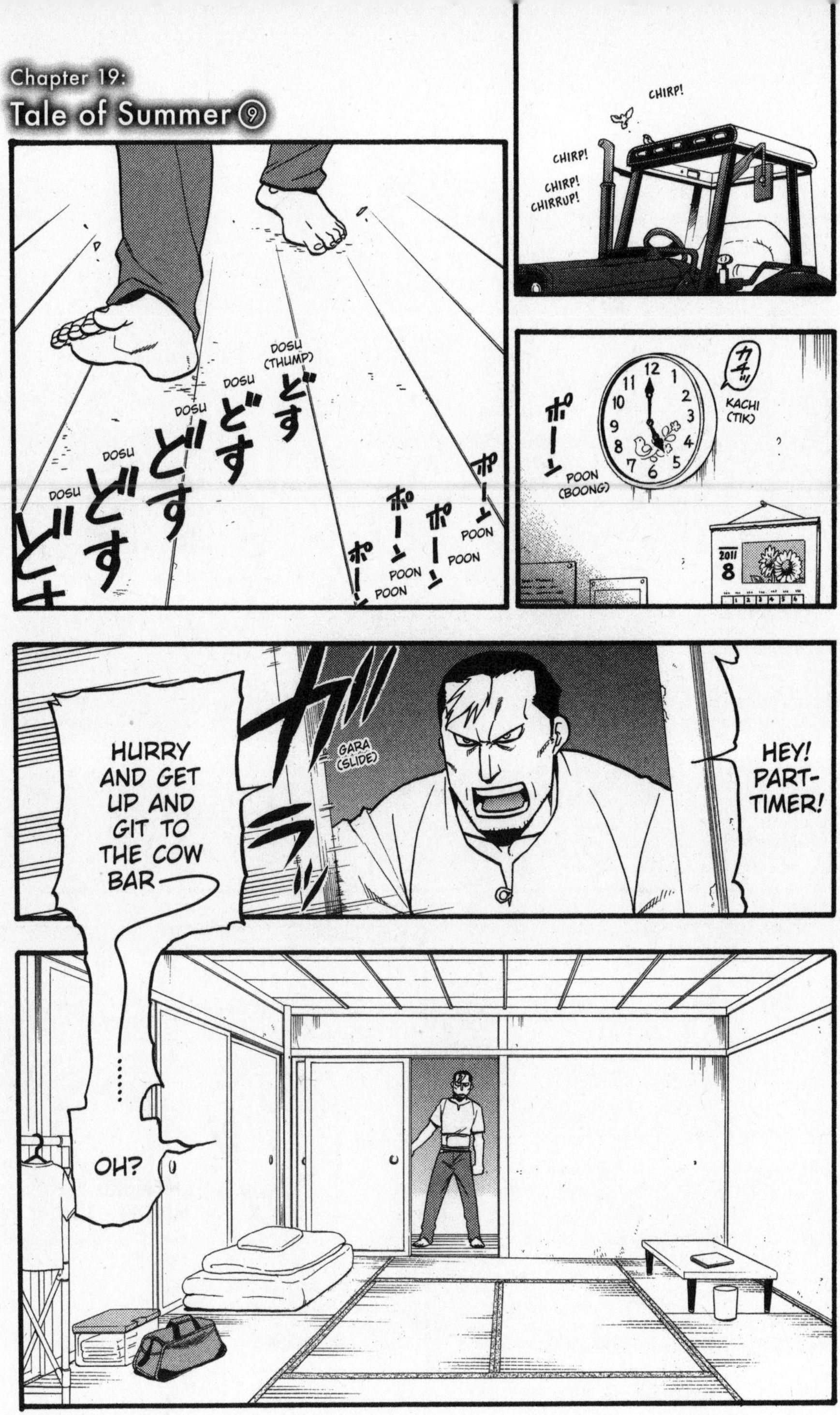

CHIRP!
CHIRP!
CHIRP!
CHIRRUP!
カチッ
KACHI (TIK)
ポーン
POON (BOONG)
どす
DOSU (THUMP)
どす
DOSU
どす
DOSU
どす
DOSU
どす
DOSU
ポーン
POON
ポーン
POON
ポーン
POON
ポーン
POON
HEY! PART-TIMER!
ガラッ
GARA (SLIDE)
HURRY AND GET UP AND GIT TO THE COW BAR—
......
OH?

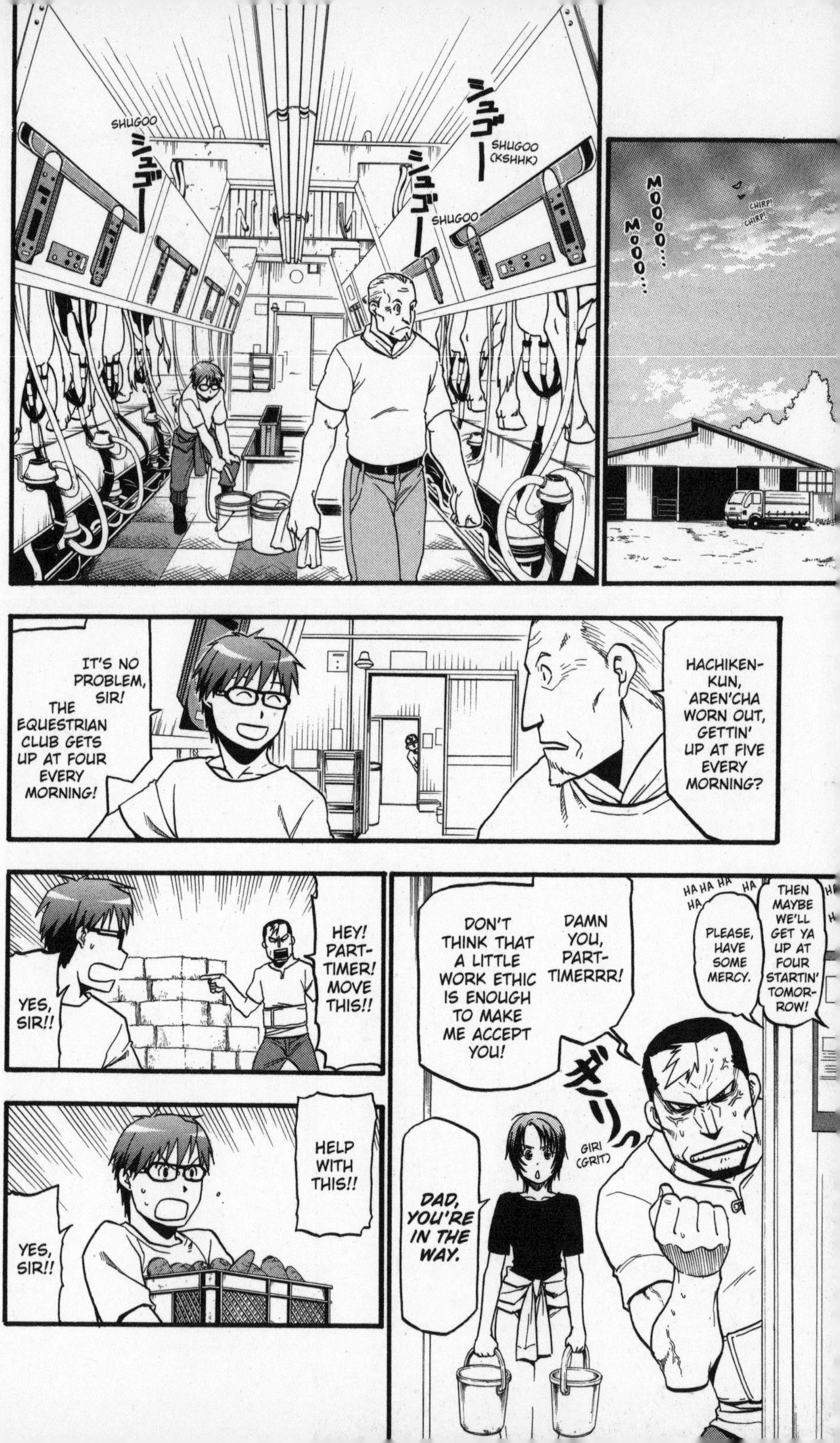
MOOOO...
MOOO...
CHIRP!
CHIRP!
シュゴー
SHUGOO (KSHHK)
シュゴー
SHUGOO
シュゴー
SHUGOO
HACHIKEN-KUN, AREN'CHA WORN OUT, GETTIN' UP AT FIVE EVERY MORNING?
IT'S NO PROBLEM, SIR!
THE EQUESTRIAN CLUB GETS UP AT FOUR EVERY MORNING!
THEN MAYBE WE'LL GET YA UP AT FOUR STARTIN' TOMORROW!
HA HA HA HA HA
PLEASE, HAVE SOME MERCY.
DAMN YOU, PART-TIMERRR!
DON'T THINK THAT A LITTLE WORK ETHIC IS ENOUGH TO MAKE ME ACCEPT YOU!
ギリッ
GIRI (GRIT)
DAD, YOU'RE IN THE WAY.
HEY! PART-TIMER! MOVE THIS!!
YES, SIR!!
HELP WITH THIS!!
YES, SIR!!

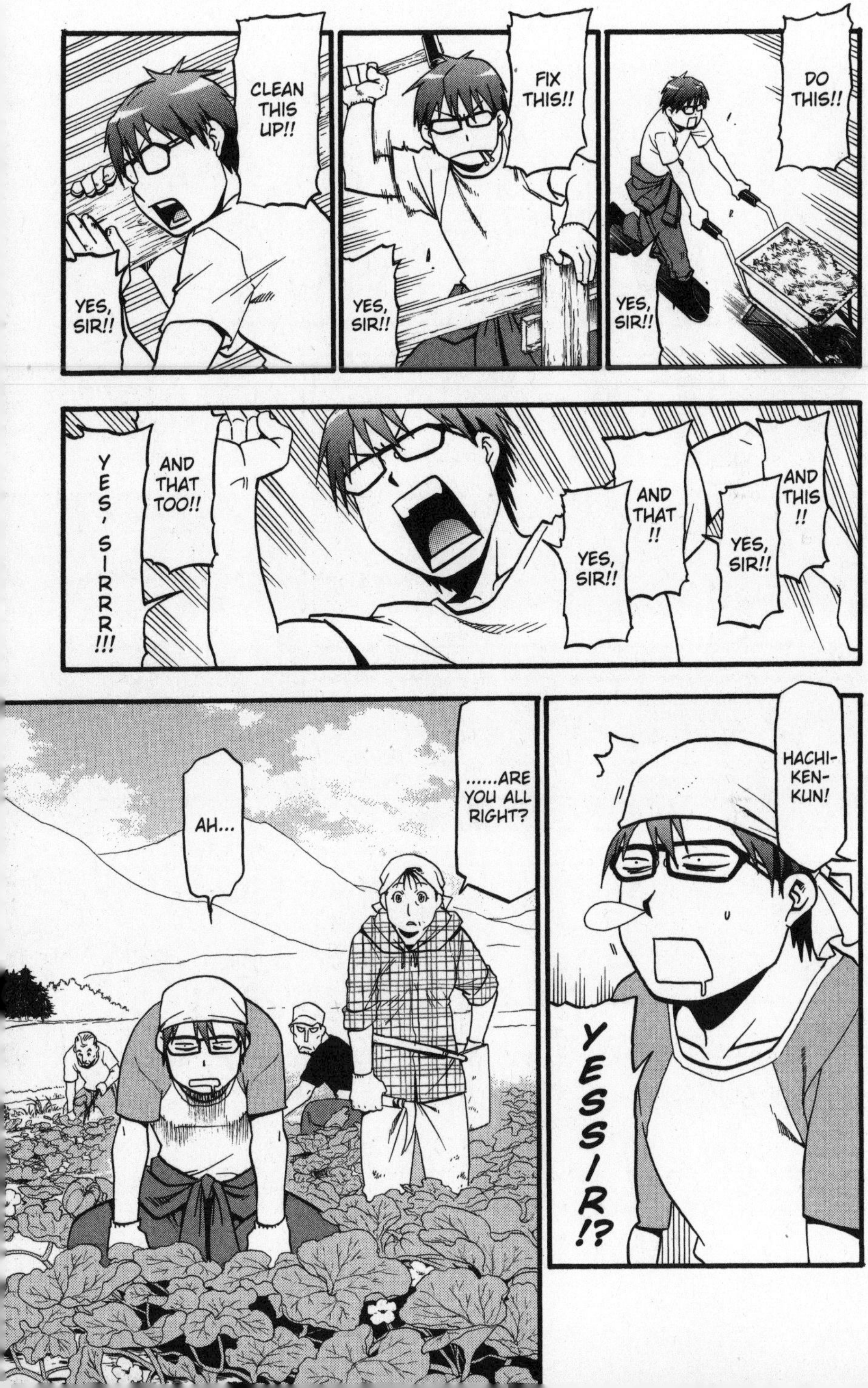
DO THIS!!
YES, SIR!!
FIX THIS!!
YES, SIR!!
CLEAN THIS UP!!
YES, SIR!!
AND THIS!!
YES, SIR!!
AND THAT!!
YES, SIR!!
AND THAT TOO!!
YES, SIRRR!!!
HACHI-KEN-KUN!
YESSIR!?
......ARE YOU ALL RIGHT?
AH...

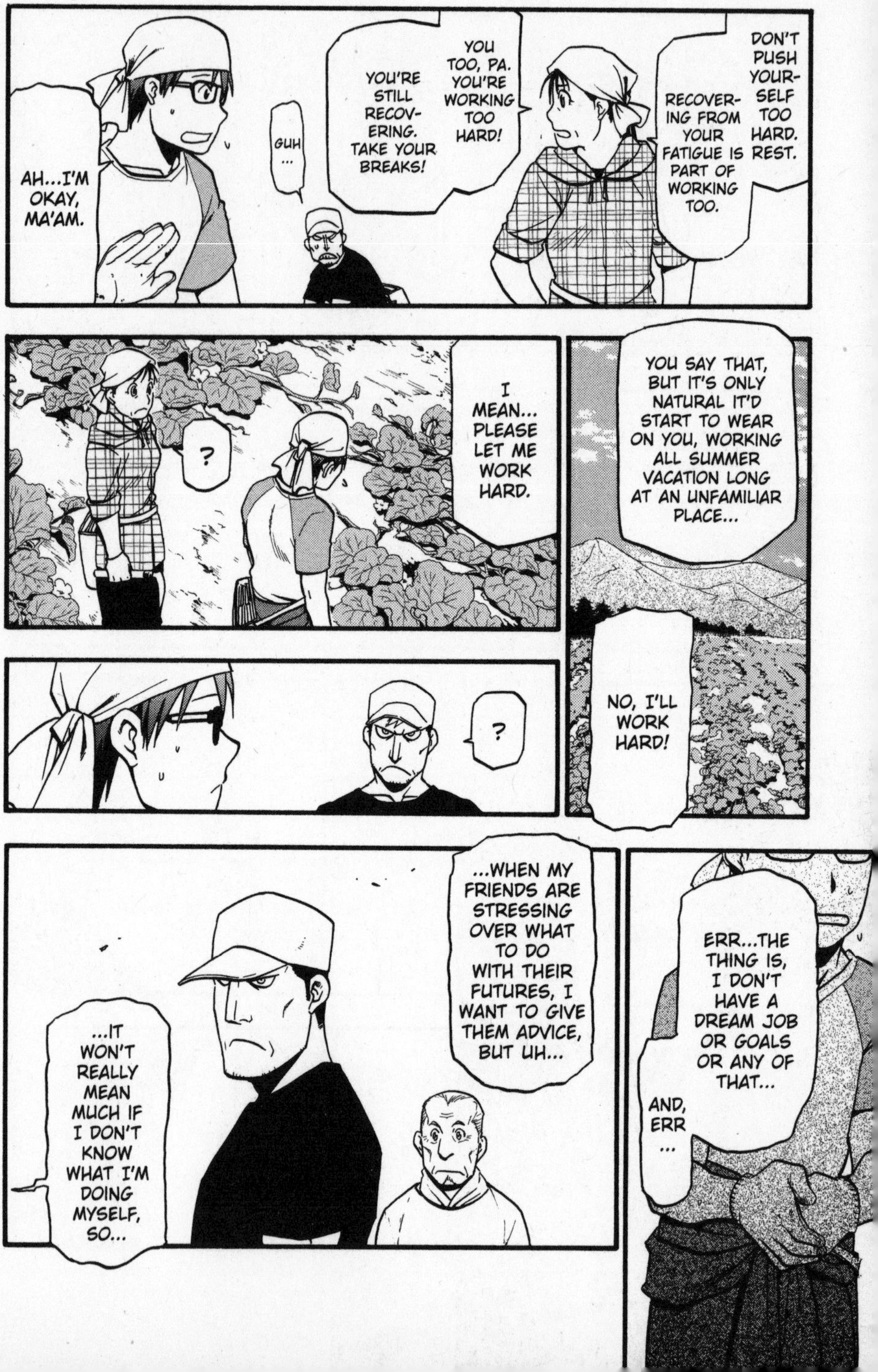
DON'T PUSH YOURSELF TOO HARD. REST.
RECOVERING FROM YOUR FATIGUE IS PART OF WORKING TOO.
YOU TOO, PA. YOU'RE WORKING TOO HARD!
YOU'RE STILL RECOVERING. TAKE YOUR BREAKS!
GUH...
AH...I'M OKAY, MA'AM.
YOU SAY THAT, BUT IT'S ONLY NATURAL IT'D START TO WEAR ON YOU, WORKING ALL SUMMER VACATION LONG AT AN UNFAMILIAR PLACE...
NO, I'LL WORK HARD!
I MEAN... PLEASE LET ME WORK HARD.
?
?
ERR...THE THING IS, I DON'T HAVE A DREAM JOB OR GOALS OR ANY OF THAT...
AND, ERR...
...WHEN MY FRIENDS ARE STRESSING OVER WHAT TO DO WITH THEIR FUTURES, I WANT TO GIVE THEM ADVICE, BUT UH...
...IT WON'T REALLY MEAN MUCH IF I DON'T KNOW WHAT I'M DOING MYSELF, SO...

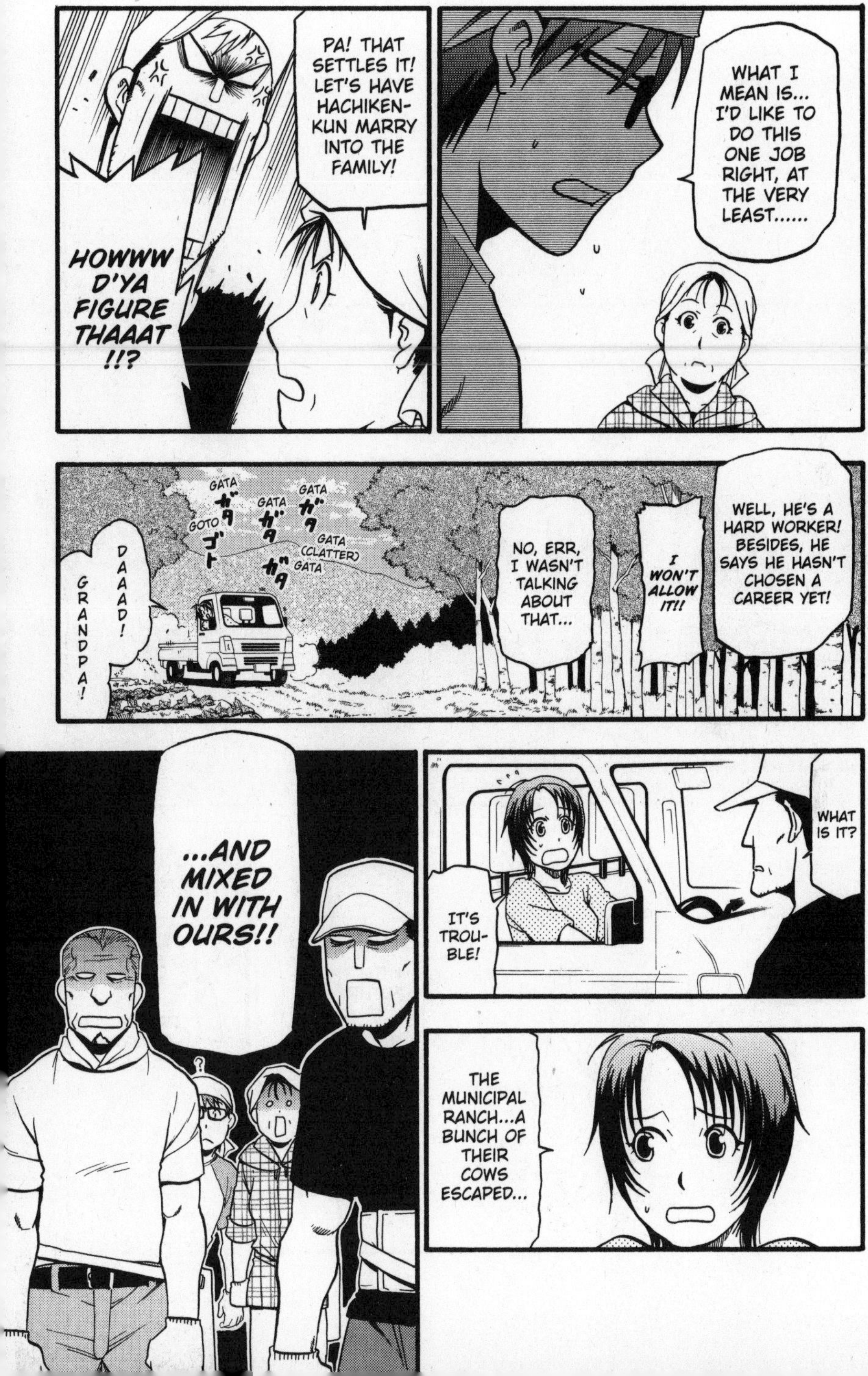
WHAT I MEAN IS... I'D LIKE TO DO THIS ONE JOB RIGHT, AT THE VERY LEAST......
PA! THAT SETTLES IT! LET'S HAVE HACHIKEN-KUN MARRY INTO THE FAMILY!
HOWWW D'YA FIGURE THAAAT!!?
WELL, HE'S A HARD WORKER! BESIDES, HE SAYS HE HASN'T CHOSEN A CAREER YET!
I WON'T ALLOW IT!!
NO, ERR, I WASN'T TALKING ABOUT THAT...
GATA GATA GATA GOTO
GATA (CLATTER) GATA
DAAAD!
GRANDPA!
WHAT IS IT?
IT'S TROUBLE!
THE MUNICIPAL RANCH...A BUNCH OF THEIR COWS ESCAPED...
...AND MIXED IN WITH OURS!!

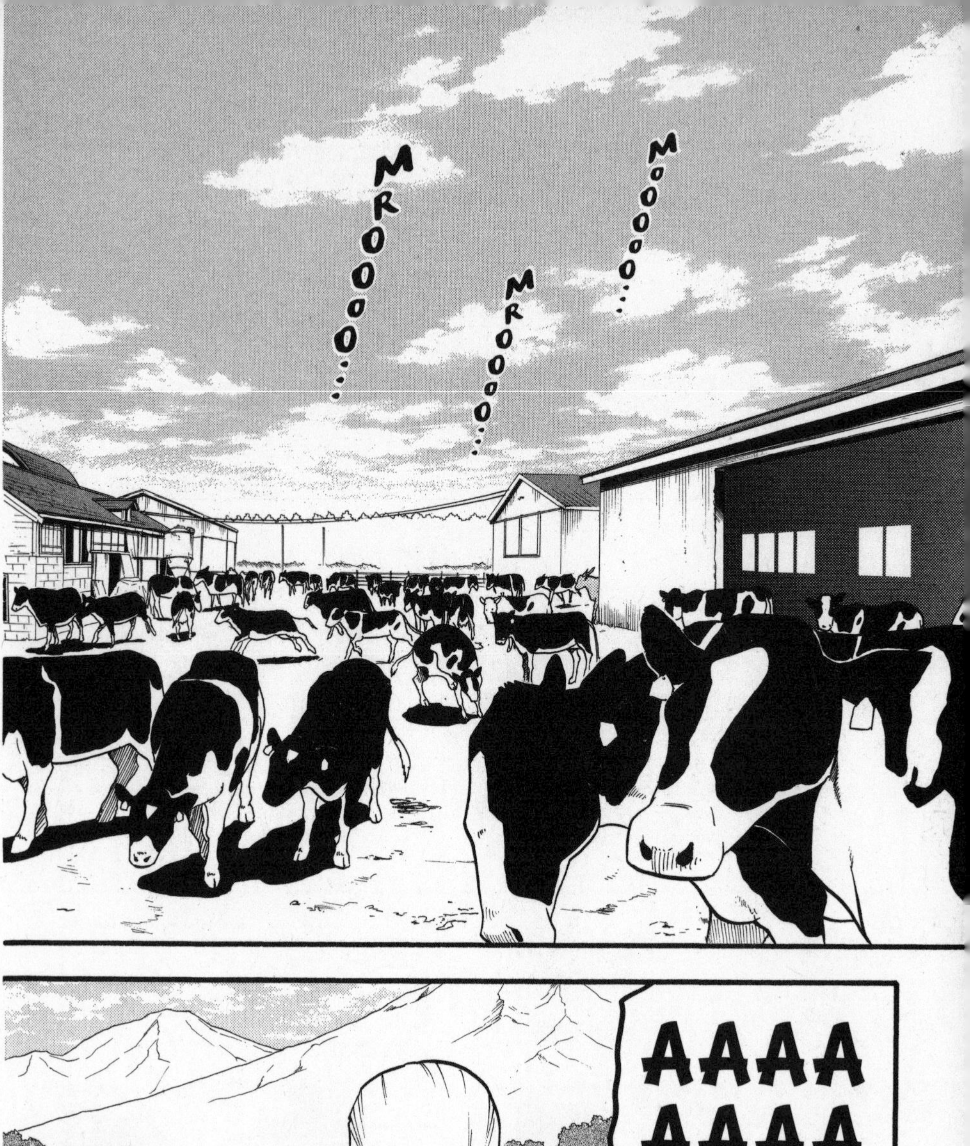
MOOOOOO...
MROOOOO...
MROOOOO...

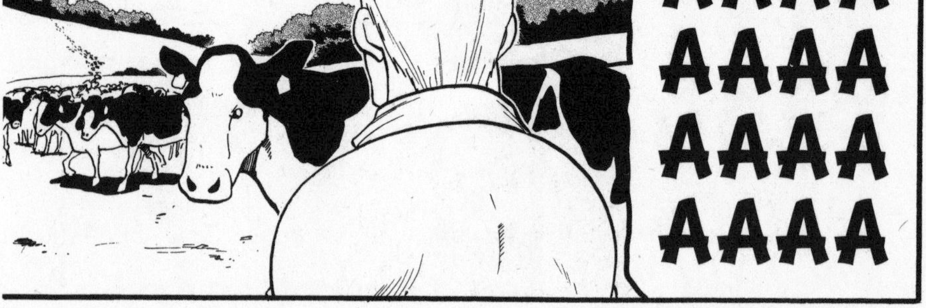
AAAA
AAAA
AAAA
AAAA
AAAA

Chapter 19: Tale of Summer 9

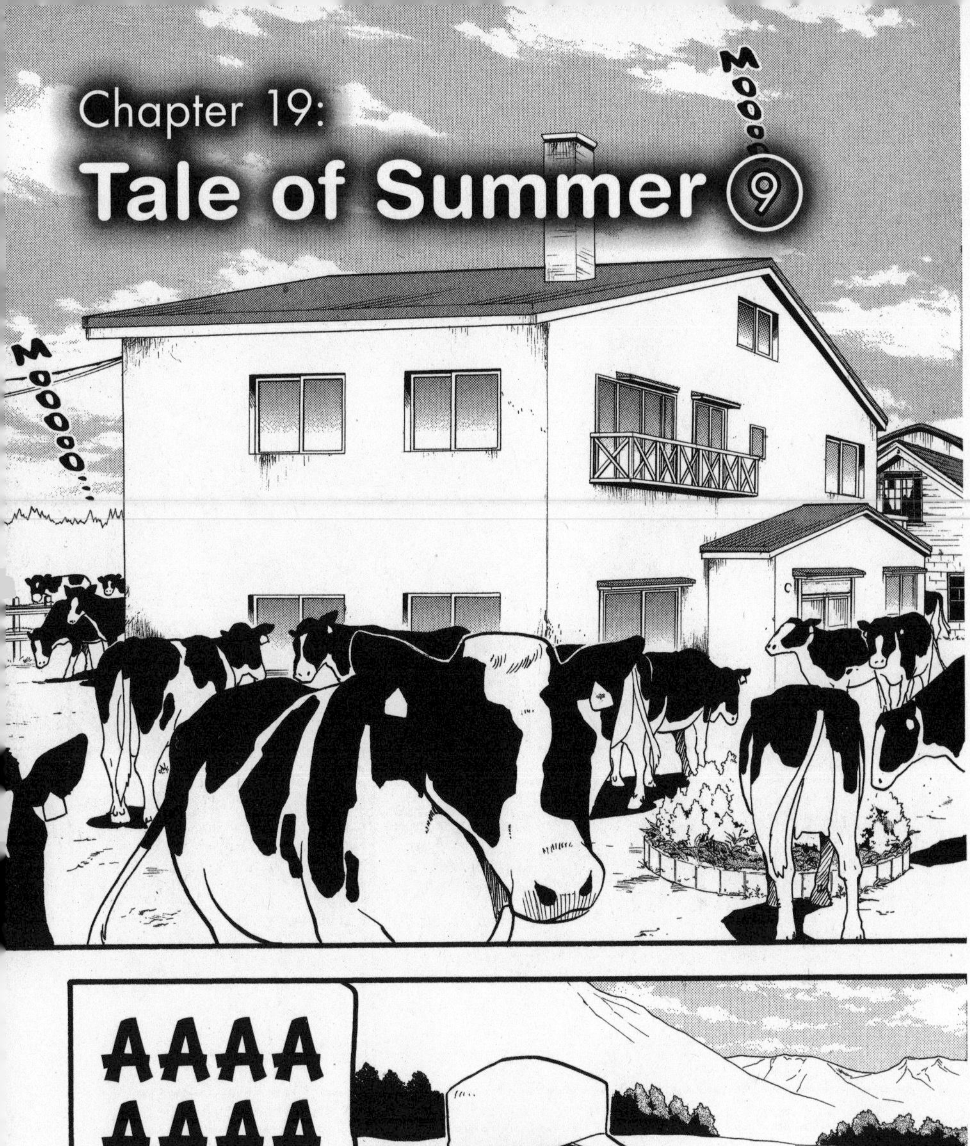
MOOOO...
MOOOOOO...

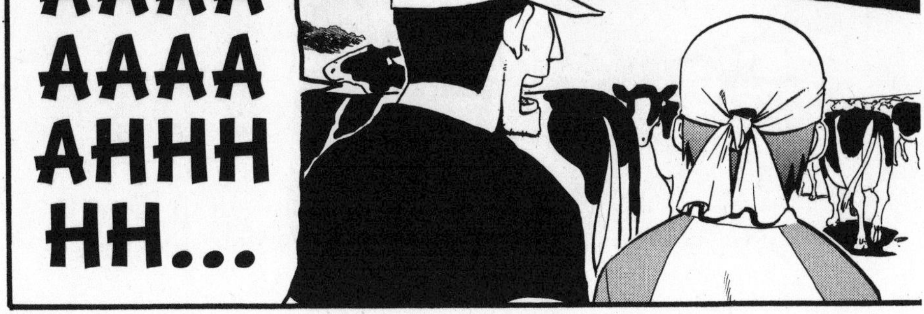
AAAA
AAAA
AAAA
AHHH
HH...

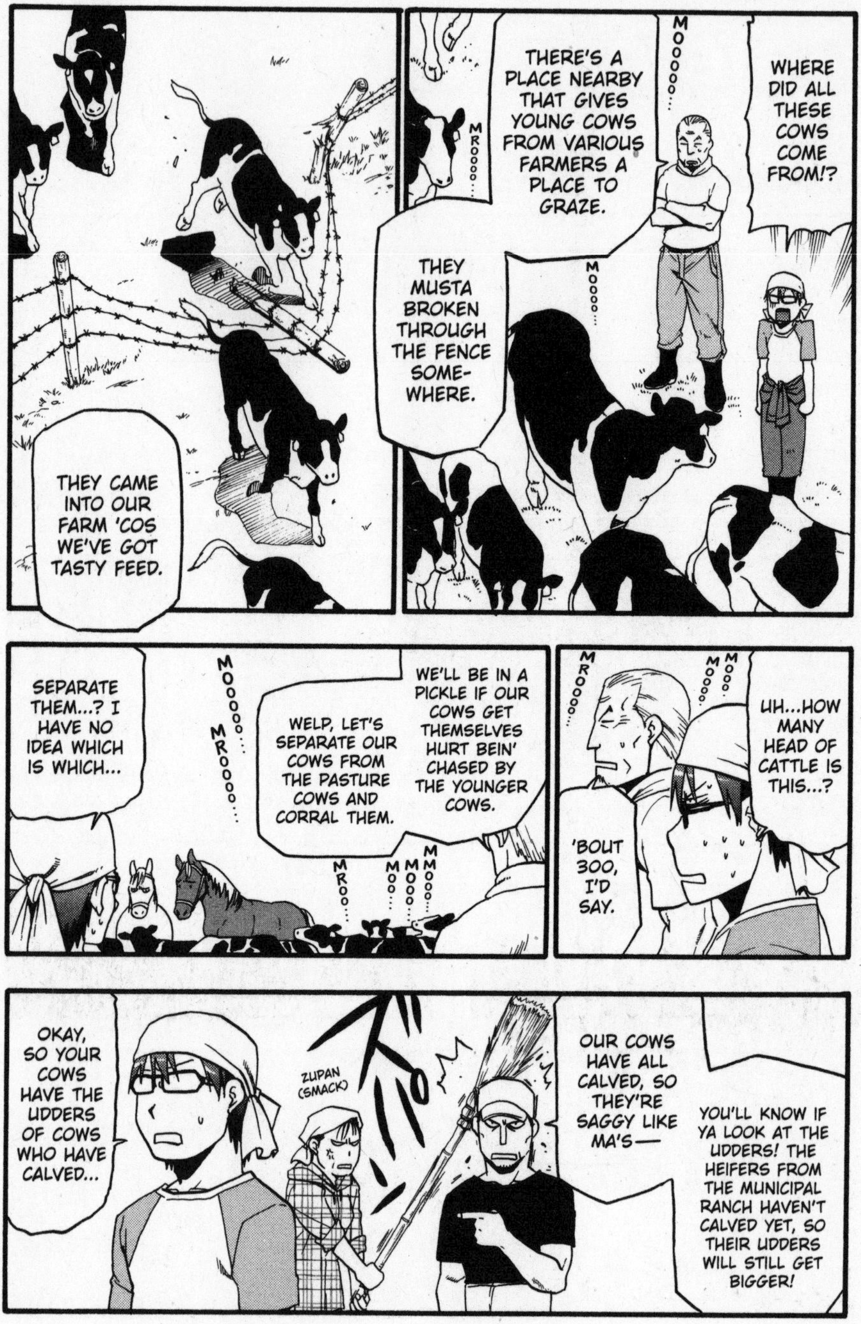
WHERE DID ALL THESE COWS COME FROM!?
MOOOOOO...
THERE'S A PLACE NEARBY THAT GIVES YOUNG COWS FROM VARIOUS FARMERS A PLACE TO GRAZE.
MROOOOO...
MOOOOO...
THEY MUSTA BROKEN THROUGH THE FENCE SOME-WHERE.
THEY CAME INTO OUR FARM 'COS WE'VE GOT TASTY FEED.
UH...HOW MANY HEAD OF CATTLE IS THIS...?
MOOOO
MOOOOO
MROOOOO...
'BOUT 300, I'D SAY.
WE'LL BE IN A PICKLE IF OUR COWS GET THEMSELVES HURT BEIN' CHASED BY THE YOUNGER COWS.
WELP, LET'S SEPARATE OUR COWS FROM THE PASTURE COWS AND CORRAL THEM.
MOOOOOO...
MROOOOO...
MMOOOO...
MOOOO...
MOO...
MROOO...
SEPARATE THEM...? I HAVE NO IDEA WHICH IS WHICH...
YOU'LL KNOW IF YA LOOK AT THE UDDERS! THE HEIFERS FROM THE MUNICIPAL RANCH HAVEN'T CALVED YET, SO THEIR UDDERS WILL STILL GET BIGGER!
OUR COWS HAVE ALL CALVED, SO THEY'RE SAGGY LIKE MA'S—
ZUPAN (SMACK)
OKAY, SO YOUR COWS HAVE THE UDDERS OF COWS WHO HAVE CALVED...

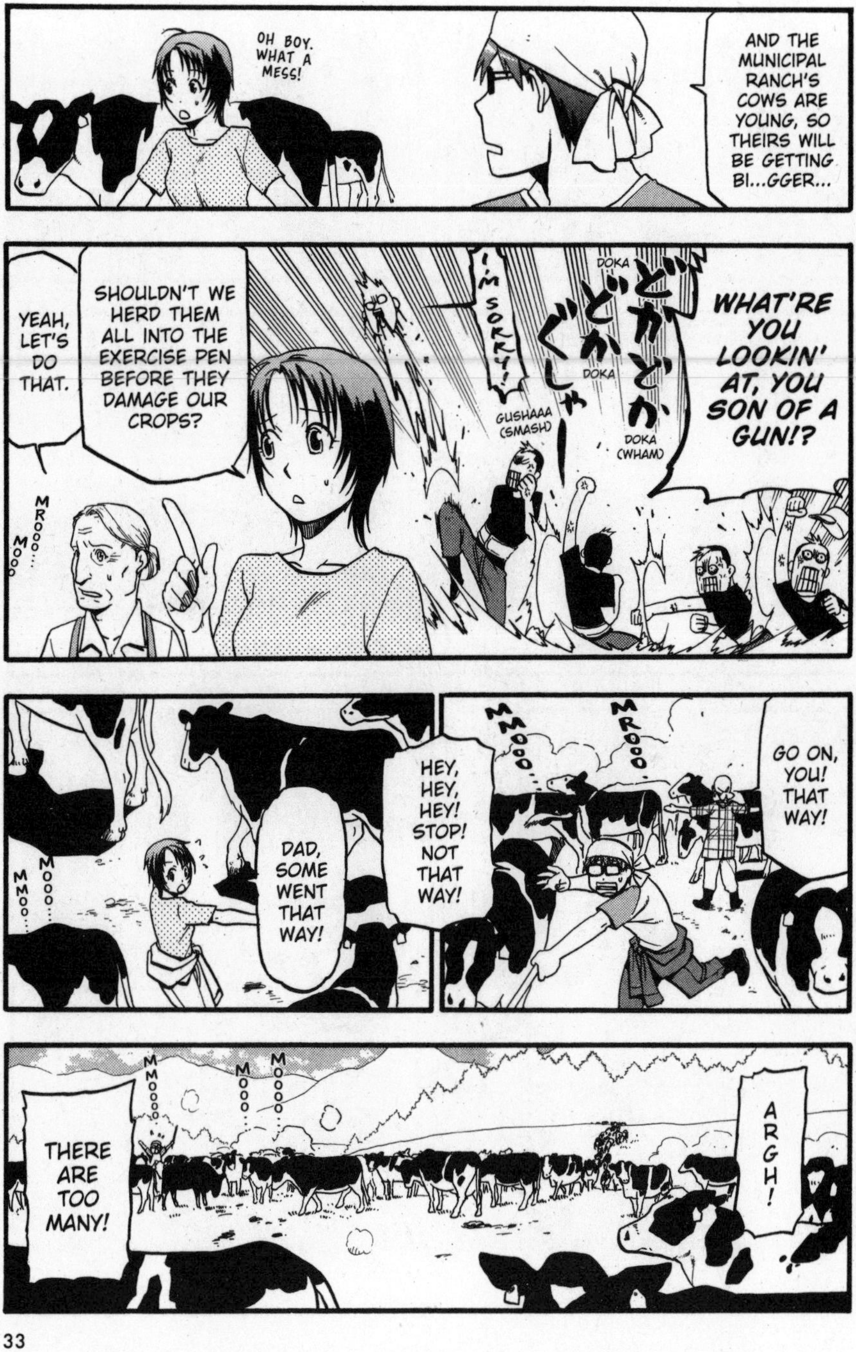
AND THE MUNICIPAL RANCH'S COWS ARE YOUNG, SO THEIRS WILL BE GETTING BI...GGER...
OH BOY. WHAT A MESS!
WHAT'RE YOU LOOKIN' AT, YOU SON OF A GUN!?
DOKA
どかどかどかぐしゃー
DOKA
DOKA (WHAM)
GUSHAAA (SMASH)
I'M SORRY!
SHOULDN'T WE HERD THEM ALL INTO THE EXERCISE PEN BEFORE THEY DAMAGE OUR CROPS?
YEAH, LET'S DO THAT.
MROOO...
MOOO
GO ON, YOU! THAT WAY!
MROOO...
HEY, HEY, HEY! STOP! NOT THAT WAY!
MMOOO...
DAD, SOME WENT THAT WAY!
MOOO...
MMOO...
ARGH!
MOOOO...
MOOO...
MMOOOO...
THERE ARE TOO MANY!

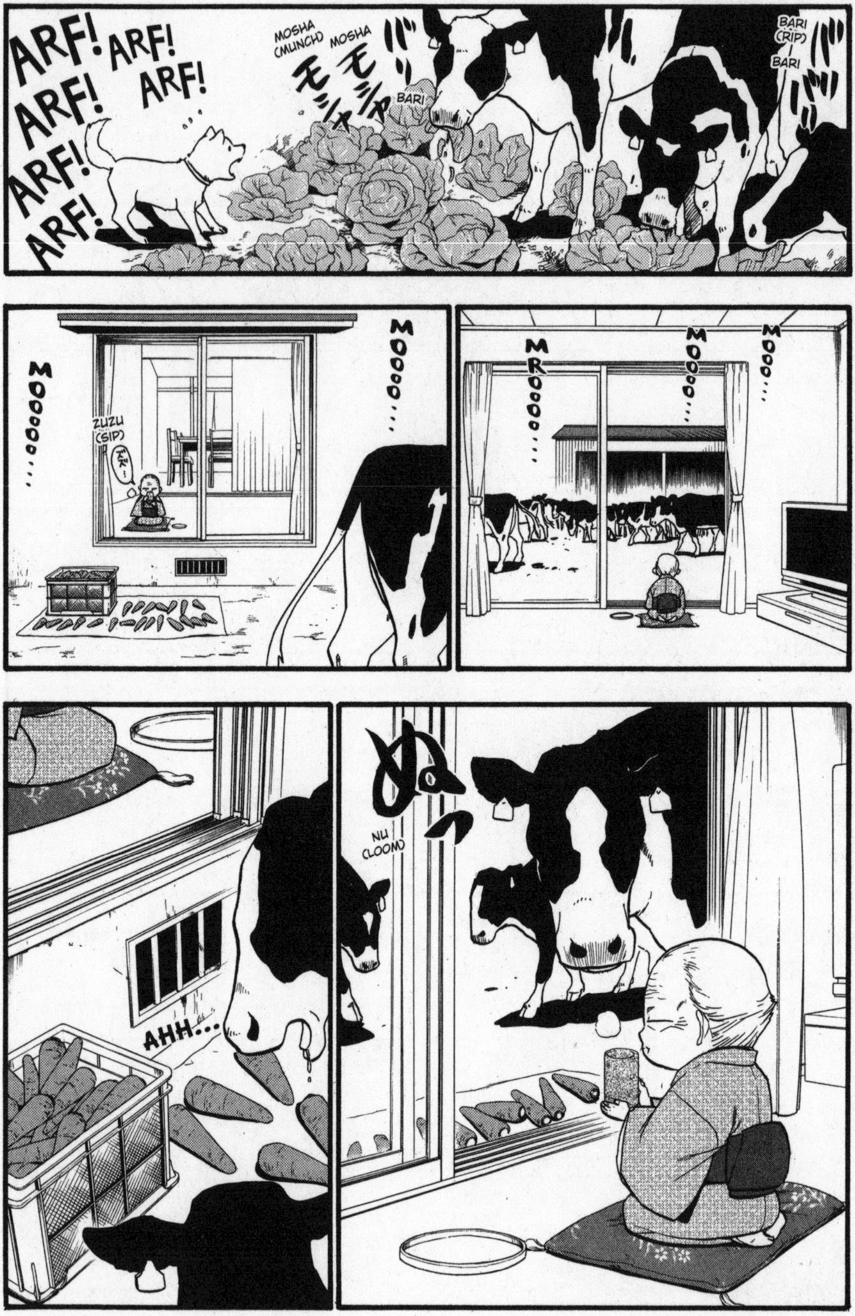

BARI (RIP) BARI
バリ
BARI!
バリ
MOSHA (MUNCH) MOSHA
モシャモシャ
ARF! ARF!
ARF! ARF! ARF! ARF!
MOOO...
MOOOO...
MROOOO...
MOOOO...
ZUZU (SIP)
MOOOOOO...
ぬっ
NU (LOOM)
AHH...

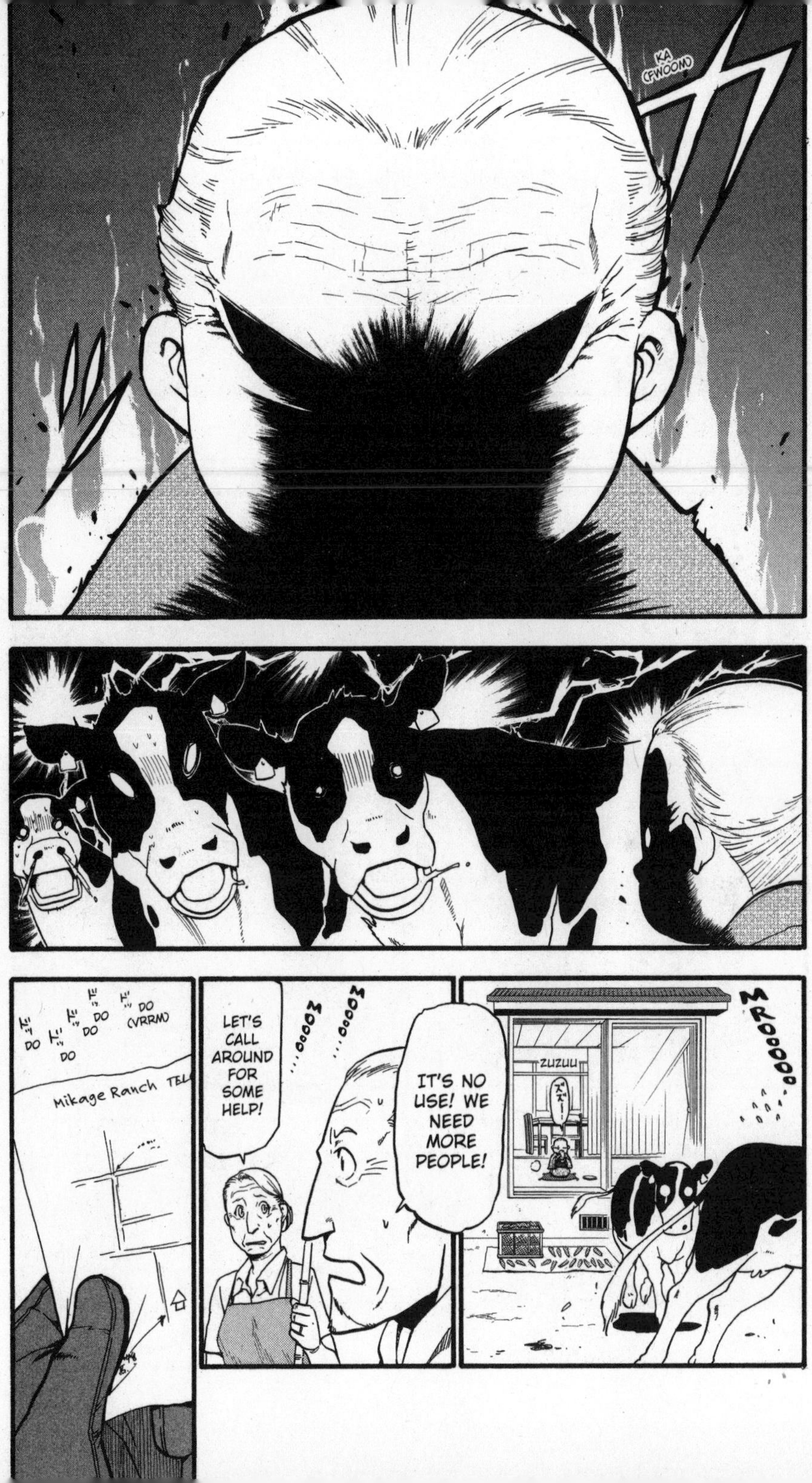
KA (FWOOM)
MROOOOOO
ZUZUU
IT'S NO USE! WE NEED MORE PEOPLE!
MOOOO...
MOOOO...
LET'S CALL AROUND FOR SOME HELP!
DO DO DO DO DO (VRRM)
Mikage Ranch TEL

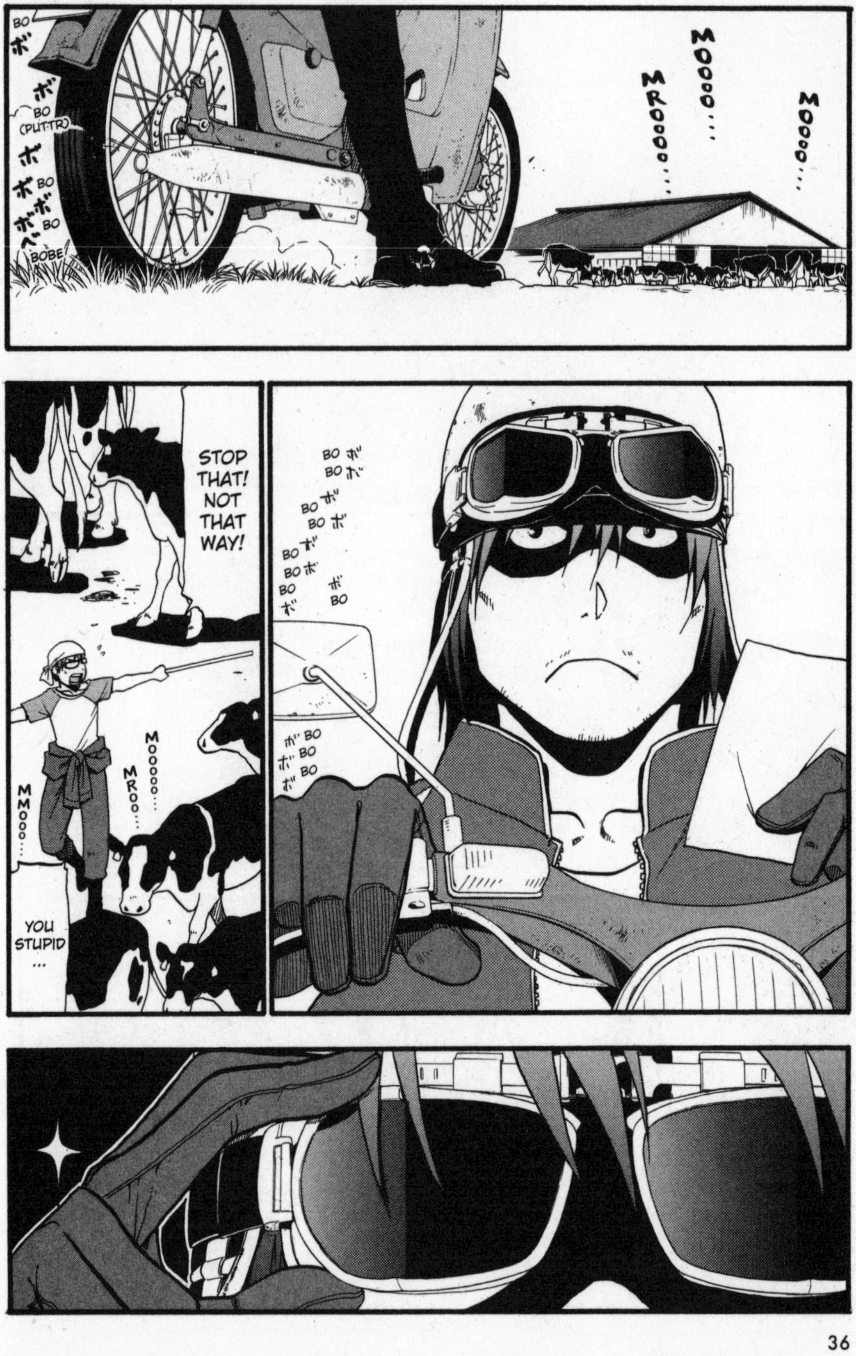
MOOOO...
MOOOO...
MROOOO...
BO
ボ
ボ
BO
(PUT-TR)
ボ
BO
ボ
ボ
BO
ボ
ベ
BOBE
BO ボ
BO ボ
BO ボ
BO ボ
BO ボ
BO ボ
BO ボ
ボ BO
ボ BO
ボ BO
ボ BO
STOP THAT! NOT THAT WAY!
MOOOOO...
MROO...
MMOOO...
YOU STUPID...

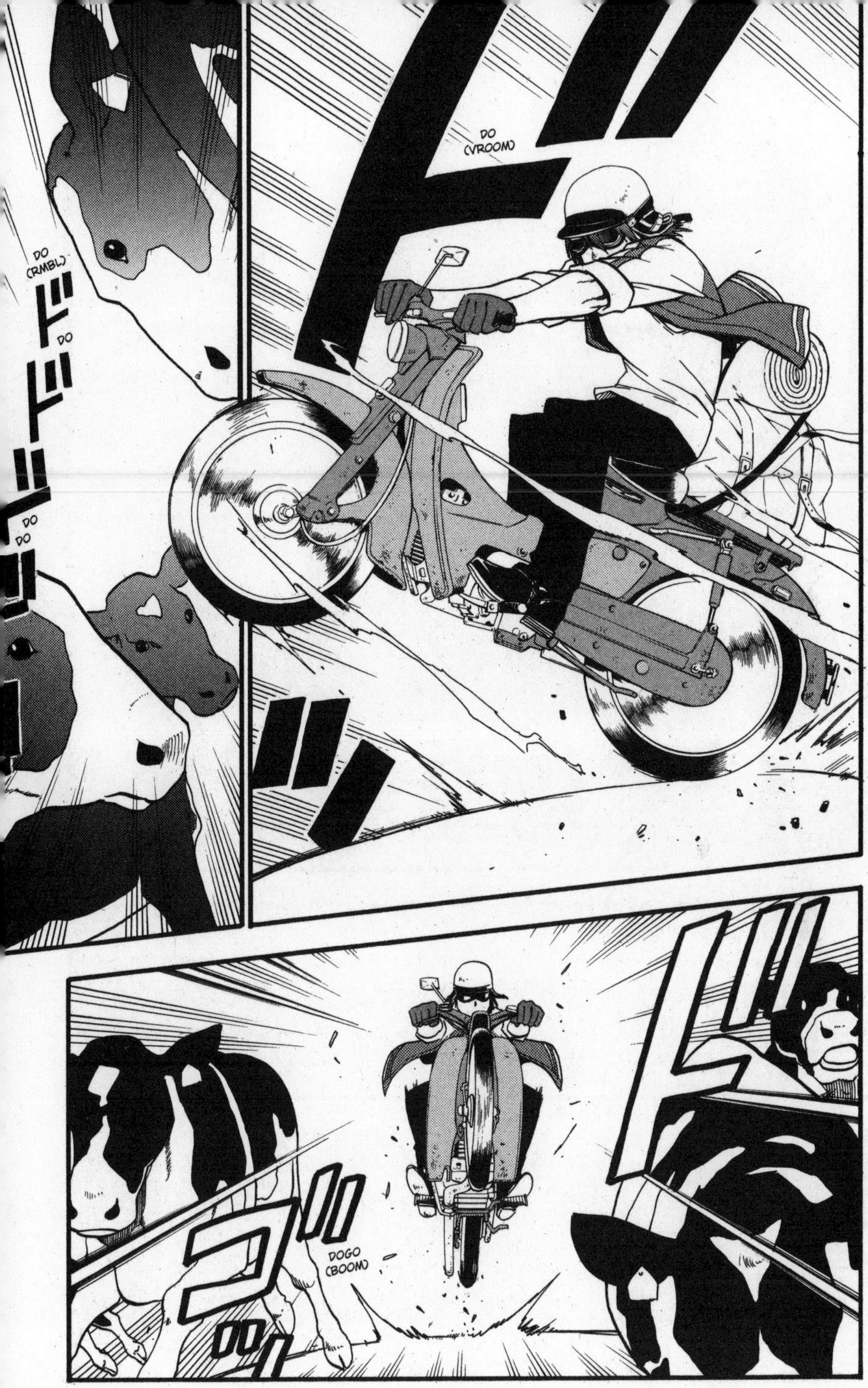
DO (VROOM)
DO (RMBL)
DO
DO DO
DOGO (BOOM)

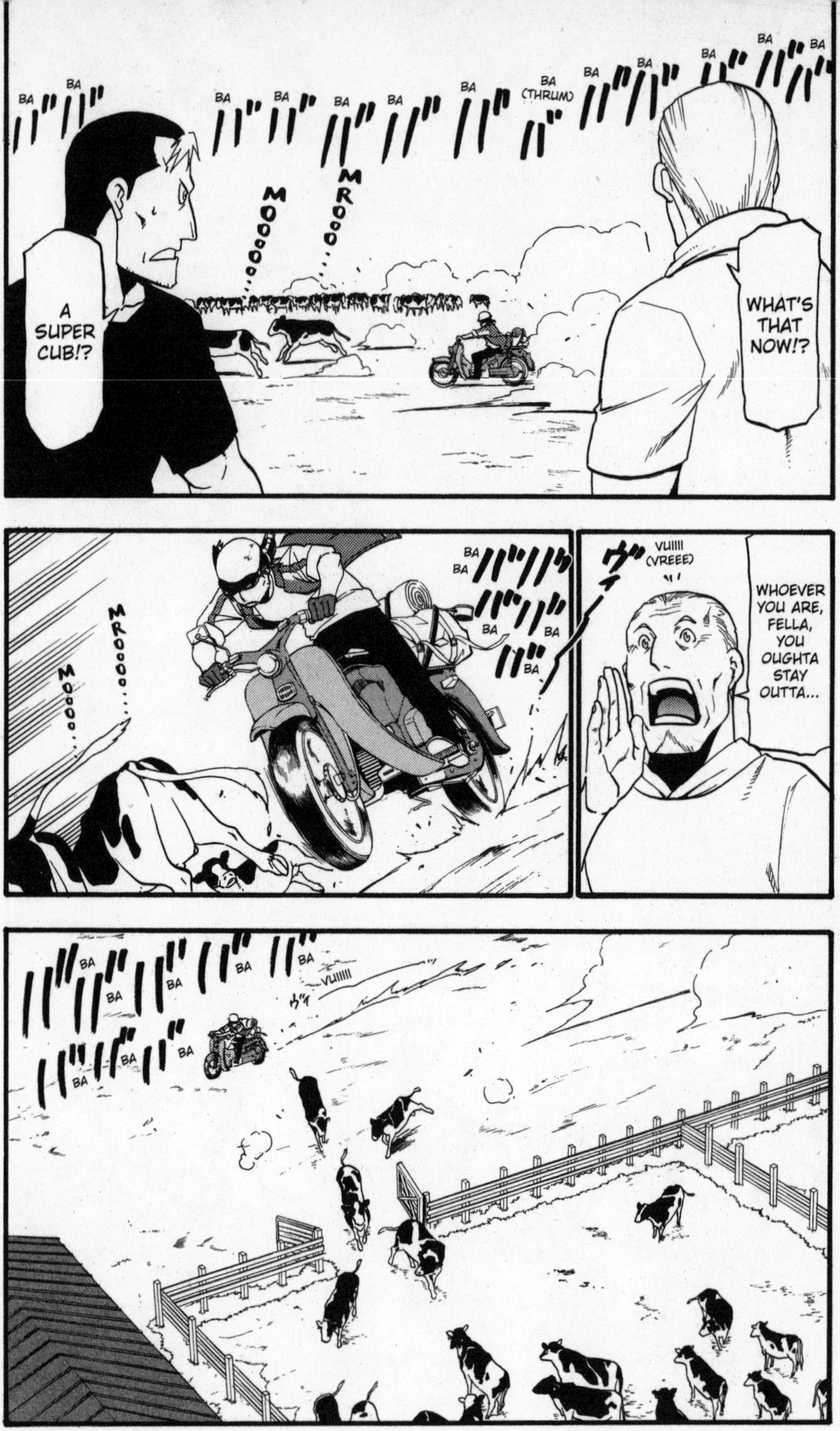
BA BA BA BA BA BA BA BA BA BA BA BA
(THRUM)
WHAT'S THAT NOW!?
MROOOO....
MOOOOOO....
A SUPER CUB!?
VUIIII (VREEE)
WHOEVER YOU ARE, FELLA, YOU OUGHTA STAY OUTTA...
BA BA BA BA BA
MROOOO....
MOOOO....
BA BA BA BA BA BA BA
VUIIIII

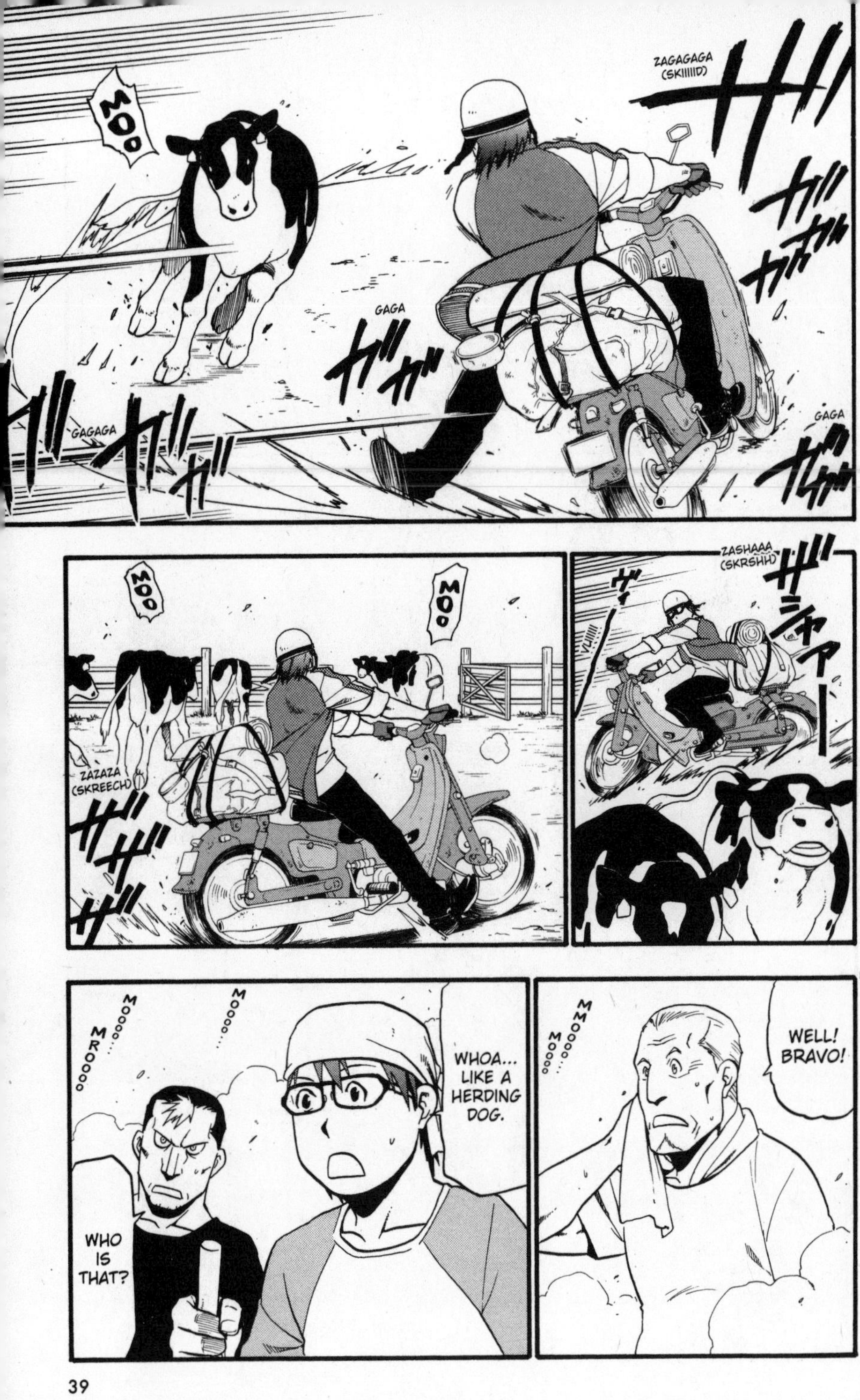
ZAGAGAGA (SKIIIIID)
MOO
GAGA
GAGA
GAGAGA
ZASHAAA (SKRSHH)
MOO
MOO
ZAZAZA (SKREECH)
WELL! BRAVO!
MMOOOO... MOOO
WHOA... LIKE A HERDING DOG.
MOOOO...
MOOOO... MROOOO
WHO IS THAT?

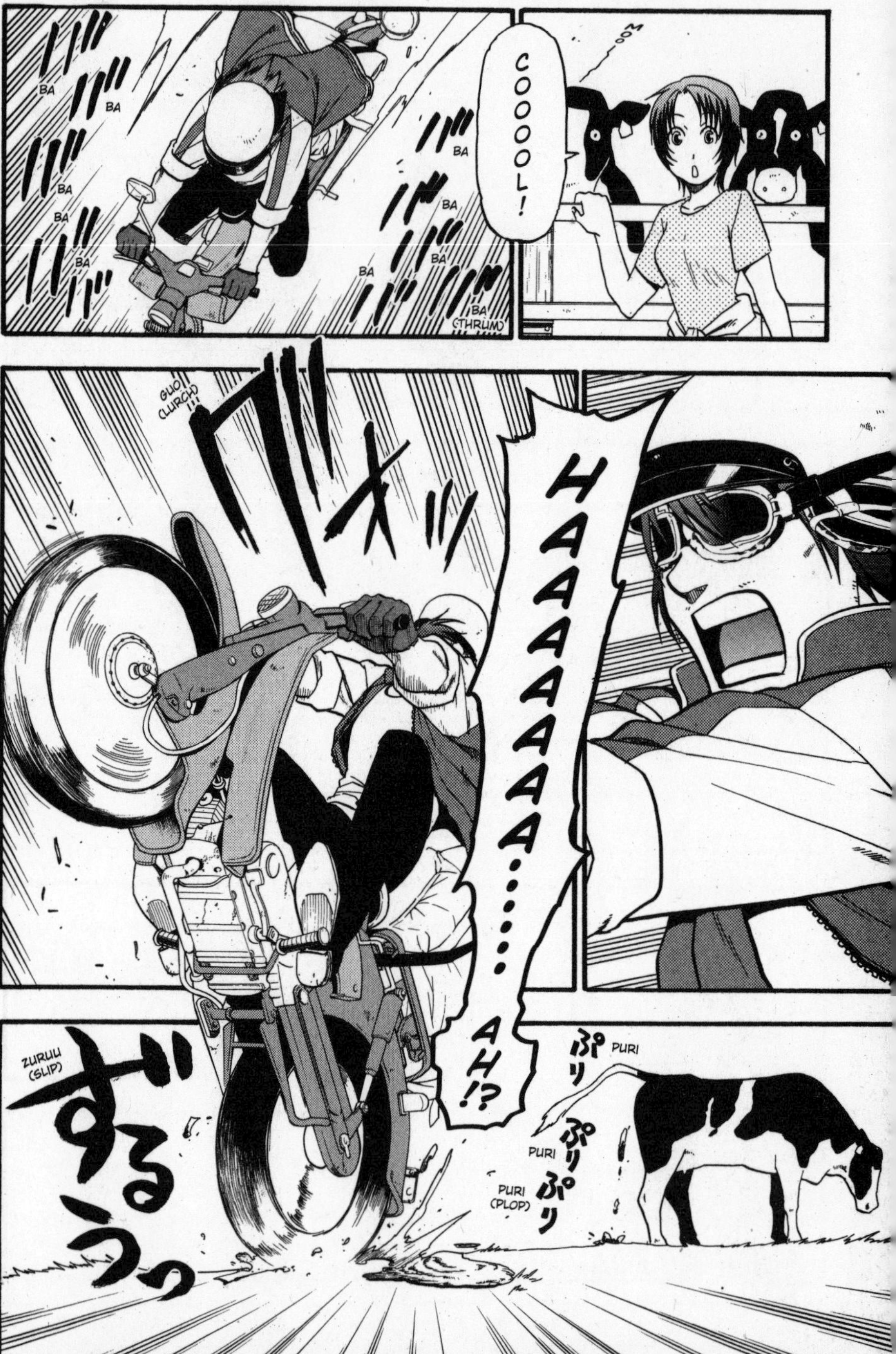
MOO~
COOOOOL!
BA BA BA BA BA BA BA BA BA
(THRUM)
HAAAAAAAAAAA......
GUO (LURCH)
グオッ
ぷり PURI
ぷり PURI
ぷり PURI (PLOP)
AH!?
ZURUU (SLIP)
するぅっ

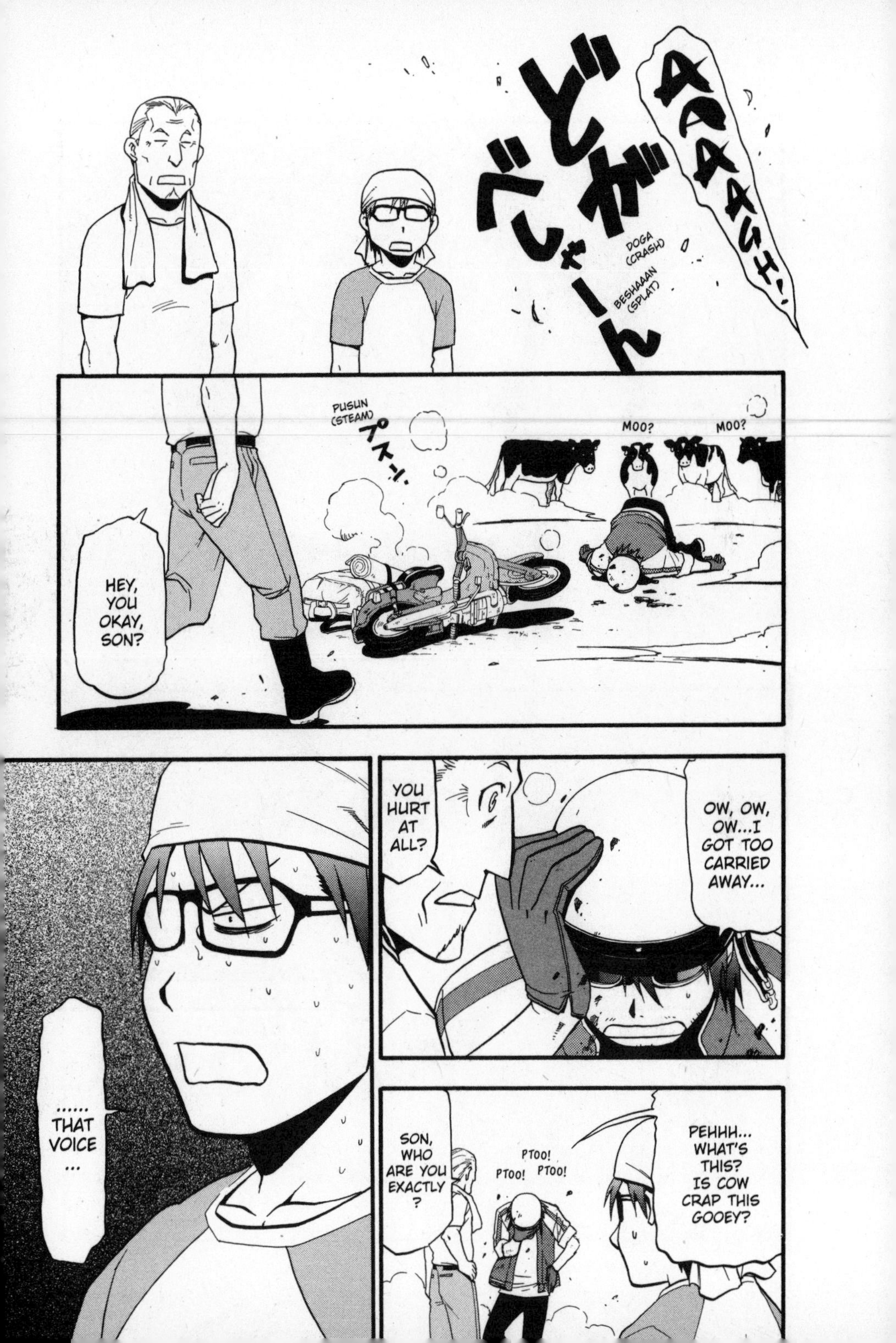
AAAAUGH!
どが
DOGA (CRASH)
べしゃーん
BESHAAAN (SPLAT)
MOO?
MOO?
PUSUN (STEAM)
プスーッ
HEY, YOU OKAY, SON?
OW, OW, OW...I GOT TOO CARRIED AWAY...
YOU HURT AT ALL?
PEHHH... WHAT'S THIS? IS COW CRAP THIS GOOEY?
PTOO! PTOO!
PTOO!
SON, WHO ARE YOU EXACTLY?
......THAT VOICE...

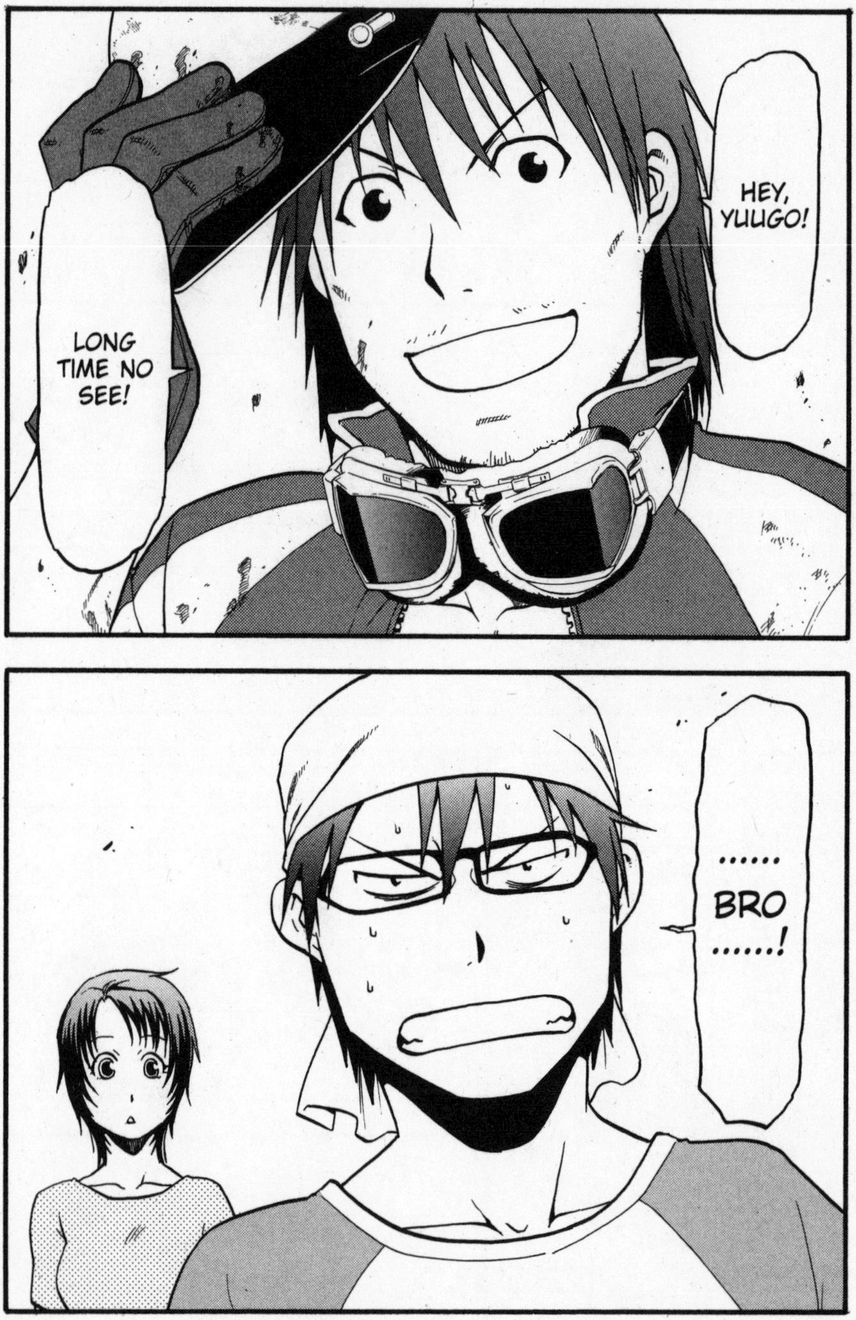
HEY, YUUGO!
LONG TIME NO SEE!
...... BRO ......!

Silver Spoon

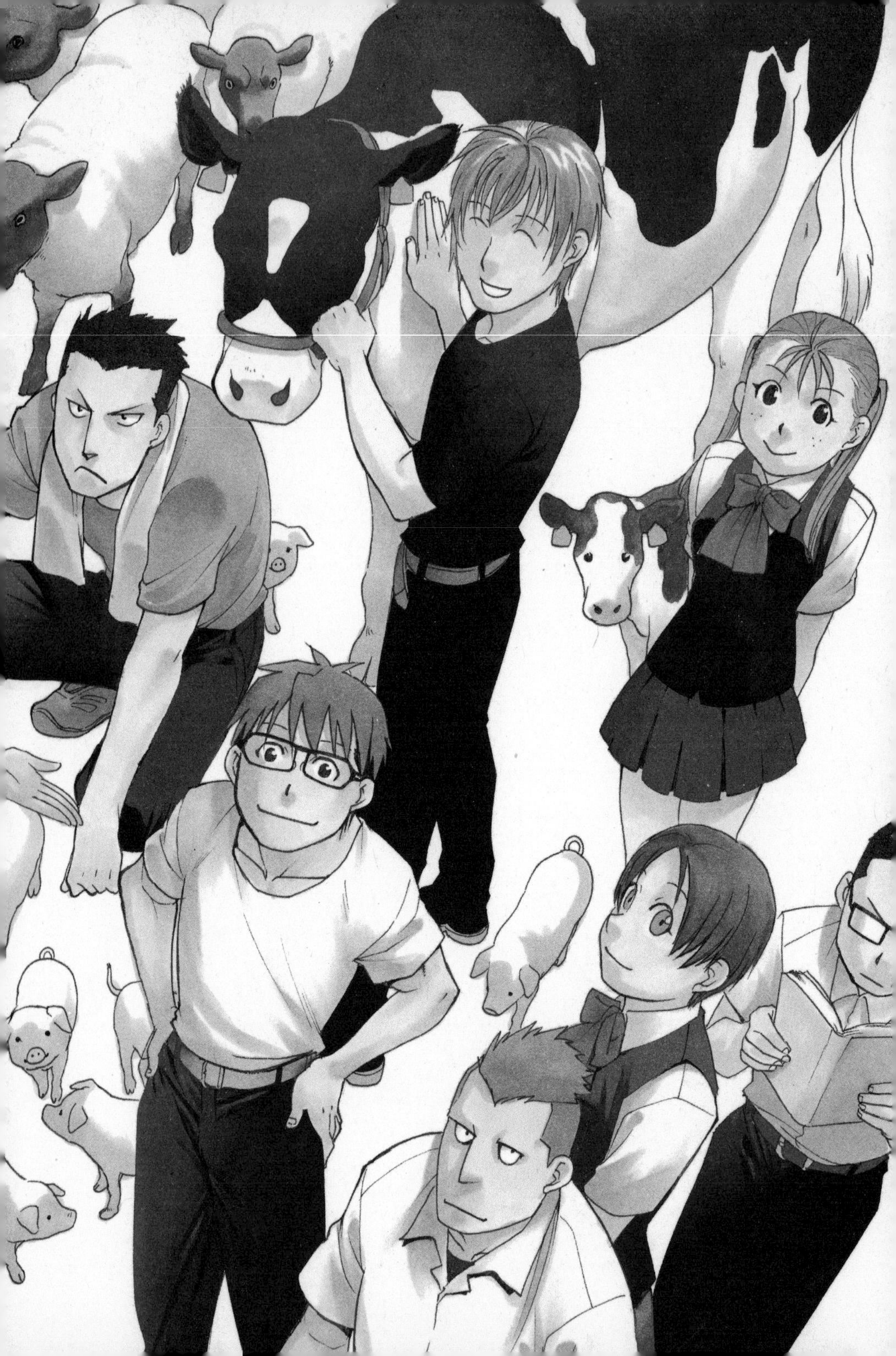

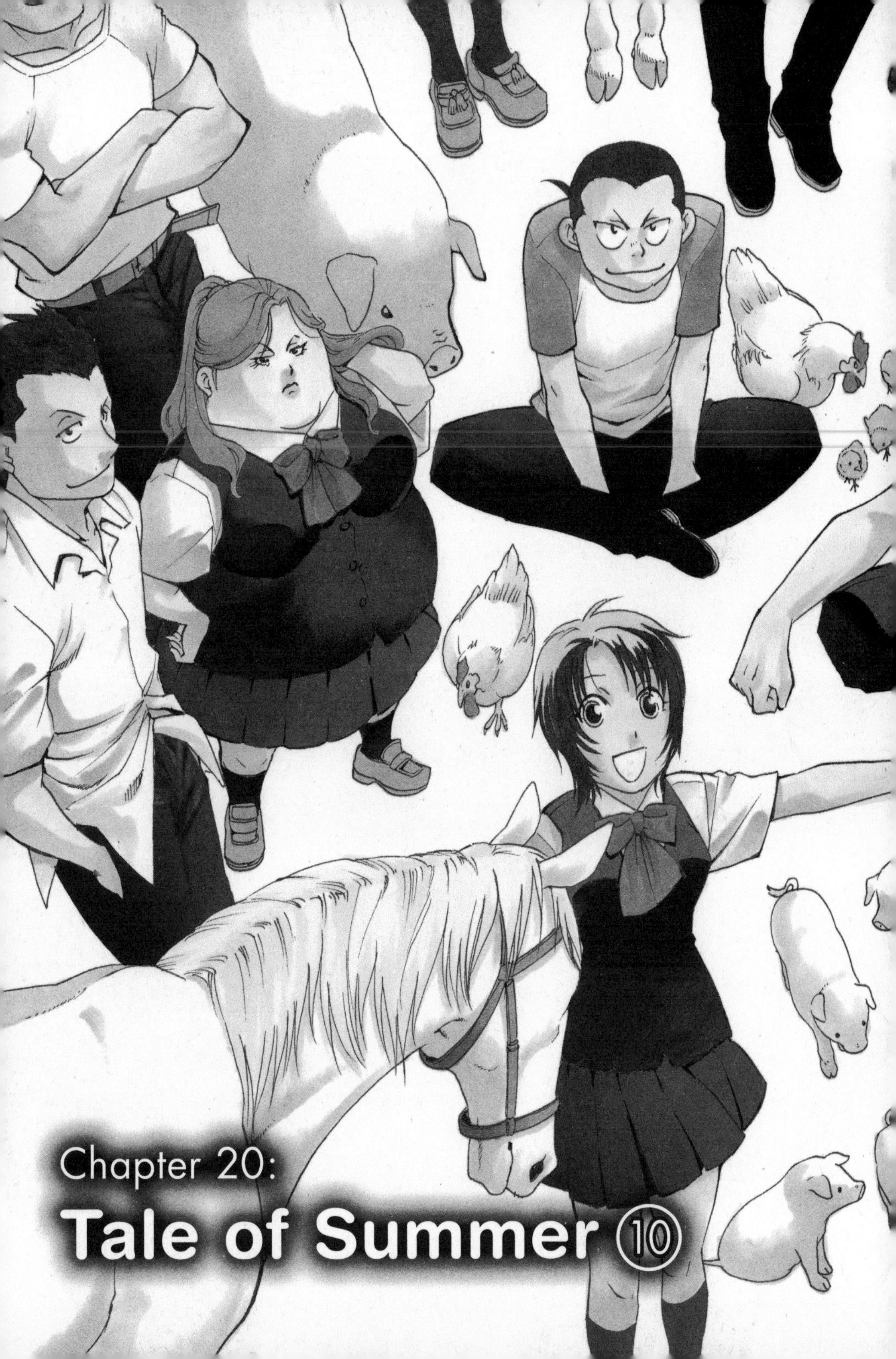
Chapter 20:
Tale of Summer ⑩

SHINNOSUKE
AIKAWA

MAKUBETSU EAST
MIDDLE SCHOOL

HOLSTEIN CLUB

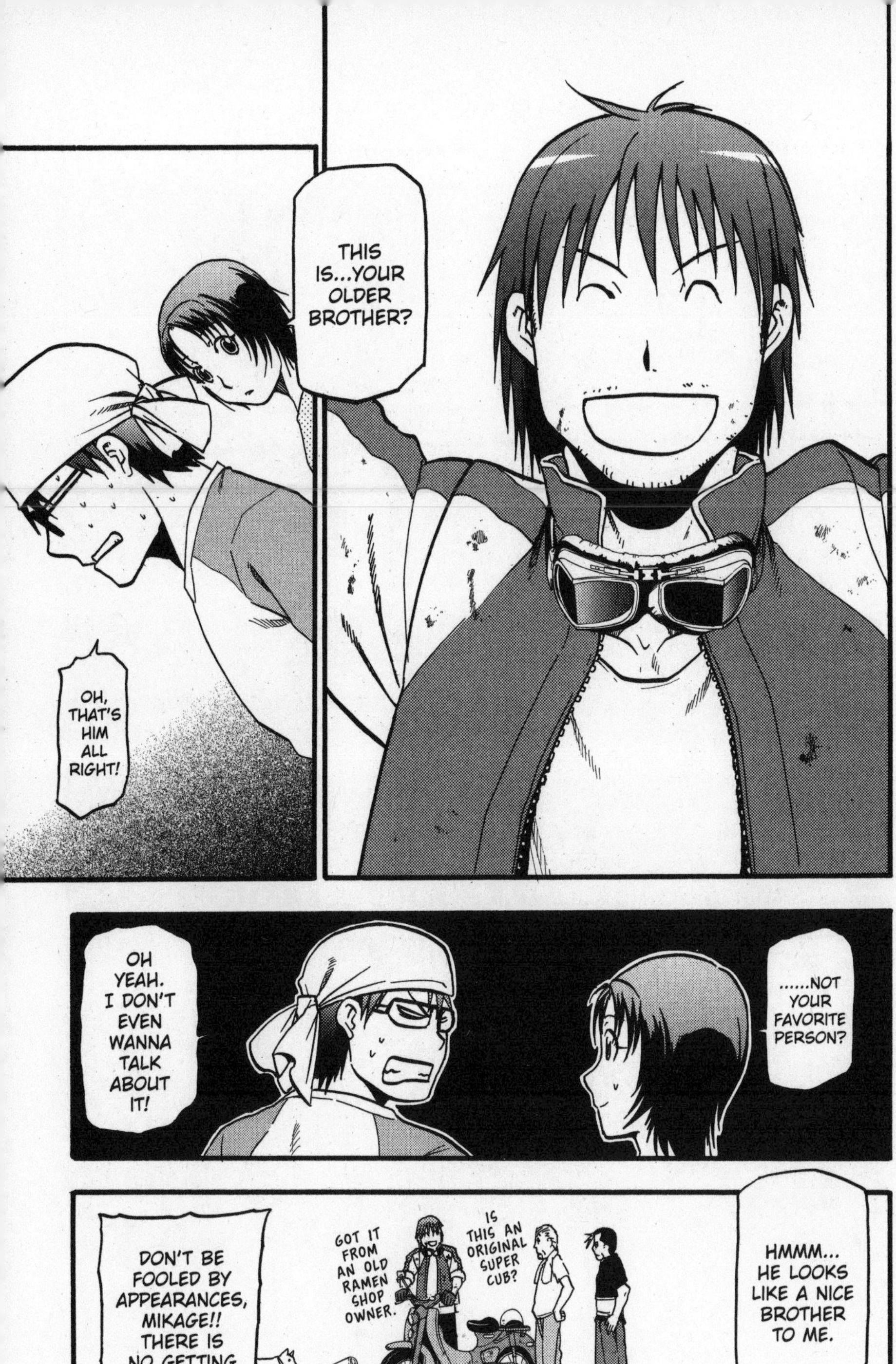
THIS IS...YOUR OLDER BROTHER?
OH, THAT'S HIM ALL RIGHT!
......NOT YOUR FAVORITE PERSON?
OH YEAH. I DON'T EVEN WANNA TALK ABOUT IT!
HMMM... HE LOOKS LIKE A NICE BROTHER TO ME.
IS THIS AN ORIGINAL SUPER CUB?
GOT IT FROM AN OLD RAMEN SHOP OWNER.
DON'T BE FOOLED BY APPEARANCES, MIKAGE!! THERE IS NO GETTING THROUGH TO THAT GUY!!

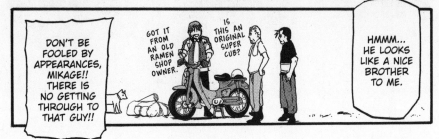

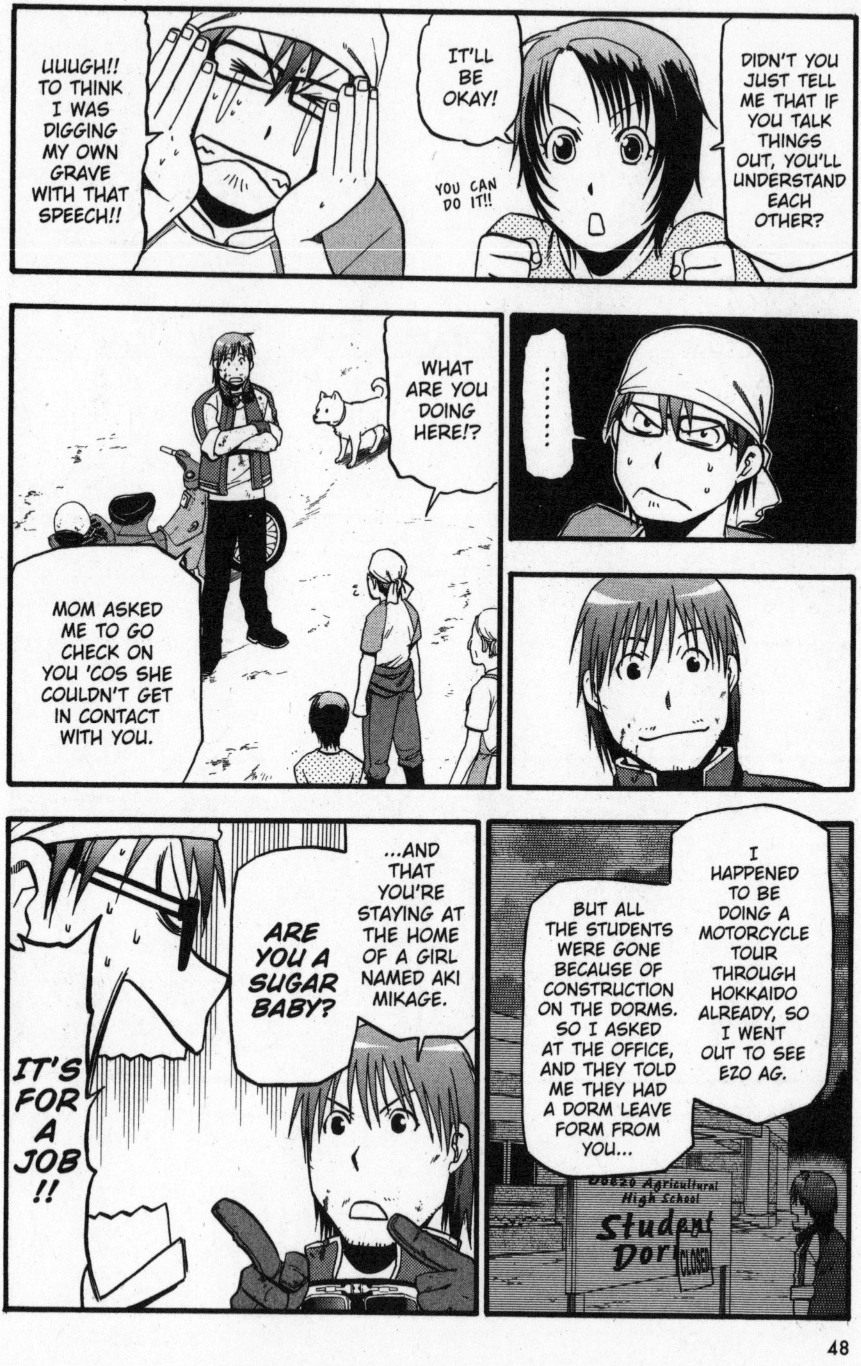
DIDN'T YOU JUST TELL ME THAT IF YOU TALK THINGS OUT, YOU'LL UNDERSTAND EACH OTHER?
IT'LL BE OKAY!
YOU CAN DO IT!!
UUUGH!! TO THINK I WAS DIGGING MY OWN GRAVE WITH THAT SPEECH!!
......
WHAT ARE YOU DOING HERE!?
MOM ASKED ME TO GO CHECK ON YOU 'COS SHE COULDN'T GET IN CONTACT WITH YOU.
I HAPPENED TO BE DOING A MOTORCYCLE TOUR THROUGH HOKKAIDO ALREADY, SO I WENT OUT TO SEE EZO AG.
BUT ALL THE STUDENTS WERE GONE BECAUSE OF CONSTRUCTION ON THE DORMS. SO I ASKED AT THE OFFICE, AND THEY TOLD ME THEY HAD A DORM LEAVE FORM FROM YOU...
Agricultural High School
CLOSED
...AND THAT YOU'RE STAYING AT THE HOME OF A GIRL NAMED AKI MIKAGE.
ARE YOU A SUGAR BABY?
IT'S FOR A JOB!!

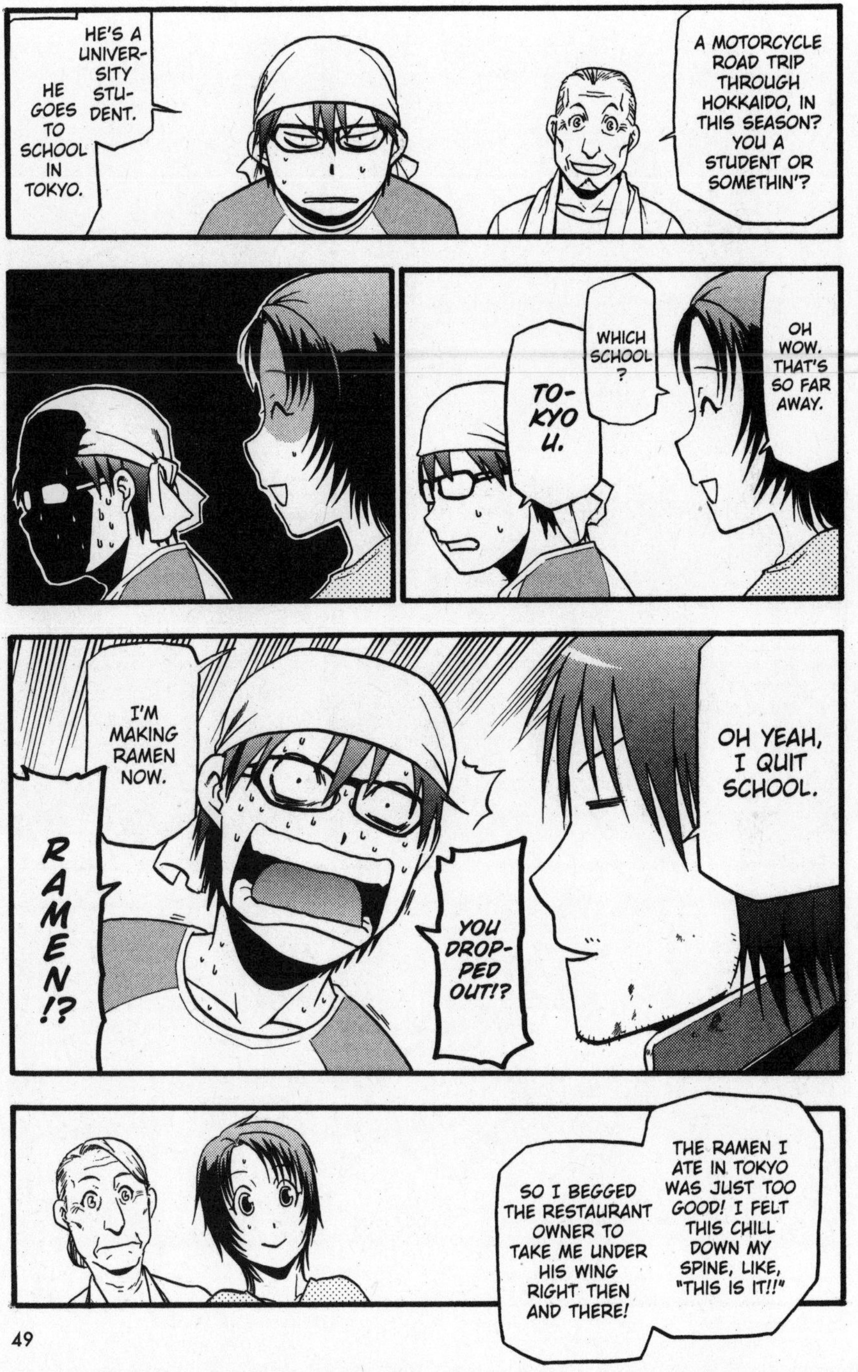
A MOTORCYCLE ROAD TRIP THROUGH HOKKAIDO, IN THIS SEASON? YOU A STUDENT OR SOMETHIN'?
HE'S A UNIVERSITY STUDENT.
HE GOES TO SCHOOL IN TOKYO.
OH WOW. THAT'S SO FAR AWAY.
WHICH SCHOOL?
TO-KYO U.
OH YEAH, I QUIT SCHOOL.
I'M MAKING RAMEN NOW.
YOU DROPPED OUT!?
RAMEN!?
THE RAMEN I ATE IN TOKYO WAS JUST TOO GOOD! I FELT THIS CHILL DOWN MY SPINE, LIKE, "THIS IS IT!!"
SO I BEGGED THE RESTAURANT OWNER TO TAKE ME UNDER HIS WING RIGHT THEN AND THERE!

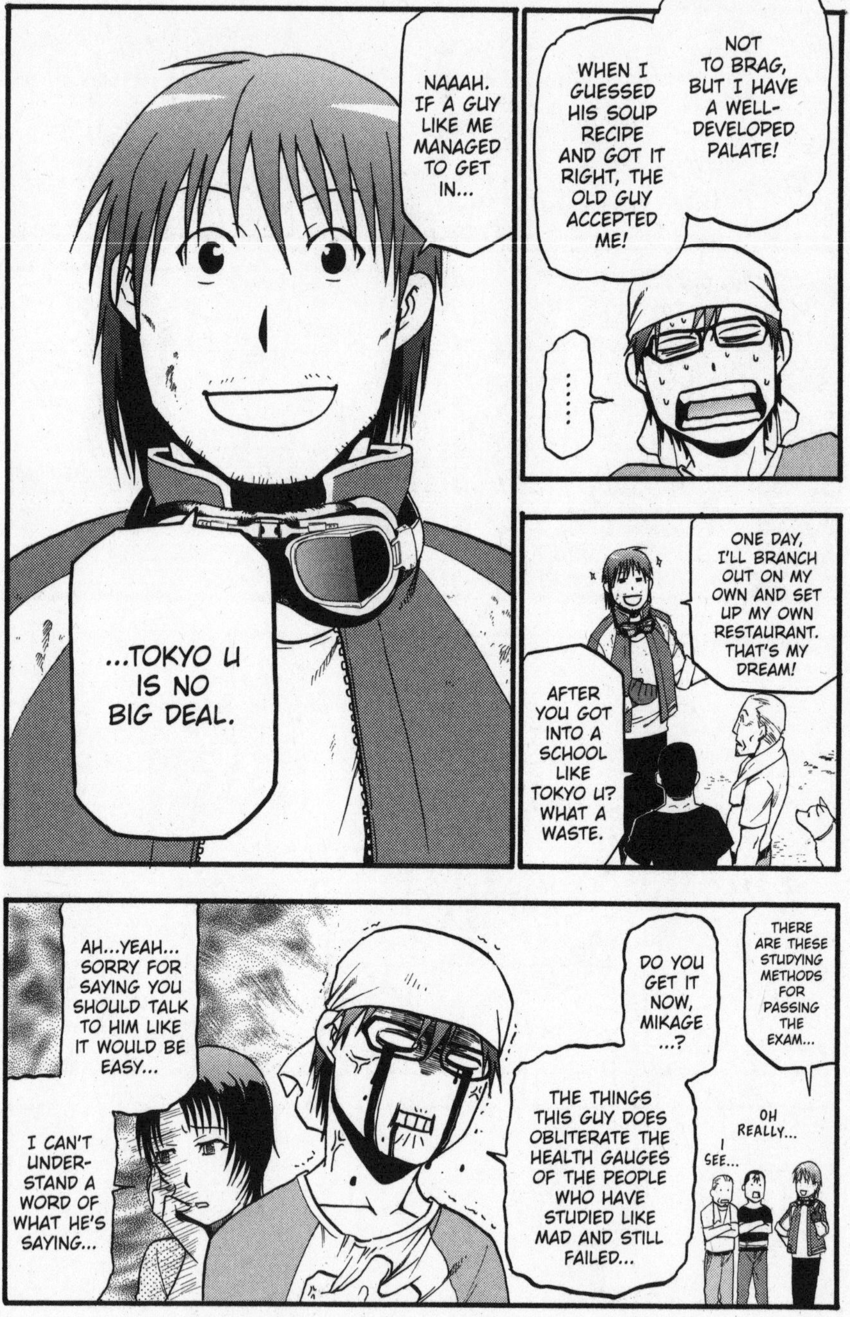
NOT TO BRAG, BUT I HAVE A WELL-DEVELOPED PALATE!
WHEN I GUESSED HIS SOUP RECIPE AND GOT IT RIGHT, THE OLD GUY ACCEPTED ME!
......
ONE DAY, I'LL BRANCH OUT ON MY OWN AND SET UP MY OWN RESTAURANT. THAT'S MY DREAM!
AFTER YOU GOT INTO A SCHOOL LIKE TOKYO U? WHAT A WASTE.
NAAAH. IF A GUY LIKE ME MANAGED TO GET IN...
...TOKYO U IS NO BIG DEAL.
THERE ARE THESE STUDYING METHODS FOR PASSING THE EXAM...
OH REALLY...
I SEE...
DO YOU GET IT NOW, MIKAGE ...?
THE THINGS THIS GUY DOES OBLITERATE THE HEALTH GAUGES OF THE PEOPLE WHO HAVE STUDIED LIKE MAD AND STILL FAILED...
AH...YEAH... SORRY FOR SAYING YOU SHOULD TALK TO HIM LIKE IT WOULD BE EASY...
I CAN'T UNDER-STAND A WORD OF WHAT HE'S SAYING...

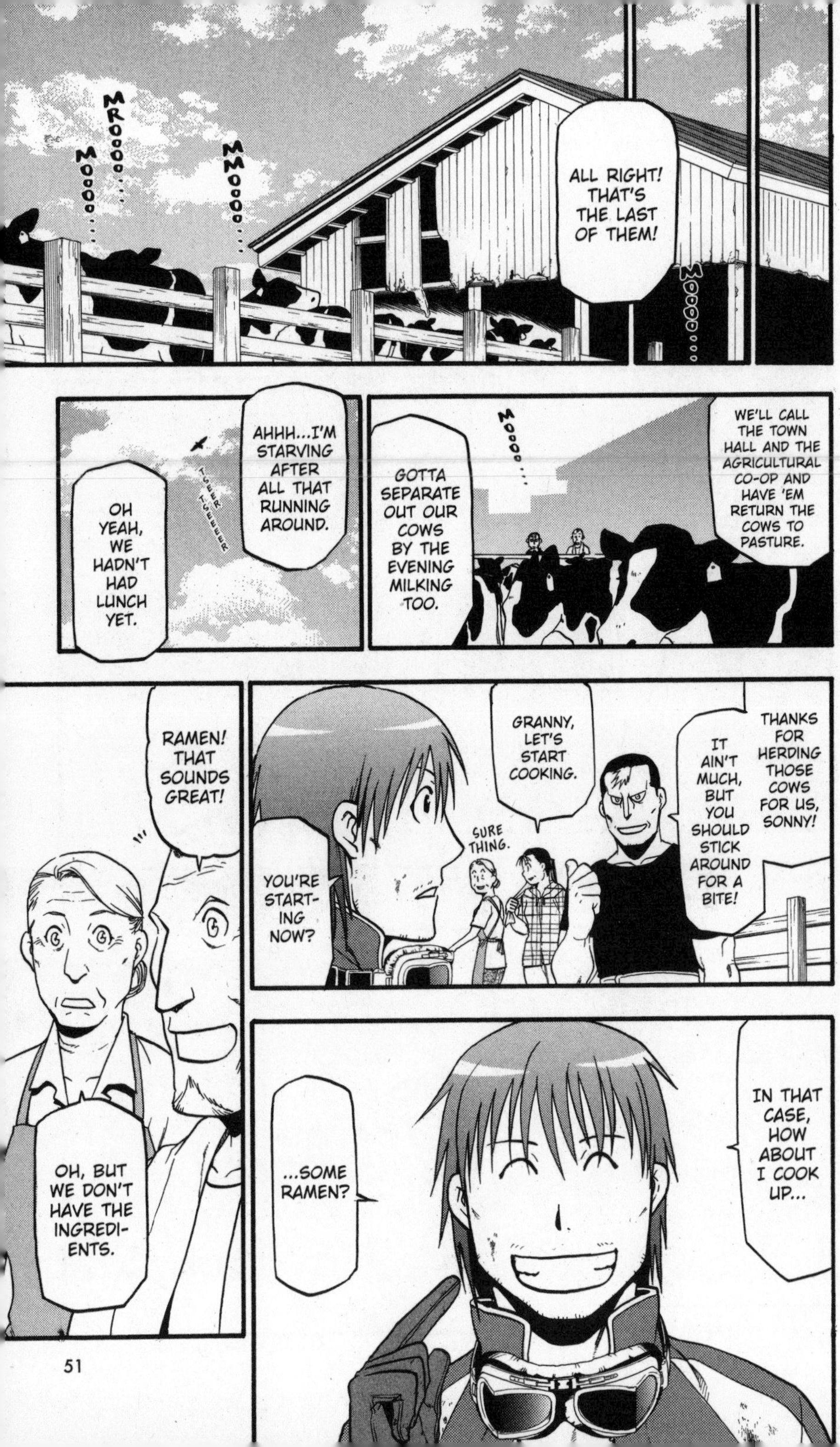
ALL RIGHT! THAT'S THE LAST OF THEM!
MOOOOO...
MMOOOOO...
MROOOOO...
MOOOOO...
WE'LL CALL THE TOWN HALL AND THE AGRICULTURAL CO-OP AND HAVE 'EM RETURN THE COWS TO PASTURE.
MOOOO...
GOTTA SEPARATE OUT OUR COWS BY THE EVENING MILKING TOO.
AHHH...I'M STARVING AFTER ALL THAT RUNNING AROUND.
TWEER TWEEEER
OH YEAH, WE HADN'T HAD LUNCH YET.
THANKS FOR HERDING THOSE COWS FOR US, SONNY!
IT AIN'T MUCH, BUT YOU SHOULD STICK AROUND FOR A BITE!
GRANNY, LET'S START COOKING.
SURE THING.
YOU'RE STARTING NOW?
IN THAT CASE, HOW ABOUT I COOK UP...
...SOME RAMEN?
RAMEN! THAT SOUNDS GREAT!
OH, BUT WE DON'T HAVE THE INGREDIENTS.

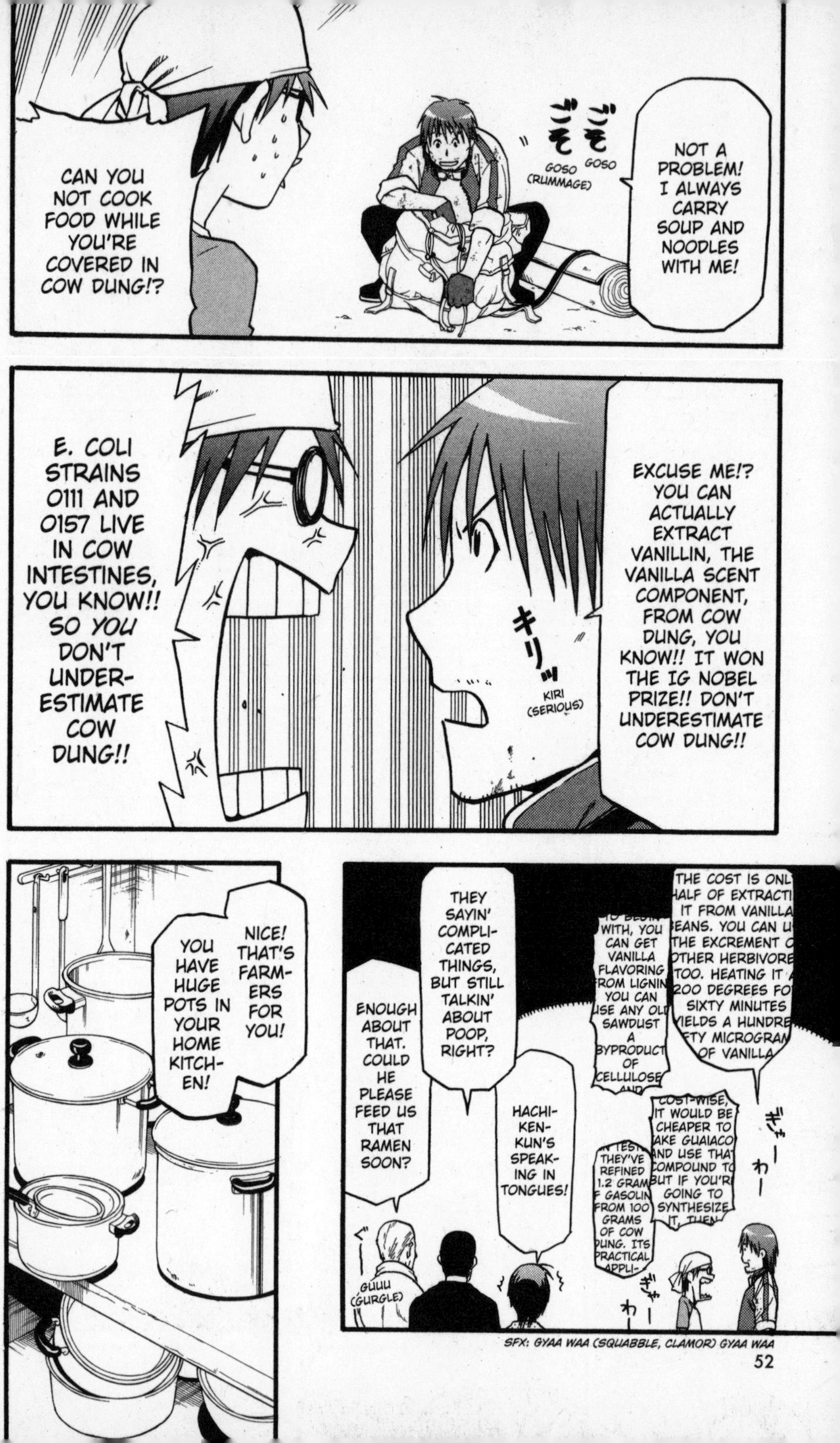
NOT A PROBLEM! I ALWAYS CARRY SOUP AND NOODLES WITH ME!
GOSO GOSO (RUMMAGE)
CAN YOU NOT COOK FOOD WHILE YOU'RE COVERED IN COW DUNG!?
EXCUSE ME!? YOU CAN ACTUALLY EXTRACT VANILLIN, THE VANILLA SCENT COMPONENT, FROM COW DUNG, YOU KNOW!! IT WON THE IG NOBEL PRIZE!! DON'T UNDERESTIMATE COW DUNG!!
KIRI (SERIOUS)
E. COLI STRAINS O111 AND O157 LIVE IN COW INTESTINES, YOU KNOW!! SO YOU DON'T UNDER-ESTIMATE COW DUNG!!
THE COST IS ONL HALF OF EXTRACTI IT FROM VANILLA EANS. YOU CAN U THE EXCREMENT O OTHER HERBIVORE TOO. HEATING IT A 200 DEGREES FO SIXTY MINUTES YIELDS A HUNDRE FTY MICROGRAM OF VANILLA
WITH, YOU CAN GET VANILLA FLAVORING FROM LIGNIN YOU CAN USE ANY OLD SAWDUST A BYPRODUCT OF CELLULOSE
THEY SAYIN' COMPLI-CATED THINGS, BUT STILL TALKIN' ABOUT POOP, RIGHT?
ENOUGH ABOUT THAT. COULD HE PLEASE FEED US THAT RAMEN SOON?
COST-WISE, IT WOULD BE CHEAPER TO AKE GUAIACO AND USE THAT COMPOUND TO BUT IF YOU'R GOING TO SYNTHESIZE IT, THEN
THEY'VE REFINED 1.2 GRAM F GASOLIN FROM 100 GRAMS OF COW DUNG. ITS PRACTICAL APPLI-
HACHI-KEN-KUN'S SPEAK-ING IN TONGUES!
GUUU (GURGLE)
NICE! THAT'S FARMERS FOR YOU!
YOU HAVE HUGE POTS IN YOUR HOME KITCH-EN!

SFX: GYAA WAA (SQUABBLE, CLAMOR) GYAA WAA

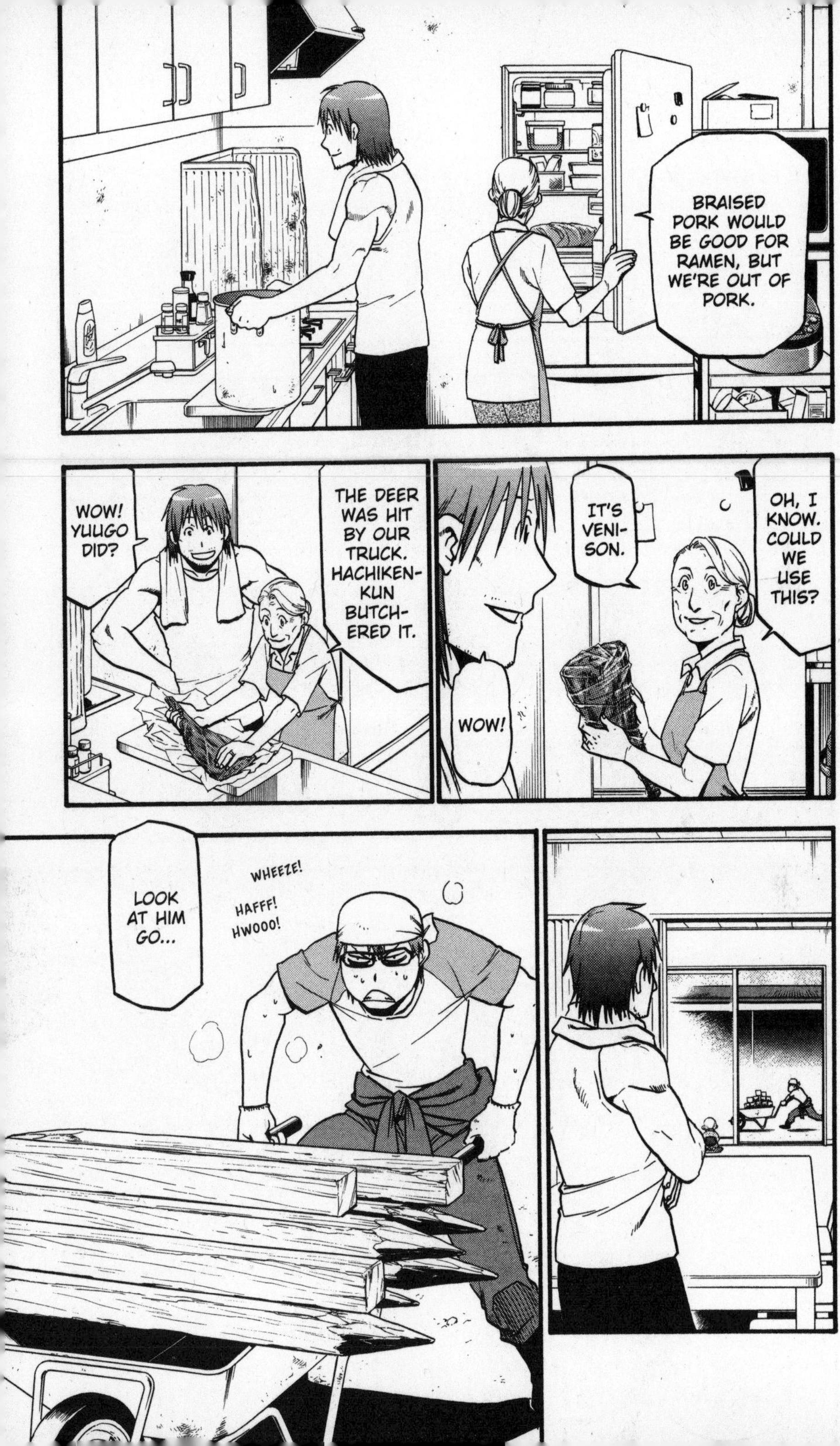
BRAISED PORK WOULD BE GOOD FOR RAMEN, BUT WE'RE OUT OF PORK.
OH, I KNOW. COULD WE USE THIS?
IT'S VENI-SON.
WOW!
THE DEER WAS HIT BY OUR TRUCK. HACHIKEN-KUN BUTCHERED IT.
WOW! YUUGO DID?
WHEEZE!
HAFFF! HWOOO!
LOOK AT HIM GO...

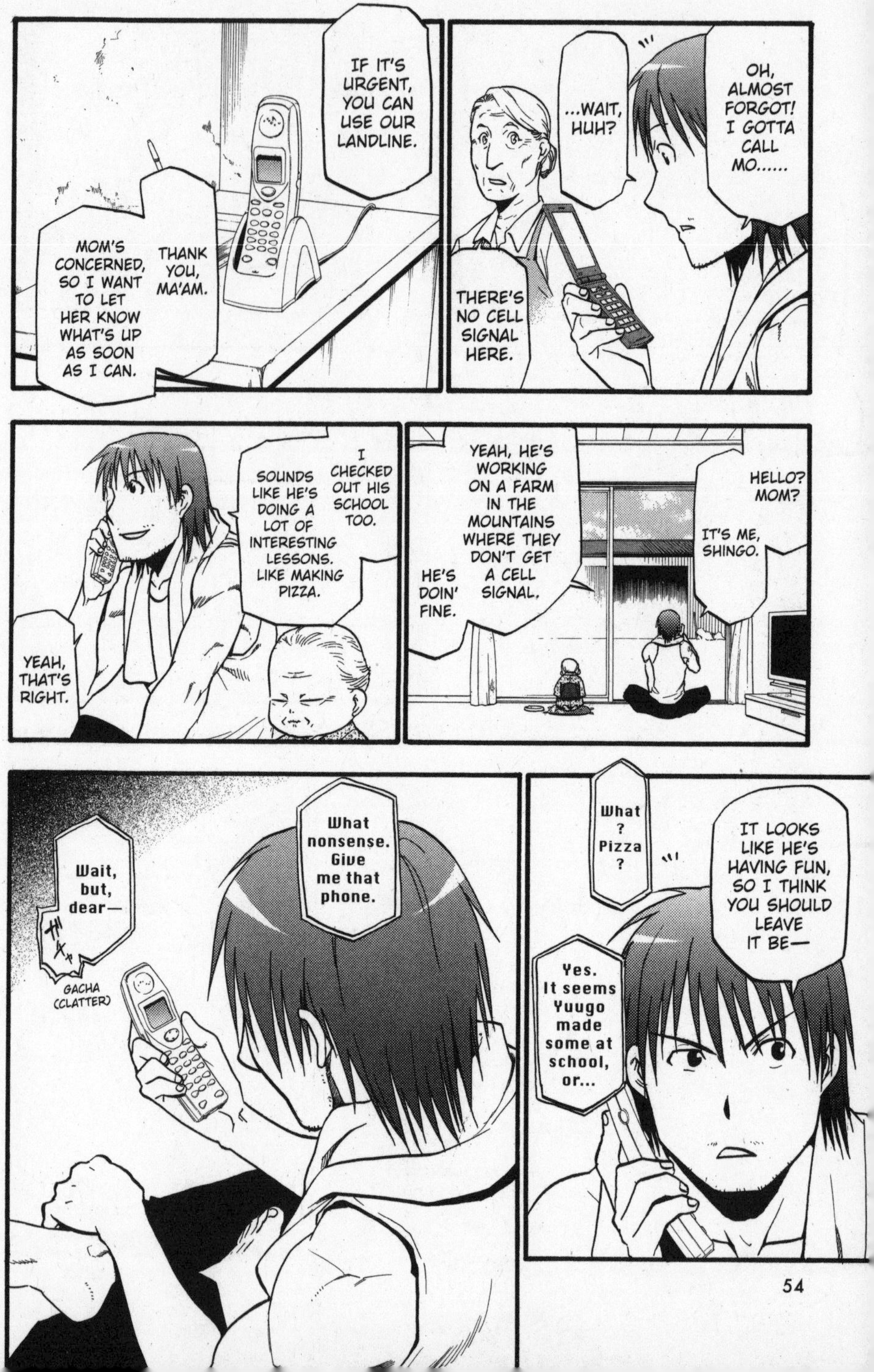
OH, ALMOST FORGOT! I GOTTA CALL MO......
...WAIT, HUH?
THERE'S NO CELL SIGNAL HERE.
IF IT'S URGENT, YOU CAN USE OUR LANDLINE.
THANK YOU, MA'AM.
MOM'S CONCERNED, SO I WANT TO LET HER KNOW WHAT'S UP AS SOON AS I CAN.
HELLO? MOM?
IT'S ME, SHINGO.
YEAH, HE'S WORKING ON A FARM IN THE MOUNTAINS WHERE THEY DON'T GET A CELL SIGNAL.
HE'S DOIN' FINE.
I CHECKED OUT HIS SCHOOL TOO.
SOUNDS LIKE HE'S DOING A LOT OF INTERESTING LESSONS. LIKE MAKING PIZZA.
YEAH, THAT'S RIGHT.
IT LOOKS LIKE HE'S HAVING FUN, SO I THINK YOU SHOULD LEAVE IT BE—
What? Pizza?
Yes. It seems Yuugo made some at school, or...
What nonsense. Give me that phone.
Wait, but, dear—
GACHA (CLATTER)

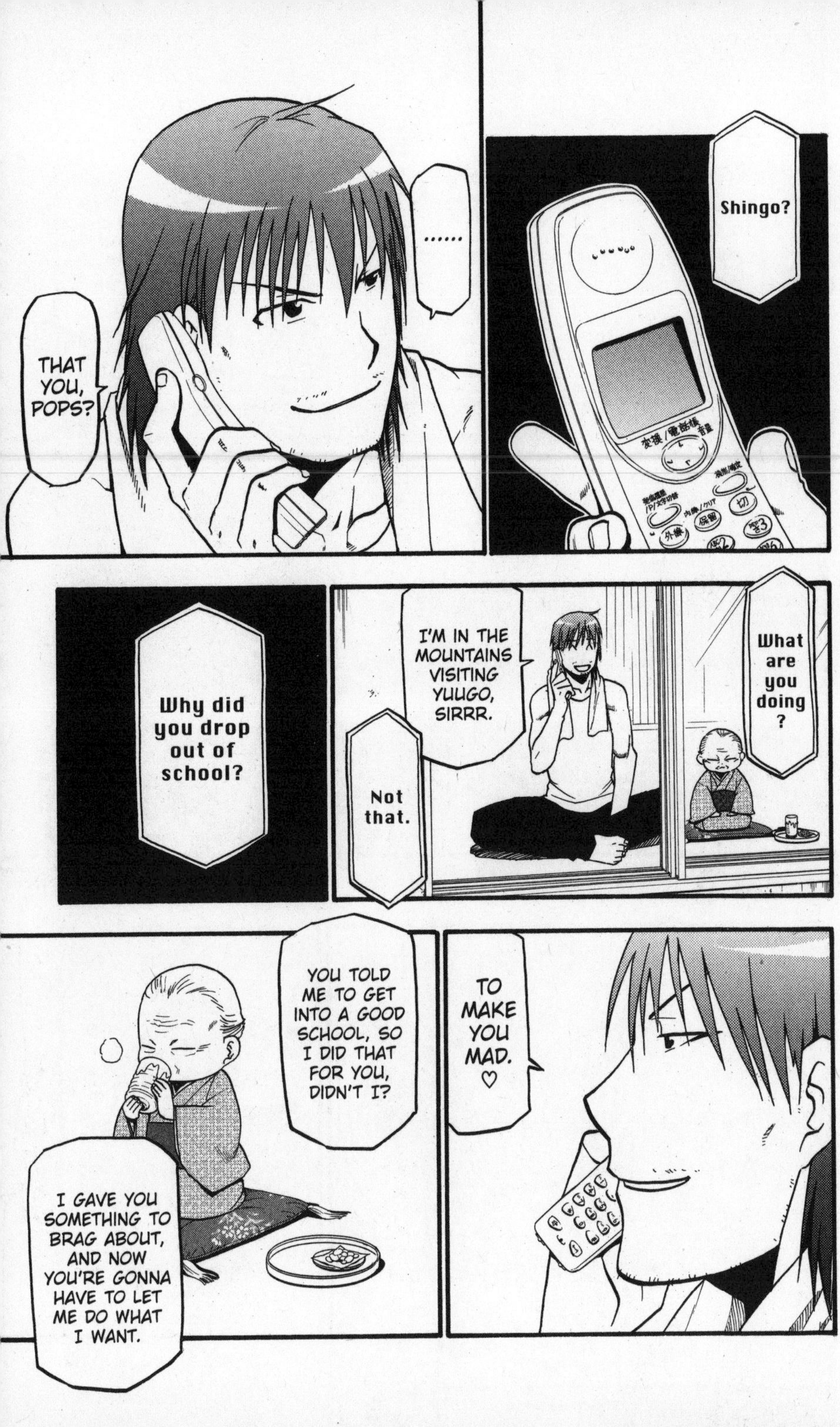
Shingo?
......
THAT YOU, POPS?
What are you doing?
I'M IN THE MOUNTAINS VISITING YUUGO, SIRRR.
Not that.
Why did you drop out of school?
TO MAKE YOU MAD. ♡
YOU TOLD ME TO GET INTO A GOOD SCHOOL, SO I DID THAT FOR YOU, DIDN'T I?
I GAVE YOU SOMETHING TO BRAG ABOUT, AND NOW YOU'RE GONNA HAVE TO LET ME DO WHAT I WANT.

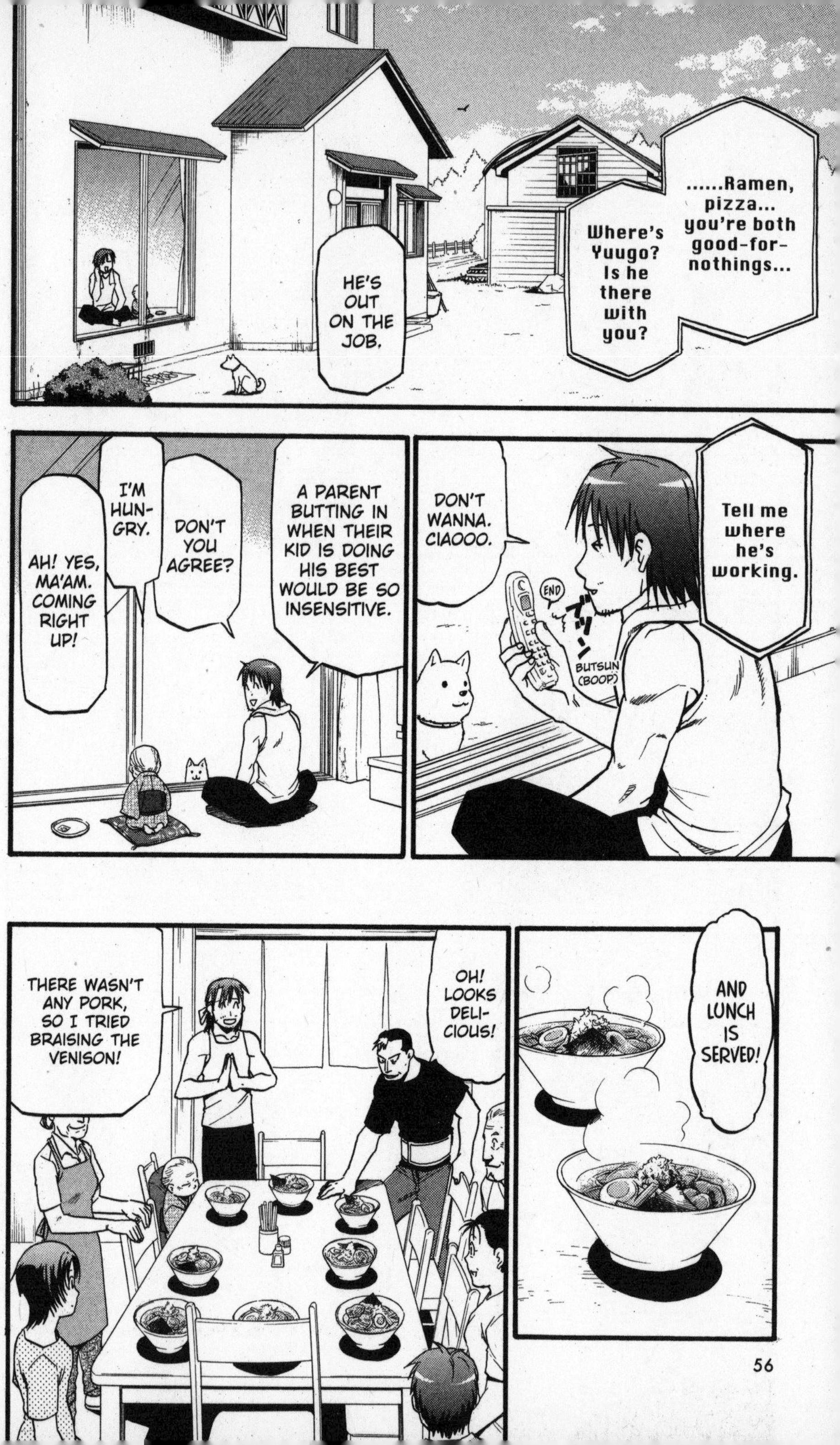
......Ramen, pizza... you're both good-for-nothings...
Where's Yuugo? Is he there with you?
HE'S OUT ON THE JOB.
Tell me where he's working.
END
BUTSUN (BOOP)
DON'T WANNA. CIAOOO.
A PARENT BUTTING IN WHEN THEIR KID IS DOING HIS BEST WOULD BE SO INSENSITIVE.
DON'T YOU AGREE?
I'M HUN-GRY.
AH! YES, MA'AM. COMING RIGHT UP!
AND LUNCH IS SERVED!
OH! LOOKS DELI-CIOUS!
THERE WASN'T ANY PORK, SO I TRIED BRAISING THE VENISON!

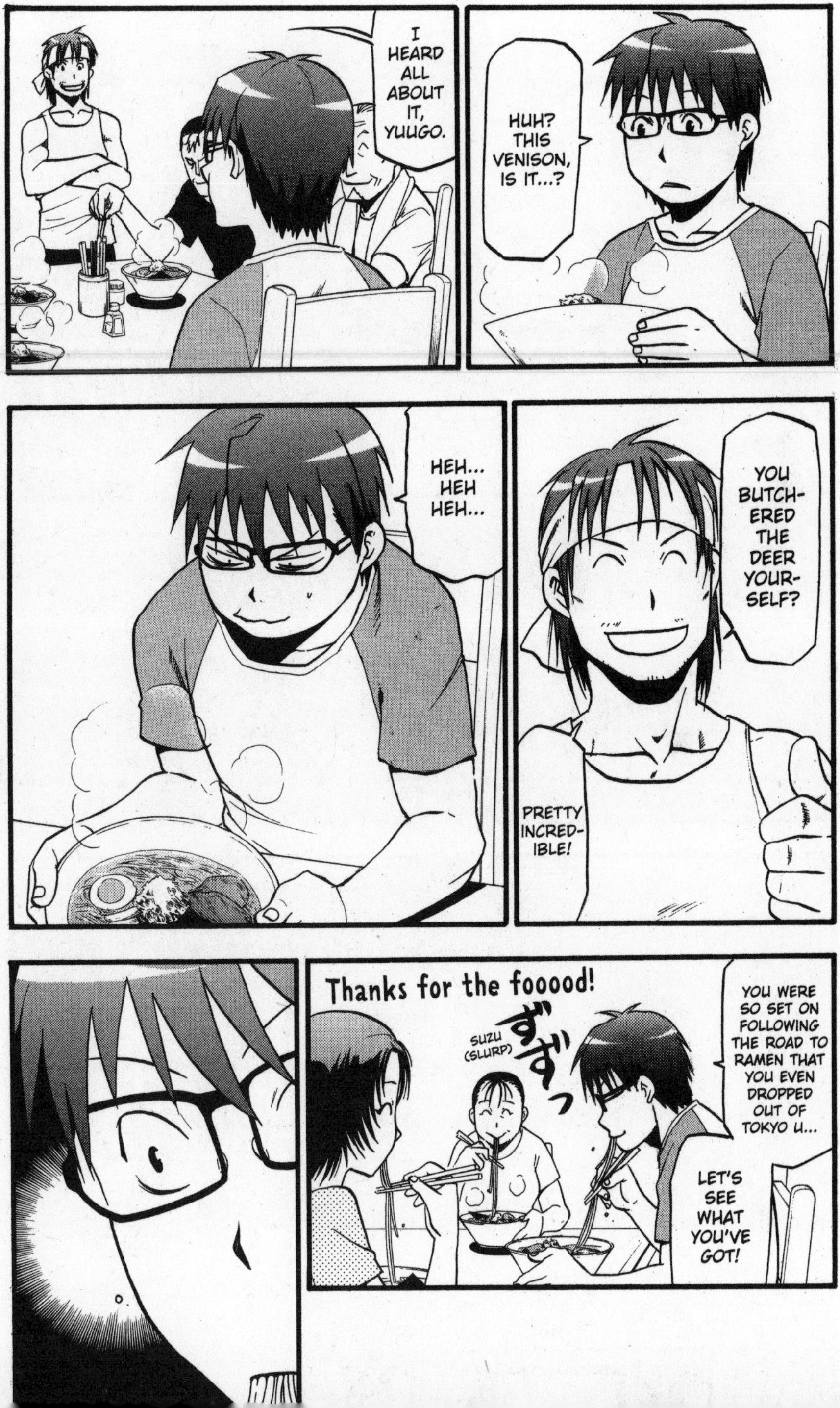
HUH? THIS VENISON, IS IT...?
I HEARD ALL ABOUT IT, YUUGO.
YOU BUTCHERED THE DEER YOURSELF?
PRETTY INCREDIBLE!
HEH... HEH HEH...
YOU WERE SO SET ON FOLLOWING THE ROAD TO RAMEN THAT YOU EVEN DROPPED OUT OF TOKYO U...
Thanks for the fooood!
ずずっ
SUZU (SLURP)
LET'S SEE WHAT YOU'VE GOT!

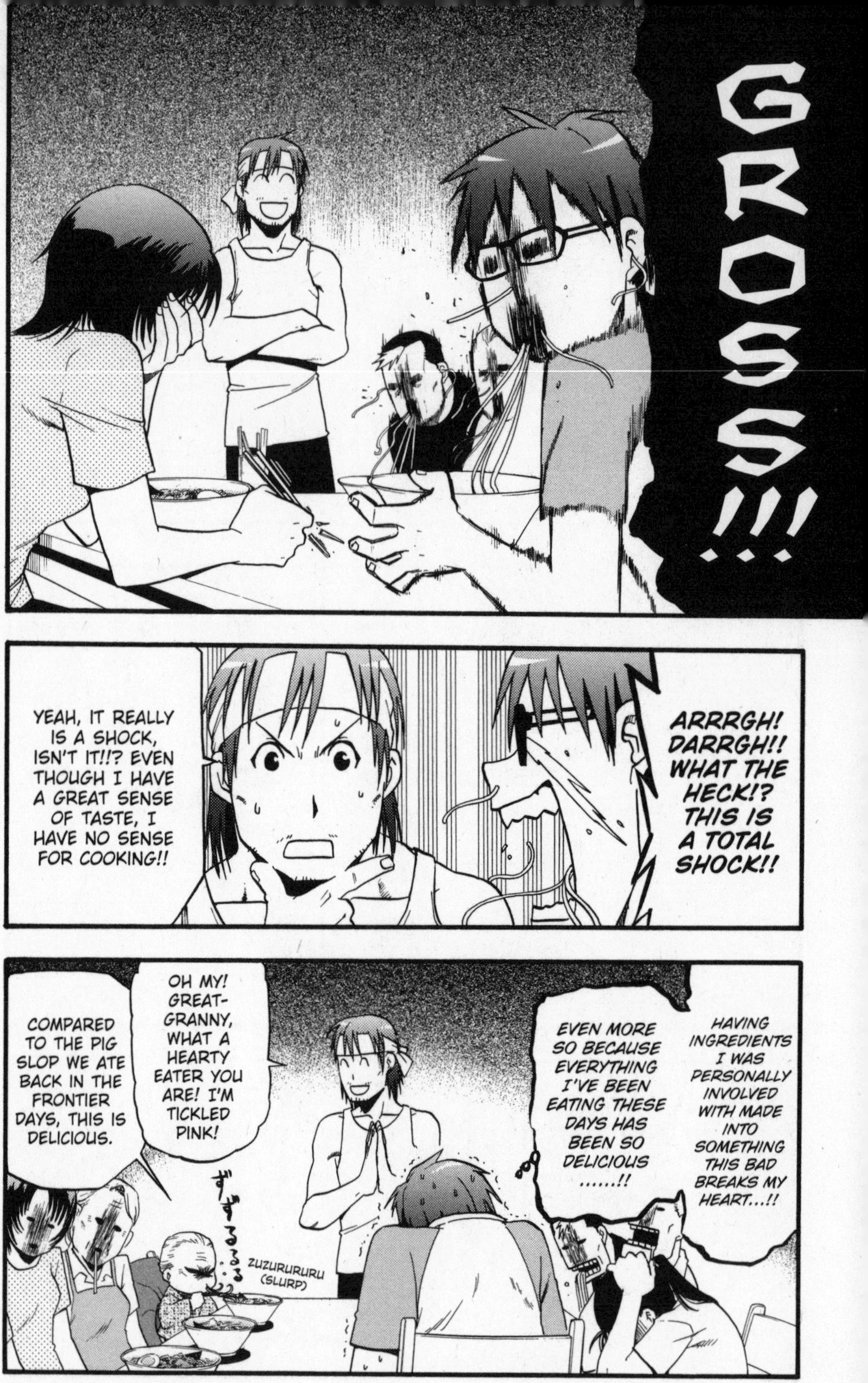
GROSS!!!
ARRRGH! DARRGH!! WHAT THE HECK!? THIS IS A TOTAL SHOCK!!
YEAH, IT REALLY IS A SHOCK, ISN'T IT!!? EVEN THOUGH I HAVE A GREAT SENSE OF TASTE, I HAVE NO SENSE FOR COOKING!!
HAVING INGREDIENTS I WAS PERSONALLY INVOLVED WITH MADE INTO SOMETHING THIS BAD BREAKS MY HEART...!!
EVEN MORE SO BECAUSE EVERYTHING I'VE BEEN EATING THESE DAYS HAS BEEN SO DELICIOUS ......!!
OH MY! GREAT-GRANNY, WHAT A HEARTY EATER YOU ARE! I'M TICKLED PINK!
COMPARED TO THE PIG SLOP WE ATE BACK IN THE FRONTIER DAYS, THIS IS DELICIOUS.
ずずるるる
ZUZURURURU (SLURP)

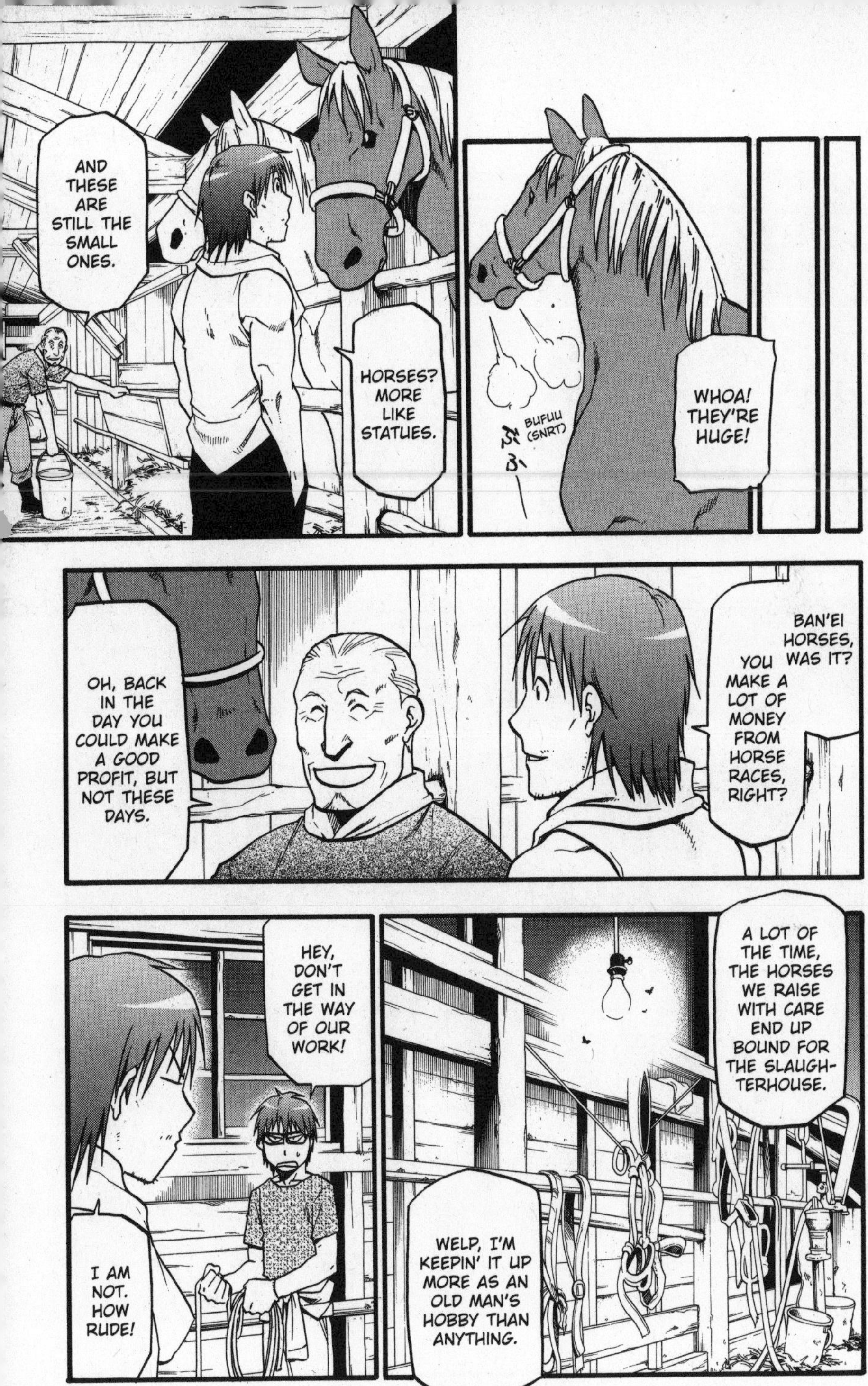

WHOA! THEY'RE HUGE!
ぶふ
BUFUU (SNRT)
HORSES? MORE LIKE STATUES.
AND THESE ARE STILL THE SMALL ONES.
BAN'EI HORSES, WAS IT? YOU MAKE A LOT OF MONEY FROM HORSE RACES, RIGHT?
OH, BACK IN THE DAY YOU COULD MAKE A GOOD PROFIT, BUT NOT THESE DAYS.
A LOT OF THE TIME, THE HORSES WE RAISE WITH CARE END UP BOUND FOR THE SLAUGHTERHOUSE.
WELP, I'M KEEPIN' IT UP MORE AS AN OLD MAN'S HOBBY THAN ANYTHING.
HEY, DON'T GET IN THE WAY OF OUR WORK!
I AM NOT. HOW RUDE!

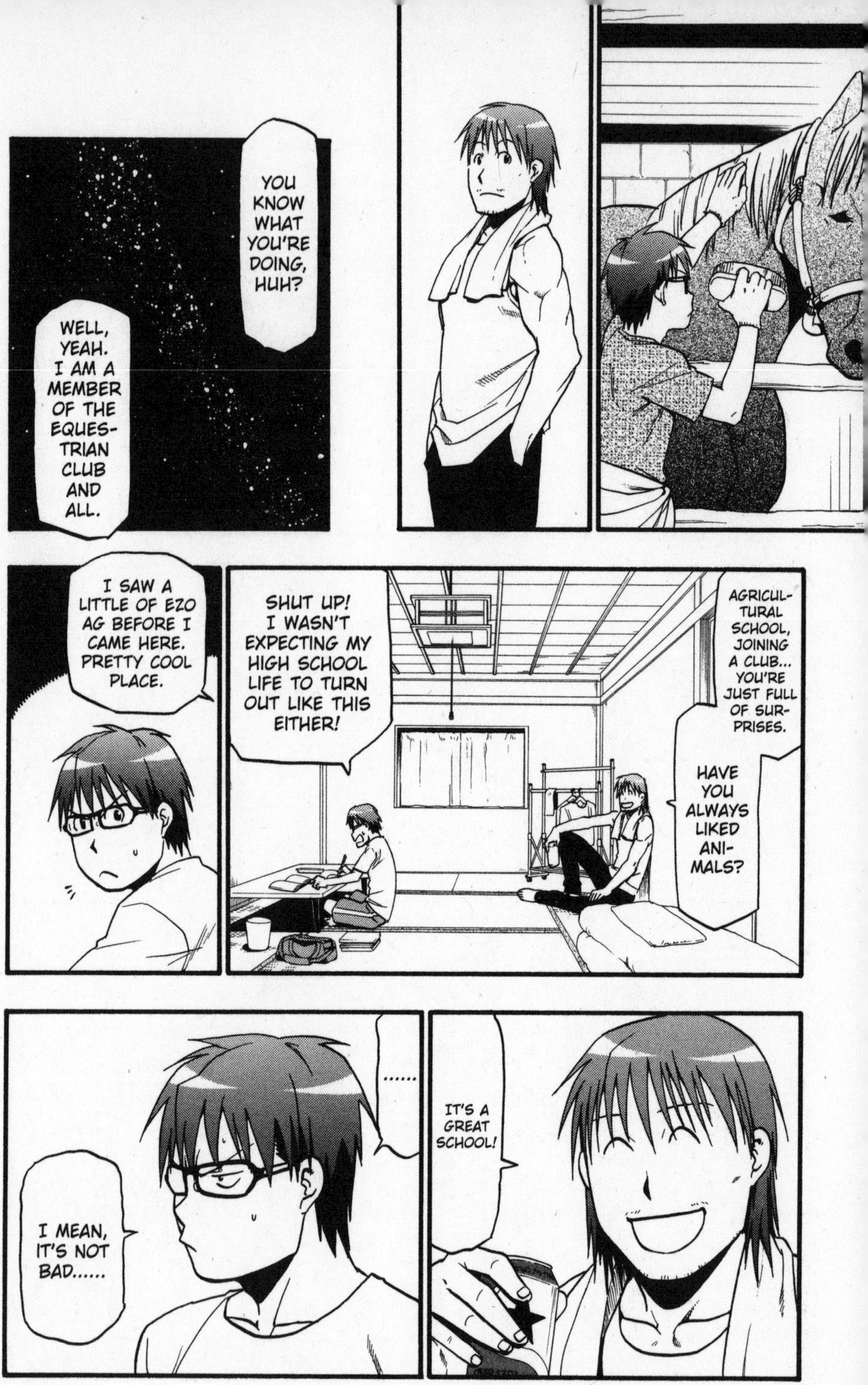
YOU KNOW WHAT YOU'RE DOING, HUH?
WELL, YEAH. I AM A MEMBER OF THE EQUES-TRIAN CLUB AND ALL.
AGRICUL-TURAL SCHOOL, JOINING A CLUB... YOU'RE JUST FULL OF SUR-PRISES.
HAVE YOU ALWAYS LIKED ANI-MALS?
SHUT UP! I WASN'T EXPECTING MY HIGH SCHOOL LIFE TO TURN OUT LIKE THIS EITHER!
I SAW A LITTLE OF EZO AG BEFORE I CAME HERE. PRETTY COOL PLACE.
IT'S A GREAT SCHOOL!
......
I MEAN, IT'S NOT BAD......

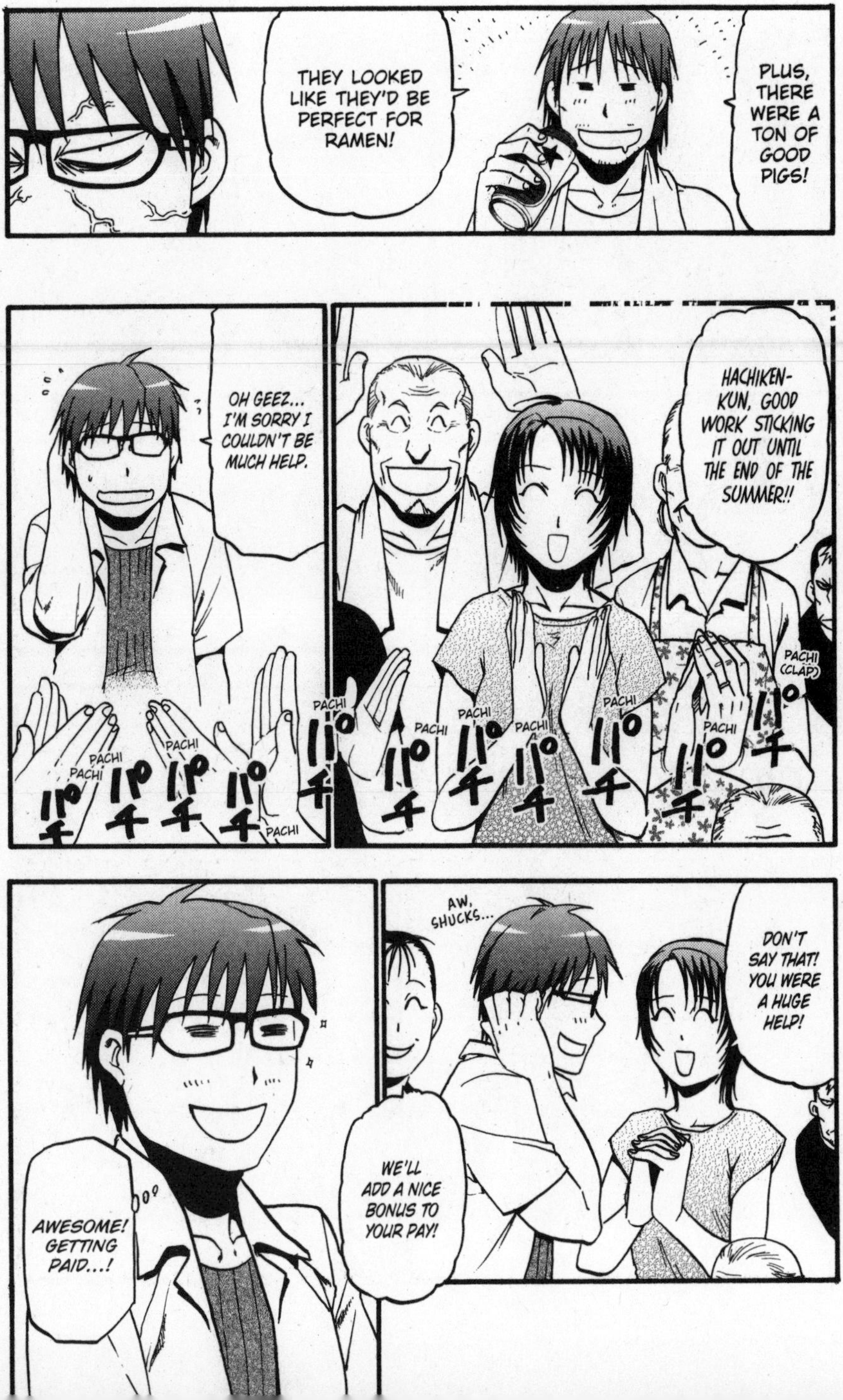
PLUS, THERE WERE A TON OF GOOD PIGS!
THEY LOOKED LIKE THEY'D BE PERFECT FOR RAMEN!
HACHIKEN-KUN, GOOD WORK STICKING IT OUT UNTIL THE END OF THE SUMMER!!
PACHI (CLAP)
PACHI
PACHI
PACHI
PACHI
PACHI
OH GEEZ... I'M SORRY I COULDN'T BE MUCH HELP.
PACHI
PACHI
PACHI
PACHI
DON'T SAY THAT! YOU WERE A HUGE HELP!
AW, SHUCKS...
WE'LL ADD A NICE BONUS TO YOUR PAY!
AWESOME! GETTING PAID...!

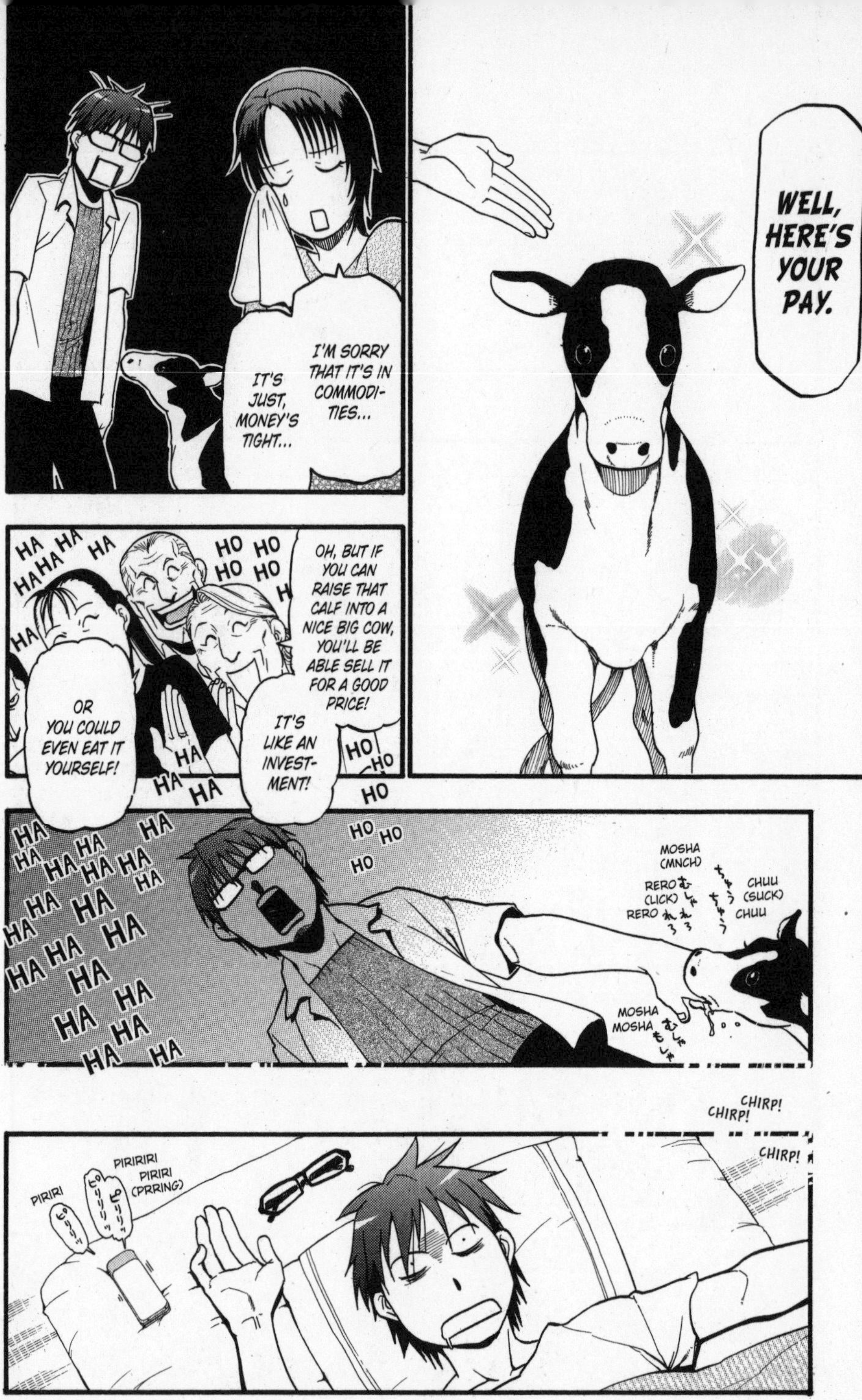

WELL, HERE'S YOUR PAY.
I'M SORRY THAT IT'S IN COMMODITIES...
IT'S JUST, MONEY'S TIGHT...
OH, BUT IF YOU CAN RAISE THAT CALF INTO A NICE BIG COW, YOU'LL BE ABLE SELL IT FOR A GOOD PRICE!
HO HO HO HO
HA HA HA HA HA HA
IT'S LIKE AN INVESTMENT!
OR YOU COULD EVEN EAT IT YOURSELF!
HO HO
HA HA
HO
HO HO HO
HA HA HA HA HA HA HA HA HA HA HA HA HA HA HA HA HA HA HA HA HA HA
CHUU (SUCK) CHUU
MOSHA (MNCH)
RERO (LICK) RERO
MOSHA MOSHA
CHIRP! CHIRP!
CHIRP!
PIRIRIRI PIRIRI (PRRING)
PIRIRI

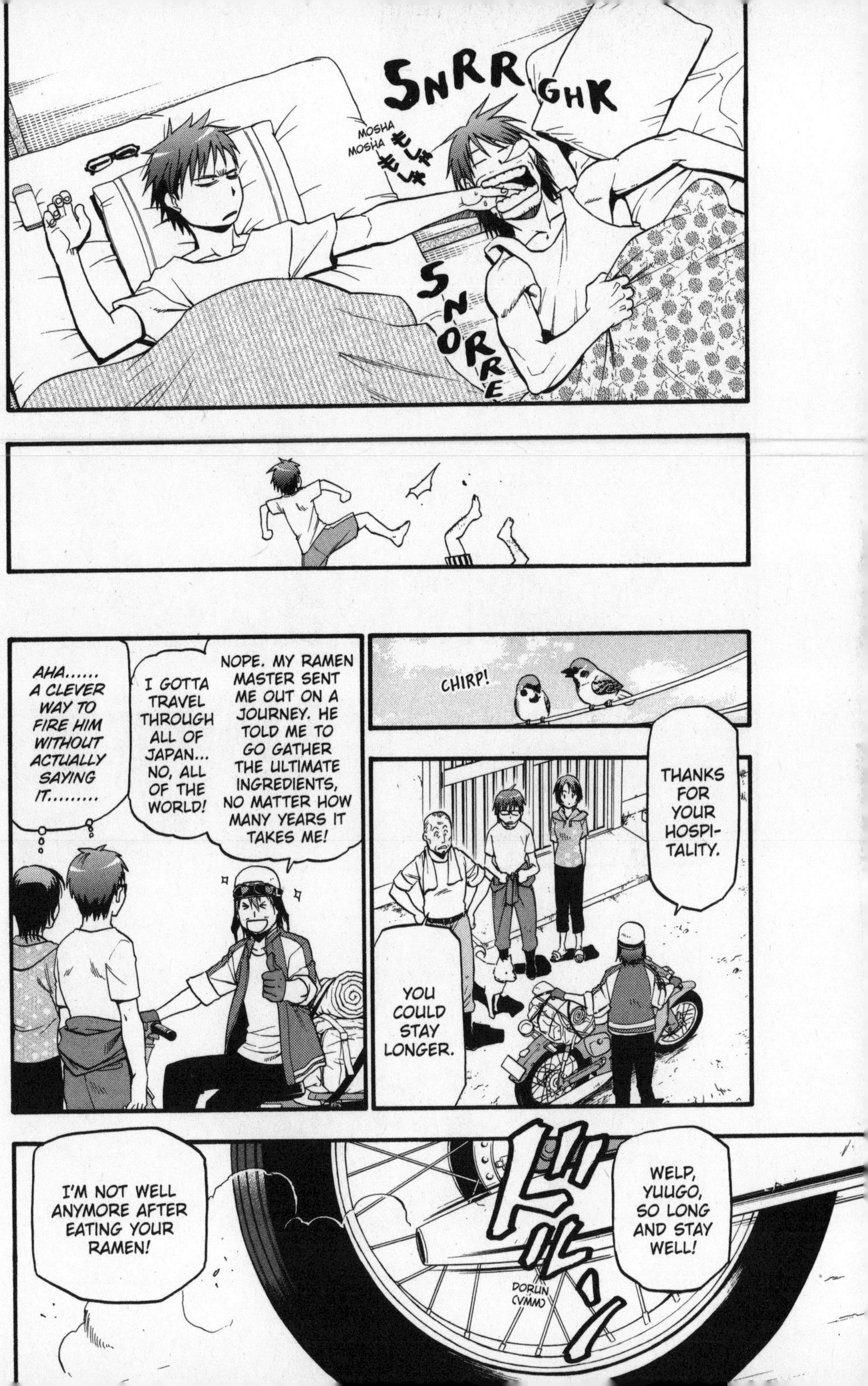
SNRRGHK
MOSHA MOSHA
もじゃ もじゃ
SNORRE
CHIRP!
THANKS FOR YOUR HOSPI-TALITY.
YOU COULD STAY LONGER.
NOPE. MY RAMEN MASTER SENT ME OUT ON A JOURNEY. HE TOLD ME TO GO GATHER THE ULTIMATE INGREDIENTS, NO MATTER HOW MANY YEARS IT TAKES ME!
I GOTTA TRAVEL THROUGH ALL OF JAPAN... NO, ALL OF THE WORLD!
AHA...... A CLEVER WAY TO FIRE HIM WITHOUT ACTUALLY SAYING IT.........
WELP, YUUGO, SO LONG AND STAY WELL!
DORUN (VMM)
I'M NOT WELL ANYMORE AFTER EATING YOUR RAMEN!

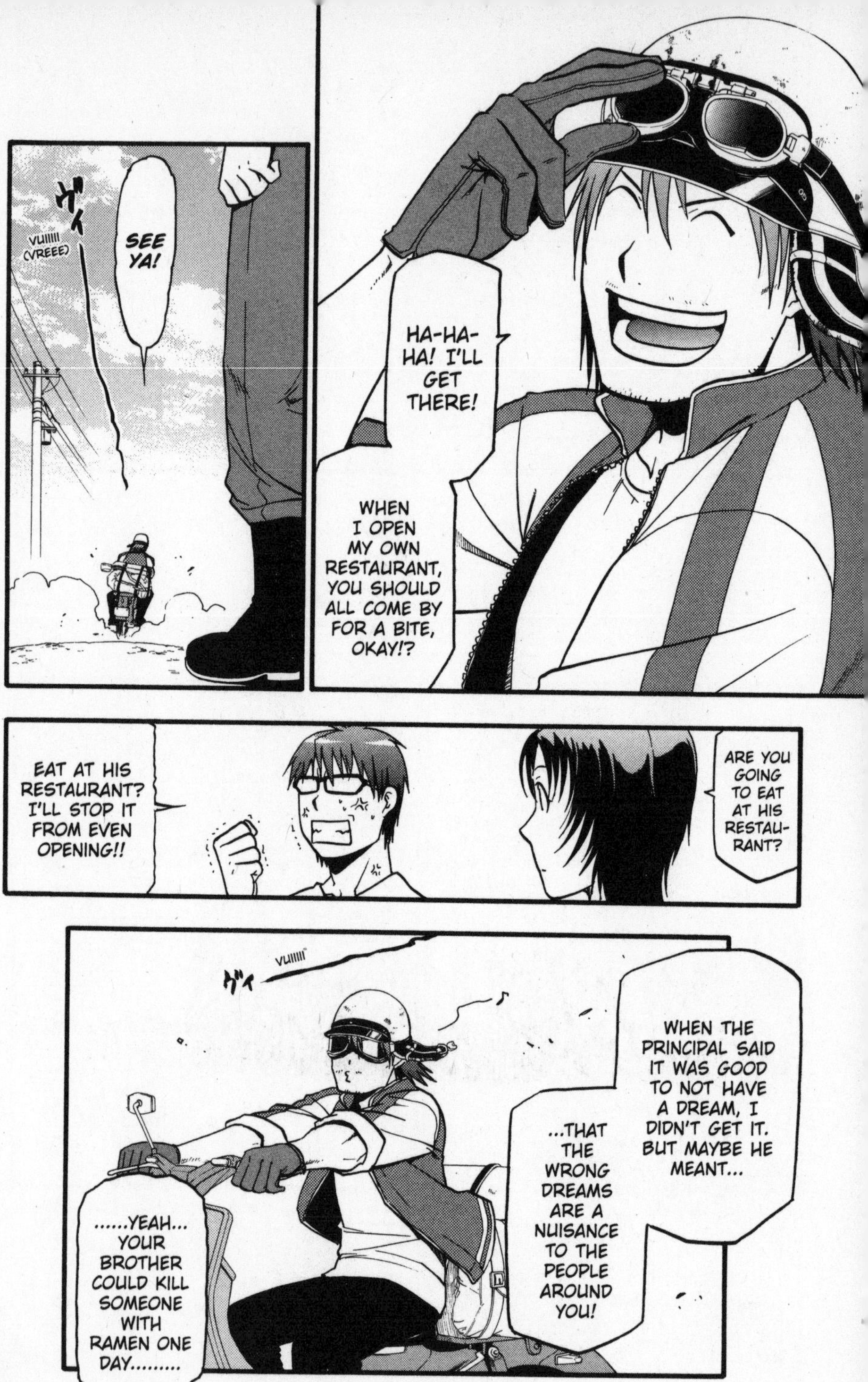
HA-HA-HA! I'LL GET THERE!
WHEN I OPEN MY OWN RESTAURANT, YOU SHOULD ALL COME BY FOR A BITE, OKAY!?
SEE YA!
ヴィ
VUIIIII (VREEE)
ARE YOU GOING TO EAT AT HIS RESTAURANT?
EAT AT HIS RESTAURANT? I'LL STOP IT FROM EVEN OPENING!!
WHEN THE PRINCIPAL SAID IT WAS GOOD TO NOT HAVE A DREAM, I DIDN'T GET IT. BUT MAYBE HE MEANT...
...THAT THE WRONG DREAMS ARE A NUISANCE TO THE PEOPLE AROUND YOU!
VUIIIII
ヴィ
......YEAH... YOUR BROTHER COULD KILL SOMEONE WITH RAMEN ONE DAY.........

Silver Spoon

MIHO
ISHIZAKA

TAIKI CENTRAL
MIDDLE SCHOOL

DAIRY FARMER
FAMILY

PING-PONG
CLUB

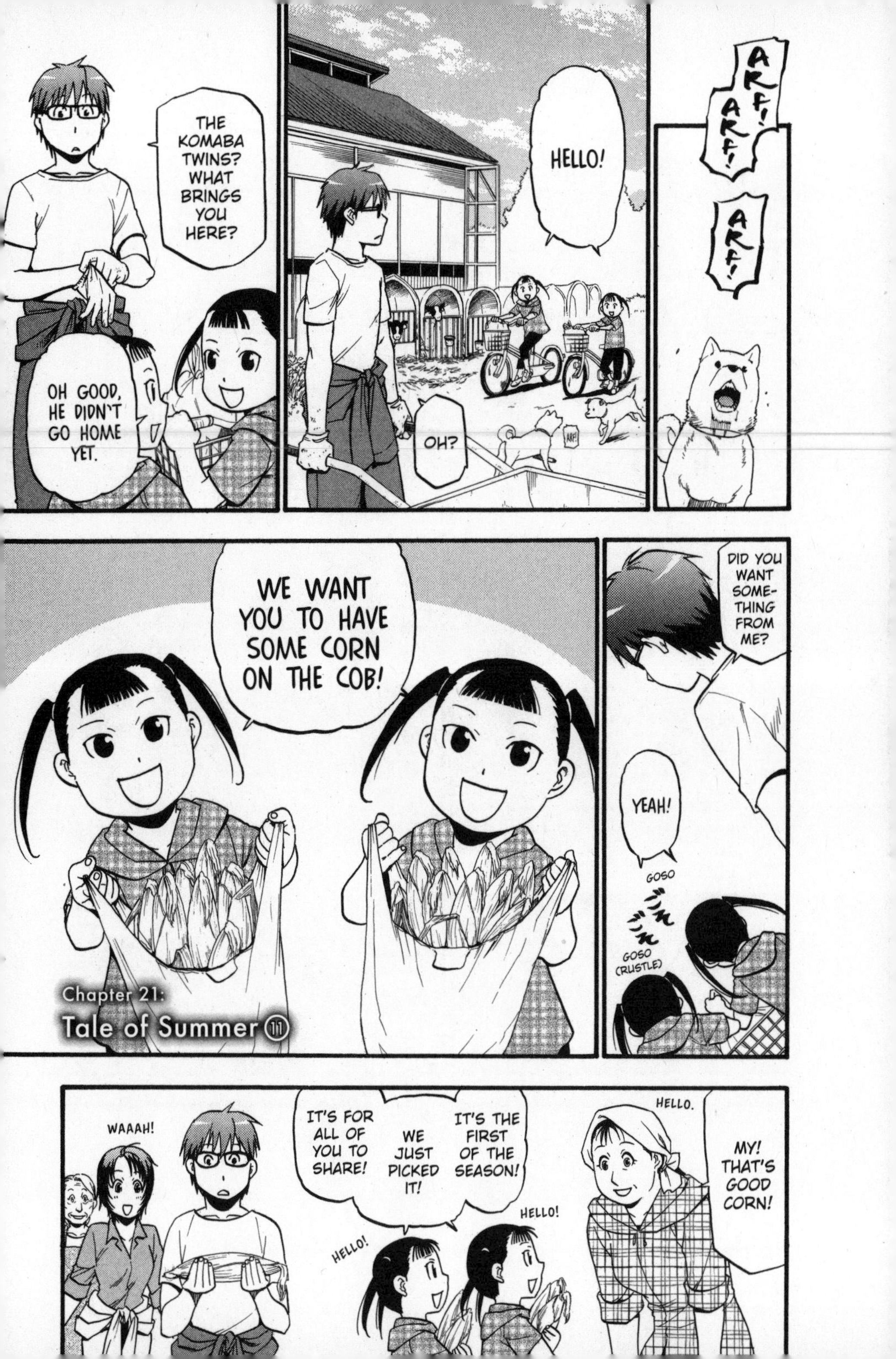
ARF! ARF!
ARF! ARF!
HELLO!
OH?
ARF!
THE KOMABA TWINS? WHAT BRINGS YOU HERE?
OH GOOD, HE DIDN'T GO HOME YET.
DID YOU WANT SOMETHING FROM ME?
YEAH!
GOSO
GOSO (RUSTLE)
WE WANT YOU TO HAVE SOME CORN ON THE COB!
Chapter 21:
Tale of Summer ⑪
HELLO.
MY! THAT'S GOOD CORN!
IT'S THE FIRST OF THE SEASON!
WE JUST PICKED IT!
IT'S FOR ALL OF YOU TO SHARE!
HELLO!
HELLO!
WAAAH!

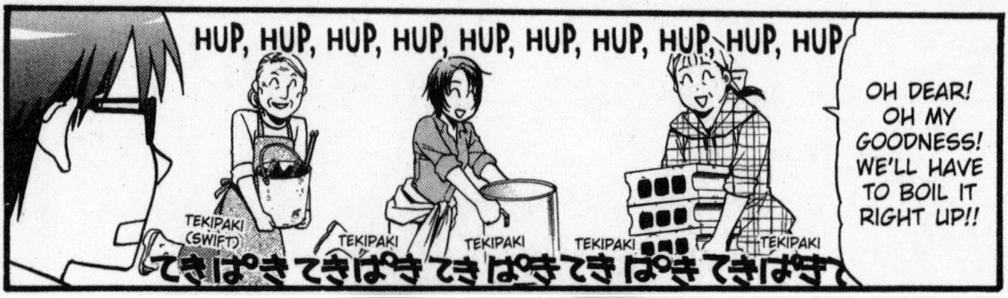
OH DEAR! OH MY GOODNESS! WE'LL HAVE TO BOIL IT RIGHT UP!!
HUP, HUP, HUP, HUP, HUP, HUP, HUP, HUP, HUP, HUP
TEKIPAKI
TEKIPAKI
TEKIPAKI
TEKIPAKI
TEKIPAKI (SWIFT)
てきぱきてきぱきてきぱきてきぱきてきぱき

Chapter 21:

Tale of Summer ⑪

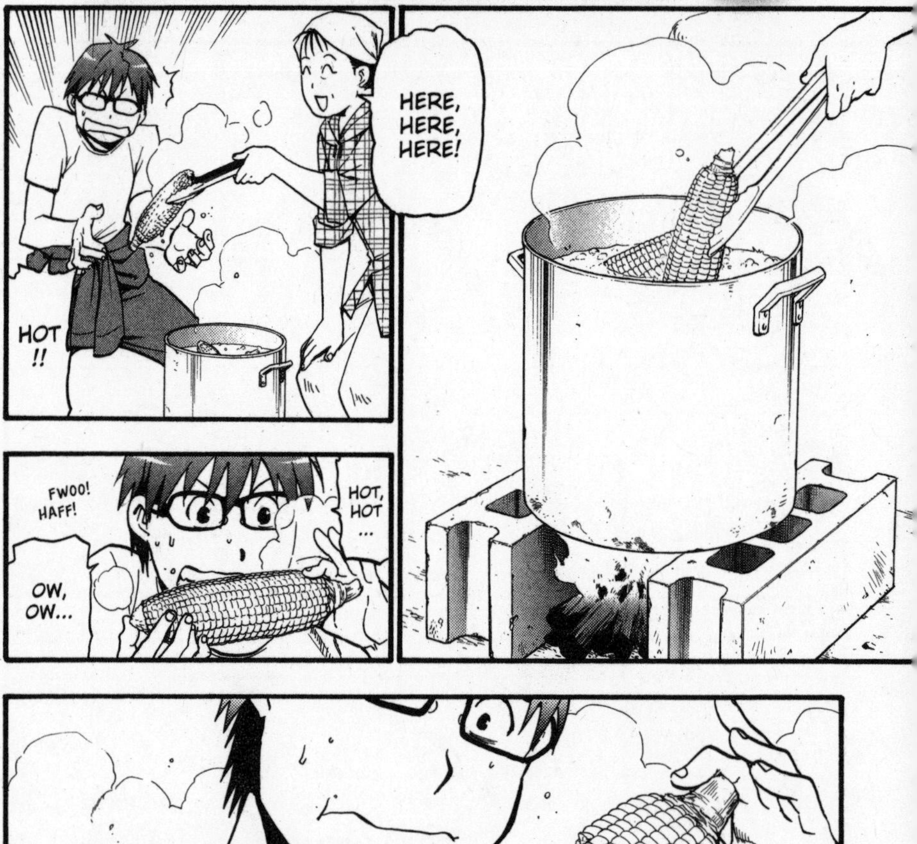
HERE, HERE, HERE!
HOT !!
HOT, HOT ...
FWOO! HAFF!
OW, OW...

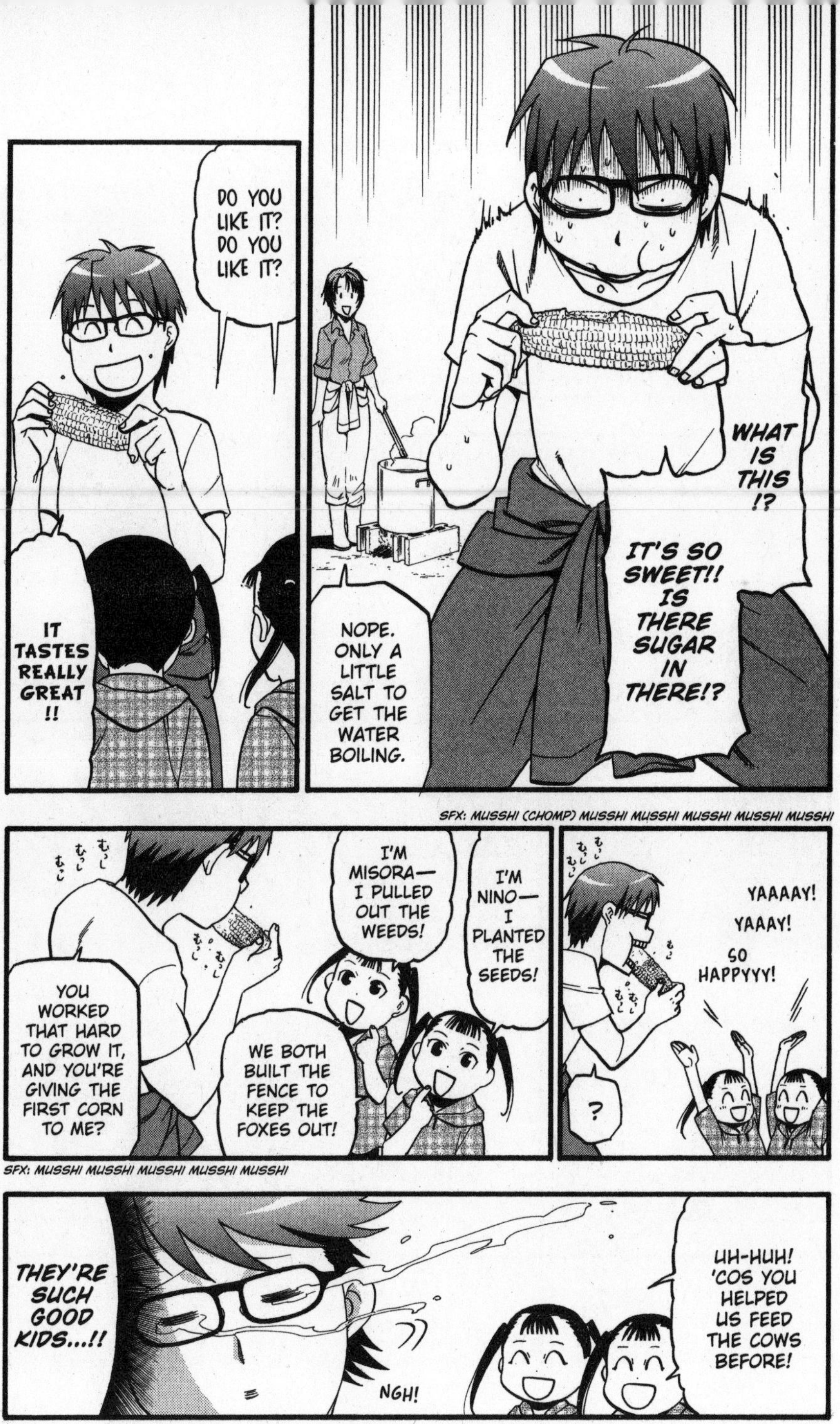
WHAT IS THIS!?
IT'S SO SWEET!! IS THERE SUGAR IN THERE!?
NOPE. ONLY A LITTLE SALT TO GET THE WATER BOILING.
DO YOU LIKE IT? DO YOU LIKE IT?
IT TASTES REALLY GREAT!!
SFX: MUSSHI (CHOMP) MUSSHI MUSSHI MUSSHI MUSSHI MUSSHI
むし むし むし
YAAAAY!
YAAAY!
SO HAPPYYY!
?
むし むし むし
I'M NINO— I PLANTED THE SEEDS!
I'M MISORA— I PULLED OUT THE WEEDS!
WE BOTH BUILT THE FENCE TO KEEP THE FOXES OUT!
YOU WORKED THAT HARD TO GROW IT, AND YOU'RE GIVING THE FIRST CORN TO ME?
SFX: MUSSHI MUSSHI MUSSHI MUSSHI MUSSHI
UH-HUH! 'COS YOU HELPED US FEED THE COWS BEFORE!
NGH!
THEY'RE SUCH GOOD KIDS...!!

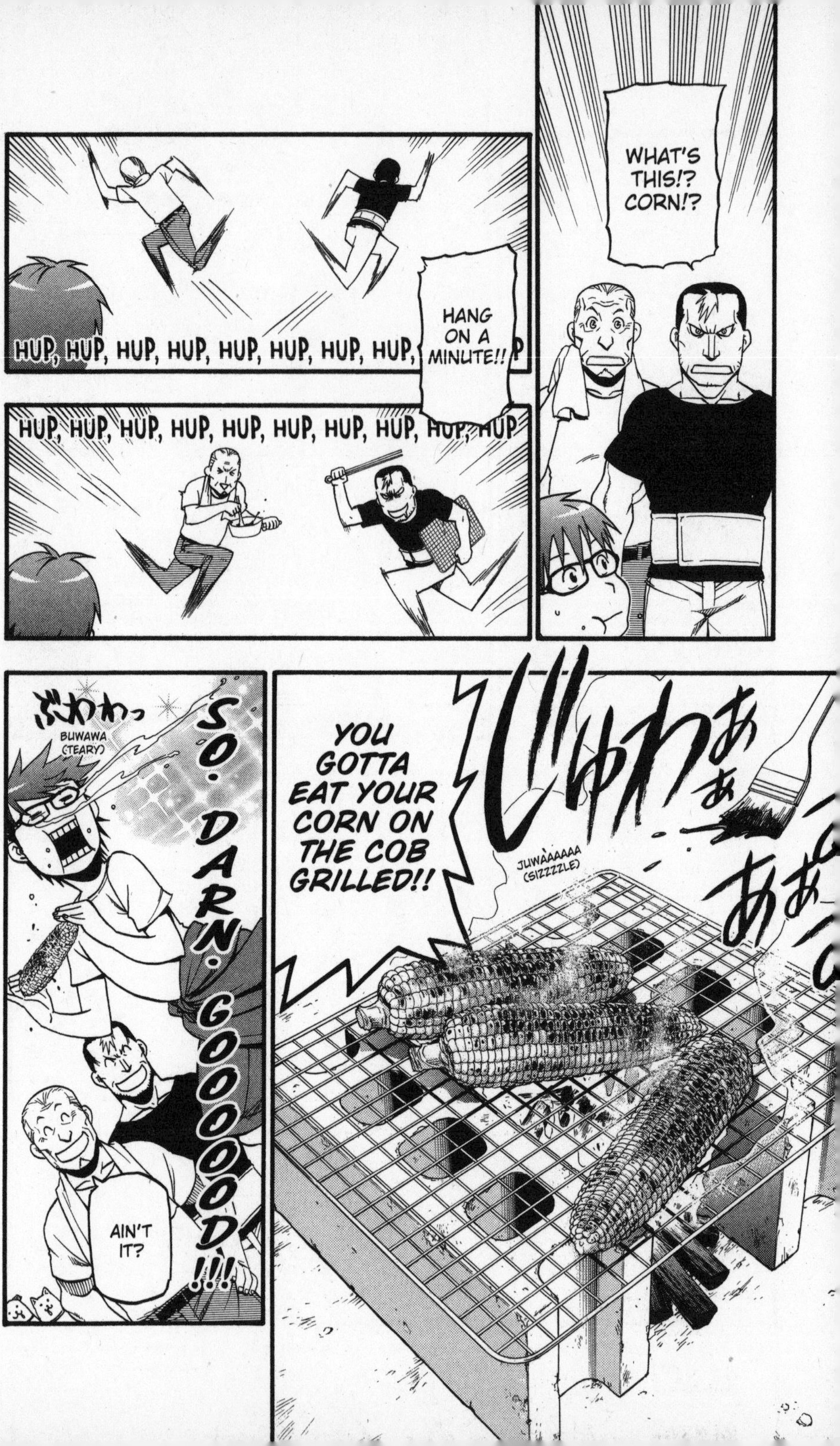

WHAT'S THIS!? CORN!?
HUP, HUP, HUP, HUP, HUP, HUP, HUP, HUP,
HANG ON A MINUTE!!
HUP, HUP, HUP, HUP, HUP, HUP, HUP, HUP, HUP
YOU GOTTA EAT YOUR CORN ON THE COB GRILLED!!
じゅわぁぁ
ああ
JUWÀAAAAA (SIZZZZLE)
ぶわわっ
BUWAWA (TEARY)
SO. DARN. GOOOOOOD!!!
AIN'T IT?

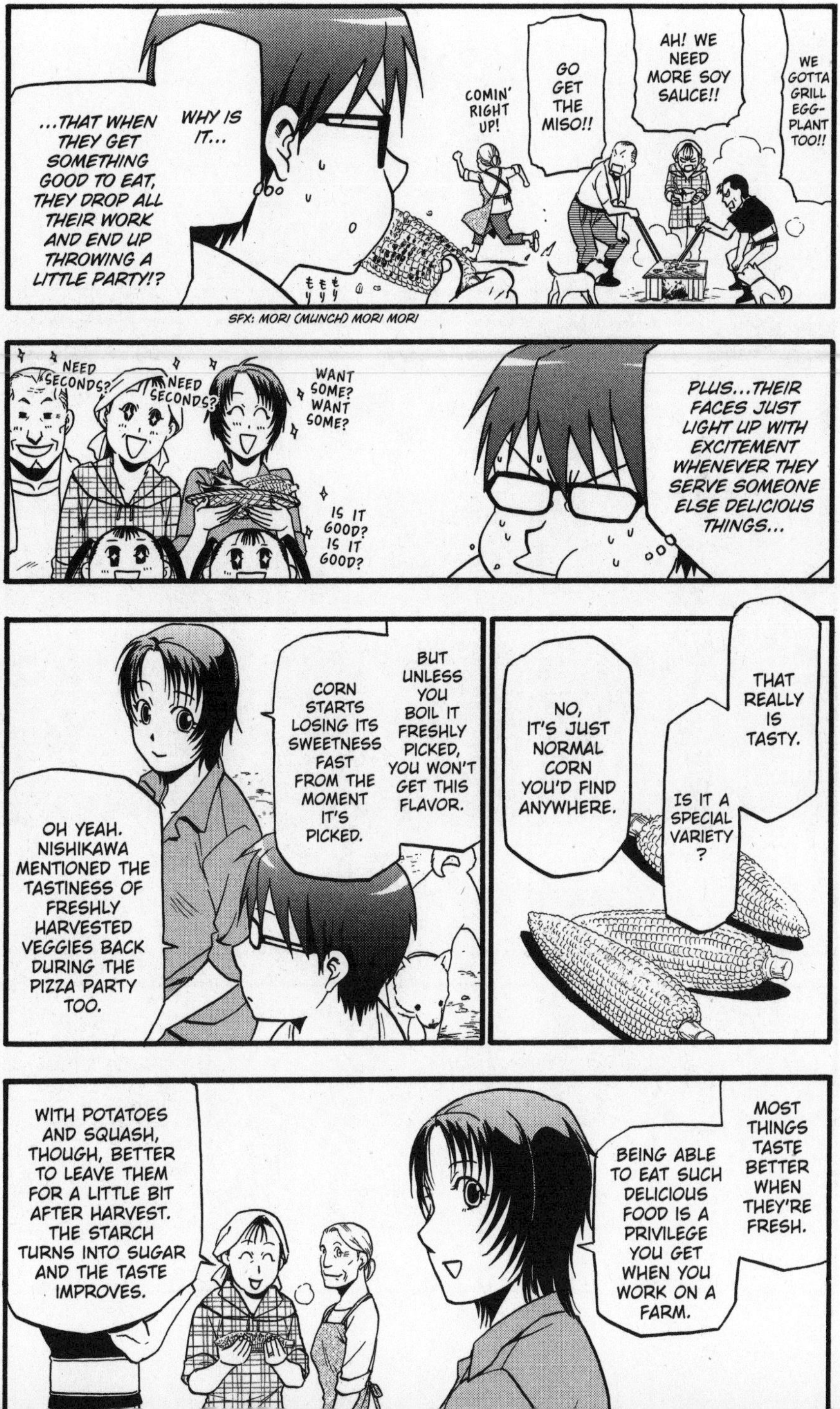
WE GOTTA GRILL EGG-PLANT TOO!!
AH! WE NEED MORE SOY SAUCE!!
GO GET THE MISO!!
COMIN' RIGHT UP!
WHY IS IT...
...THAT WHEN THEY GET SOMETHING GOOD TO EAT, THEY DROP ALL THEIR WORK AND END UP THROWING A LITTLE PARTY!?
SFX: MORI (MUNCH) MORI MORI
PLUS...THEIR FACES JUST LIGHT UP WITH EXCITEMENT WHENEVER THEY SERVE SOMEONE ELSE DELICIOUS THINGS...
IS IT GOOD? IS IT GOOD?
WANT SOME? WANT SOME?
NEED SECONDS?
NEED SECONDS?
THAT REALLY IS TASTY.
IS IT A SPECIAL VARIETY?
NO, IT'S JUST NORMAL CORN YOU'D FIND ANYWHERE.
BUT UNLESS YOU BOIL IT FRESHLY PICKED, YOU WON'T GET THIS FLAVOR.
CORN STARTS LOSING ITS SWEETNESS FAST FROM THE MOMENT IT'S PICKED.
OH YEAH. NISHIKAWA MENTIONED THE TASTINESS OF FRESHLY HARVESTED VEGGIES BACK DURING THE PIZZA PARTY TOO.
MOST THINGS TASTE BETTER WHEN THEY'RE FRESH.
BEING ABLE TO EAT SUCH DELICIOUS FOOD IS A PRIVILEGE YOU GET WHEN YOU WORK ON A FARM.
WITH POTATOES AND SQUASH, THOUGH, BETTER TO LEAVE THEM FOR A LITTLE BIT AFTER HARVEST. THE STARCH TURNS INTO SUGAR AND THE TASTE IMPROVES.

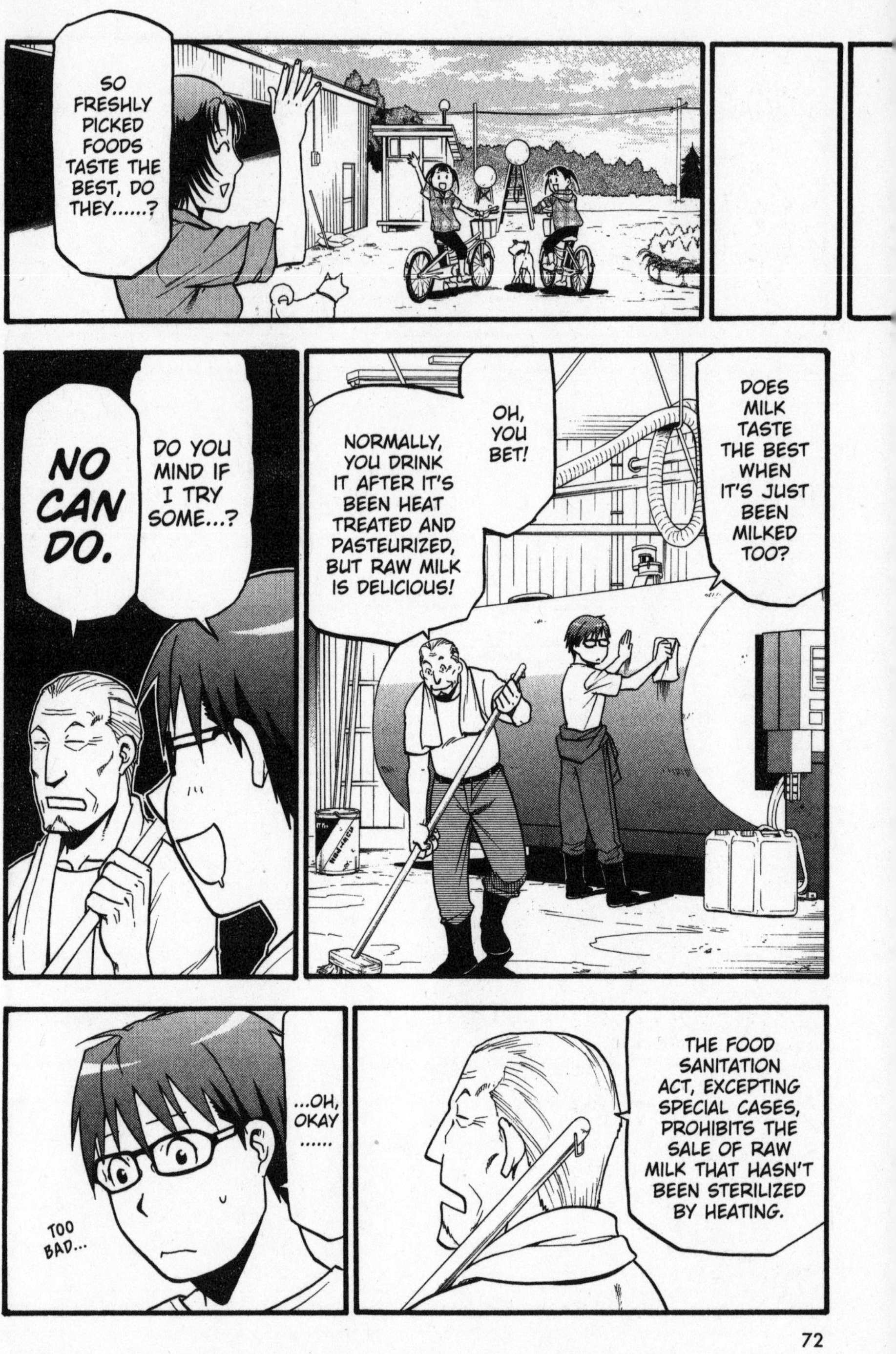
SO FRESHLY PICKED FOODS TASTE THE BEST, DO THEY......?
DOES MILK TASTE THE BEST WHEN IT'S JUST BEEN MILKED TOO?
OH, YOU BET!
NORMALLY, YOU DRINK IT AFTER IT'S BEEN HEAT TREATED AND PASTEURIZED, BUT RAW MILK IS DELICIOUS!
DO YOU MIND IF I TRY SOME...?
NO CAN DO.
THE FOOD SANITATION ACT, EXCEPTING SPECIAL CASES, PROHIBITS THE SALE OF RAW MILK THAT HASN'T BEEN STERILIZED BY HEATING.
...OH, OKAY ......
TOO BAD...

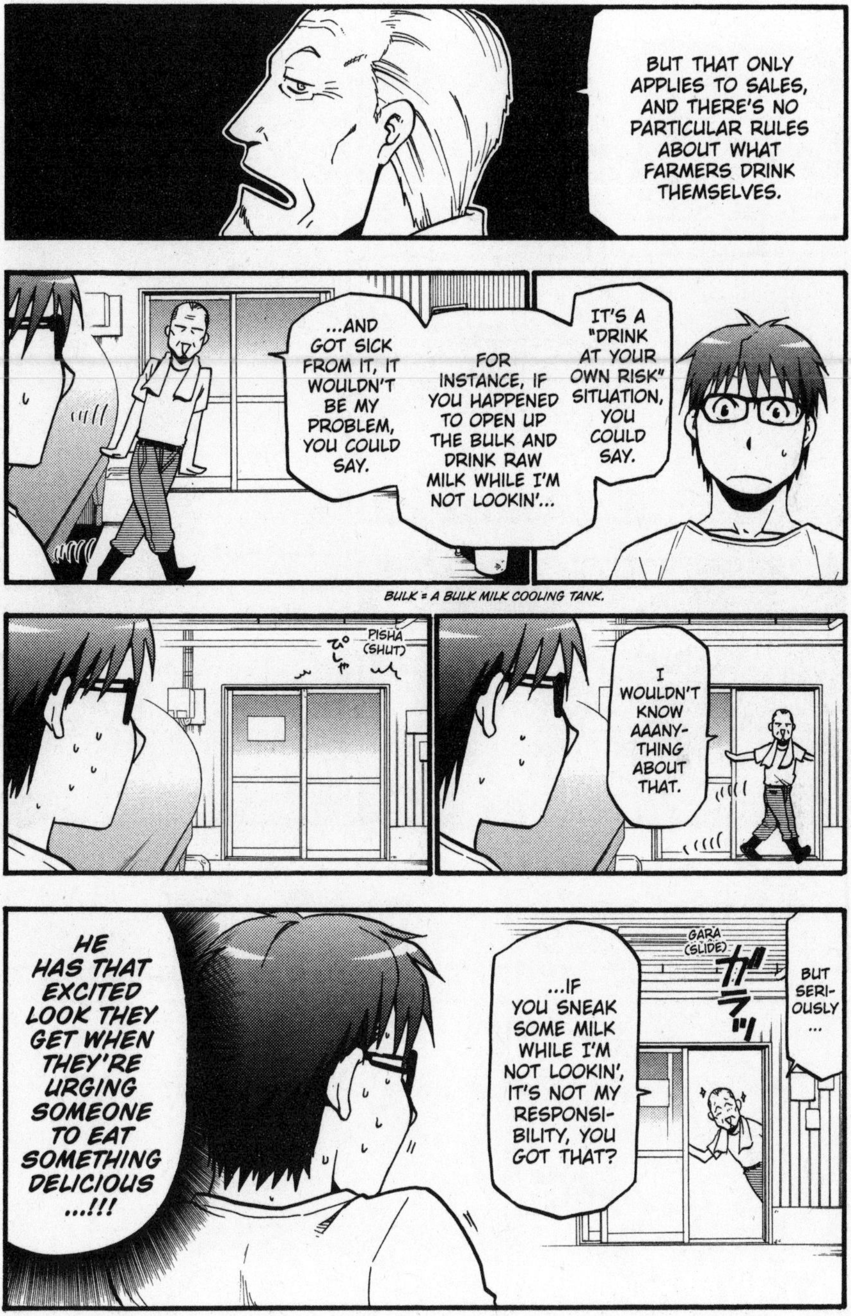
BUT THAT ONLY APPLIES TO SALES, AND THERE'S NO PARTICULAR RULES ABOUT WHAT FARMERS DRINK THEMSELVES.
IT'S A "DRINK AT YOUR OWN RISK" SITUATION, YOU COULD SAY.
FOR INSTANCE, IF YOU HAPPENED TO OPEN UP THE BULK AND DRINK RAW MILK WHILE I'M NOT LOOKIN'...
...AND GOT SICK FROM IT, IT WOULDN'T BE MY PROBLEM, YOU COULD SAY.
BULK = A BULK MILK COOLING TANK.
I WOULDN'T KNOW AAANY-THING ABOUT THAT.
PISHA (SHUT)
ぴしゃ
BUT SERI-OUSLY...
GARA (SLIDE)
ガラッ
...IF YOU SNEAK SOME MILK WHILE I'M NOT LOOKIN', IT'S NOT MY RESPONSI-BILITY, YOU GOT THAT?
HE HAS THAT EXCITED LOOK THEY GET WHEN THEY'RE URGING SOMEONE TO EAT SOMETHING DELICIOUS ...!!!

PAKA
(POP)

DOKI
DOKI
(BADUM)

DOKI
DOKI
DOKI
DOKI

DOKI
DOKI
DOKI
DOKI

DRINK
AT
YOUR
OWN
RISK...

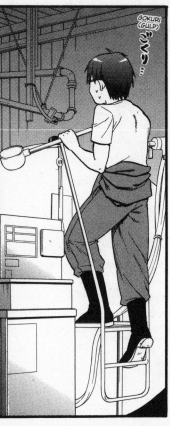

GOKURI
(GULP)

THEEERE'S
A GOOD
GIRL...

GUBI
(GULP)

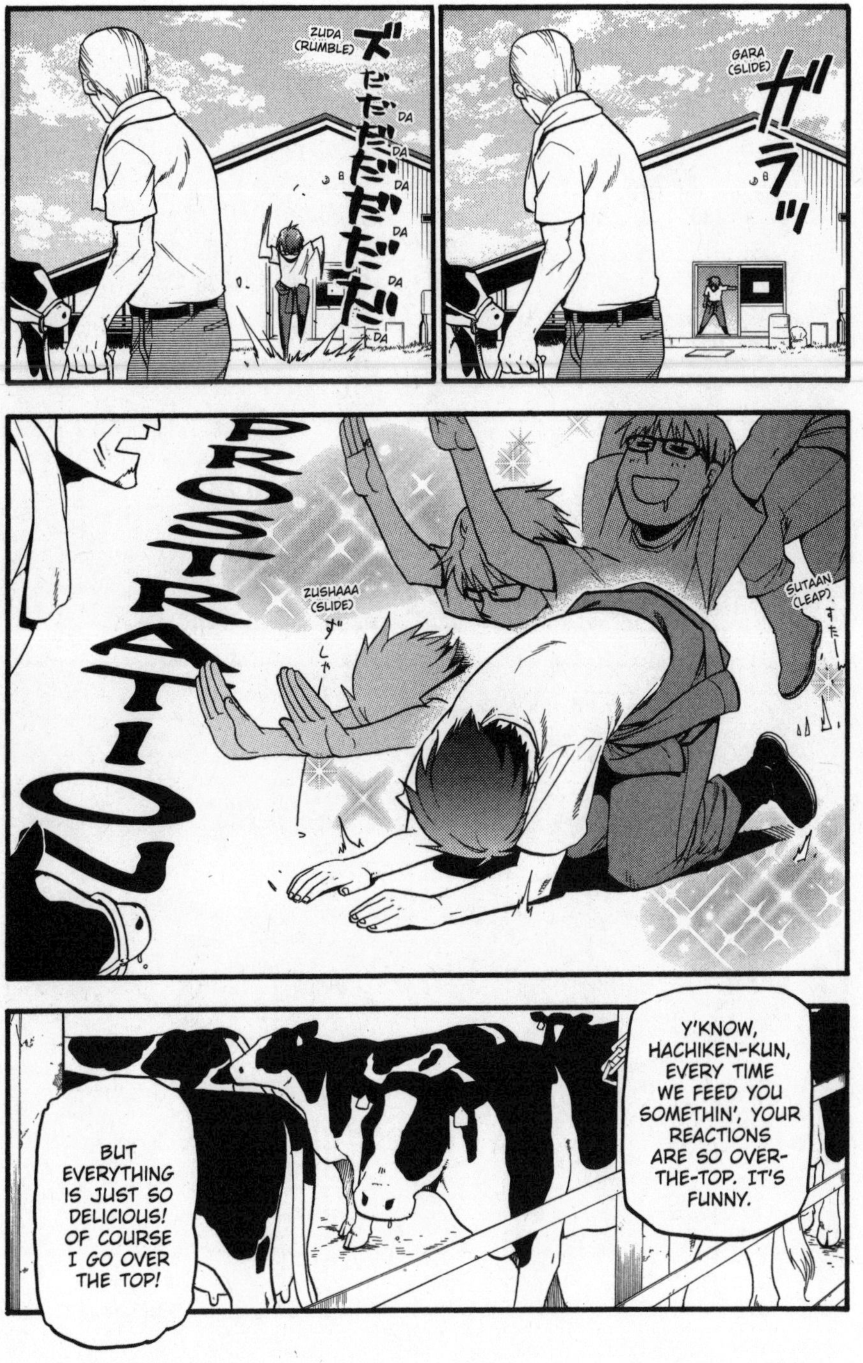
GARA (SLIDE)
ガラッ
ZUDA (RUMBLE)
ズだだだだだだ
DA DA DA DA DA DA
PROSTRATION
SUTAAN (LEAP)
ZUSHAAA (SLIDE)
Y'KNOW, HACHIKEN-KUN, EVERY TIME WE FEED YOU SOMETHIN', YOUR REACTIONS ARE SO OVER-THE-TOP. IT'S FUNNY.
BUT EVERYTHING IS JUST SO DELICIOUS! OF COURSE I GO OVER THE TOP!

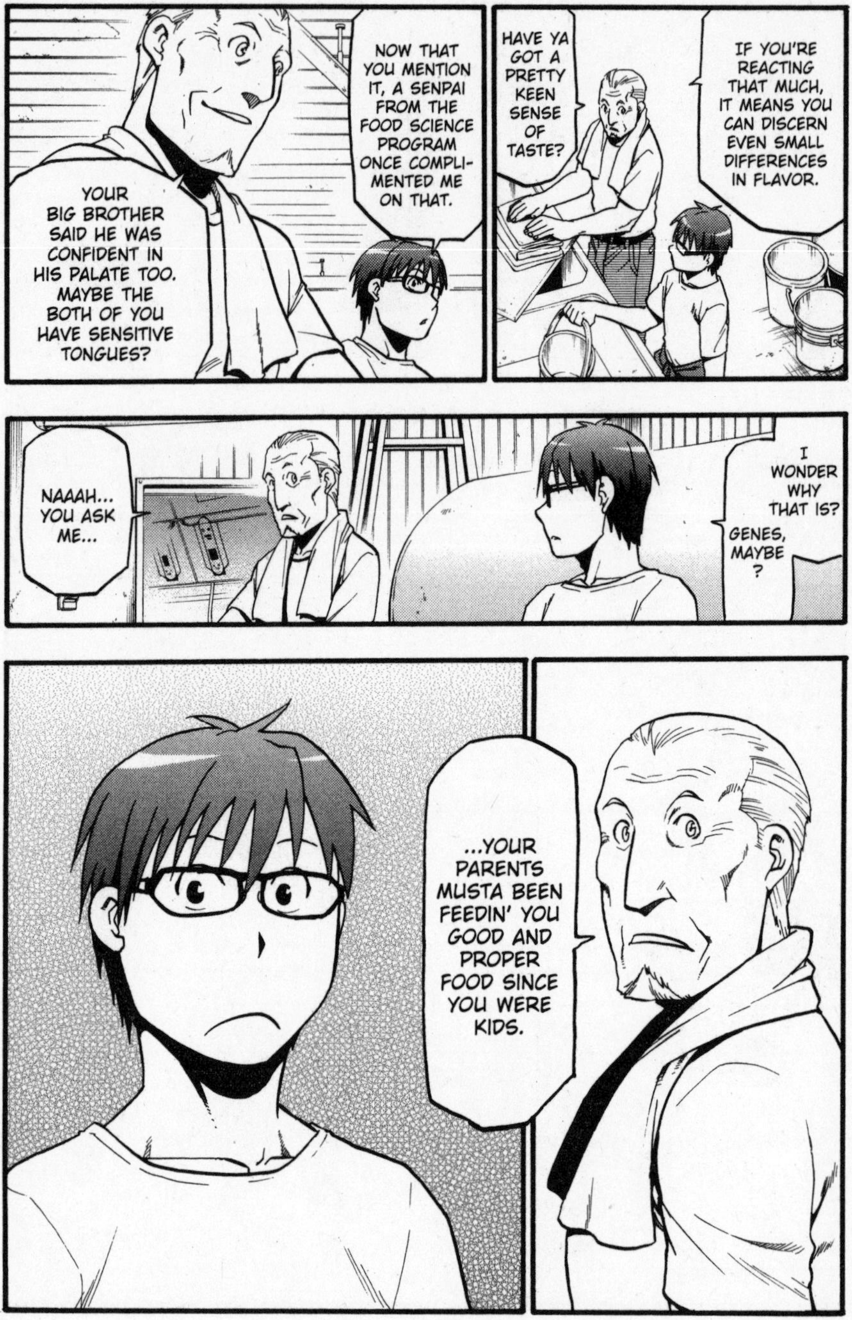
IF YOU'RE REACTING THAT MUCH, IT MEANS YOU CAN DISCERN EVEN SMALL DIFFERENCES IN FLAVOR.
HAVE YA GOT A PRETTY KEEN SENSE OF TASTE?
NOW THAT YOU MENTION IT, A SENPAI FROM THE FOOD SCIENCE PROGRAM ONCE COMPLIMENTED ME ON THAT.
YOUR BIG BROTHER SAID HE WAS CONFIDENT IN HIS PALATE TOO. MAYBE THE BOTH OF YOU HAVE SENSITIVE TONGUES?
I WONDER WHY THAT IS? GENES, MAYBE?
NAAAH... YOU ASK ME...
...YOUR PARENTS MUSTA BEEN FEEDIN' YOU GOOD AND PROPER FOOD SINCE YOU WERE KIDS.

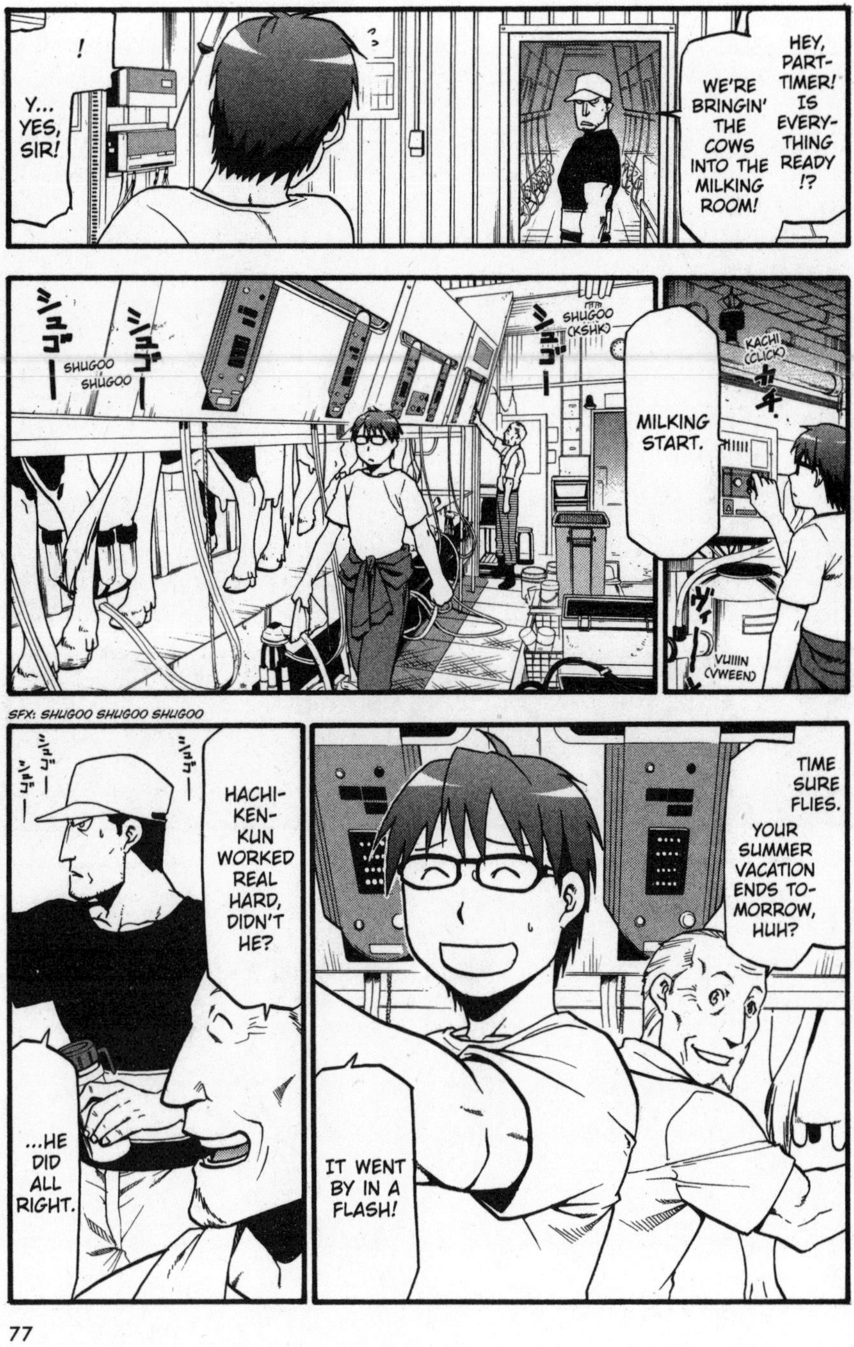

HEY, PART-TIMER! IS EVERYTHING READY!?
WE'RE BRINGIN' THE COWS INTO THE MILKING ROOM!
!
Y... YES, SIR!
KACHI (CLICK)
MILKING START.
VUIIIN (VWEEND)
SHUGOO (KSHK)
SHUGOO
SHUGOO
SFX: SHUGOO SHUGOO SHUGOO
TIME SURE FLIES.
YOUR SUMMER VACATION ENDS TOMORROW, HUH?
IT WENT BY IN A FLASH!
HACHIKEN-KUN WORKED REAL HARD, DIDN'T HE?
...HE DID ALL RIGHT.

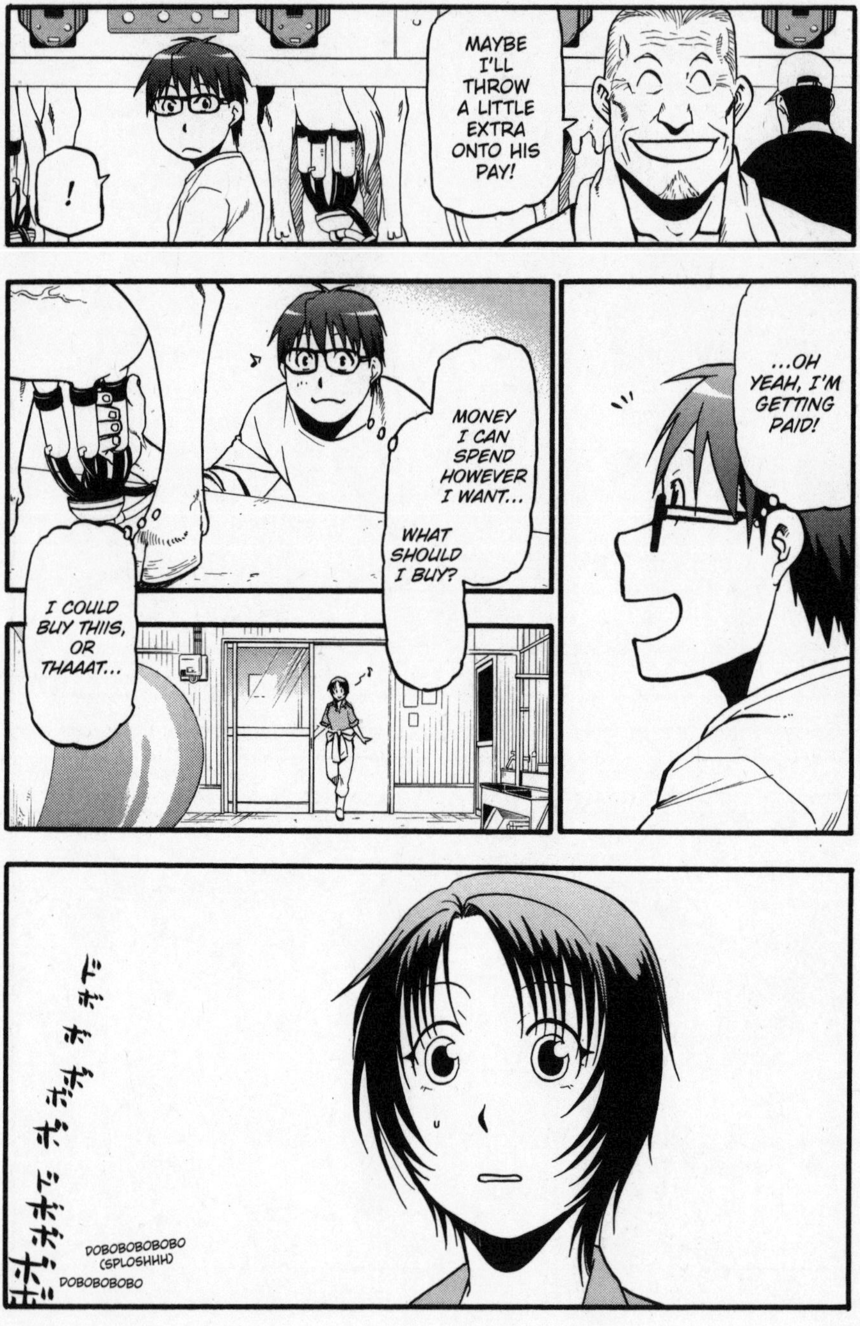
MAYBE I'LL THROW A LITTLE EXTRA ONTO HIS PAY!
!
...OH YEAH, I'M GETTING PAID!
MONEY I CAN SPEND HOWEVER I WANT...
WHAT SHOULD I BUY?
I COULD BUY THIIS, OR THAAAT...
DOBOBOBOBO (SPLOSHHH)
DOBOBOBO

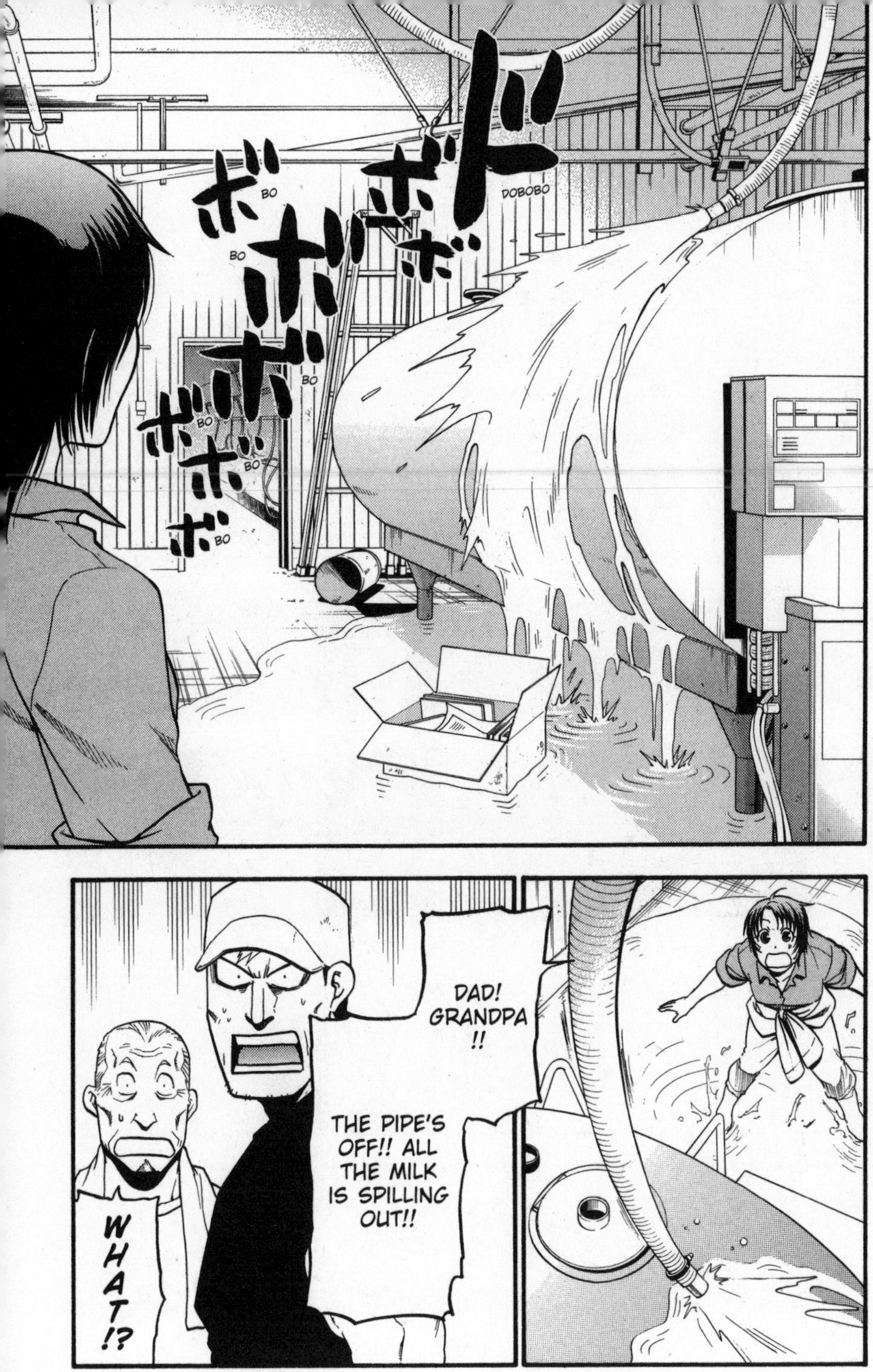
DOBOBO
BO
BO
BO
BO
BO
BO
DAD! GRANDPA !!
THE PIPE'S OFF!! ALL THE MILK IS SPILLING OUT!!
WHAT!?

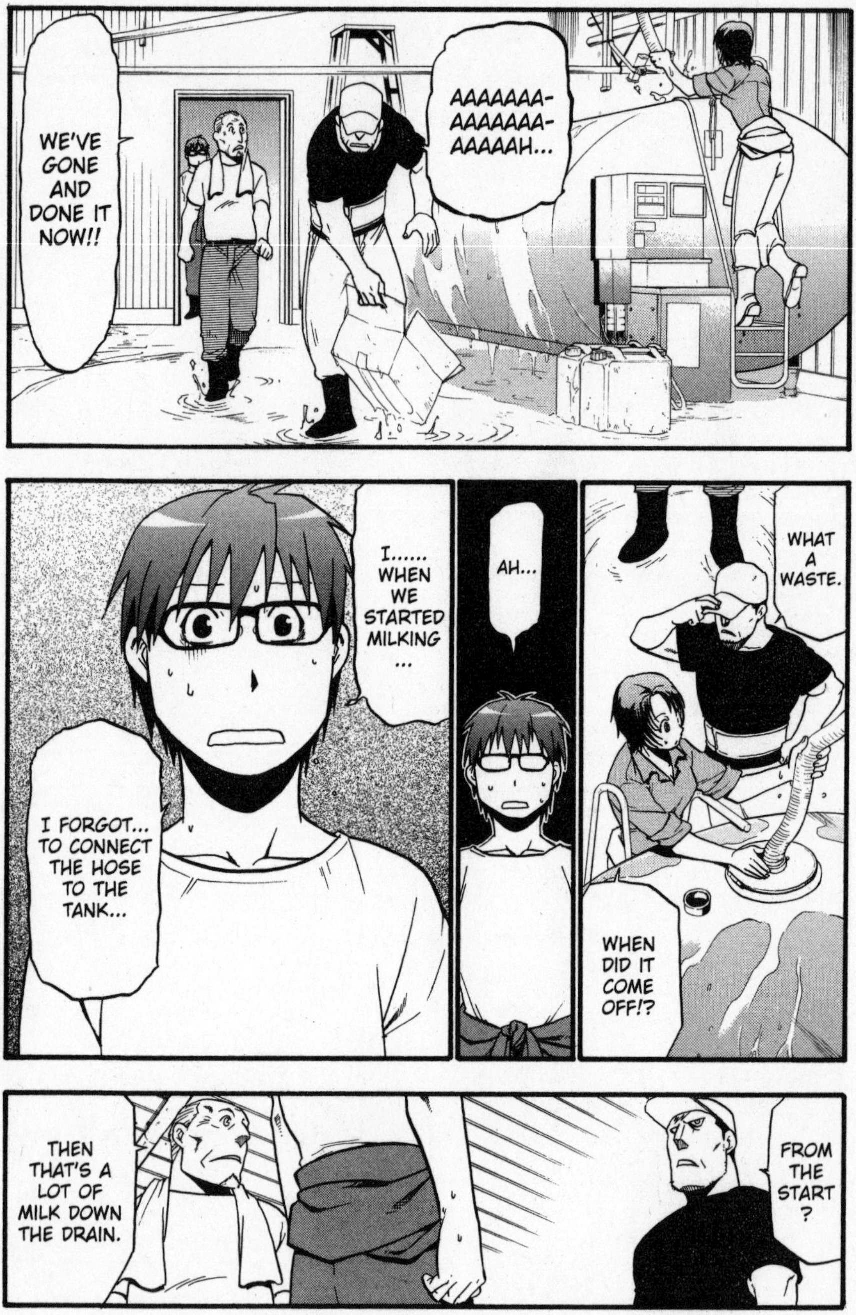
AAAAAAA-AAAAAAA-AAAAAAH...
WE'VE GONE AND DONE IT NOW!!
WHAT A WASTE.
WHEN DID IT COME OFF!?
AH...
I...... WHEN WE STARTED MILKING ...
I FORGOT... TO CONNECT THE HOSE TO THE TANK...
FROM THE START?
THEN THAT'S A LOT OF MILK DOWN THE DRAIN.

SFX: JABABABABABA (FSSSH)

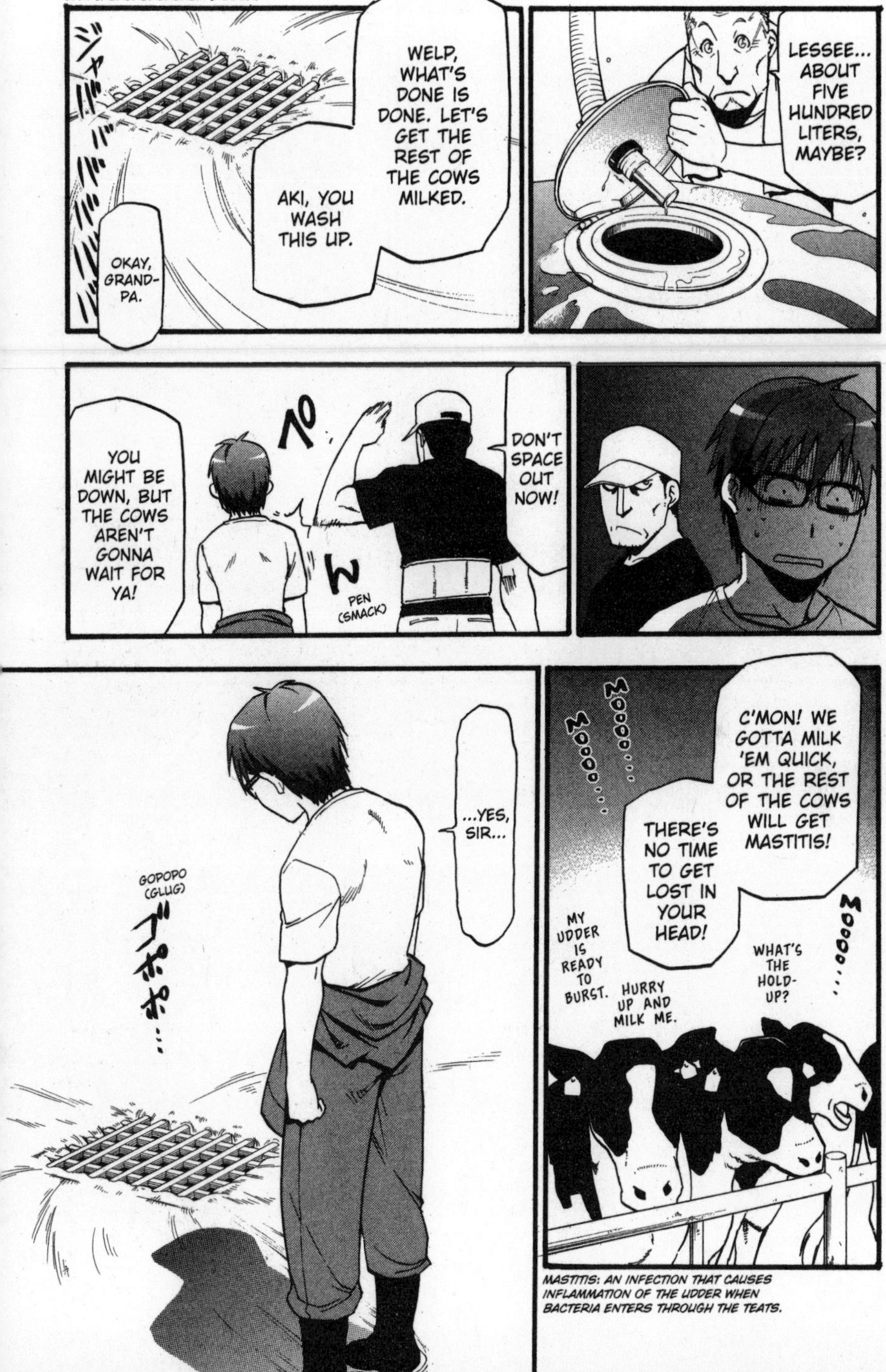
LESSEE... ABOUT FIVE HUNDRED LITERS, MAYBE?
WELP, WHAT'S DONE IS DONE. LET'S GET THE REST OF THE COWS MILKED.
AKI, YOU WASH THIS UP.
OKAY, GRANDPA.
DON'T SPACE OUT NOW!
PEN (SMACK)
YOU MIGHT BE DOWN, BUT THE COWS AREN'T GONNA WAIT FOR YA!
C'MON! WE GOTTA MILK 'EM QUICK, OR THE REST OF THE COWS WILL GET MASTITIS!
THERE'S NO TIME TO GET LOST IN YOUR HEAD!
MOOOO...
MOOOO...
MOOOO...
WHAT'S THE HOLD-UP?
HURRY UP AND MILK ME.
MY UDDER IS READY TO BURST.
...YES, SIR...
GOPOPO (GLUG)

MASTITIS: AN INFECTION THAT CAUSES INFLAMMATION OF THE UDDER WHEN BACTERIA ENTERS THROUGH THE TEATS.

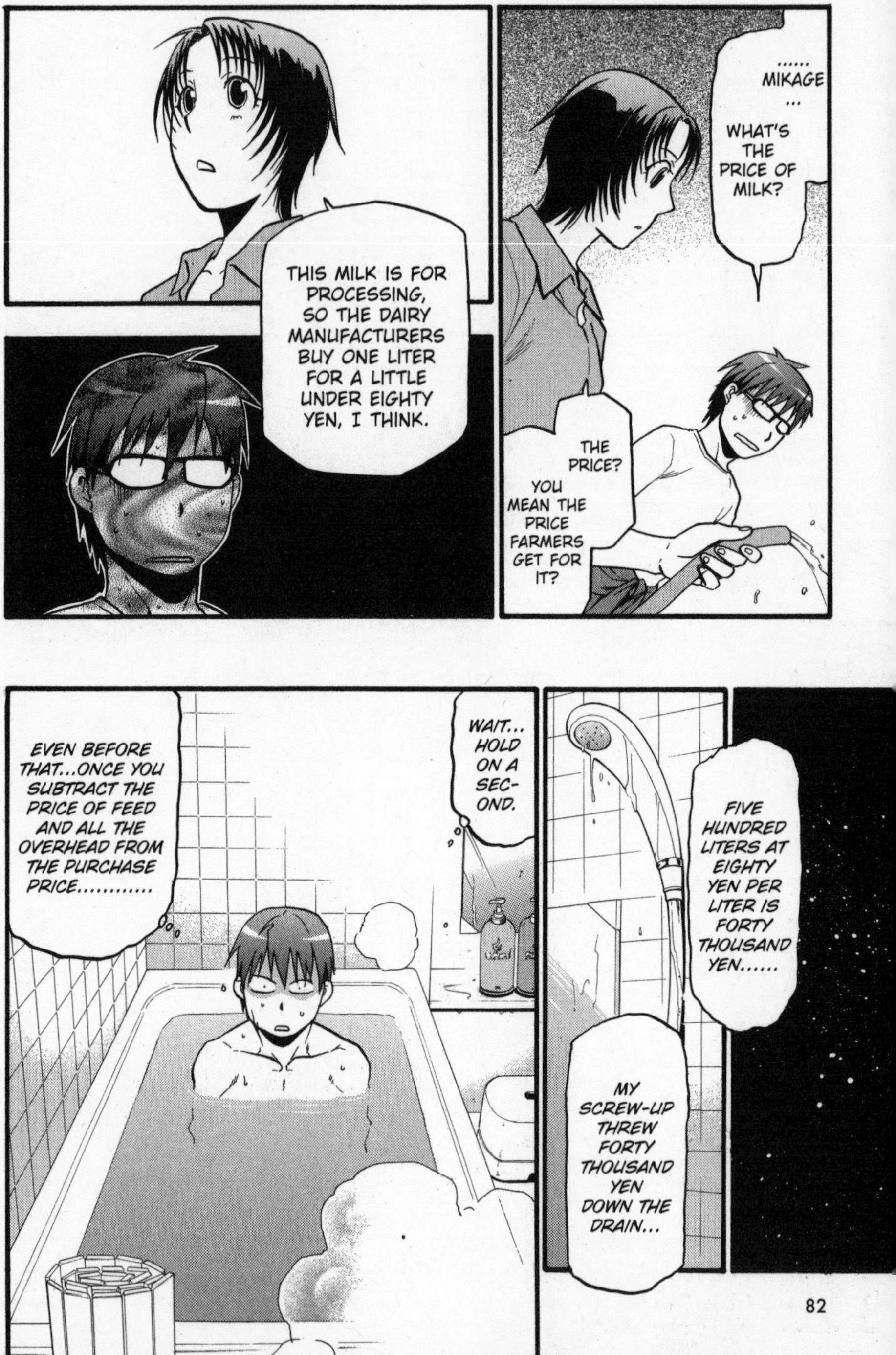
......MIKAGE ... WHAT'S THE PRICE OF MILK?
THE PRICE? YOU MEAN THE PRICE FARMERS GET FOR IT?
THIS MILK IS FOR PROCESSING, SO THE DAIRY MANUFACTURERS BUY ONE LITER FOR A LITTLE UNDER EIGHTY YEN, I THINK.
FIVE HUNDRED LITERS AT EIGHTY YEN PER LITER IS FORTY THOUSAND YEN......
MY SCREW-UP THREW FORTY THOUSAND YEN DOWN THE DRAIN...
WAIT... HOLD ON A SEC-OND.
EVEN BEFORE THAT...ONCE YOU SUBTRACT THE PRICE OF FEED AND ALL THE OVERHEAD FROM THE PURCHASE PRICE...........

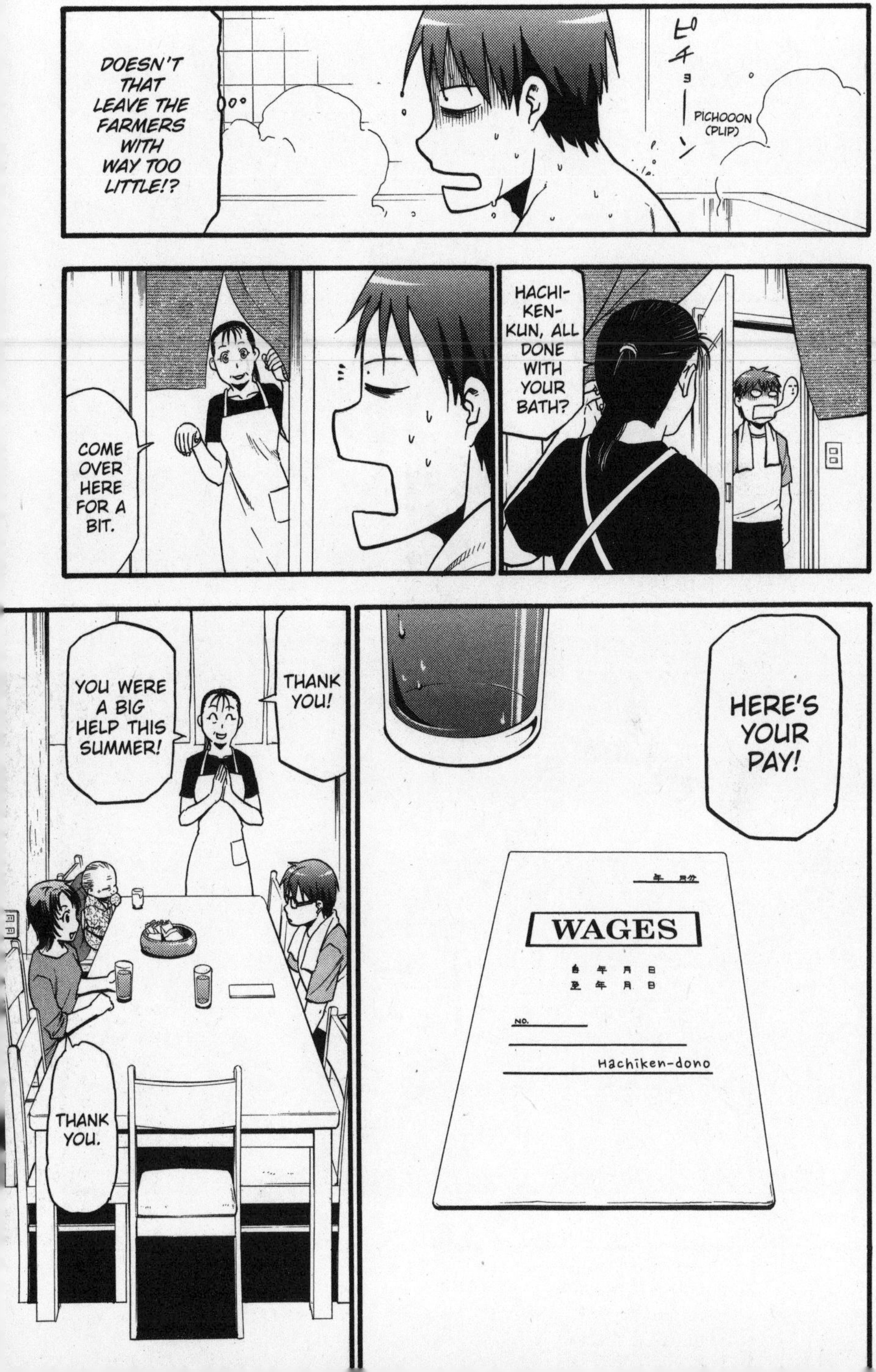
ピチョーン
PICHOOON (PLIP)
DOESN'T THAT LEAVE THE FARMERS WITH WAY TOO LITTLE!?
HACHI-KEN-KUN, ALL DONE WITH YOUR BATH?
COME OVER HERE FOR A BIT.
HERE'S YOUR PAY!
年 月分
WAGES
自 年 月 日
至 年 月 日
NO.
Hachiken-dono
THANK YOU!
YOU WERE A BIG HELP THIS SUMMER!
THANK YOU.

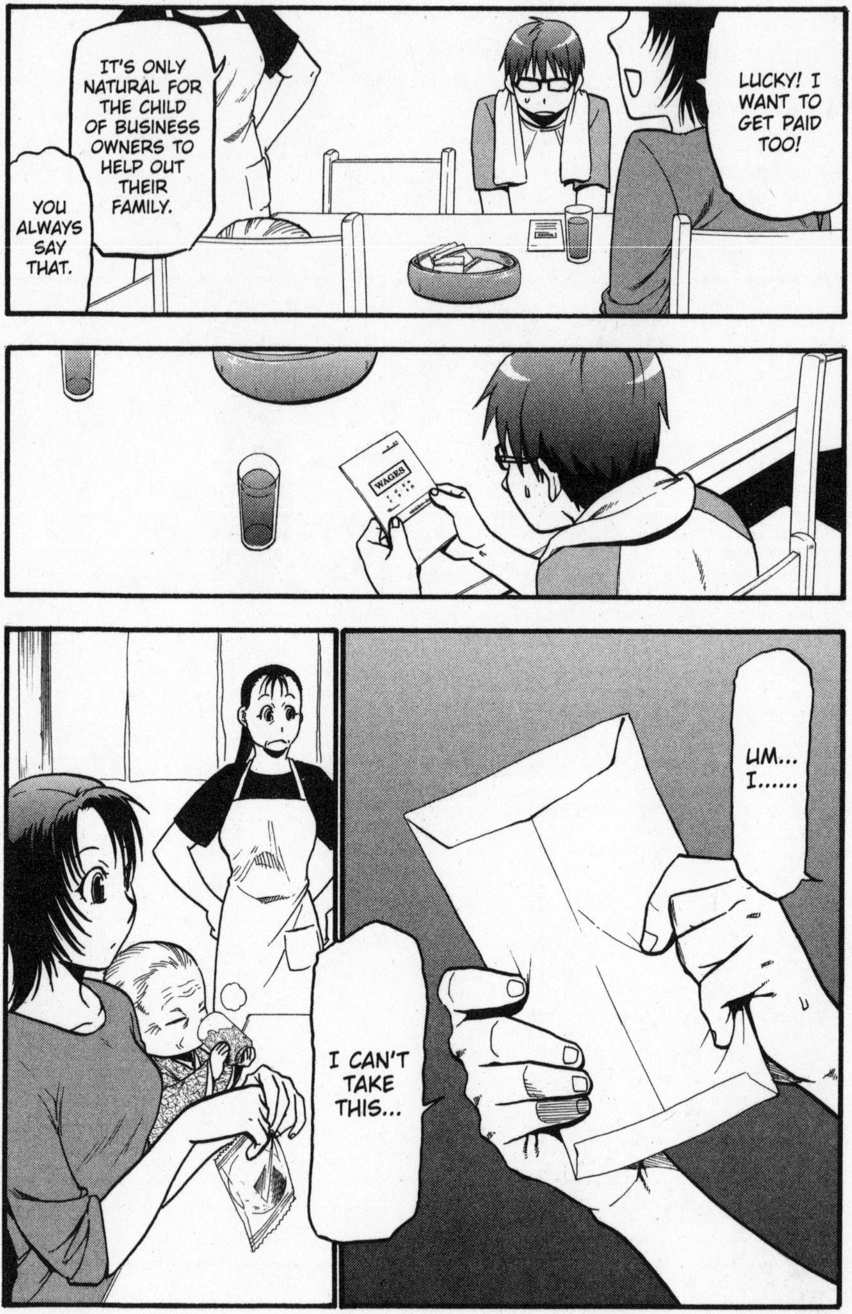
LUCKY! I WANT TO GET PAID TOO!
IT'S ONLY NATURAL FOR THE CHILD OF BUSINESS OWNERS TO HELP OUT THEIR FAMILY.
YOU ALWAYS SAY THAT.
WAGES
UM... I......
I CAN'T TAKE THIS...

Silver Spoon

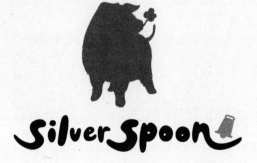

TAKU
SANJOU

SHINTOKU TOMURAUSHI
MIDDLE SCHOOL

SOCCER TEAM

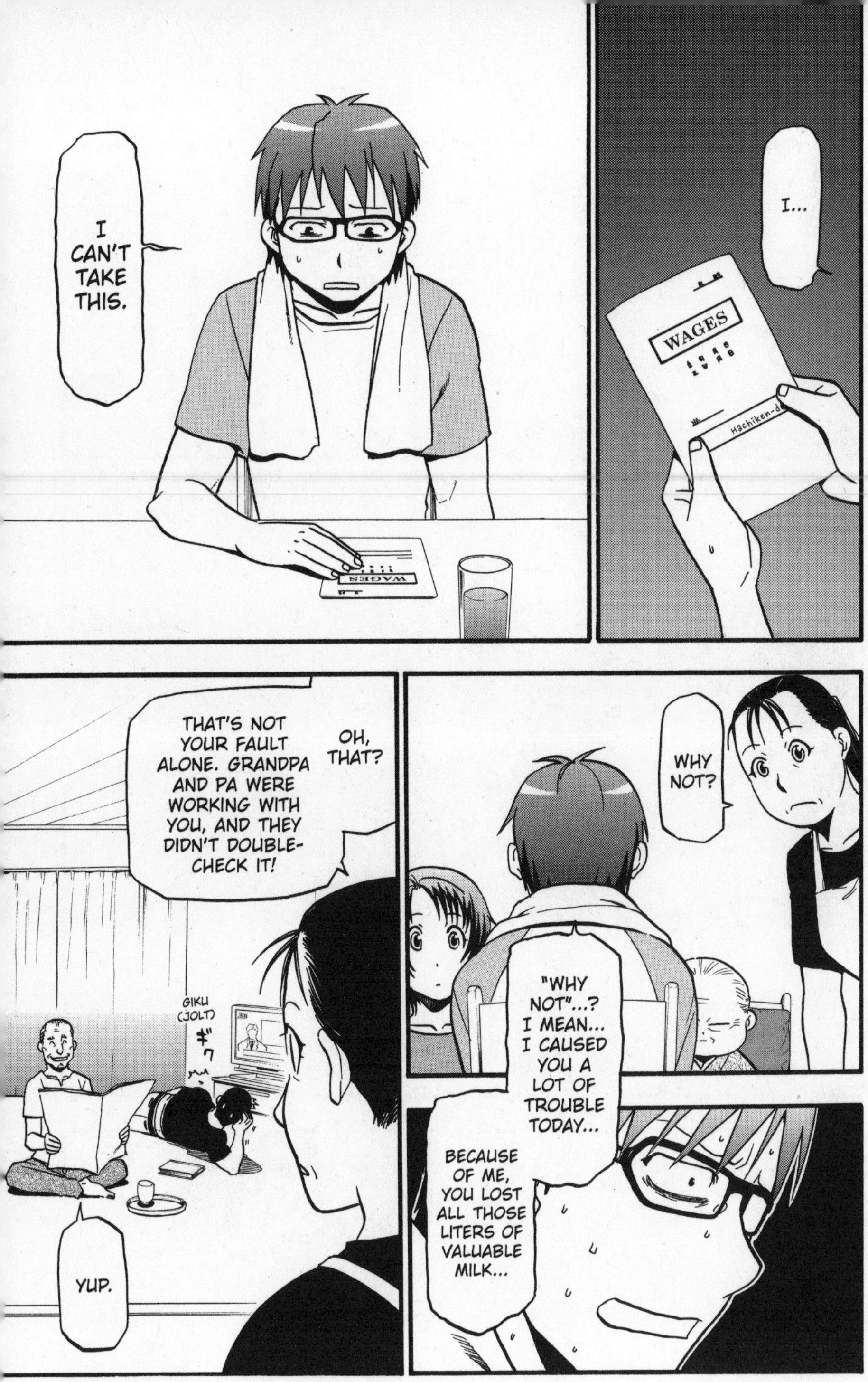
I...
WAGES
Hachiken-d
I CAN'T TAKE THIS.
WHY NOT?
"WHY NOT"...? I MEAN... I CAUSED YOU A LOT OF TROUBLE TODAY...
BECAUSE OF ME, YOU LOST ALL THOSE LITERS OF VALUABLE MILK...
OH, THAT?
THAT'S NOT YOUR FAULT ALONE. GRANDPA AND PA WERE WORKING WITH YOU, AND THEY DIDN'T DOUBLE-CHECK IT!
GIKU (JOLT)
YUP.

Chapter 22:
Tale of Summer ⑫

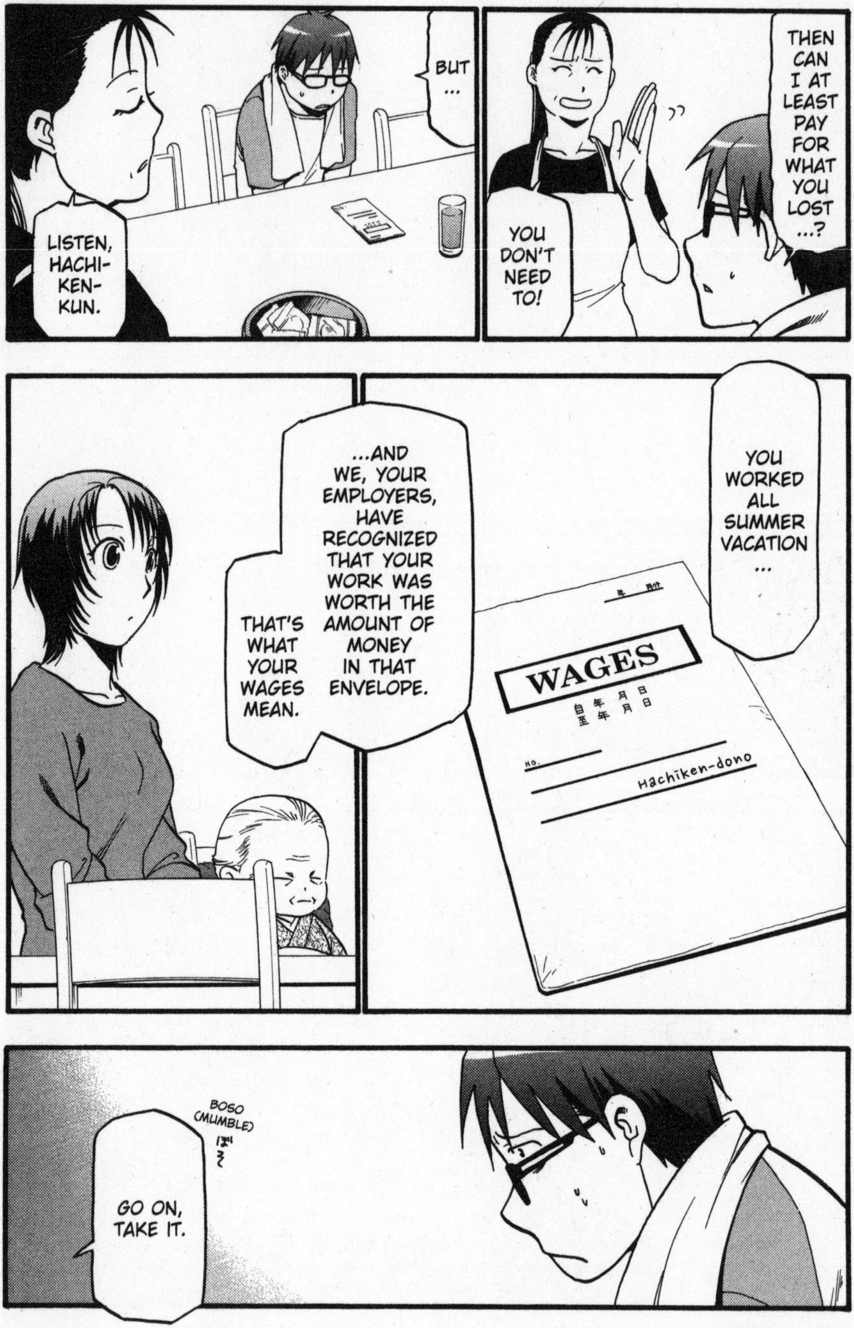
THEN CAN I AT LEAST PAY FOR WHAT YOU LOST ...?
YOU DON'T NEED TO!
BUT ...
LISTEN, HACHI-KEN-KUN.
YOU WORKED ALL SUMMER VACATION ...
WAGES
自 年 月 日
至 年 月 日
NO.
Hachiken-dono
...AND WE, YOUR EMPLOYERS, HAVE RECOGNIZED THAT YOUR WORK WAS WORTH THE AMOUNT OF MONEY IN THAT ENVELOPE.
THAT'S WHAT YOUR WAGES MEAN.
BOSO (MUMBLE)
ぼそ
GO ON, TAKE IT.

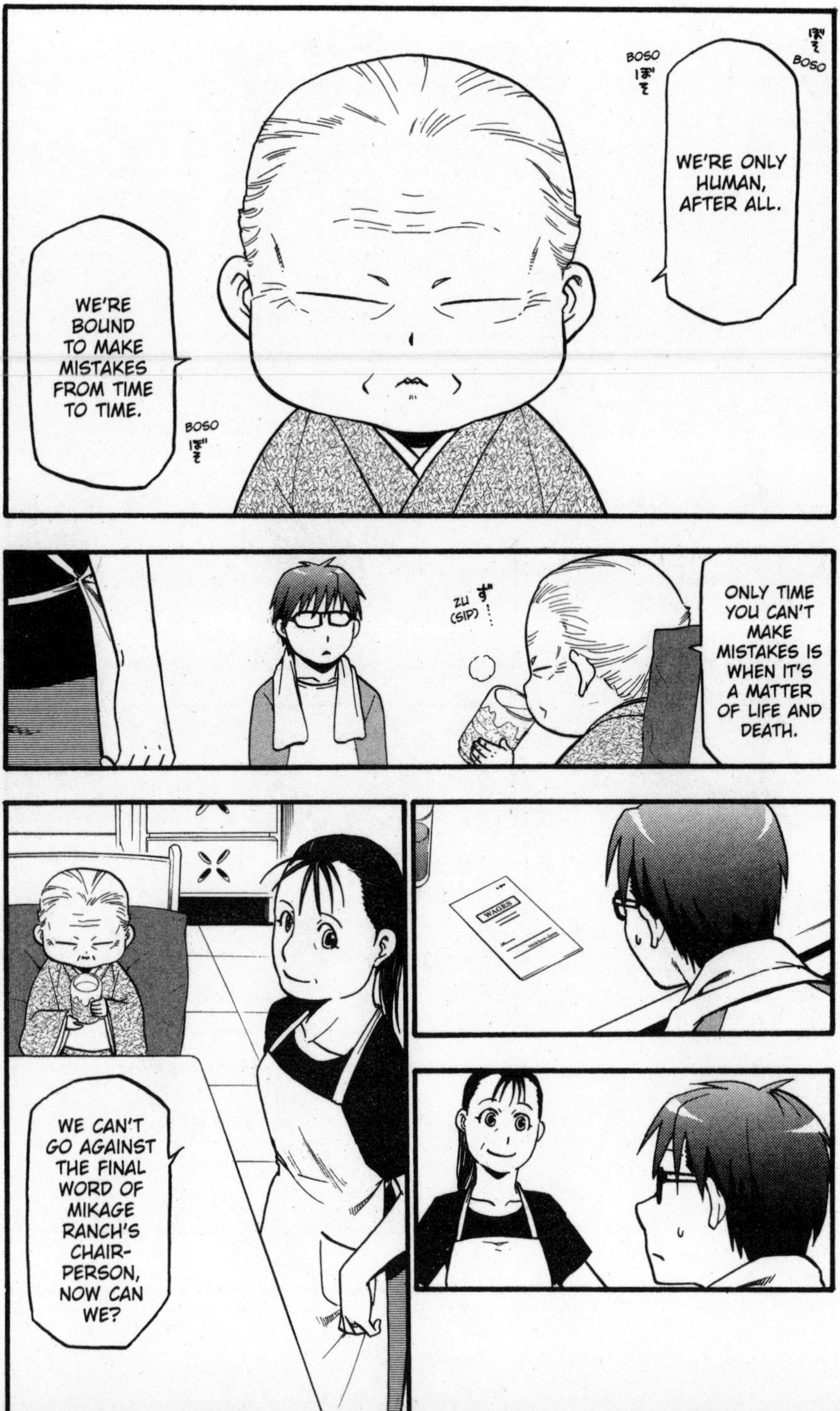

ぼそ BOSO
BOSO ぼそ
WE'RE ONLY HUMAN, AFTER ALL.
WE'RE BOUND TO MAKE MISTAKES FROM TIME TO TIME.
BOSO ぼそ
ONLY TIME YOU CAN'T MAKE MISTAKES IS WHEN IT'S A MATTER OF LIFE AND DEATH.
ZU (SIP) ず…
WAGES
WE CAN'T GO AGAINST THE FINAL WORD OF MIKAGE RANCH'S CHAIR-PERSON, NOW CAN WE?

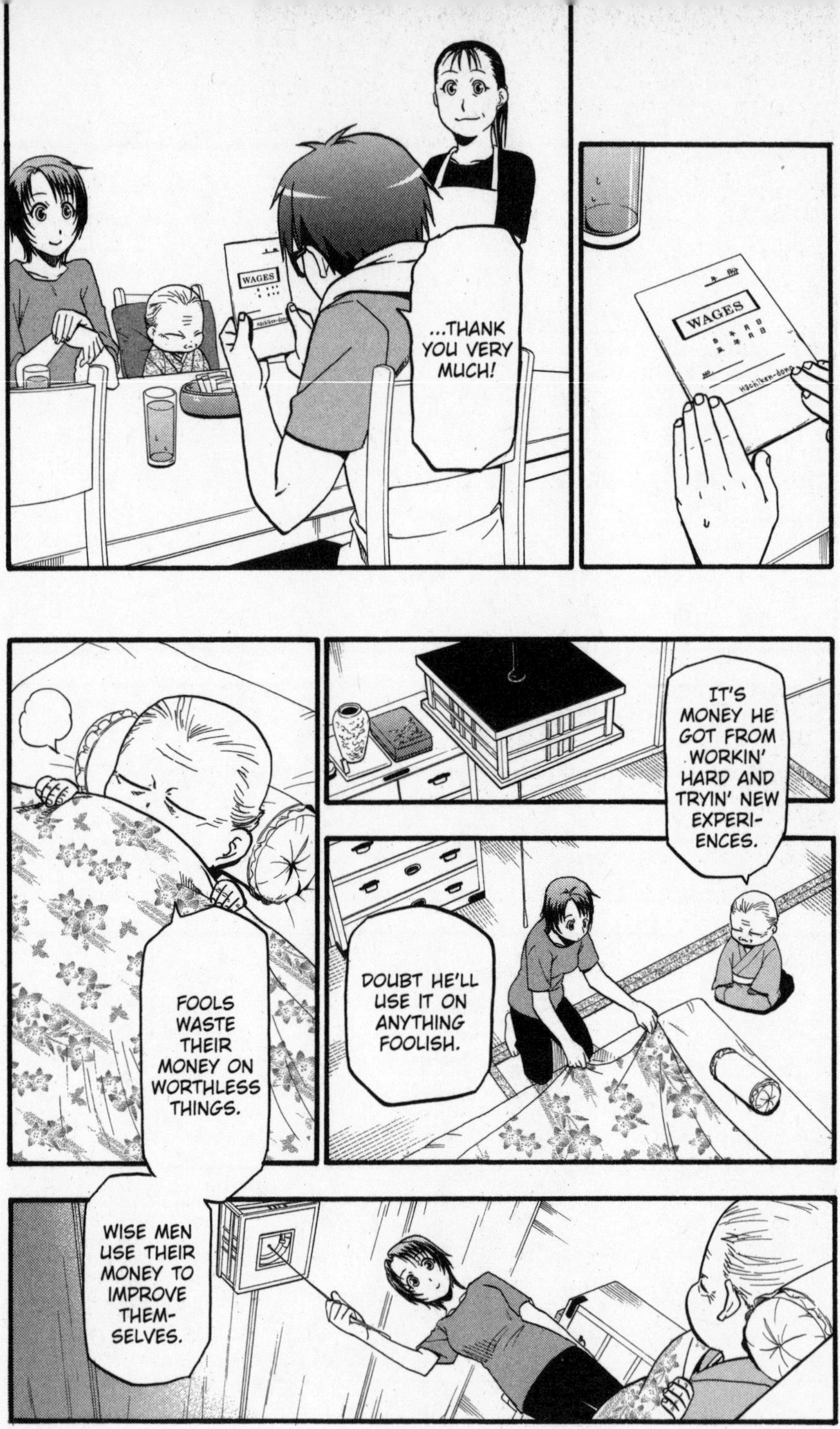
WAGES
...THANK YOU VERY MUCH!
IT'S MONEY HE GOT FROM WORKIN' HARD AND TRYIN' NEW EXPERIENCES.
DOUBT HE'LL USE IT ON ANYTHING FOOLISH.
FOOLS WASTE THEIR MONEY ON WORTHLESS THINGS.
WISE MEN USE THEIR MONEY TO IMPROVE THEMSELVES.

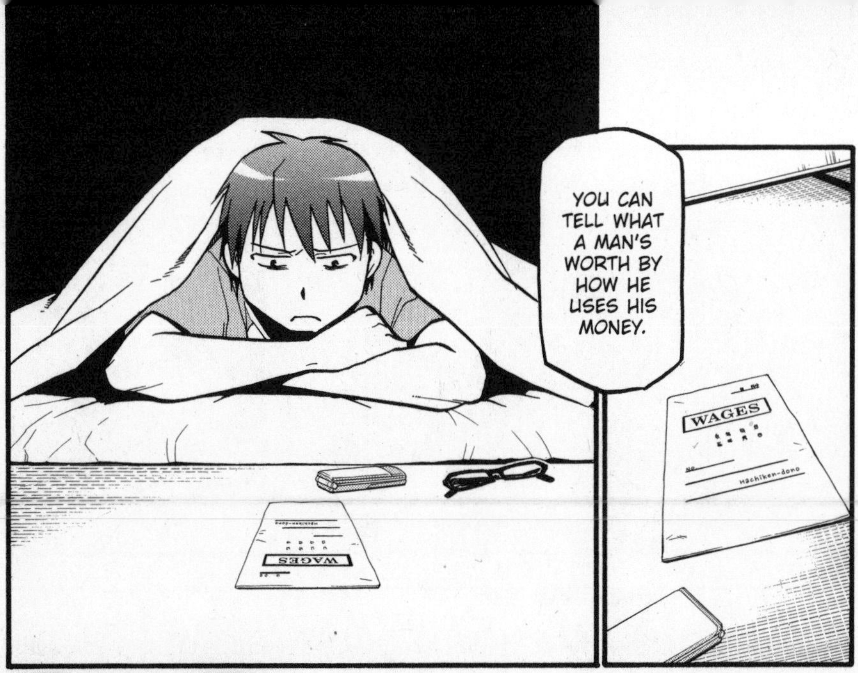
WAGES
Hachiken-dono
YOU CAN TELL WHAT A MAN'S WORTH BY HOW HE USES HIS MONEY.

Chapter 22: Tale of Summer ⑫

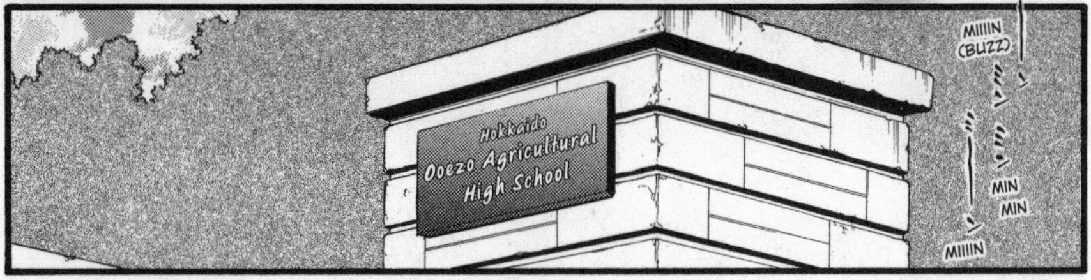
MIIIN (BUZZ)
MIN MIN
MIIIN
Hokkaido Ooezo Agricultural High School

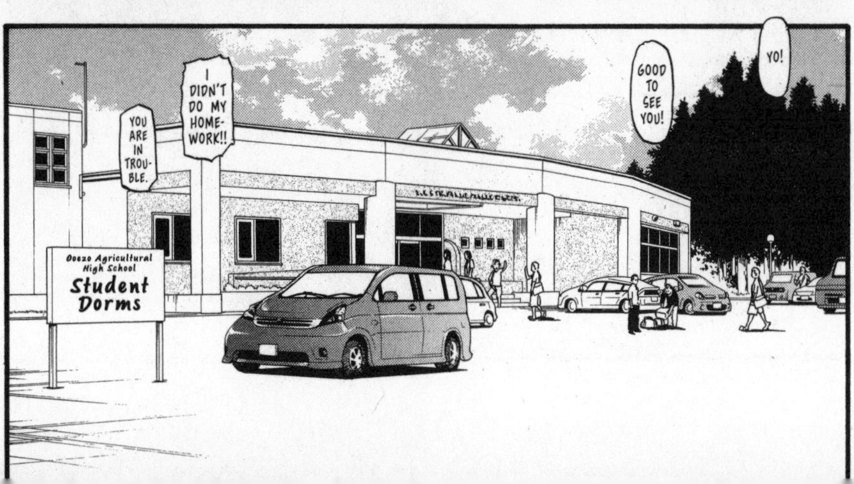
YO!
GOOD TO SEE YOU!
I DIDN'T DO MY HOME-WORK!!
YOU ARE IN TROU-BLE.
Ooezo Agricultural High School Student Dorms

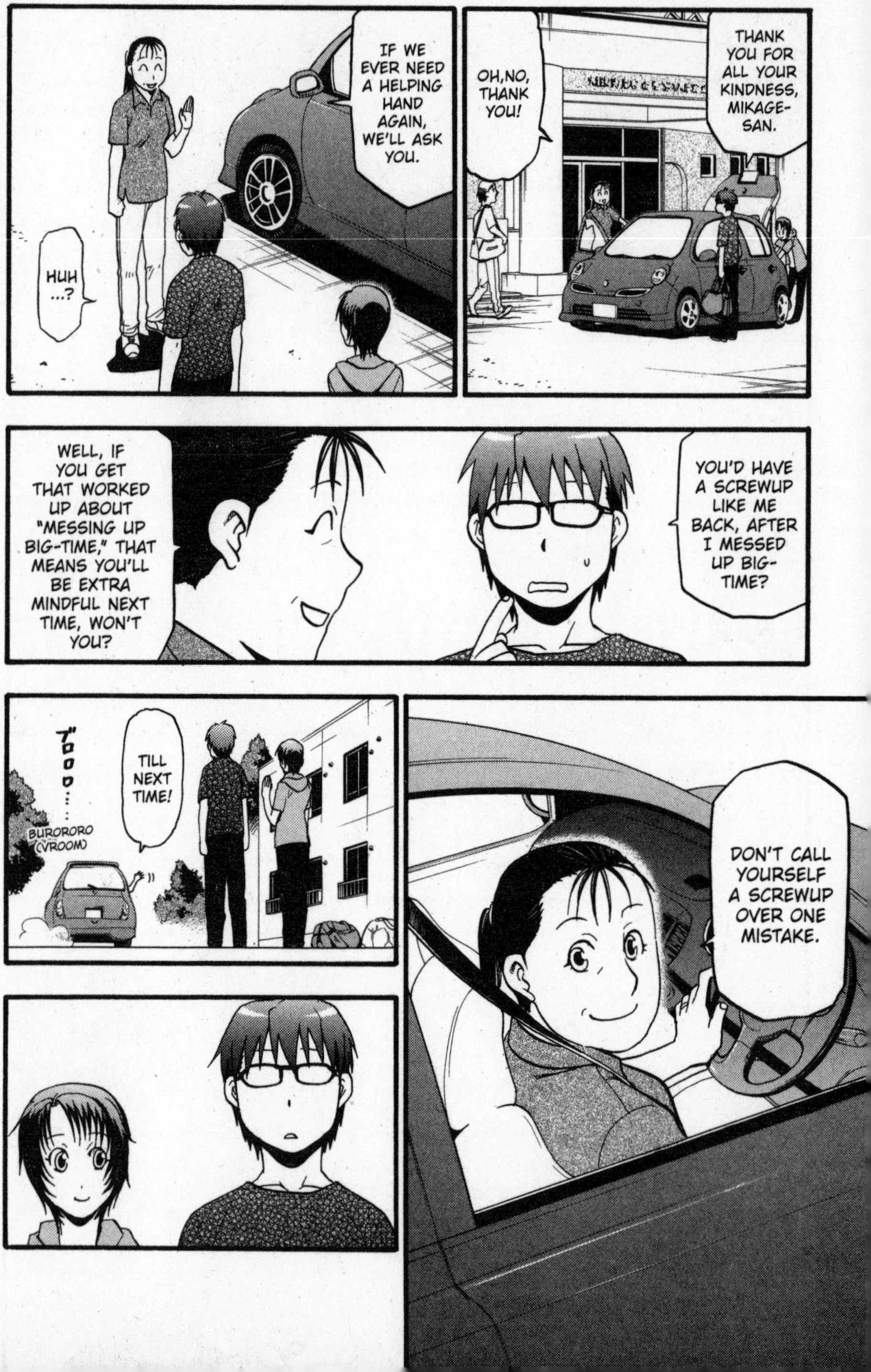
THANK YOU FOR ALL YOUR KINDNESS, MIKAGE-SAN.
OH,NO, THANK YOU!
IF WE EVER NEED A HELPING HAND AGAIN, WE'LL ASK YOU.
HUH ...?
YOU'D HAVE A SCREWUP LIKE ME BACK, AFTER I MESSED UP BIG-TIME?
WELL, IF YOU GET THAT WORKED UP ABOUT "MESSING UP BIG-TIME," THAT MEANS YOU'LL BE EXTRA MINDFUL NEXT TIME, WON'T YOU?
DON'T CALL YOURSELF A SCREWUP OVER ONE MISTAKE.
TILL NEXT TIME!
ブロロロ…
BURORORO (VROOM)

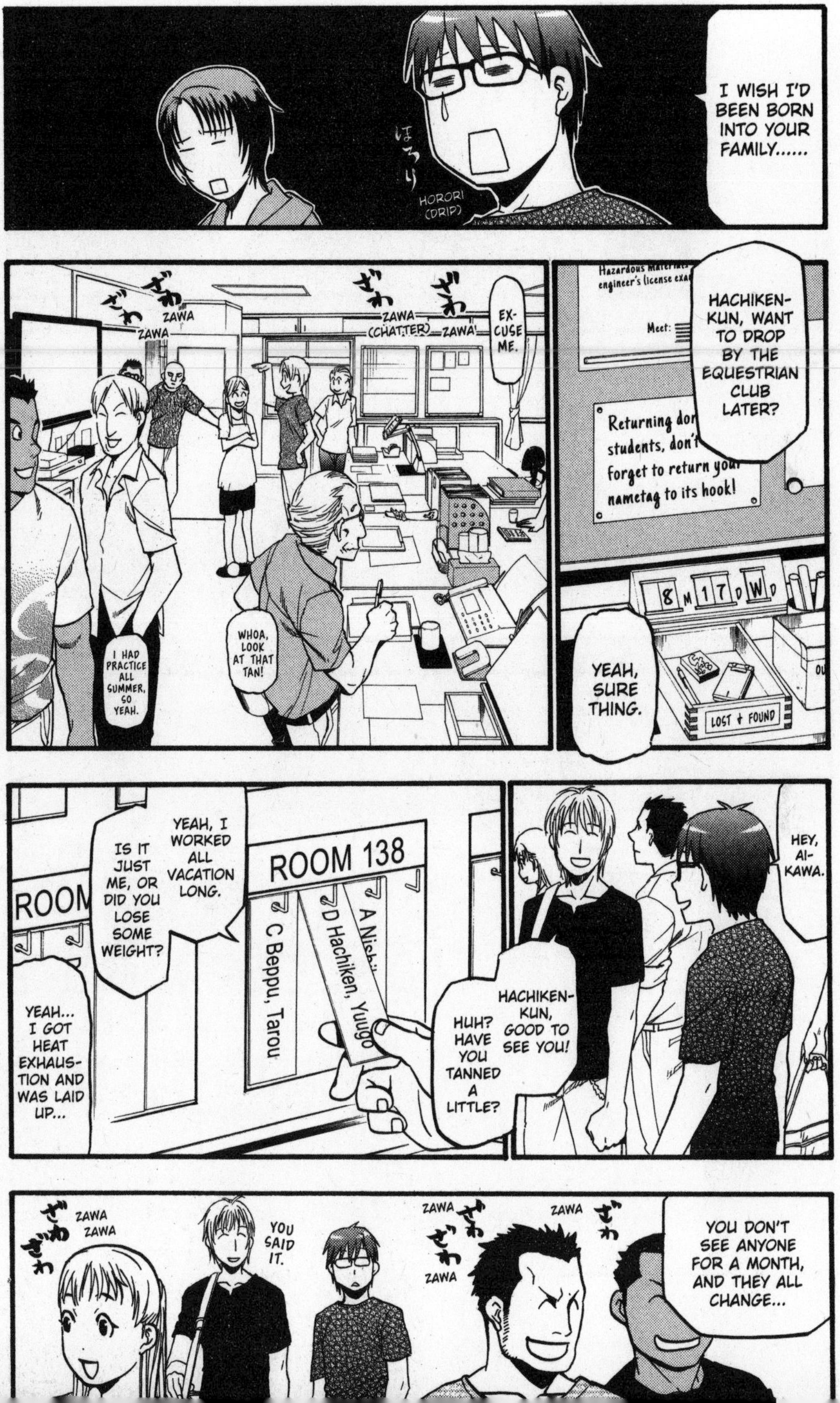
I WISH I'D BEEN BORN INTO YOUR FAMILY......
ほろり
HORORI (DRIP)
HACHIKEN-KUN, WANT TO DROP BY THE EQUESTRIAN CLUB LATER?
Meet:
Returning dor students, don't forget to return you nametag to its hook!
8 M 17 D W D
YEAH, SURE THING.
LOST & FOUND
ざわ ざわ
ZAWA (CHATTER) ZAWA
EX-CUSE ME.
ざわ ざわ
ZAWA ZAWA
WHOA, LOOK AT THAT TAN!
I HAD PRACTICE ALL SUMMER, SO YEAH.
HEY, AI-KAWA.
HACHIKEN-KUN, GOOD TO SEE YOU!
HUH? HAVE YOU TANNED A LITTLE?
ROOM 138
D Hachiken, Yuugo
C Beppu, Tarou
YEAH, I WORKED ALL VACATION LONG.
IS IT JUST ME, OR DID YOU LOSE SOME WEIGHT?
ROOM
YEAH... I GOT HEAT EXHAUS-TION AND WAS LAID UP...
YOU DON'T SEE ANYONE FOR A MONTH, AND THEY ALL CHANGE...
ざわ ZAWA
ざわ ざわ ZAWA ZAWA
YOU SAID IT.
ざわ ざわ ZAWA ZAWA

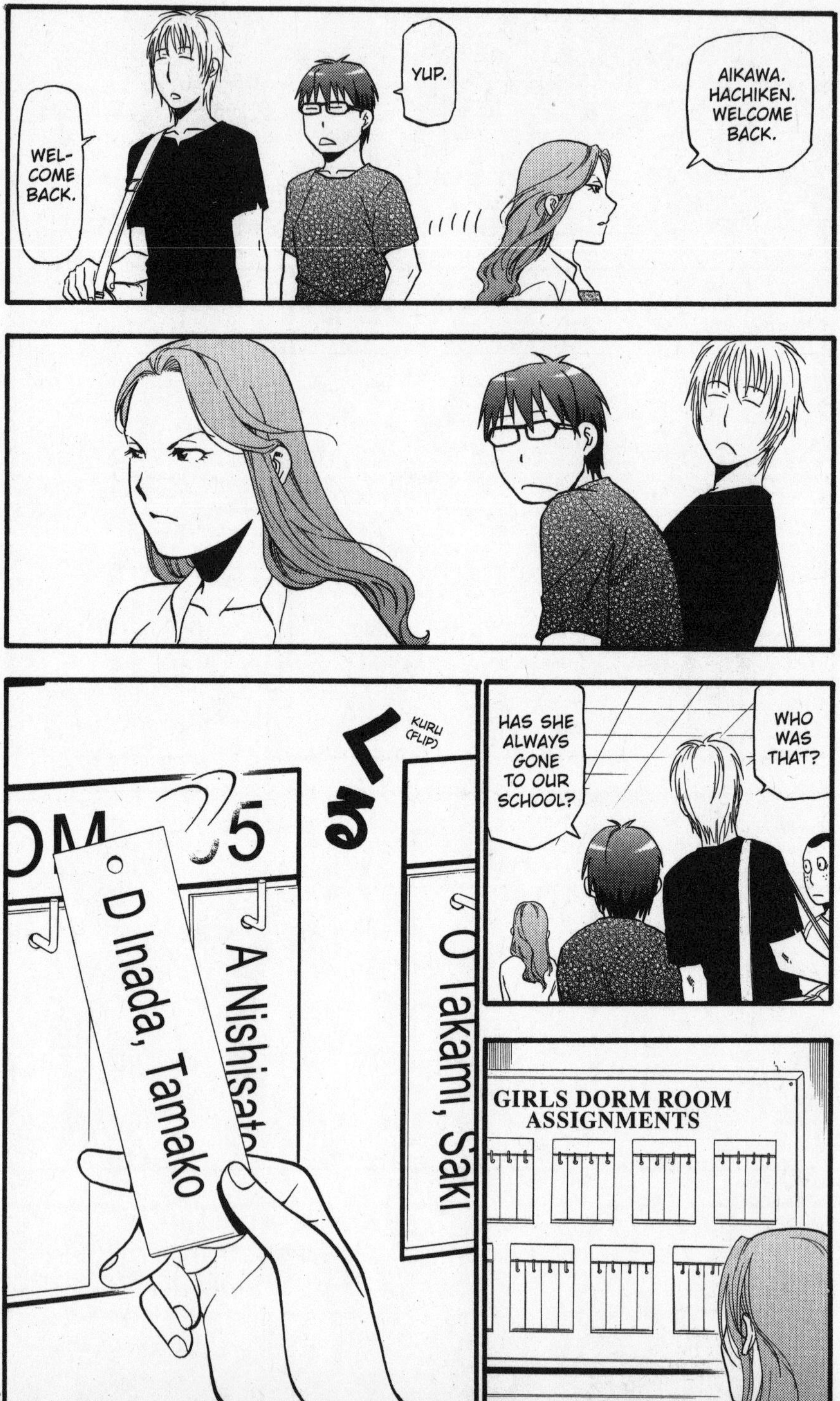
AIKAWA. HACHIKEN. WELCOME BACK.
YUP.
WEL-COME BACK.
WHO WAS THAT?
HAS SHE ALWAYS GONE TO OUR SCHOOL?
GIRLS DORM ROOM ASSIGNMENTS
KURU (FLIP)
くる
O Takami, Saki
A Nishisat
D Inada, Tamako

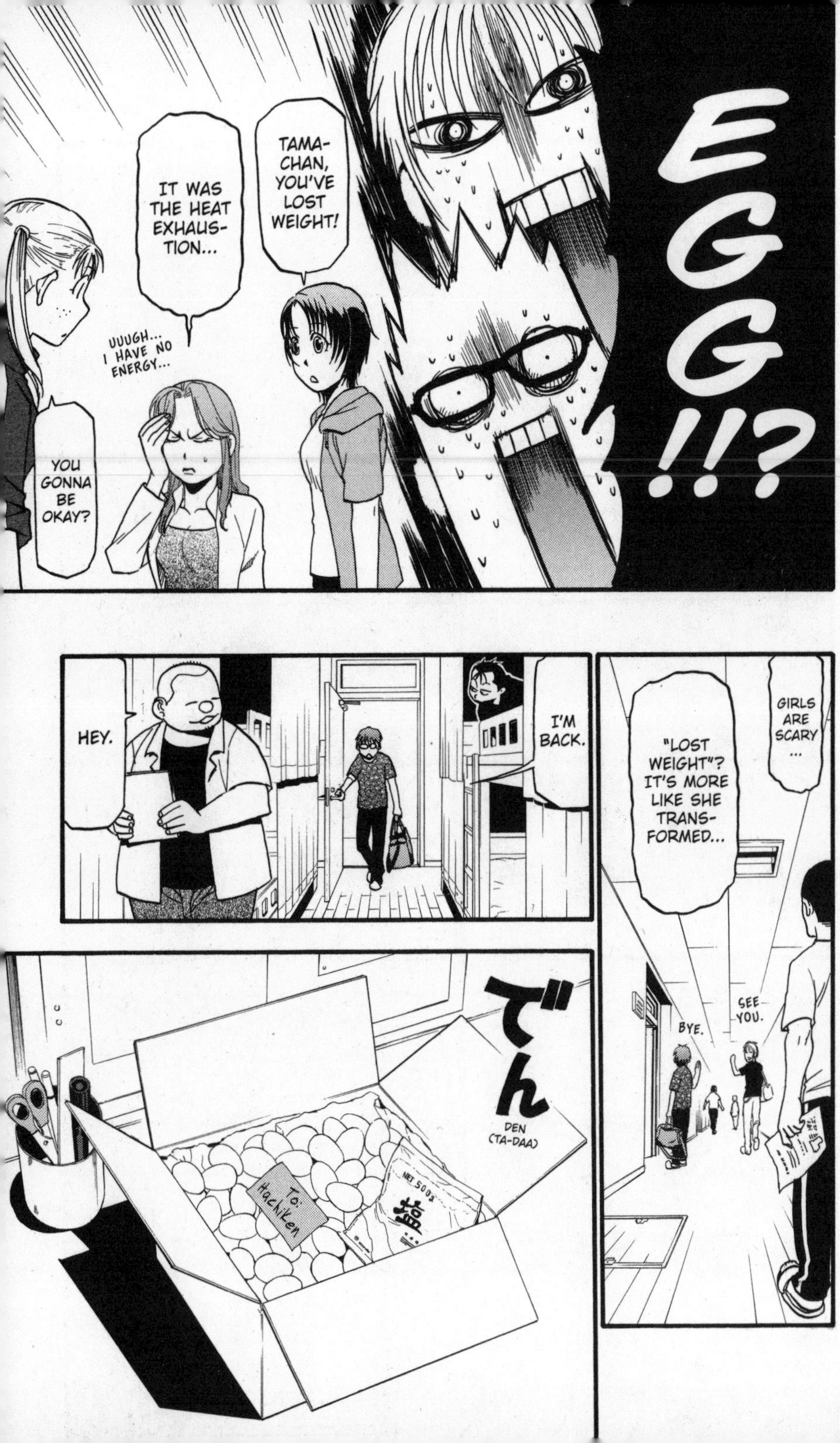
EGG!!?
TAMA-CHAN, YOU'VE LOST WEIGHT!
IT WAS THE HEAT EXHAUSTION...
UUUGH... I HAVE NO ENERGY...
YOU GONNA BE OKAY?
GIRLS ARE SCARY...
"LOST WEIGHT"? IT'S MORE LIKE SHE TRANSFORMED...
SEE YOU.
BYE.
I'M BACK.
HEY.
でん
DEN (TA-DAA)
NET 500g
To: Hachiken

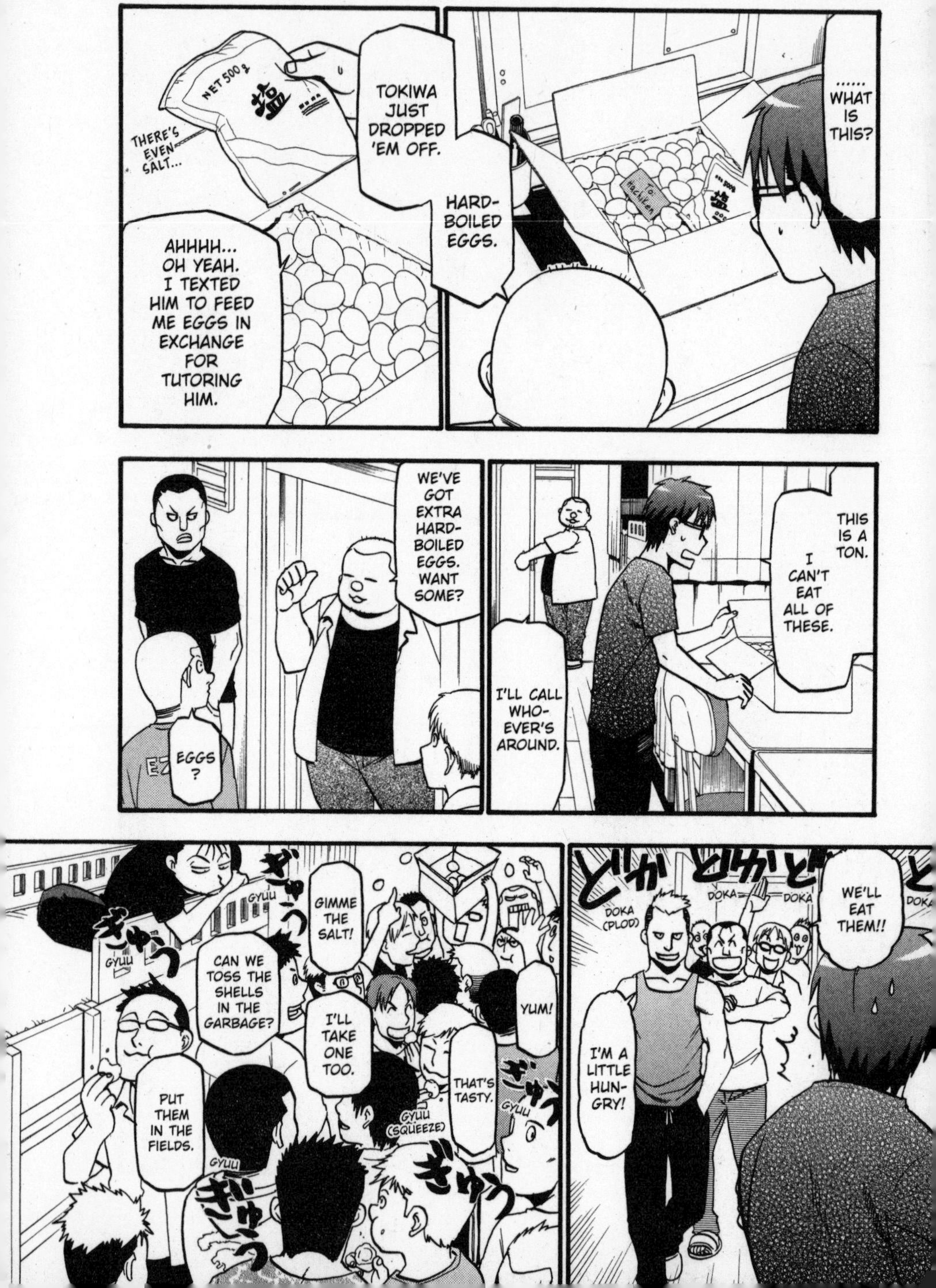

......WHAT IS THIS?
TOKIWA JUST DROPPED 'EM OFF.
HARD-BOILED EGGS.
To: Hachiken
NET 500g 塩
THERE'S EVEN SALT...
AHHHH... OH YEAH. I TEXTED HIM TO FEED ME EGGS IN EXCHANGE FOR TUTORING HIM.
THIS IS A TON.
I CAN'T EAT ALL OF THESE.
I'LL CALL WHO-EVER'S AROUND.
WE'VE GOT EXTRA HARD-BOILED EGGS. WANT SOME?
EGGS?
どか DOKA (PLOD)
どか DOKA
どか DOKA
ど DOKA
WE'LL EAT THEM!!
I'M A LITTLE HUN-GRY!
ぎゅう GYUU
ぎゅう GYUU
GIMME THE SALT!
CAN WE TOSS THE SHELLS IN THE GARBAGE?
YUM!
I'LL TAKE ONE TOO.
THAT'S TASTY.
ぎゅう GYUU
ぎゅう GYUU (SQUEEZE)
PUT THEM IN THE FIELDS.
ぎゅう GYUU
ぎゅう

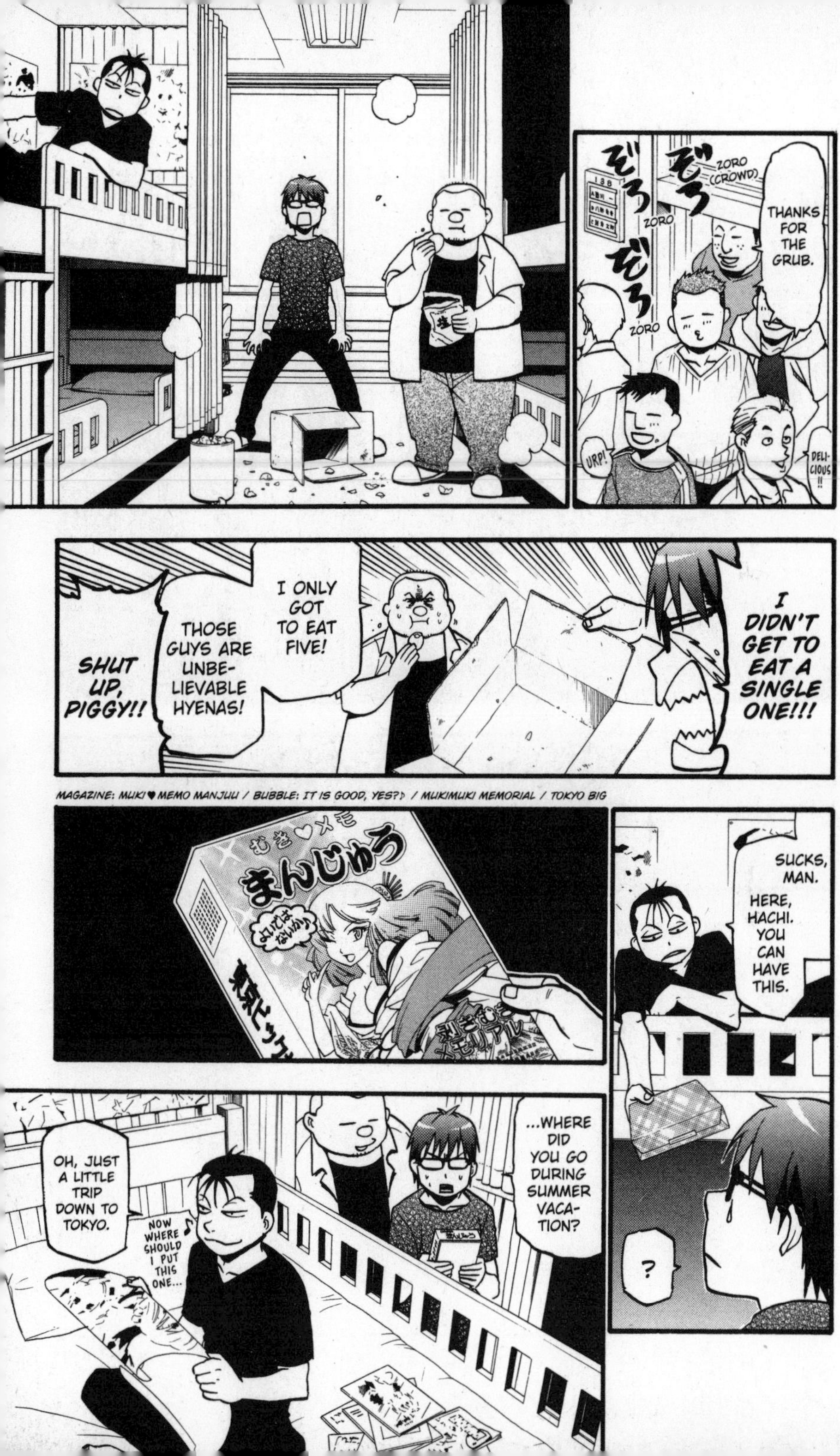

ZORO (CROWD)
ZORO
ZORO
THANKS FOR THE GRUB.
URP!
DELICIOUS!!
I DIDN'T GET TO EAT A SINGLE ONE!!!
I ONLY GOT TO EAT FIVE!
THOSE GUYS ARE UNBE-LIEVABLE HYENAS!
SHUT UP, PIGGY!!
MAGAZINE: MUKI♥MEMO MANJUU / BUBBLE: IT IS GOOD, YES?♪ / MUKIMUKI MEMORIAL / TOKYO BIG
SUCKS, MAN.
HERE, HACHI. YOU CAN HAVE THIS.
まんじゅう
...WHERE DID YOU GO DURING SUMMER VACA-TION?
OH, JUST A LITTLE TRIP DOWN TO TOKYO.
NOW WHERE SHOULD I PUT THIS ONE...
?

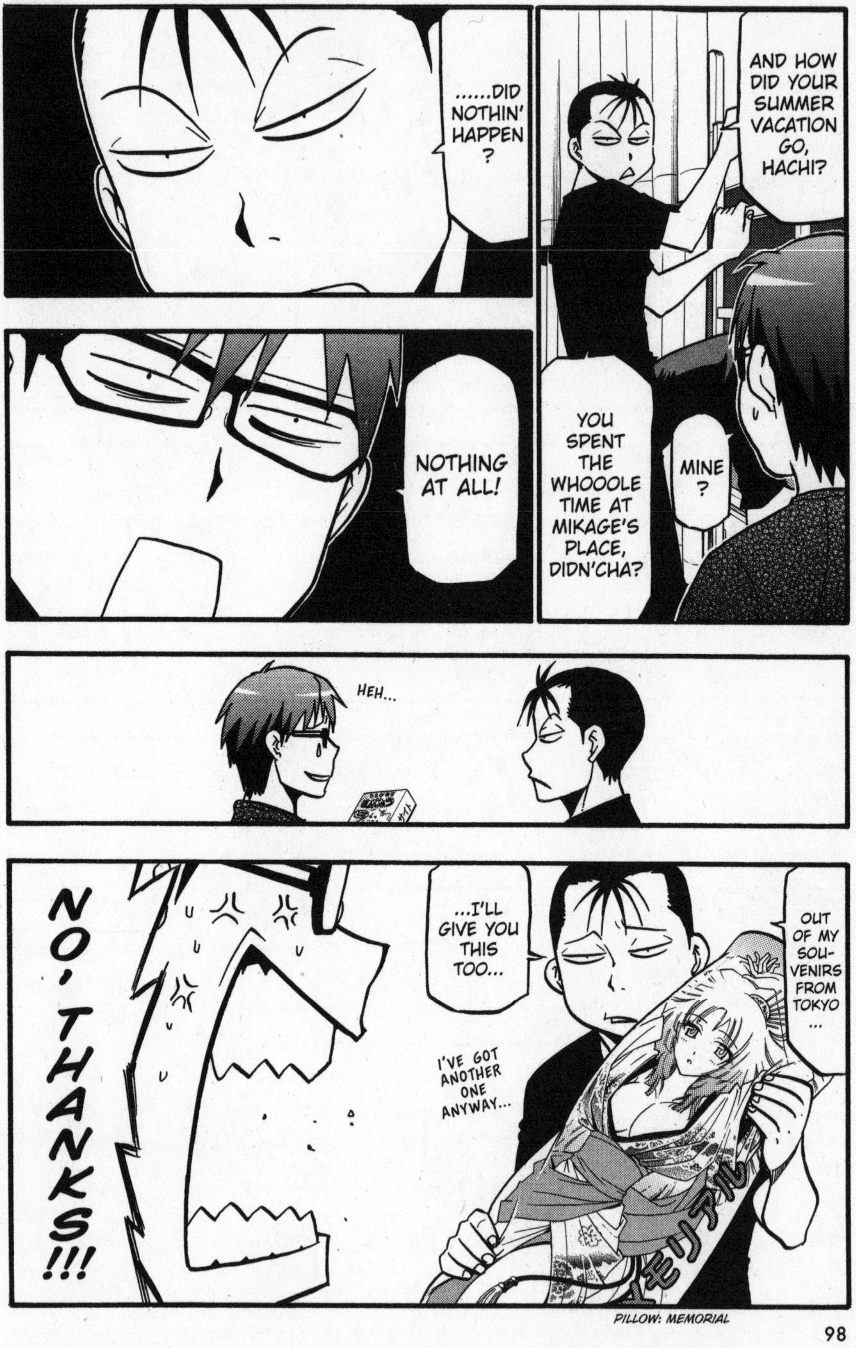
AND HOW DID YOUR SUMMER VACATION GO, HACHI?
MINE?
YOU SPENT THE WHOOOLE TIME AT MIKAGE'S PLACE, DIDN'CHA?
......DID NOTHIN' HAPPEN?
NOTHING AT ALL!
HEH...
OUT OF MY SOUVENIRS FROM TOKYO...
...I'LL GIVE YOU THIS TOO...
I'VE GOT ANOTHER ONE ANYWAY...
NO, THANKS!!!

PILLOW: MEMORIAL

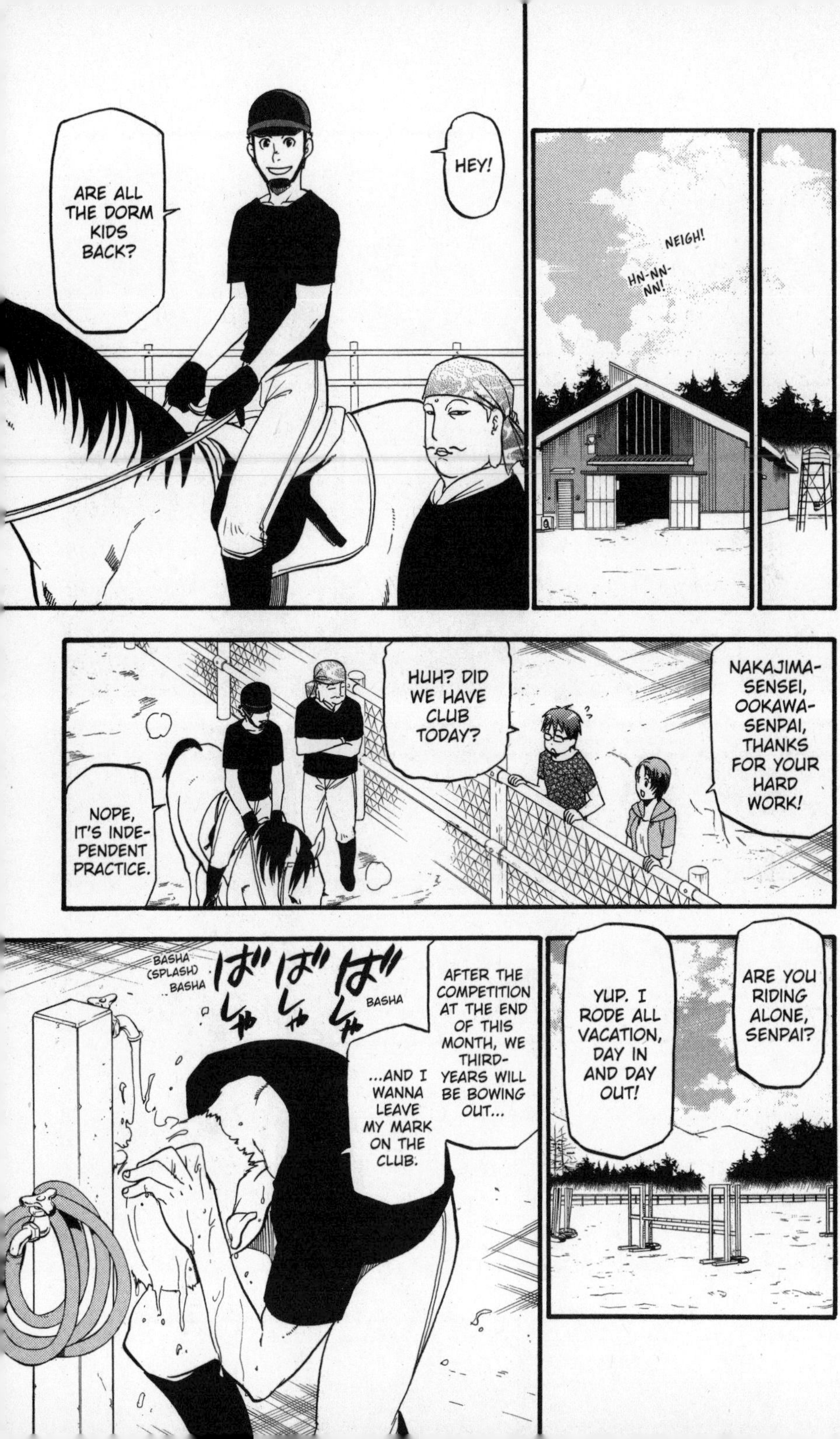
NEIGH!
HN-NN-NN!
HEY!
ARE ALL THE DORM KIDS BACK?
NAKAJIMA-SENSEI, OOKAWA-SENPAI, THANKS FOR YOUR HARD WORK!
HUH? DID WE HAVE CLUB TODAY?
NOPE, IT'S INDEPENDENT PRACTICE.
ARE YOU RIDING ALONE, SENPAI?
YUP. I RODE ALL VACATION, DAY IN AND DAY OUT!
AFTER THE COMPETITION AT THE END OF THIS MONTH, WE THIRD-YEARS WILL BE BOWING OUT...
...AND I WANNA LEAVE MY MARK ON THE CLUB.
ばしゃ
BASHA
ばしゃ
ばしゃ
BASHA (SPLASH) BASHA

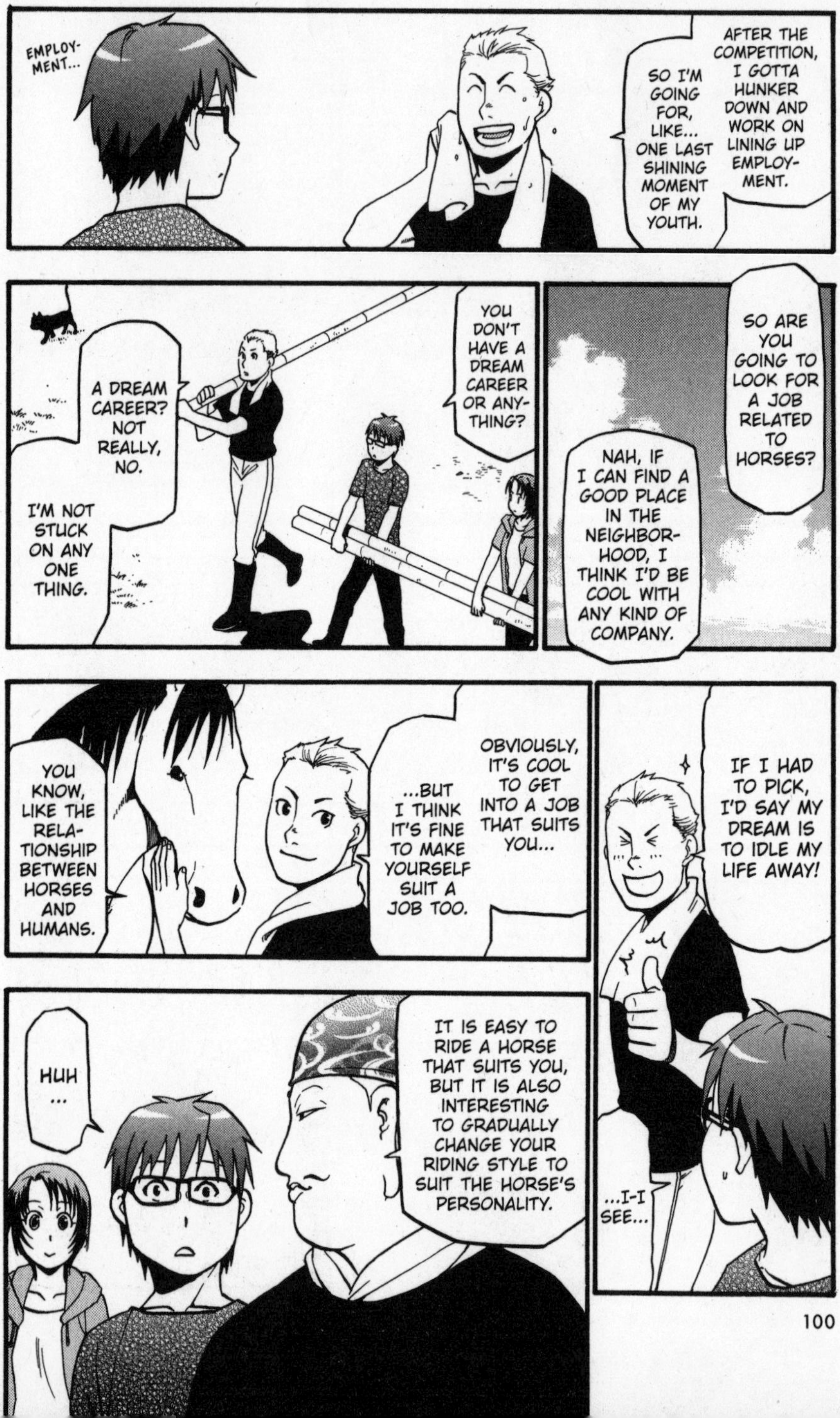

AFTER THE COMPETITION, I GOTTA HUNKER DOWN AND WORK ON LINING UP EMPLOYMENT.
SO I'M GOING FOR, LIKE... ONE LAST SHINING MOMENT OF MY YOUTH.
EMPLOYMENT...
SO ARE YOU GOING TO LOOK FOR A JOB RELATED TO HORSES?
NAH, IF I CAN FIND A GOOD PLACE IN THE NEIGHBORHOOD, I THINK I'D BE COOL WITH ANY KIND OF COMPANY.
YOU DON'T HAVE A DREAM CAREER OR ANYTHING?
A DREAM CAREER? NOT REALLY, NO.
I'M NOT STUCK ON ANY ONE THING.
IF I HAD TO PICK, I'D SAY MY DREAM IS TO IDLE MY LIFE AWAY!
...I-I SEE...
OBVIOUSLY, IT'S COOL TO GET INTO A JOB THAT SUITS YOU...
...BUT I THINK IT'S FINE TO MAKE YOURSELF SUIT A JOB TOO.
YOU KNOW, LIKE THE RELATIONSHIP BETWEEN HORSES AND HUMANS.
IT IS EASY TO RIDE A HORSE THAT SUITS YOU, BUT IT IS ALSO INTERESTING TO GRADUALLY CHANGE YOUR RIDING STYLE TO SUIT THE HORSE'S PERSONALITY.
HUH...

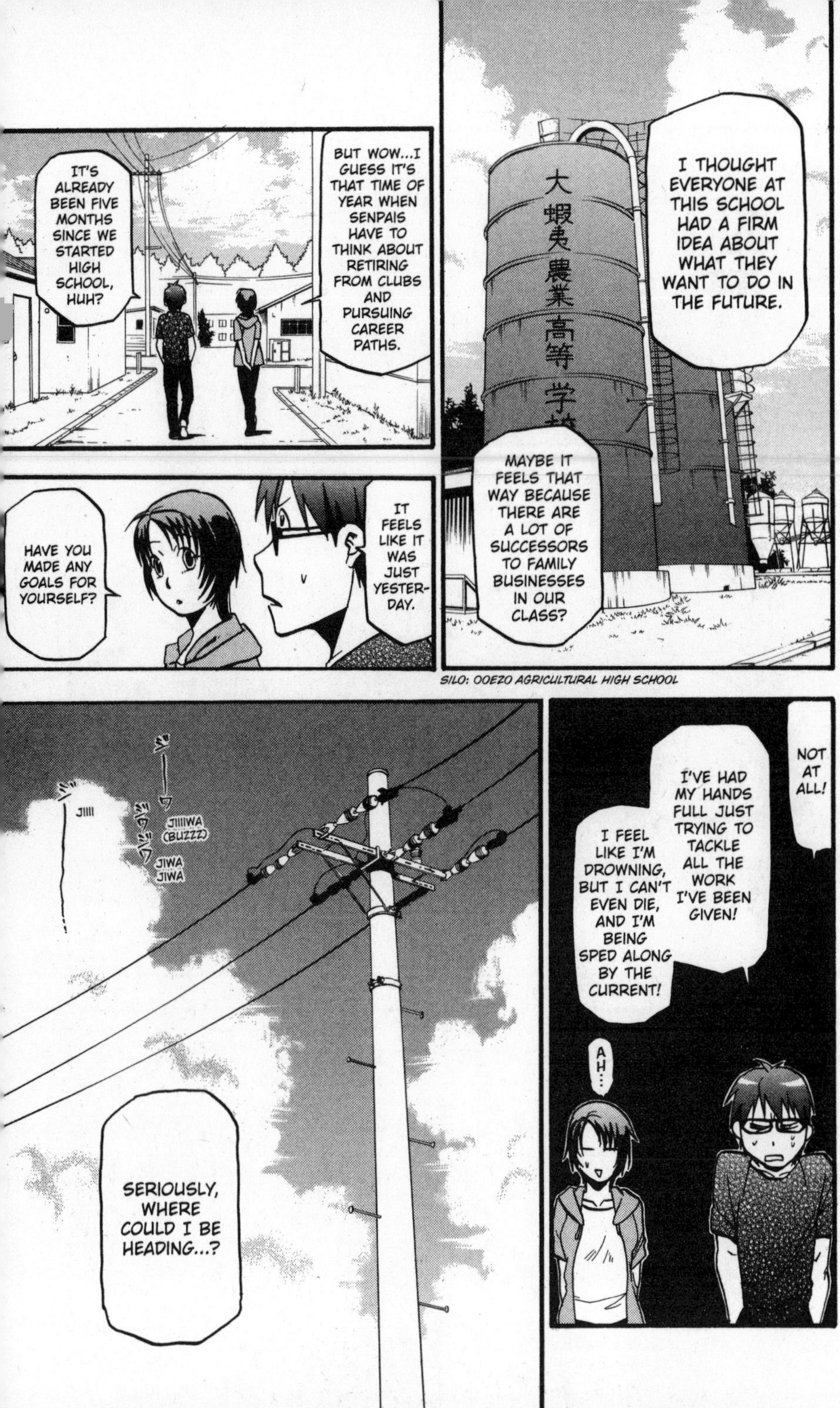
I THOUGHT EVERYONE AT THIS SCHOOL HAD A FIRM IDEA ABOUT WHAT THEY WANT TO DO IN THE FUTURE.
MAYBE IT FEELS THAT WAY BECAUSE THERE ARE A LOT OF SUCCESSORS TO FAMILY BUSINESSES IN OUR CLASS?
BUT WOW...I GUESS IT'S THAT TIME OF YEAR WHEN SENPAIS HAVE TO THINK ABOUT RETIRING FROM CLUBS AND PURSUING CAREER PATHS.
IT'S ALREADY BEEN FIVE MONTHS SINCE WE STARTED HIGH SCHOOL, HUH?
IT FEELS LIKE IT WAS JUST YESTER-DAY.
HAVE YOU MADE ANY GOALS FOR YOURSELF?
SILO: OOEZO AGRICULTURAL HIGH SCHOOL
NOT AT ALL!
I'VE HAD MY HANDS FULL JUST TRYING TO TACKLE ALL THE WORK I'VE BEEN GIVEN!
I FEEL LIKE I'M DROWNING, BUT I CAN'T EVEN DIE, AND I'M BEING SPED ALONG BY THE CURRENT!
AH...
JIIIIWA (BUZZZ)
JIWA JIWA
JIIII
SERIOUSLY, WHERE COULD I BE HEADING...?

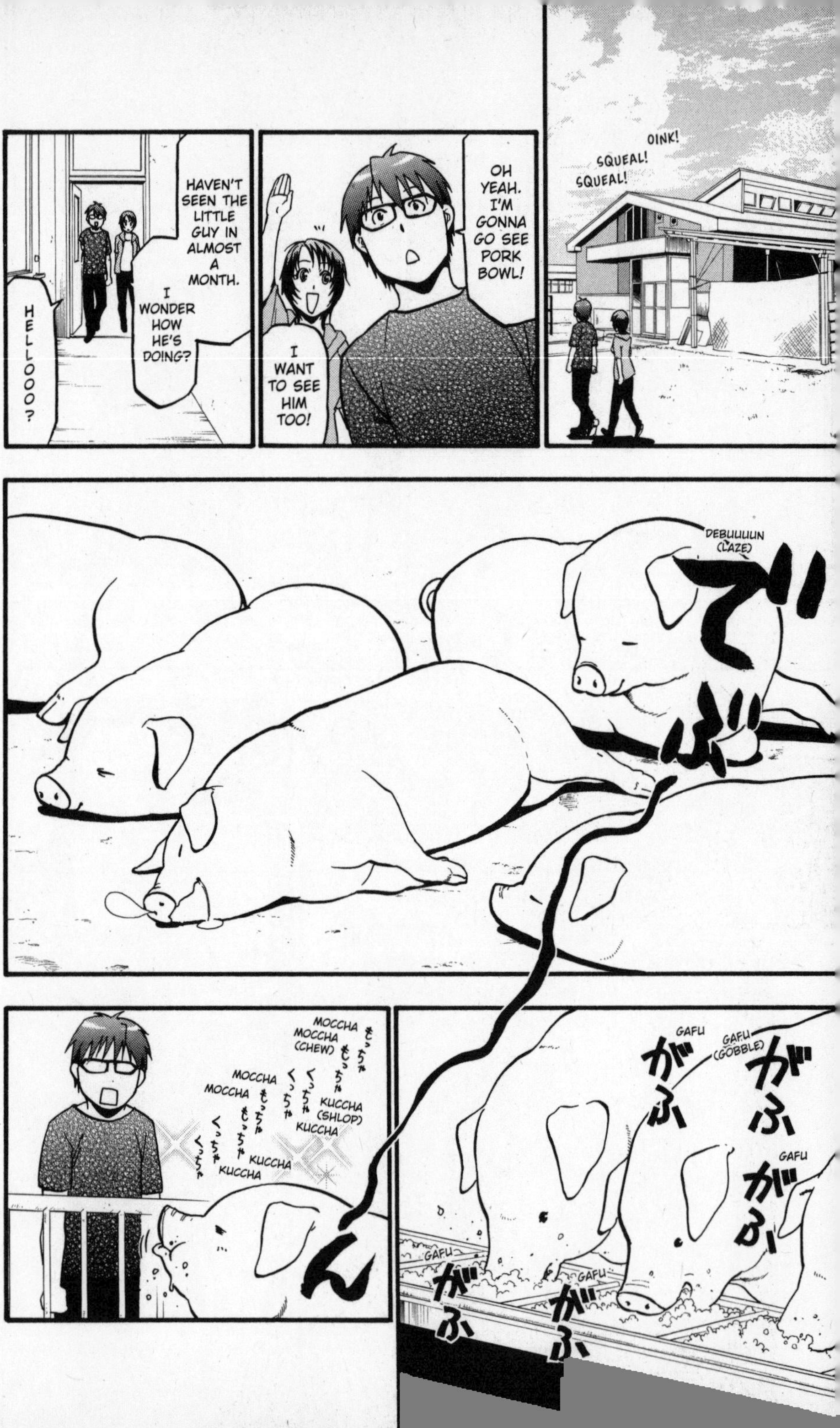
OINK!
SQUEAL!
SQUEAL!
OH YEAH. I'M GONNA GO SEE PORK BOWL!
I WANT TO SEE HIM TOO!
HAVEN'T SEEN THE LITTLE GUY IN ALMOST A MONTH.
I WONDER HOW HE'S DOING?
HELLOOO?
DEBUUUUN (LAZE)
でぶ
ん
GAFU GAFU (GOBBLE)
がふ がふ
GAFU
がふ
GAFU
がふ
GAFU
がふ
MOCCHA MOCCHA (CHEW)
もっちゃ もっちゃ
KUCCHA (SHLOP) KUCCHA
くっちゃ くっちゃ
MOCCHA MOCCHA
もっちゃ もっちゃ
KUCCHA KUCCHA
くっちゃ くっちゃ

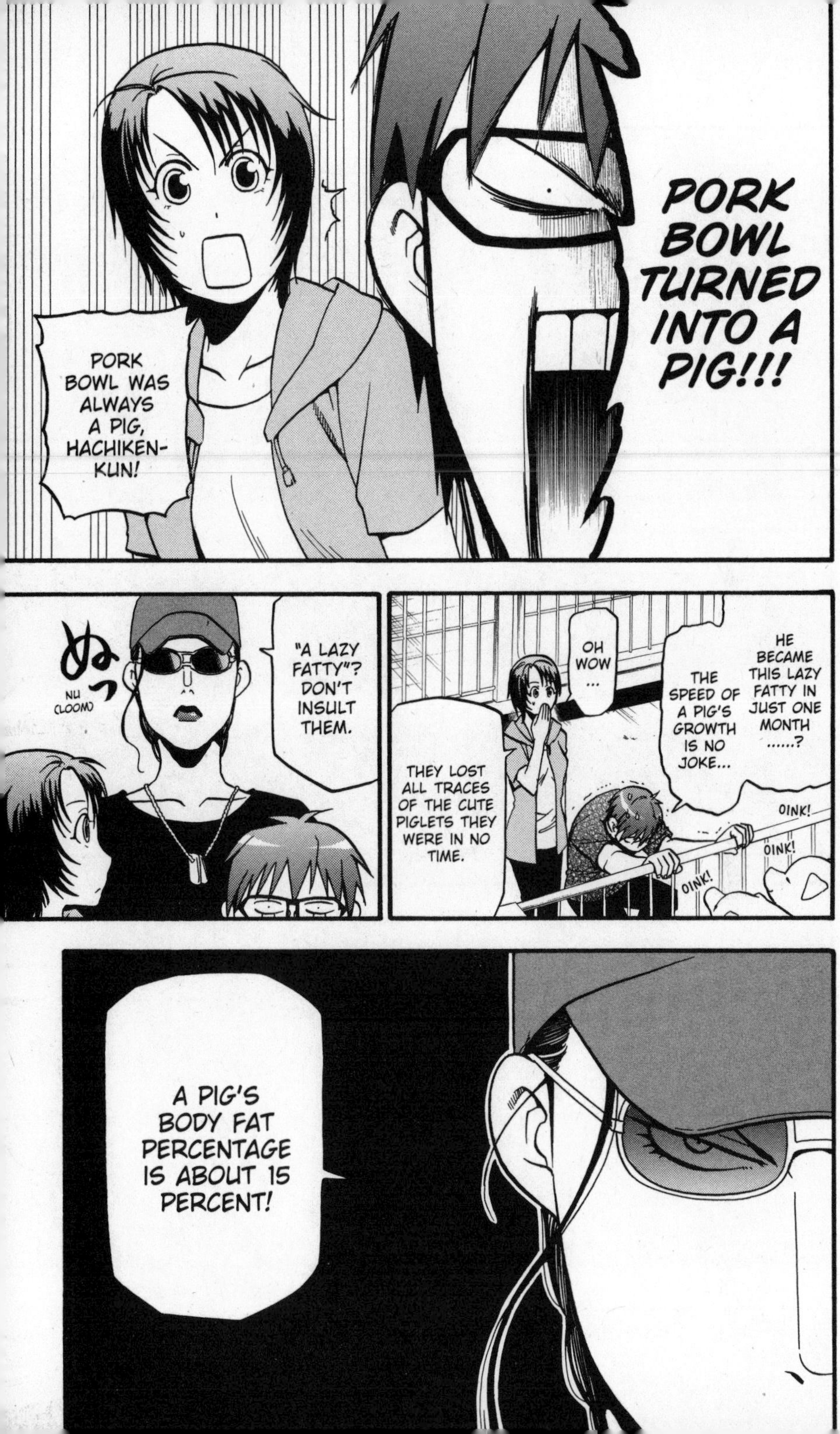
PORK BOWL TURNED INTO A PIG!!!
PORK BOWL WAS ALWAYS A PIG, HACHIKEN-KUN!
HE BECAME THIS LAZY FATTY IN JUST ONE MONTH ......?
THE SPEED OF A PIG'S GROWTH IS NO JOKE...
OH WOW ...
THEY LOST ALL TRACES OF THE CUTE PIGLETS THEY WERE IN NO TIME.
OINK!
OINK!
OINK!
"A LAZY FATTY"? DON'T INSULT THEM.
ぬっ
NU (LOOM)
A PIG'S BODY FAT PERCENTAGE IS ABOUT 15 PERCENT!

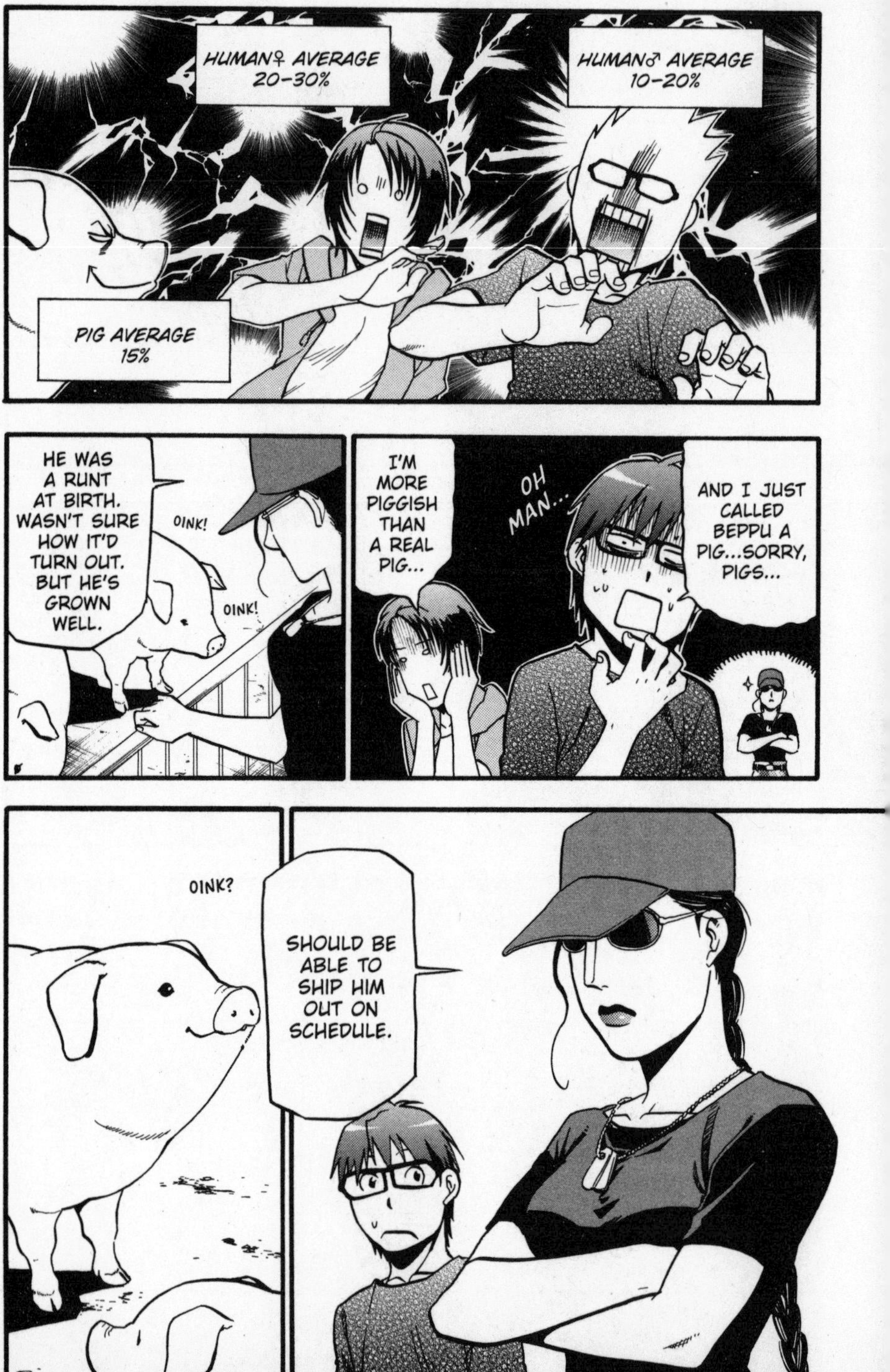
HUMAN♂ AVERAGE 10–20%
HUMAN♀ AVERAGE 20–30%
PIG AVERAGE 15%
AND I JUST CALLED BEPPU A PIG...SORRY, PIGS...
OH MAN...
I'M MORE PIGGISH THAN A REAL PIG...
HE WAS A RUNT AT BIRTH. WASN'T SURE HOW IT'D TURN OUT. BUT HE'S GROWN WELL.
OINK!
OINK!
SHOULD BE ABLE TO SHIP HIM OUT ON SCHEDULE.
OINK?

Silver Spoon

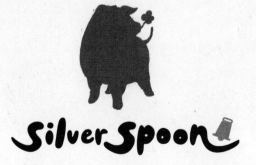

YUUICHI
MATSUYAMA

TAIKI CENTRAL
MIDDLE SCHOOL

BASEBALL TEAM

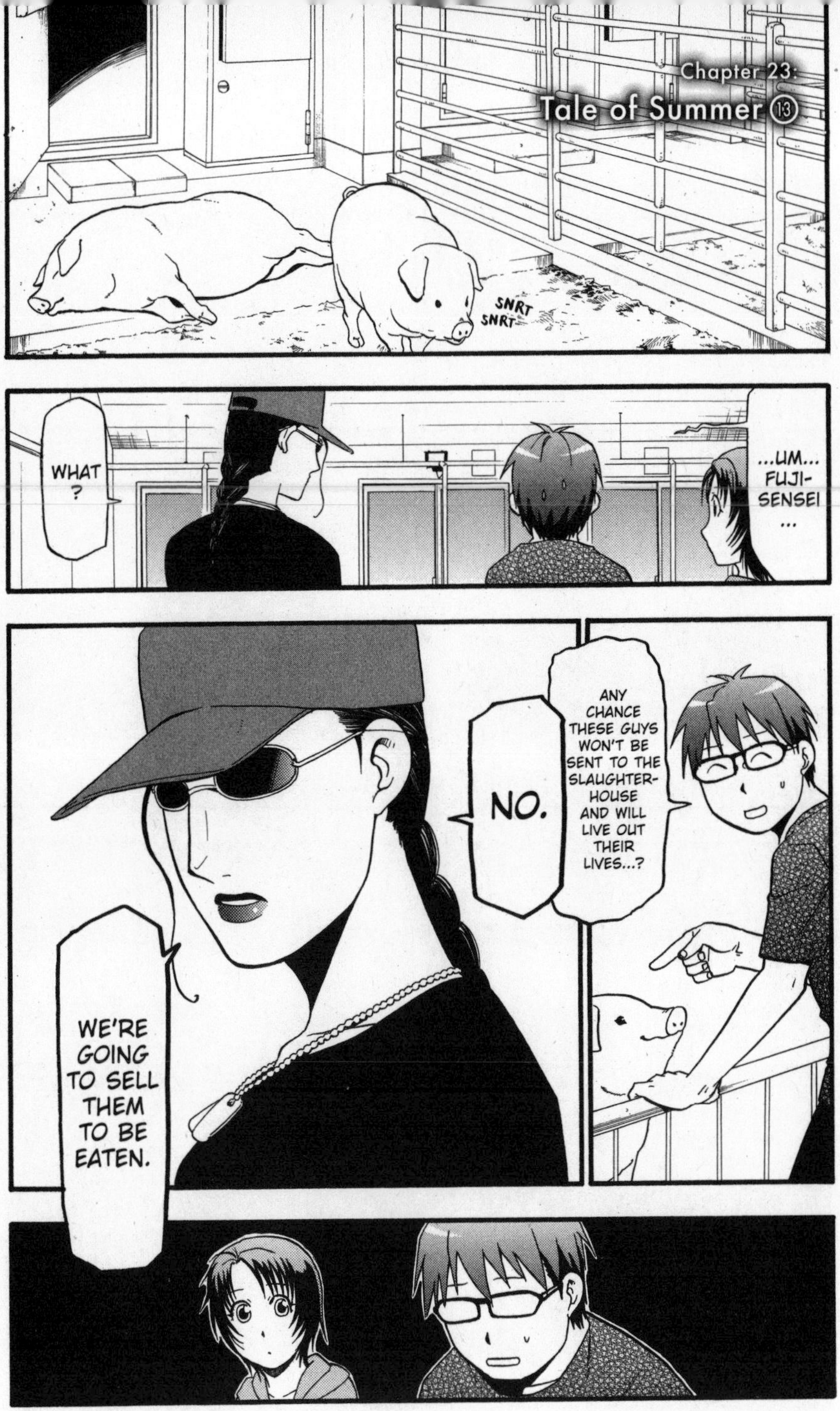
Chapter 23:
Tale of Summer ⑬
SNRT
SNRT
...UM... FUJI-SENSEI ...
WHAT?
ANY CHANCE THESE GUYS WON'T BE SENT TO THE SLAUGHTER-HOUSE AND WILL LIVE OUT THEIR LIVES...?
NO.
WE'RE GOING TO SELL THEM TO BE EATEN.

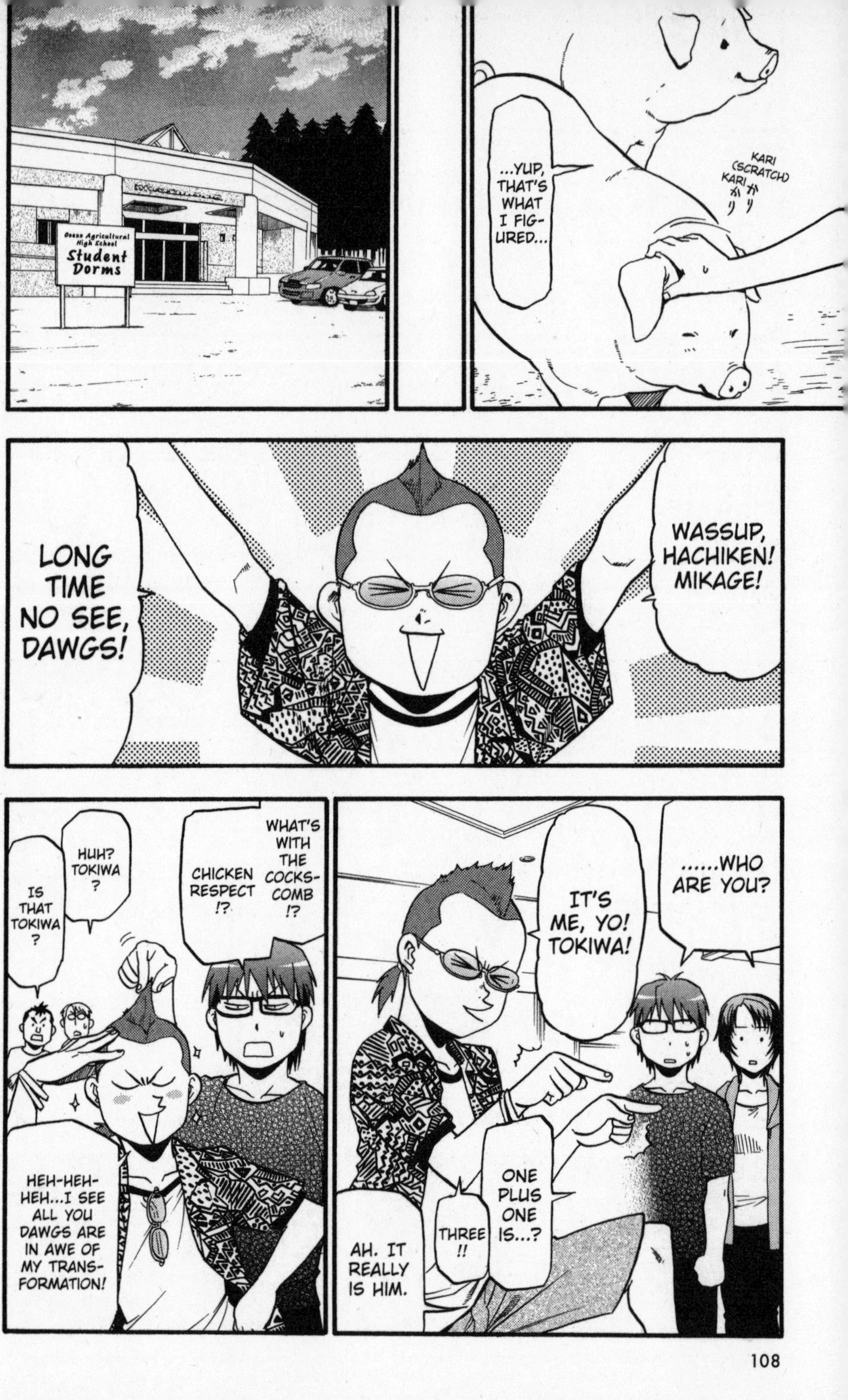
...YUP, THAT'S WHAT I FIGURED...
KARI (SCRATCH) KARI かり
Oezo Agricultural High School Student Dorms
WASSUP, HACHIKEN! MIKAGE!
LONG TIME NO SEE, DAWGS!
......WHO ARE YOU?
IT'S ME, YO! TOKIWA!
ONE PLUS ONE IS...?
THREE!!
AH. IT REALLY IS HIM.
WHAT'S WITH THE COCKS-COMB!?
CHICKEN RESPECT!?
HUH? TOKIWA?
IS THAT TOKIWA?
HEH-HEH-HEH...I SEE ALL YOU DAWGS ARE IN AWE OF MY TRANS-FORMATION!

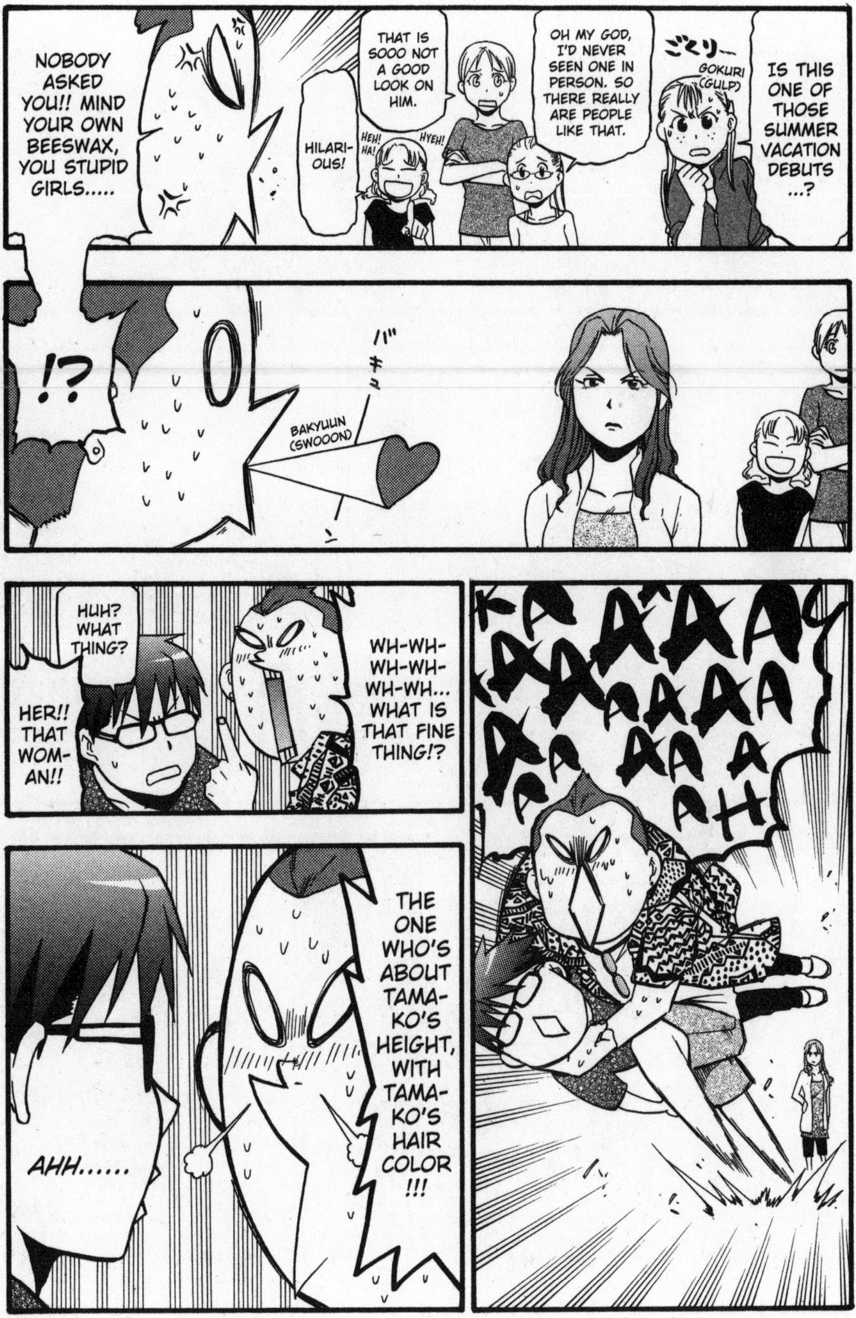
IS THIS ONE OF THOSE SUMMER VACATION DEBUTS ...?
ごくりー
GOKURI (GULP)
OH MY GOD, I'D NEVER SEEN ONE IN PERSON. SO THERE REALLY ARE PEOPLE LIKE THAT.
THAT IS SOOO NOT A GOOD LOOK ON HIM.
HYEH!
HEH! HA!
HILARI-OUS!
NOBODY ASKED YOU!! MIND YOUR OWN BEESWAX, YOU STUPID GIRLS.....
バキュン
BAKYUUN (SWOOON)
!?
KAAAAAAAAAAAAAAAAAAAAAAAAH
WH-WH-WH-WH-WH-WH... WHAT IS THAT FINE THING!?
HUH? WHAT THING?
HER!! THAT WOM-AN!!
THE ONE WHO'S ABOUT TAMA-KO'S HEIGHT, WITH TAMA-KO'S HAIR COLOR !!!
AHH......

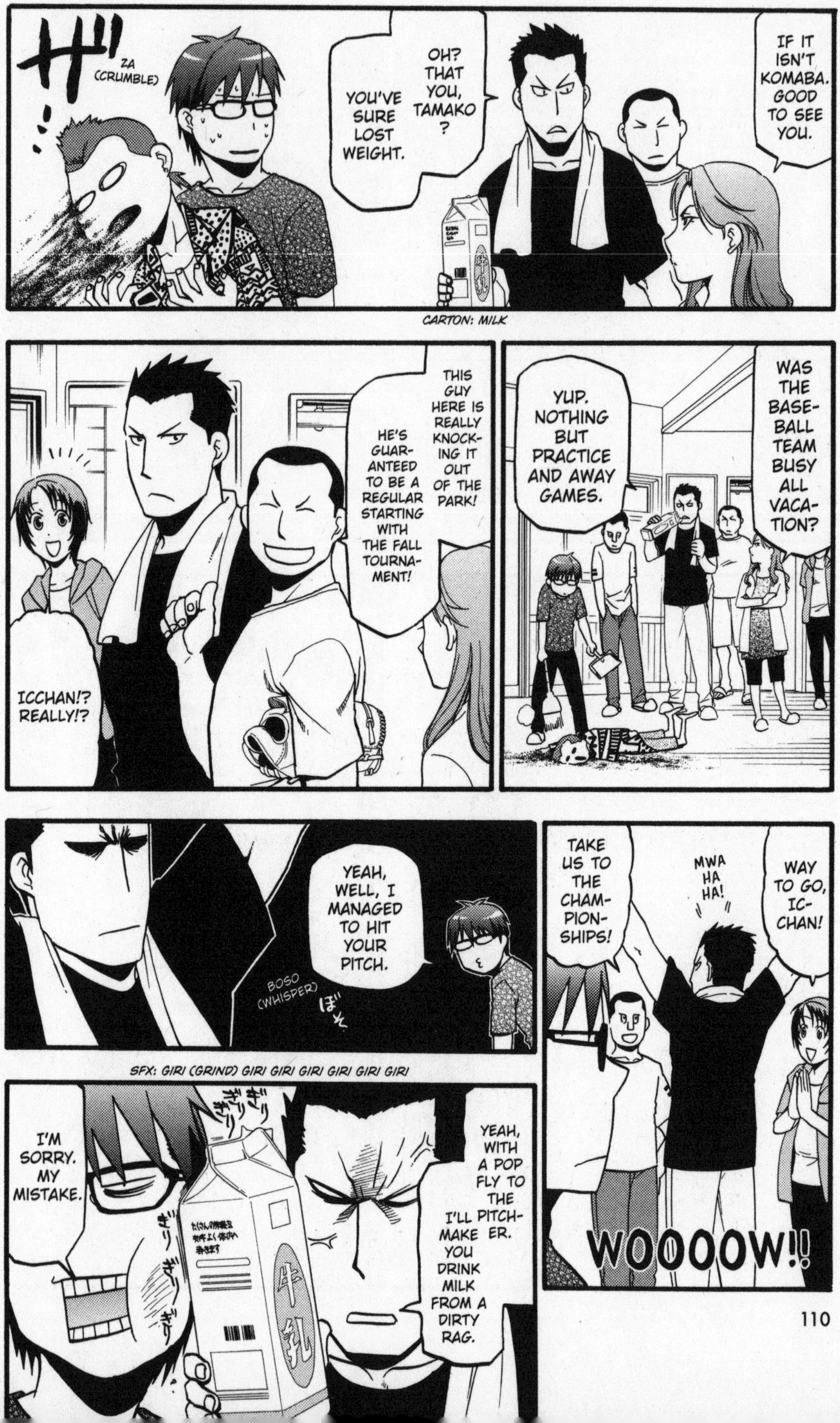
IF IT ISN'T KOMABA. GOOD TO SEE YOU.
OH? THAT YOU, TAMAKO?
YOU'VE SURE LOST WEIGHT.
ZA (CRUMBLE)
CARTON: MILK
WAS THE BASE-BALL TEAM BUSY ALL VACA-TION?
YUP. NOTHING BUT PRACTICE AND AWAY GAMES.
THIS GUY HERE IS REALLY KNOCK-ING IT OUT OF THE PARK!
HE'S GUAR-ANTEED TO BE A REGULAR STARTING WITH THE FALL TOURNA-MENT!
ICCHAN!? REALLY!?
WAY TO GO, IC-CHAN!
MWA HA HA!
TAKE US TO THE CHAM-PION-SHIPS!
WOOOOW!!
YEAH, WELL, I MANAGED TO HIT YOUR PITCH.
BOSO (WHISPER)
SFX: GIRI (GRIND) GIRI GIRI GIRI GIRI GIRI GIRI
YEAH, WITH A POP FLY TO THE PITCH-ER.
I'LL MAKE YOU DRINK MILK FROM A DIRTY RAG.
I'M SORRY. MY MISTAKE.

SIGN: SCHOOL PRECEPTS: WORK, COLLABORATE, DEFY LOGIC

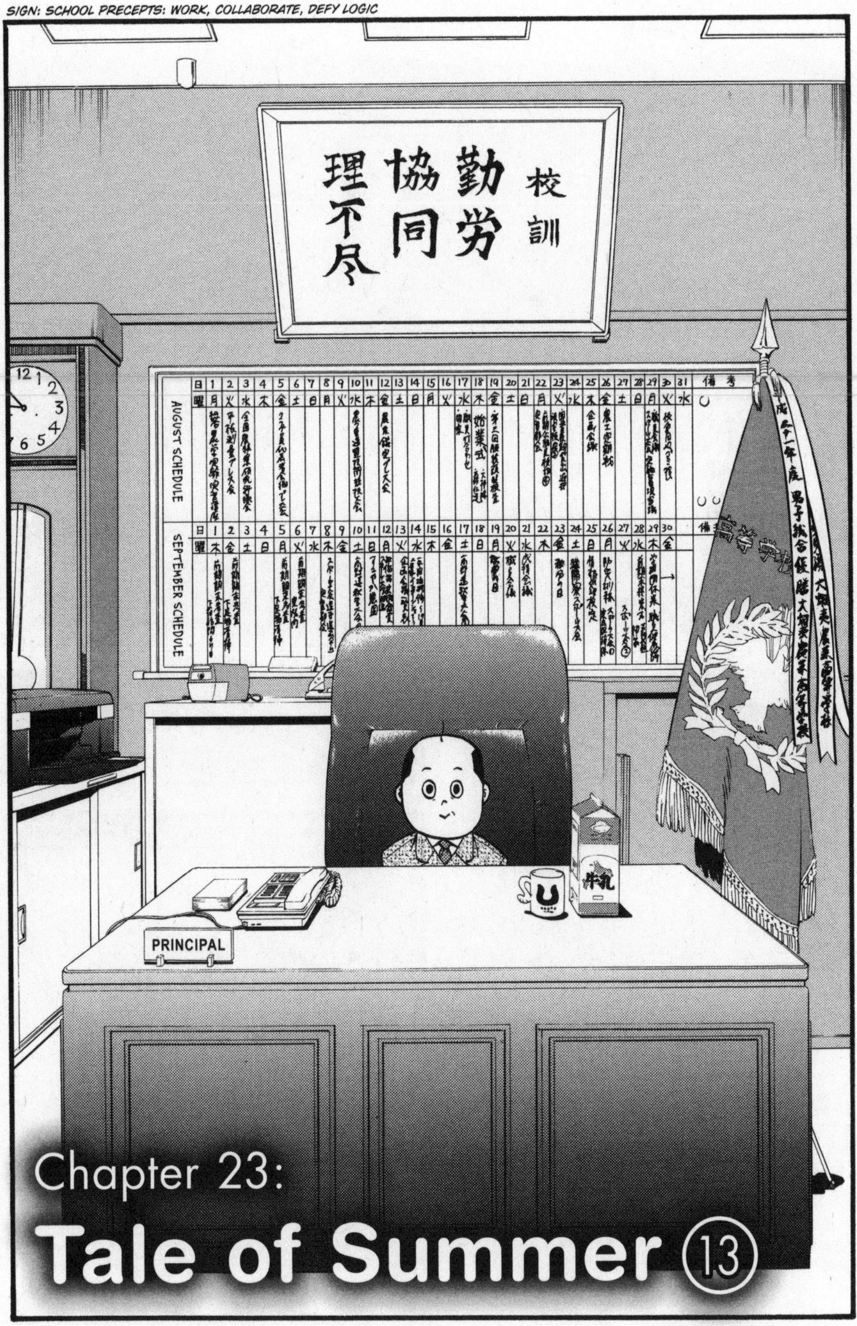
校訓
勤労
協同
理不尽
AUGUST SCHEDULE
SEPTEMBER SCHEDULE
PRINCIPAL
牛乳

Chapter 23: Tale of Summer ⑬

SIGN: SCHOOL PRECEPTS: WORK, COLLABORATE, DEFY LOGIC

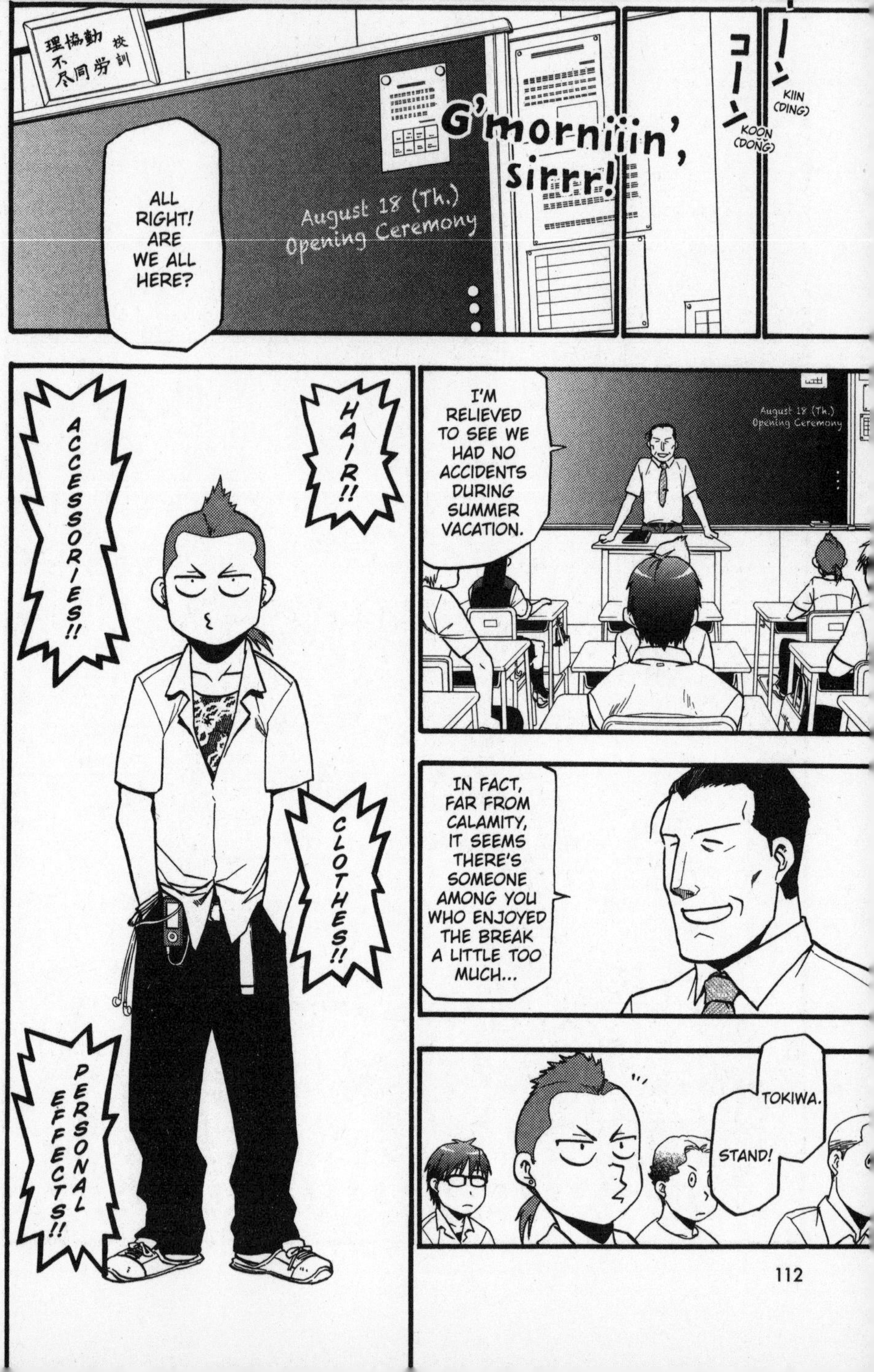
キーン
KIIN (DING)
コーン
KOON (DONG)
校訓 勤労 協同 理不尽
G'morniiin', sirrr!
August 18 (Th.) Opening Ceremony
ALL RIGHT! ARE WE ALL HERE?
August 18 (Th.) Opening Ceremony
I'M RELIEVED TO SEE WE HAD NO ACCIDENTS DURING SUMMER VACATION.
IN FACT, FAR FROM CALAMITY, IT SEEMS THERE'S SOMEONE AMONG YOU WHO ENJOYED THE BREAK A LITTLE TOO MUCH...
TOKIWA.
STAND!
HAIR!!
ACCESSORIES!!
CLOTHES!!
PERSONAL EFFECTS!!

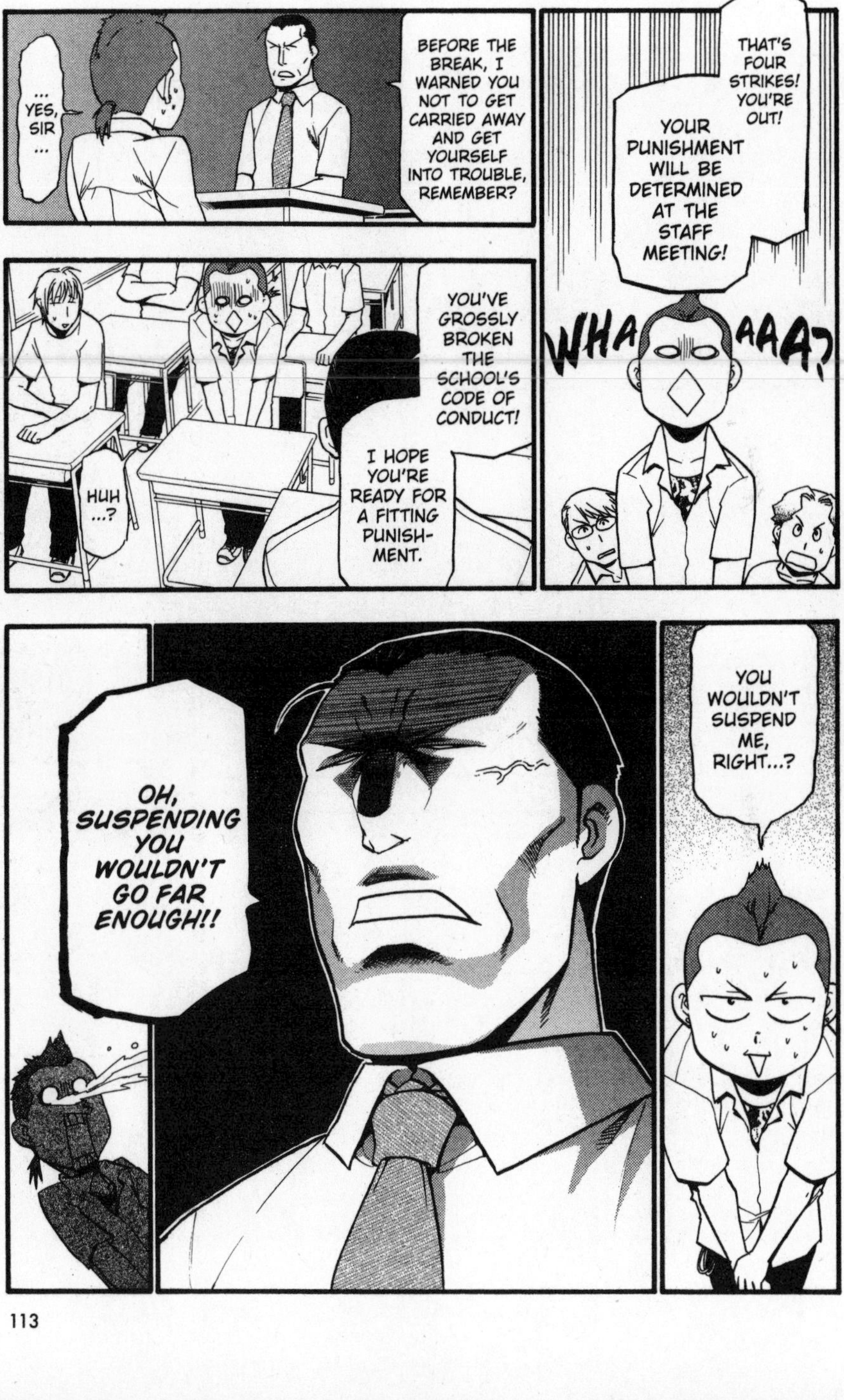
THAT'S FOUR STRIKES! YOU'RE OUT!
YOUR PUNISHMENT WILL BE DETERMINED AT THE STAFF MEETING!
WHAAAA?
BEFORE THE BREAK, I WARNED YOU NOT TO GET CARRIED AWAY AND GET YOURSELF INTO TROUBLE, REMEMBER?
... YES, SIR ...
YOU'VE GROSSLY BROKEN THE SCHOOL'S CODE OF CONDUCT!
I HOPE YOU'RE READY FOR A FITTING PUNISH-MENT.
HUH ...?
YOU WOULDN'T SUSPEND ME, RIGHT...?
OH, SUSPENDING YOU WOULDN'T GO FAR ENOUGH!!

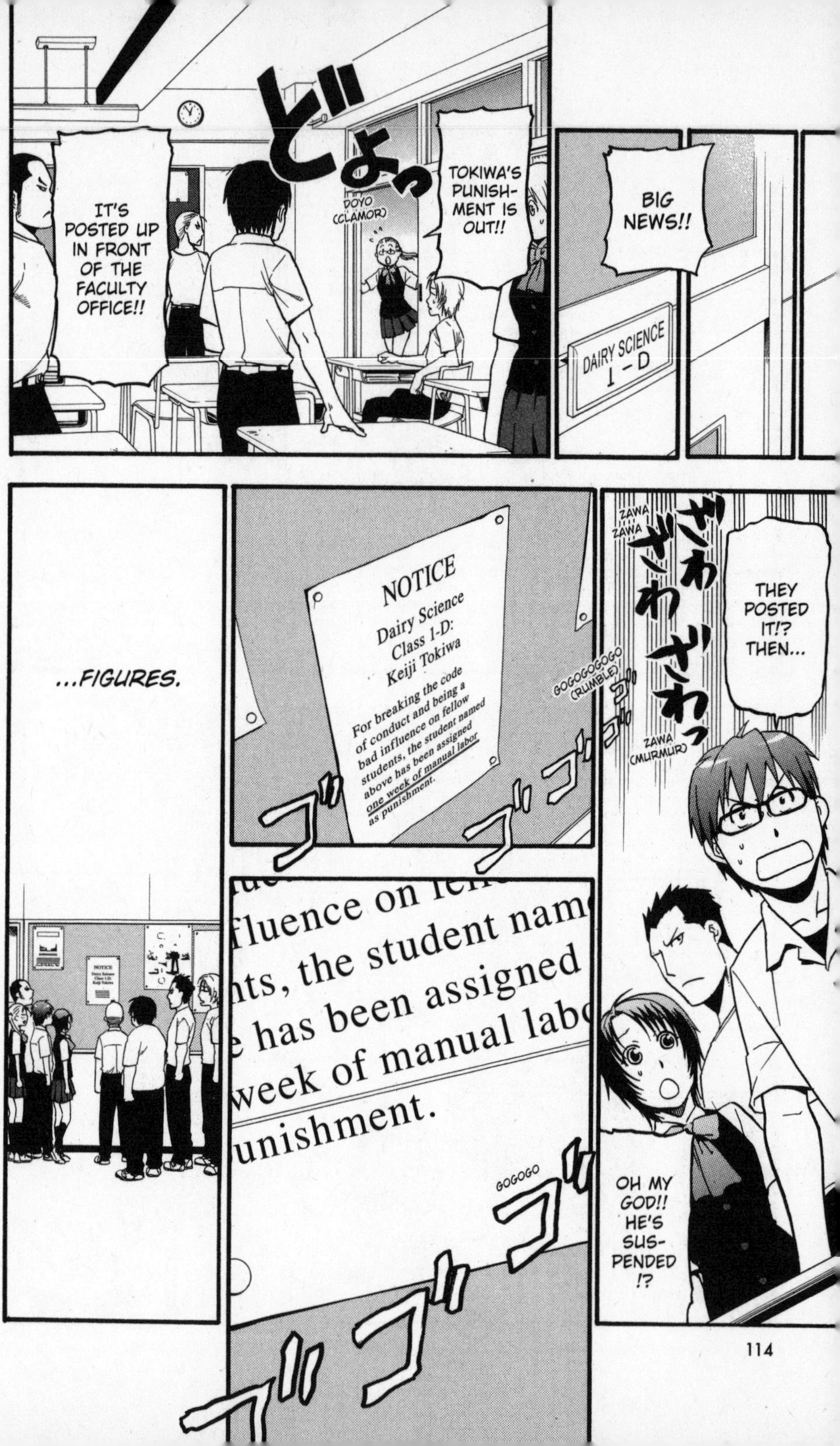

BIG NEWS!!
DAIRY SCIENCE 1-D
TOKIWA'S PUNISHMENT IS OUT!!
DOYO (CLAMOR)
IT'S POSTED UP IN FRONT OF THE FACULTY OFFICE!!
ZAWA ZAWA
THEY POSTED IT!? THEN...
ZAWA (MURMUR)
OH MY GOD!! HE'S SUSPENDED!?
NOTICE
Dairy Science Class 1-D: Keiji Tokiwa
For breaking the code of conduct and being a bad influence on fellow students, the student named above has been assigned one week of manual labor as punishment.
GOGOGOGOGO (RUMBLE)
fluence on fell
nts, the student nam
e has been assigned
week of manual labo
unishment.
GOGOGO
...FIGURES.

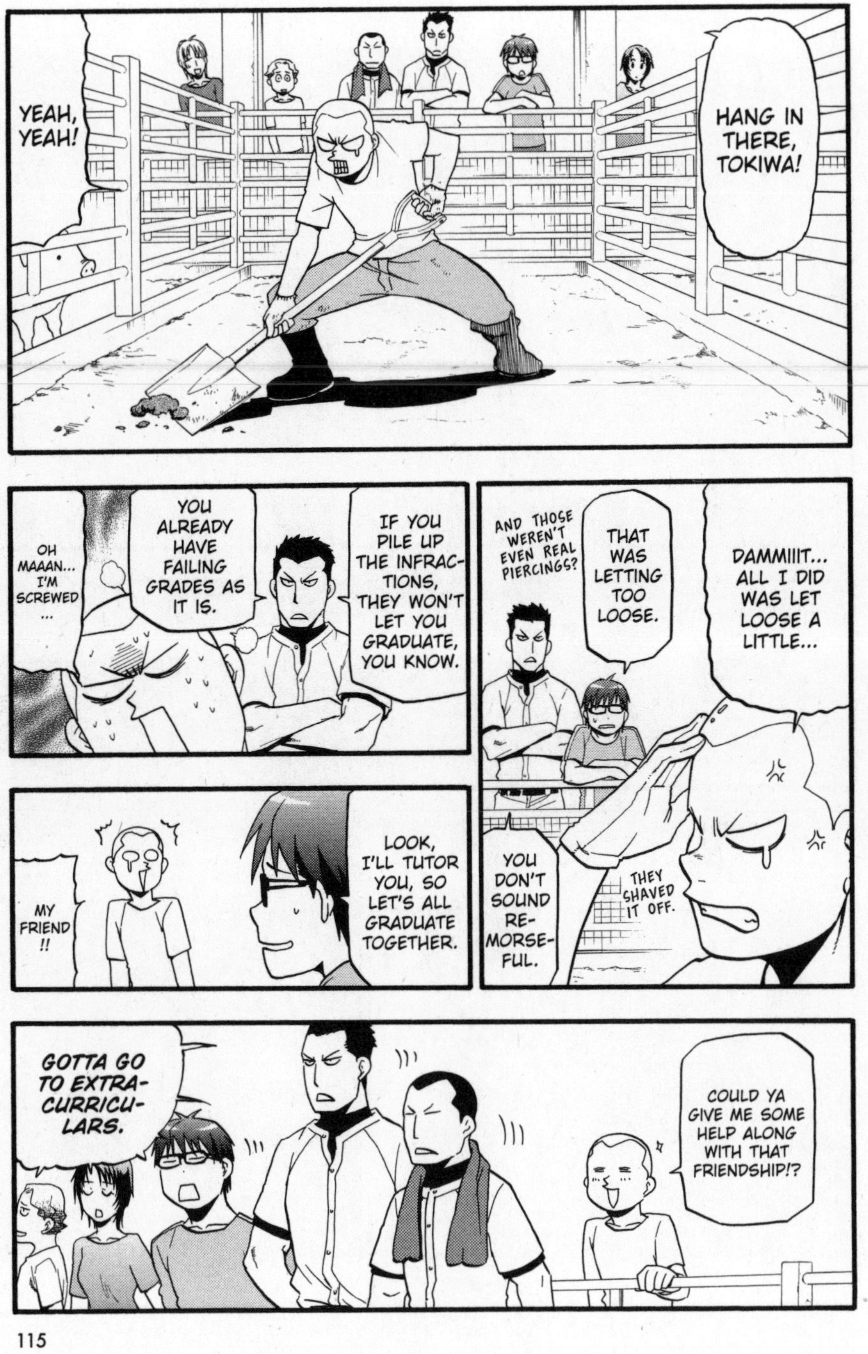
HANG IN THERE, TOKIWA!
YEAH, YEAH!
DAMMIIIT... ALL I DID WAS LET LOOSE A LITTLE...
THAT WAS LETTING TOO LOOSE.
AND THOSE WEREN'T EVEN REAL PIERCINGS?
THEY SHAVED IT OFF.
YOU DON'T SOUND RE-MORSE-FUL.
IF YOU PILE UP THE INFRAC-TIONS, THEY WON'T LET YOU GRADUATE, YOU KNOW.
YOU ALREADY HAVE FAILING GRADES AS IT IS.
OH MAAAN... I'M SCREWED ...
LOOK, I'LL TUTOR YOU, SO LET'S ALL GRADUATE TOGETHER.
MY FRIEND !!
COULD YA GIVE ME SOME HELP ALONG WITH THAT FRIENDSHIP!?
GOTTA GO TO EXTRA-CURRICU-LARS.

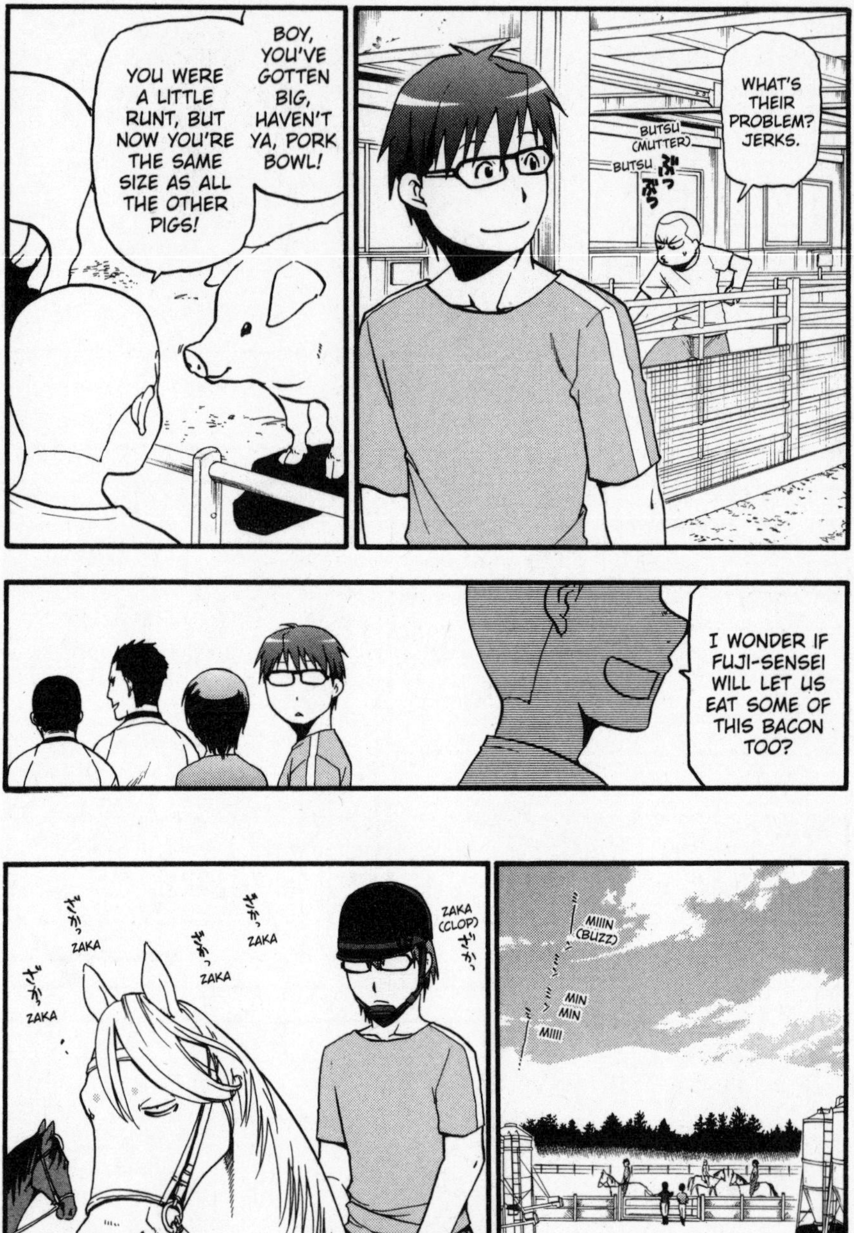
WHAT'S THEIR PROBLEM? JERKS.
BUTSU (MUTTER) BUTSU ぶつ ぶつ
BOY, YOU'VE GOTTEN BIG, HAVEN'T YA, PORK BOWL!
YOU WERE A LITTLE RUNT, BUT NOW YOU'RE THE SAME SIZE AS ALL THE OTHER PIGS!
I WONDER IF FUJI-SENSEI WILL LET US EAT SOME OF THIS BACON TOO?
MIIIN (BUZZ)
MIN MIN
MIIII
ZAKA (CLOP) ざかっ
ざかっ ZAKA
ざかっ ZAKA
ざかっ ZAKA
ざかっ ZAKA

PORK BOWL......
ZAKA
ZAKA
ZAKA
ZAKA
ARE WE ALL GOING TO EAT YOU...?
NO, NO, COME ON. HE'S FOOD!
ZAKA
ZAKA
ZAKA
ZAKA
ZAKA
NOT A PET!
ARRGH... BUT, BUT......
BFF!
ピタッ
PITA (STOP)
WHOA! WHOA! WHOOOOOOOA!!
ぶんぶんっ
BUN (SWING) BUN

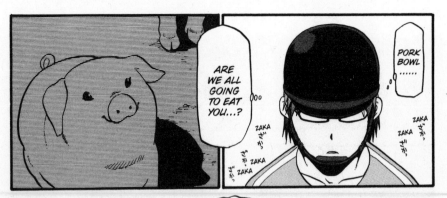

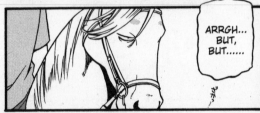

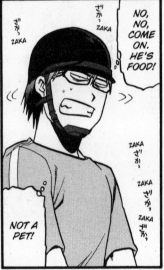

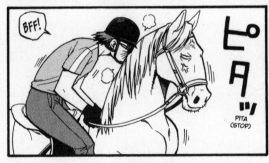

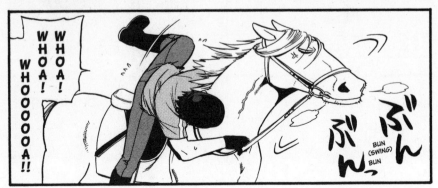

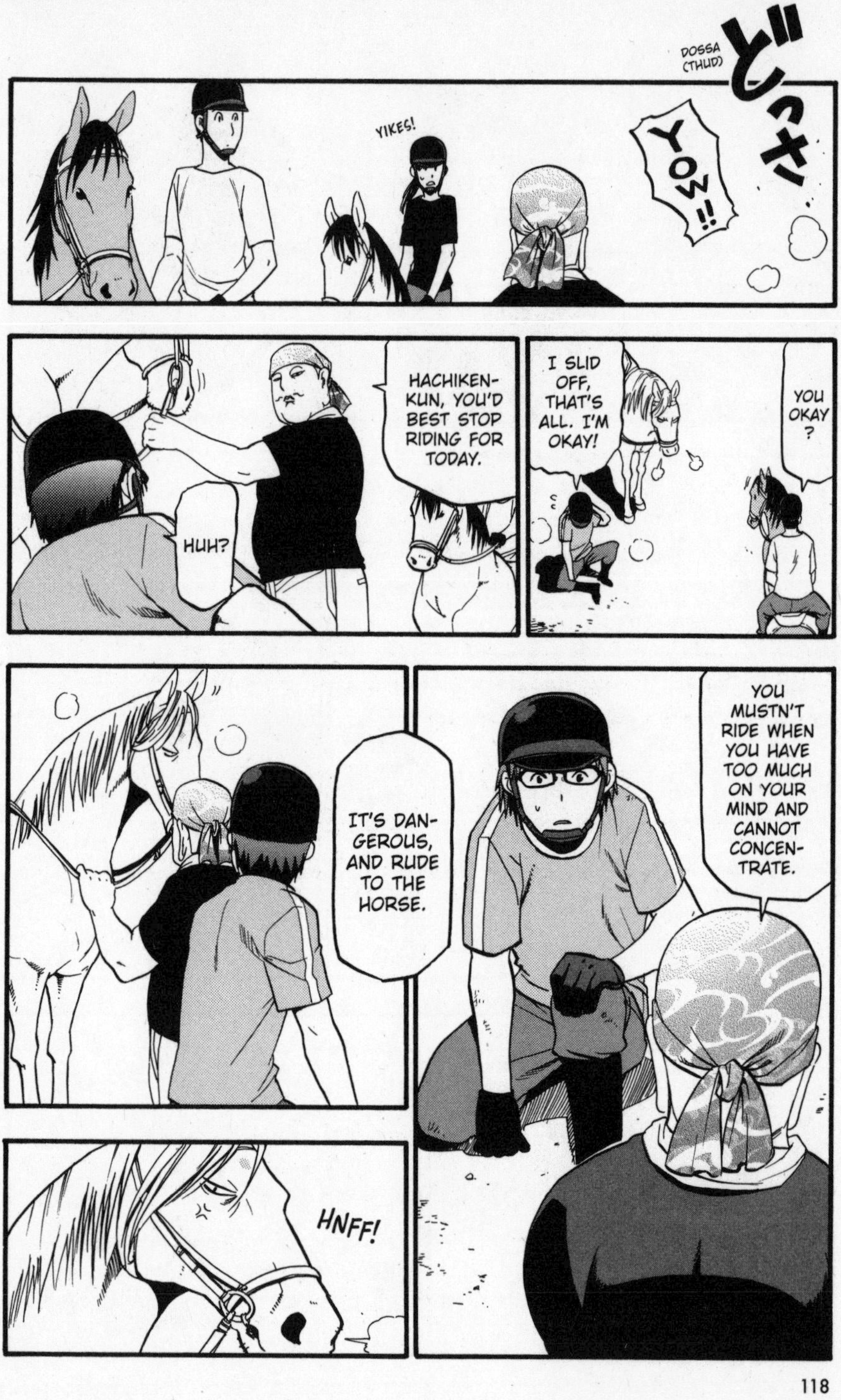
どっさ
DOSSA (THUD)
YOW!!
YIKES!
YOU OKAY?
I SLID OFF, THAT'S ALL. I'M OKAY!
HACHIKEN-KUN, YOU'D BEST STOP RIDING FOR TODAY.
HUH?
YOU MUSTN'T RIDE WHEN YOU HAVE TOO MUCH ON YOUR MIND AND CANNOT CONCENTRATE.
IT'S DANGEROUS, AND RUDE TO THE HORSE.
HNFF!

...I'M SORRY, SIR.

HACHIKEN SEEMS DOWN.

HE DOES.

MAYBE SOMETHING HAPPENED DURING SUMMER BREAK.

HE WORKED AT YOUR PLACE THE WHOLE TIME, RIGHT?

THAT'S RIGHT.

NOT A THING.

SAKU

SAKU (CLOP)

......DID ANYTHING HAPPEN BETWEEN YOU TWO?

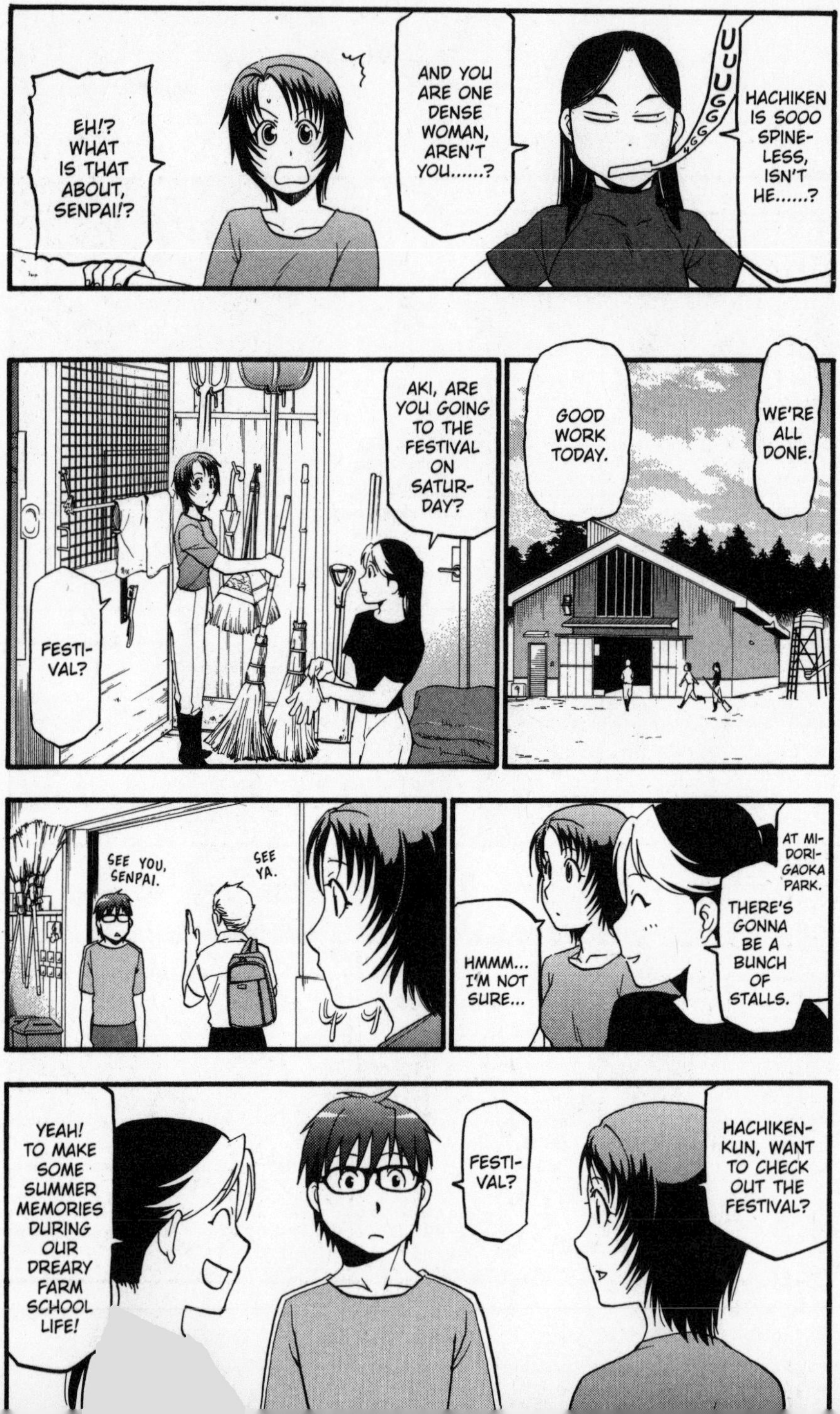

UUUGGG
HACHIKEN IS SOOO SPINE-LESS, ISN'T HE......?
AND YOU ARE ONE DENSE WOMAN, AREN'T YOU......?
EH!? WHAT IS THAT ABOUT, SENPAI!?
WE'RE ALL DONE.
GOOD WORK TODAY.
AKI, ARE YOU GOING TO THE FESTIVAL ON SATUR-DAY?
FESTI-VAL?
AT MI-DORI-GAOKA PARK.
THERE'S GONNA BE A BUNCH OF STALLS.
HMMM... I'M NOT SURE...
SEE YA.
SEE YOU, SENPAI.
HACHIKEN-KUN, WANT TO CHECK OUT THE FESTIVAL?
FESTI-VAL?
YEAH! TO MAKE SOME SUMMER MEMORIES DURING OUR DREARY FARM SCHOOL LIFE!

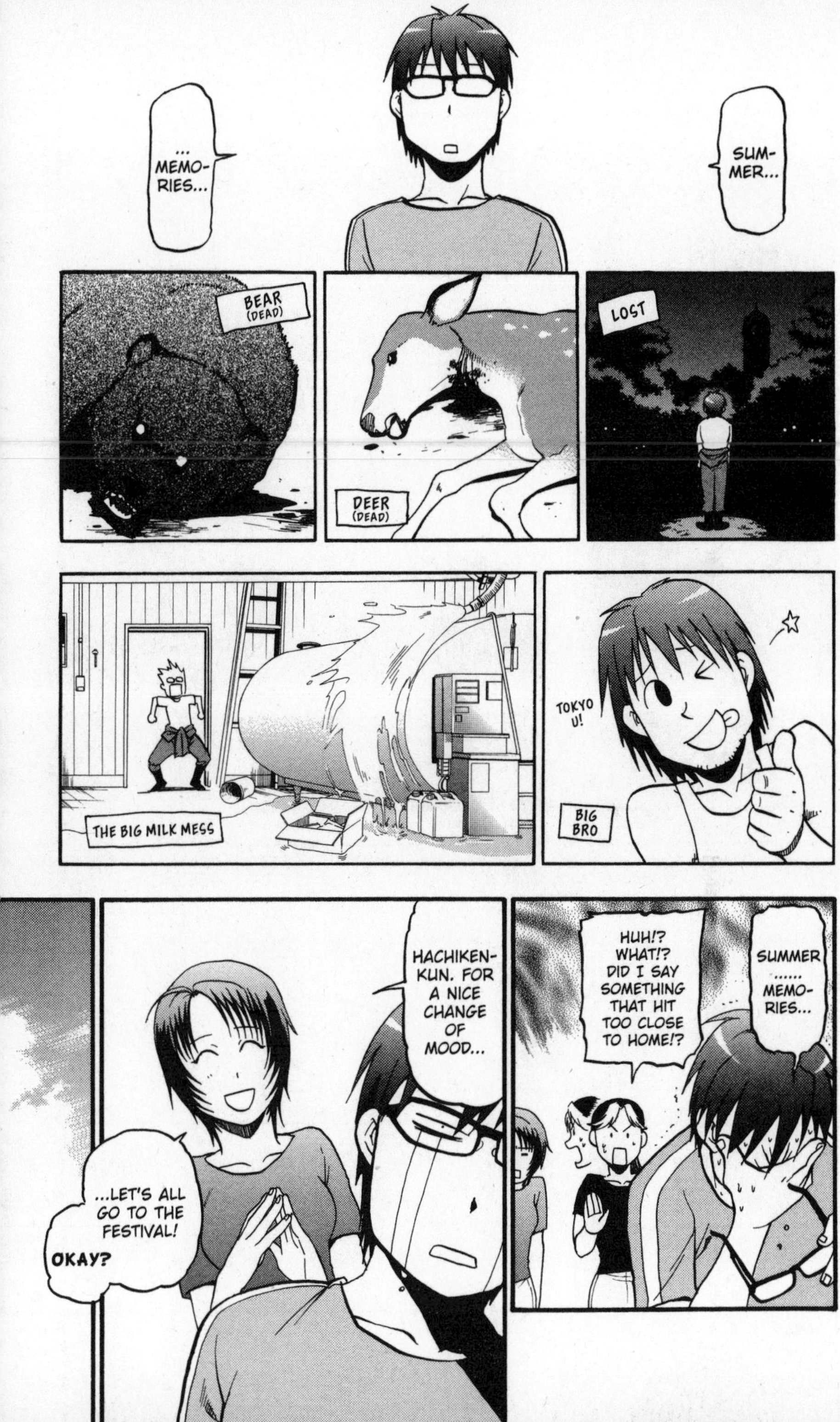
SUM-MER...
...MEMO-RIES...
LOST
DEER (DEAD)
BEAR (DEAD)
BIG BRO
TOKYO U!
THE BIG MILK MESS
SUMMER ...... MEMO-RIES...
HUH!? WHAT!? DID I SAY SOMETHING THAT HIT TOO CLOSE TO HOME!?
HACHIKEN-KUN. FOR A NICE CHANGE OF MOOD...
...LET'S ALL GO TO THE FESTIVAL!
OKAY?

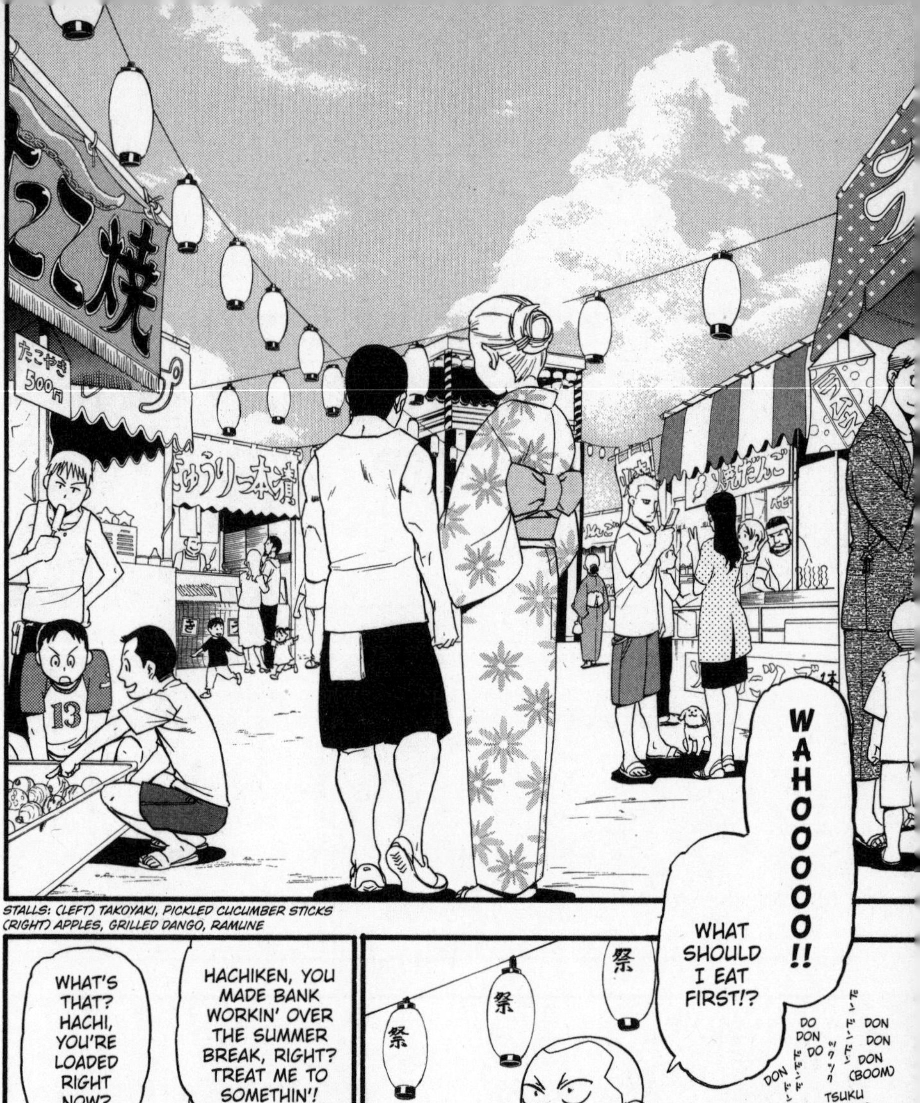
たこ焼
たこやき
500円
きゅうり一本漬
焼だんご

STALLS: (LEFT) TAKOYAKI, PICKLED CUCUMBER STICKS
(RIGHT) APPLES, GRILLED DANGO, RAMUNE

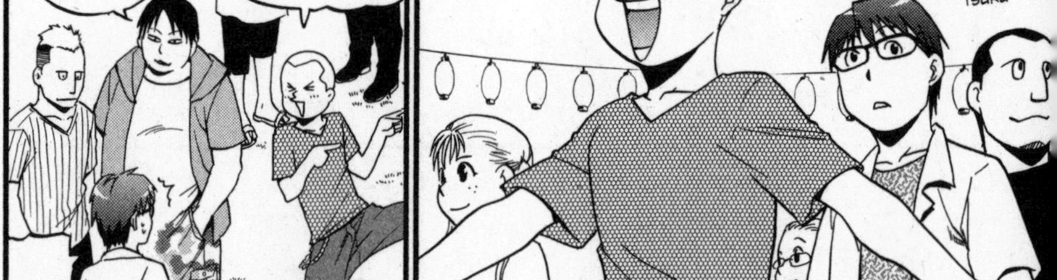
WAHOOOOOO!!
WHAT SHOULD I EAT FIRST!?
祭
祭
祭
DO DON DO DON
DON DON DON (BOOM)
TSUKU (JINGLE) TSUKU
HACHIKEN, YOU MADE BANK WORKIN' OVER THE SUMMER BREAK, RIGHT? TREAT ME TO SOMETHIN'!
WHAT'S THAT? HACHI, YOU'RE LOADED RIGHT NOW?
HUH!?

LANTERNS: FESTIVAL

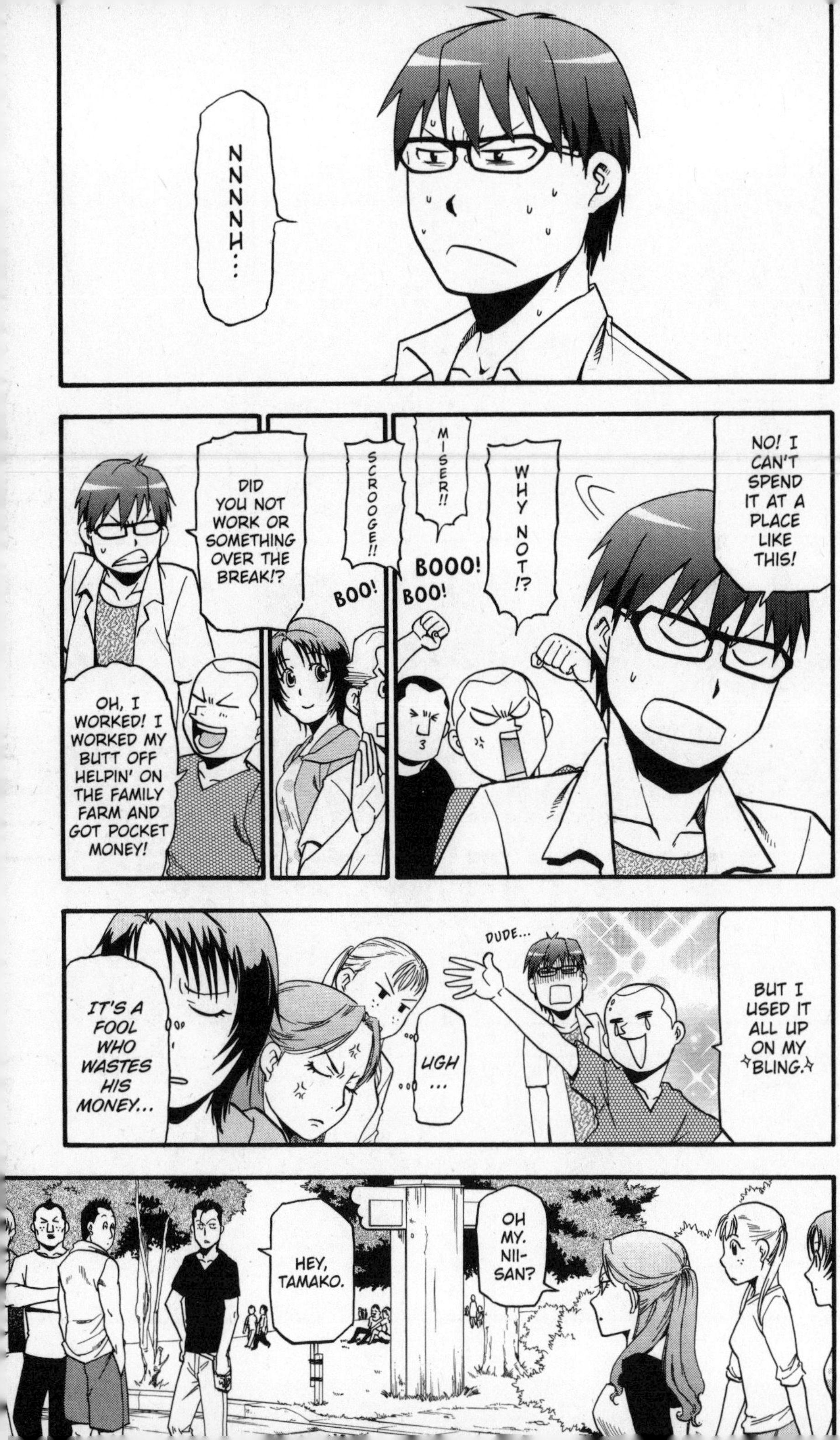
NNNNH...
NO! I CAN'T SPEND IT AT A PLACE LIKE THIS!
WHY NOT!?
MISER!!
BOOO!
BOO!
SCROOGE!!
BOO!
DID YOU NOT WORK OR SOMETHING OVER THE BREAK!?
OH, I WORKED! I WORKED MY BUTT OFF HELPIN' ON THE FAMILY FARM AND GOT POCKET MONEY!
BUT I USED IT ALL UP ON MY ✧BLING.✧
DUDE...
UGH...
IT'S A FOOL WHO WASTES HIS MONEY...
OH MY. NII-SAN?
HEY, TAMAKO.

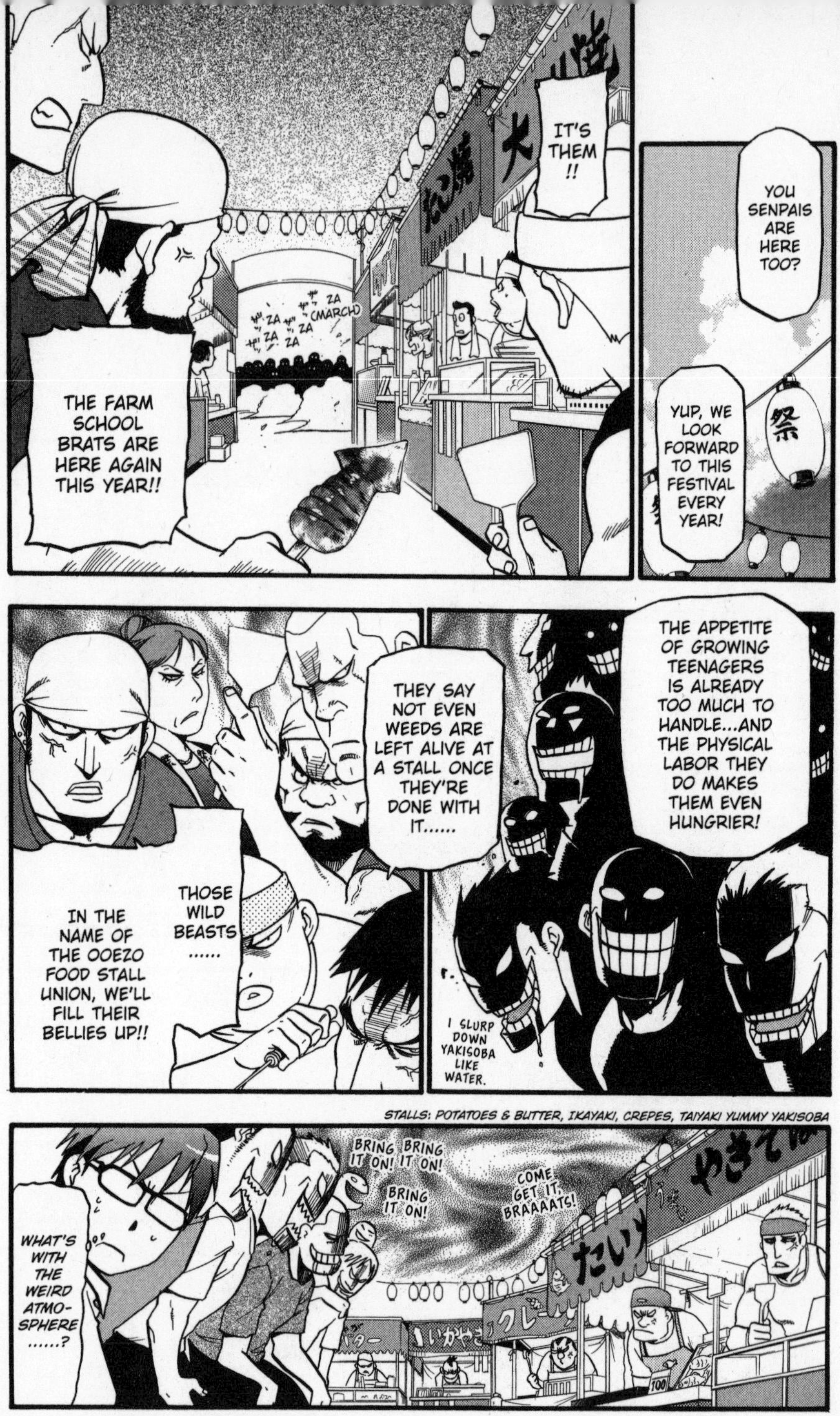

YOU SENPAIS ARE HERE TOO?
YUP, WE LOOK FORWARD TO THIS FESTIVAL EVERY YEAR!
祭
IT'S THEM!!
ZA ZA ZA ZA ZA ZA (MARCH)
THE FARM SCHOOL BRATS ARE HERE AGAIN THIS YEAR!!
THE APPETITE OF GROWING TEENAGERS IS ALREADY TOO MUCH TO HANDLE...AND THE PHYSICAL LABOR THEY DO MAKES THEM EVEN HUNGRIER!
I SLURP DOWN YAKISOBA LIKE WATER.
THEY SAY NOT EVEN WEEDS ARE LEFT ALIVE AT A STALL ONCE THEY'RE DONE WITH IT......
THOSE WILD BEASTS......
IN THE NAME OF THE OOEZO FOOD STALL UNION, WE'LL FILL THEIR BELLIES UP!!
STALLS: POTATOES & BUTTER, IKAYAKI, CREPES, TAIYAKI YUMMY YAKISOBA
BRING IT ON! BRING IT ON!
BRING IT ON!
COME GET IT, BRAAAATS!
WHAT'S WITH THE WEIRD ATMOSPHERE......?

Silver Spoon

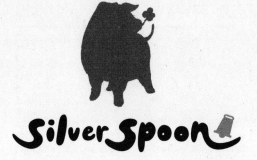

**JIN
ASHIRABETSU**

HIROO MOMOJIDORI
MIDDLE SCHOOL

KARATE CLUB

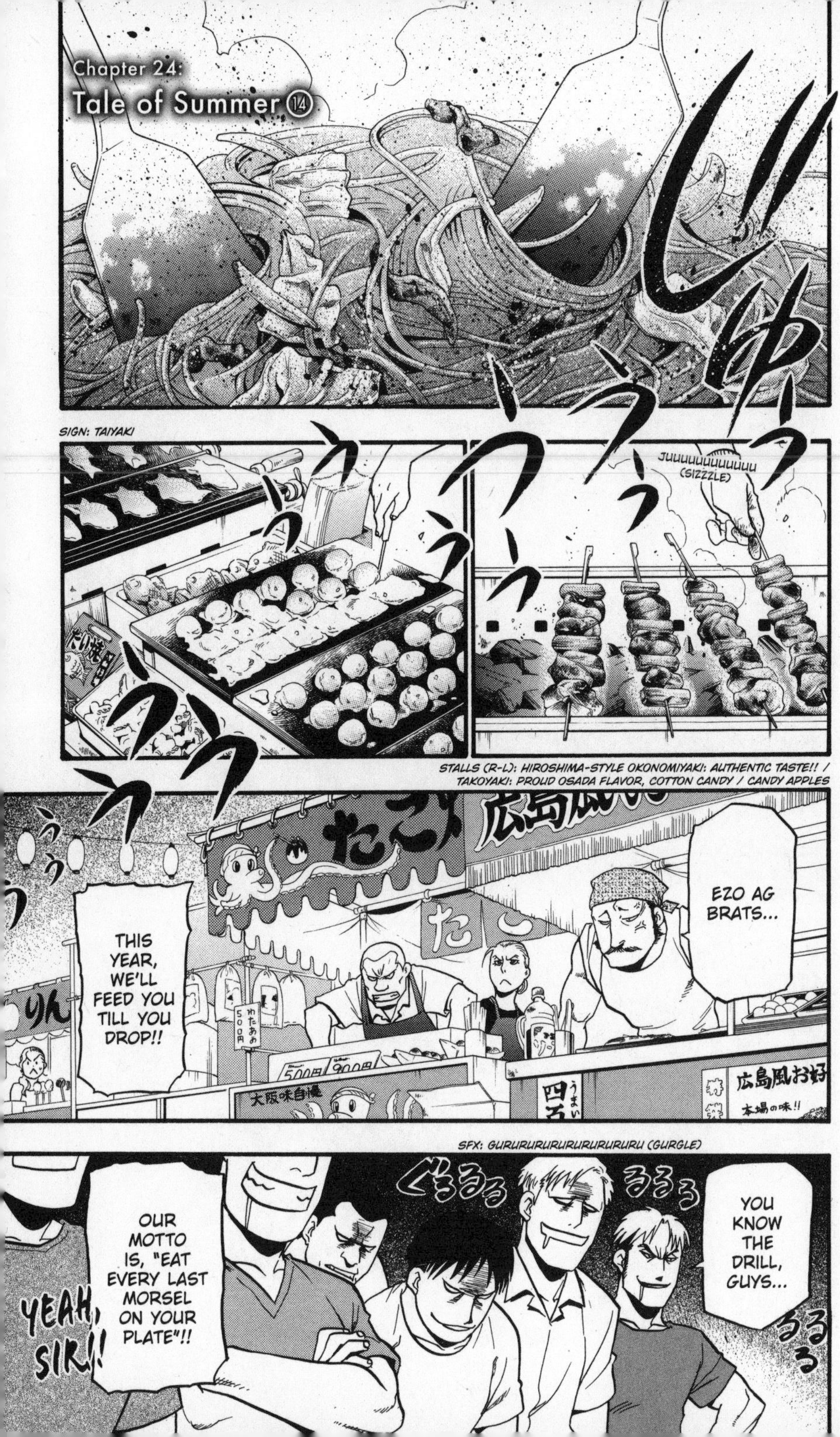
Chapter 24:
Tale of Summer ⑭
JUUUUUUUUUUUU (SIZZZLE)
SIGN: TAIYAKI
STALLS (R-L): HIROSHIMA-STYLE OKONOMIYAKI: AUTHENTIC TASTE!! / TAKOYAKI: PROUD OSADA FLAVOR, COTTON CANDY / CANDY APPLES
EZO AG BRATS...
THIS YEAR, WE'LL FEED YOU TILL YOU DROP!!
SFX: GURURURURURURURURURU (GURGLE)
YOU KNOW THE DRILL, GUYS...
OUR MOTTO IS, "EAT EVERY LAST MORSEL ON YOUR PLATE"!!
YEAH, SIR!!

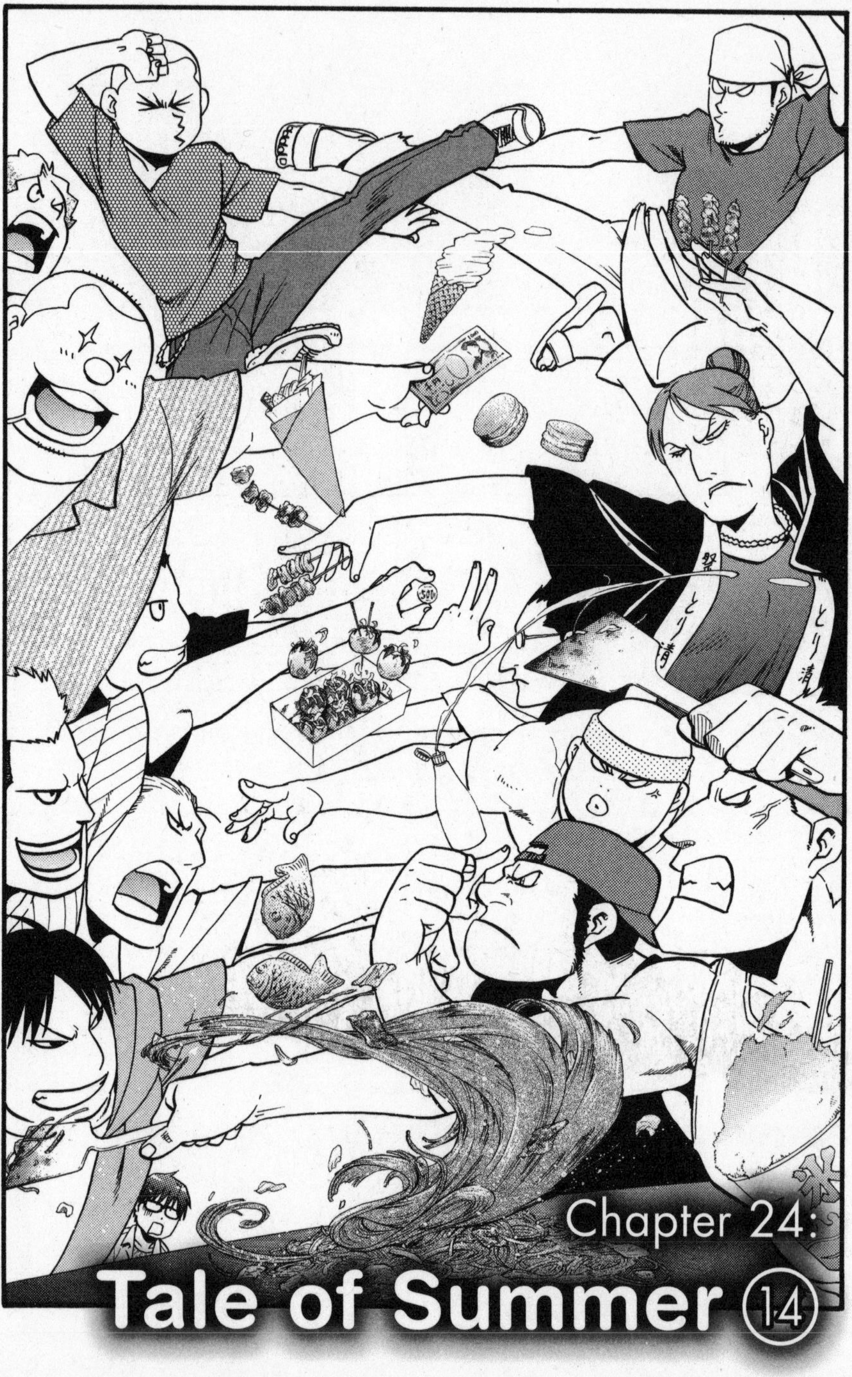
とり清

Chapter 24:
Tale of Summer ⑭

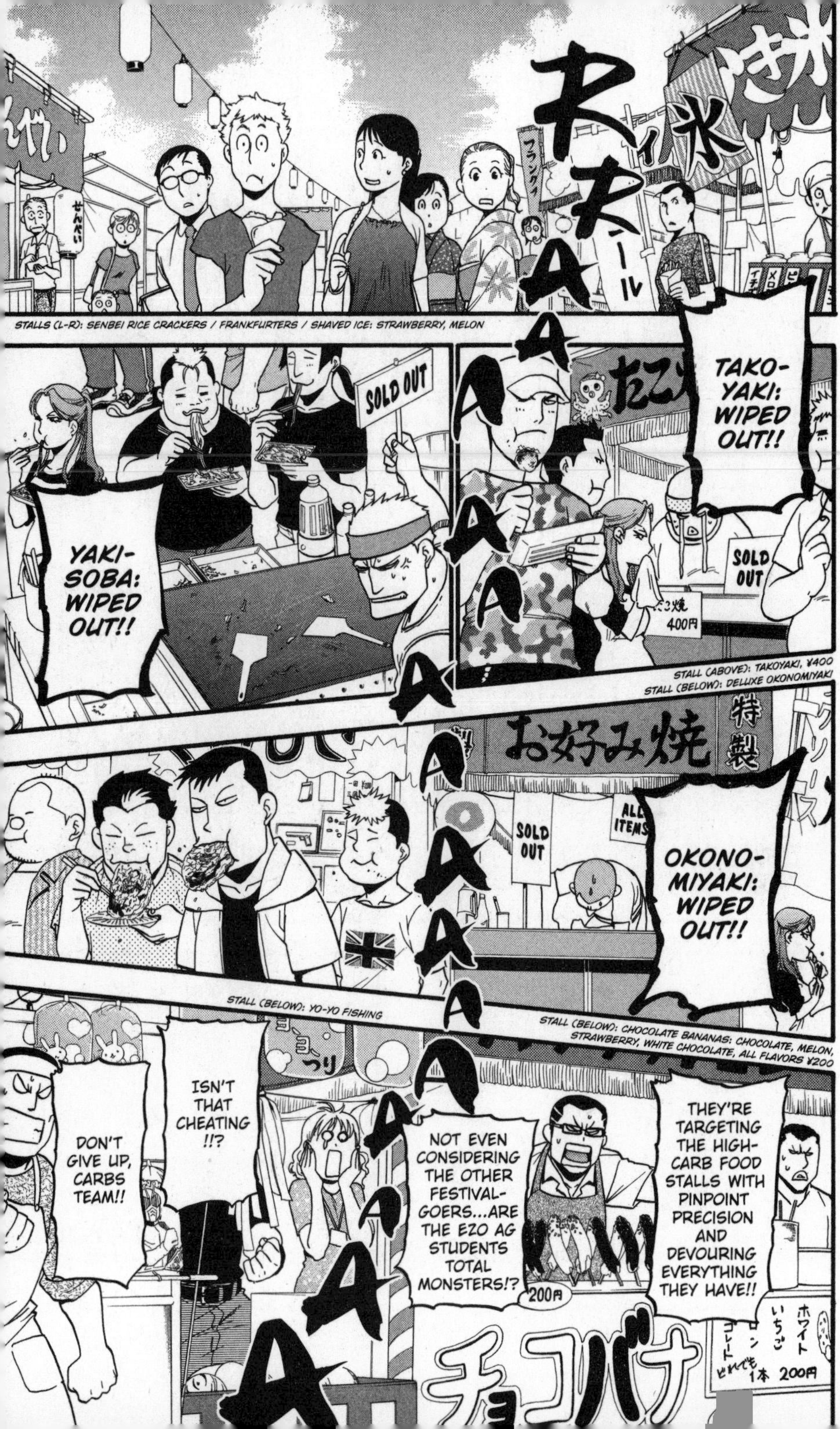
AAAAAAAAAAAAAAA
STALLS (L-R): SENBEI RICE CRACKERS / FRANKFURTERS / SHAVED ICE: STRAWBERRY, MELON
TAKO-YAKI: WIPED OUT!!
SOLD OUT
たこ焼 400円
SOLD OUT
YAKI-SOBA: WIPED OUT!!
STALL (ABOVE): TAKOYAKI, ¥400
STALL (BELOW): DELUXE OKONOMIYAKI
お好み焼
特製
OKONOMI-MIYAKI: WIPED OUT!!
ALL ITEMS
SOLD OUT
STALL (BELOW): CHOCOLATE BANANAS: CHOCOLATE, MELON, STRAWBERRY, WHITE CHOCOLATE, ALL FLAVORS ¥200
STALL (BELOW): YO-YO FISHING
THEY'RE TARGETING THE HIGH-CARB FOOD STALLS WITH PINPOINT PRECISION AND DEVOURING EVERYTHING THEY HAVE!!
NOT EVEN CONSIDERING THE OTHER FESTIVAL-GOERS...ARE THE EZO AG STUDENTS TOTAL MONSTERS!?
200円
ISN'T THAT CHEATING!!?
DON'T GIVE UP, CARBS TEAM!!
ホワイト いちご メロン チョコレート どれでも1本 200円
チョコバナ

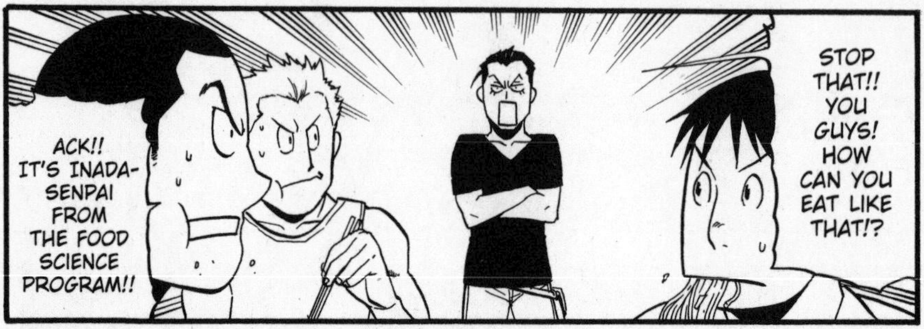
STOP THAT!! YOU GUYS! HOW CAN YOU EAT LIKE THAT!?
ACK!! IT'S INADA-SENPAI FROM THE FOOD SCIENCE PROGRAM!!

BANNER: CANDY APPLES

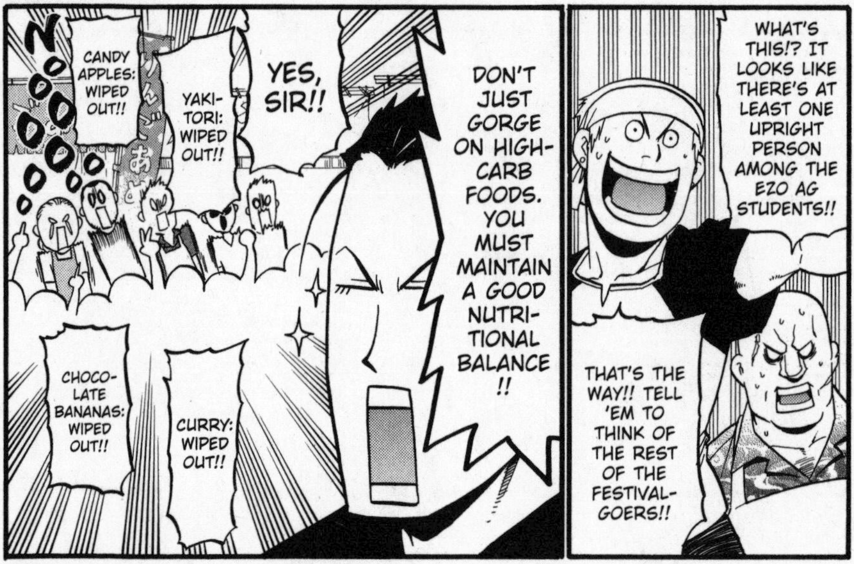
WHAT'S THIS!? IT LOOKS LIKE THERE'S AT LEAST ONE UPRIGHT PERSON AMONG THE EZO AG STUDENTS!!
THAT'S THE WAY!! TELL 'EM TO THINK OF THE REST OF THE FESTIVAL-GOERS!!
DON'T JUST GORGE ON HIGH-CARB FOODS. YOU MUST MAINTAIN A GOOD NUTRITIONAL BALANCE!!
YES, SIR!!
YAKITORI: WIPED OUT!!
CANDY APPLES: WIPED OUT!!
NOOOOOOOOOO
CURRY: WIPED OUT!!
CHOCOLATE BANANAS: WIPED OUT!!

STALLS (R-L): CREPES, SQUID

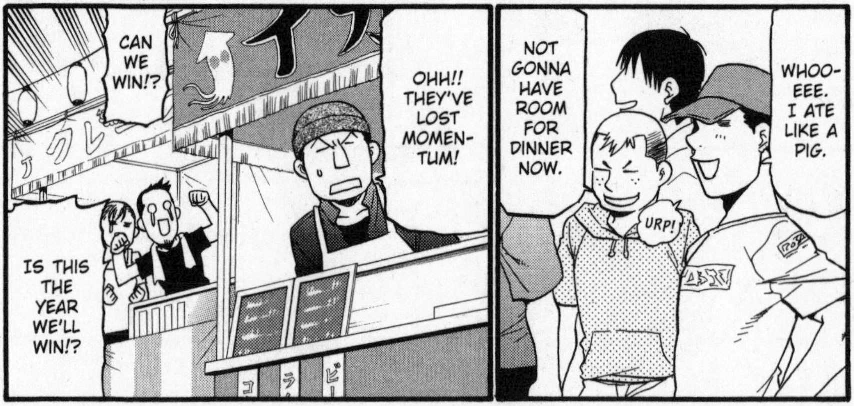
WHOOEEE. I ATE LIKE A PIG.
NOT GONNA HAVE ROOM FOR DINNER NOW.
URP!
OHH!! THEY'VE LOST MOMENTUM!
CAN WE WIN!?
IS THIS THE YEAR WE'LL WIN!?

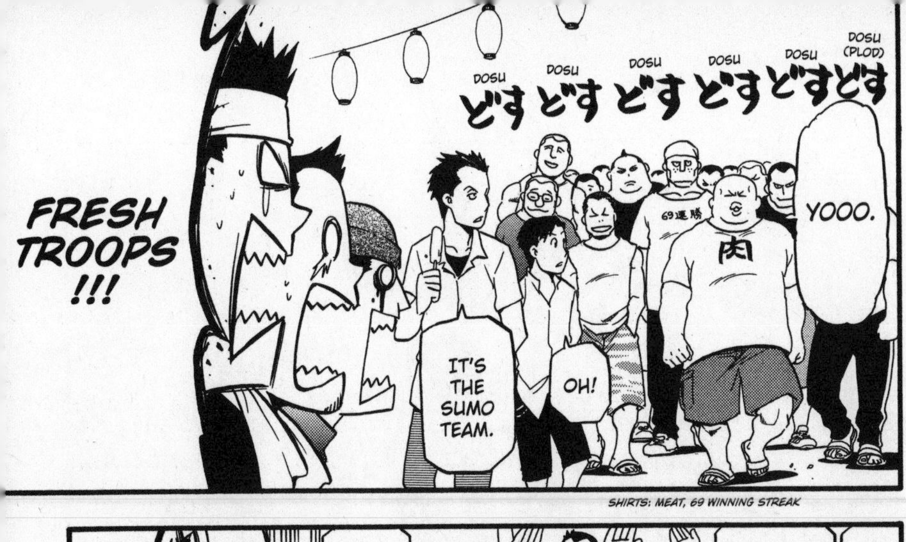
DOSU DOSU DOSU DOSU DOSU DOSU (PLOD)
どすどすどすどすどすどす
YOOO.
FRESH TROOPS!!!
OH!
IT'S THE SUMO TEAM.
SHIRTS: MEAT, 69 WINNING STREAK

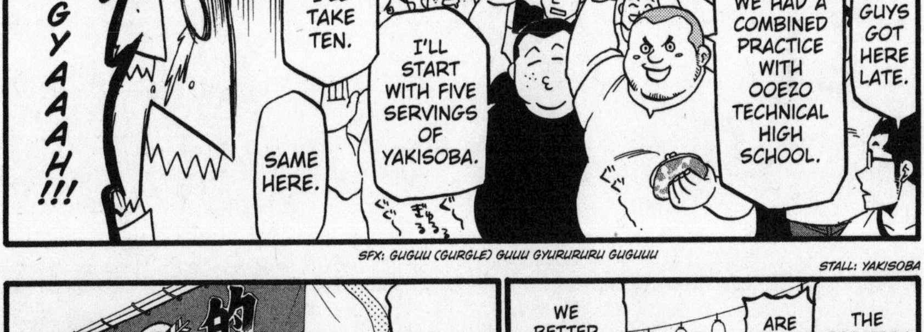
YOU GUYS GOT HERE LATE.
WE HAD A COMBINED PRACTICE WITH OOEZO TECHNICAL HIGH SCHOOL.
I'LL START WITH FIVE SERVINGS OF YAKISOBA.
I'LL TAKE TEN.
SAME HERE.
GYAAAAH!!!
SFX: GUGUU (GURGLE) GUUU GYURURURU GUGUUU

STALL: YAKISOBA

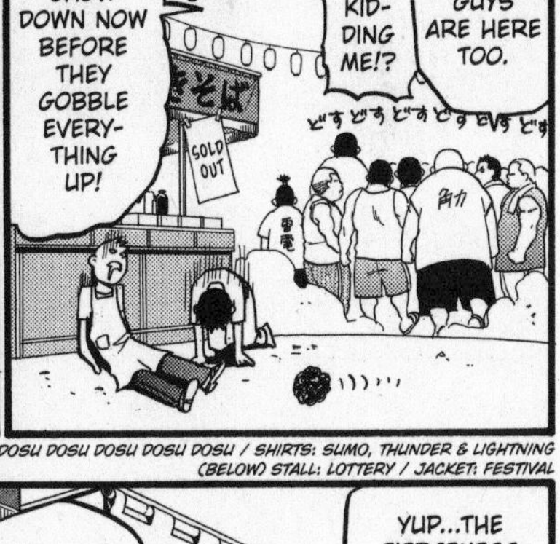
THE EZO TECH GUYS ARE HERE TOO.
ARE YOU KID-DING ME!?
WE BETTER CHOW DOWN NOW BEFORE THEY GOBBLE EVERY-THING UP!
SOLD OUT
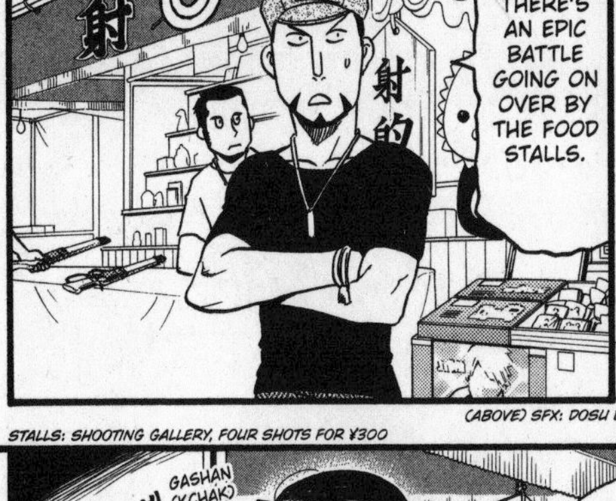
THERE'S AN EPIC BATTLE GOING ON OVER BY THE FOOD STALLS.
(ABOVE) SFX: DOSU DOSU DOSU DOSU DOSU DOSU / SHIRTS: SUMO, THUNDER & LIGHTNING

STALLS: SHOOTING GALLERY, FOUR SHOTS FOR ¥300

(BELOW) STALL: LOTTERY / JACKET: FESTIVAL

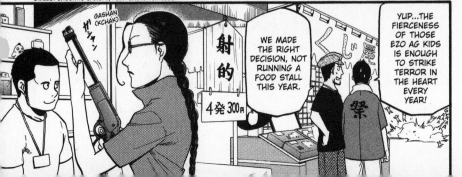

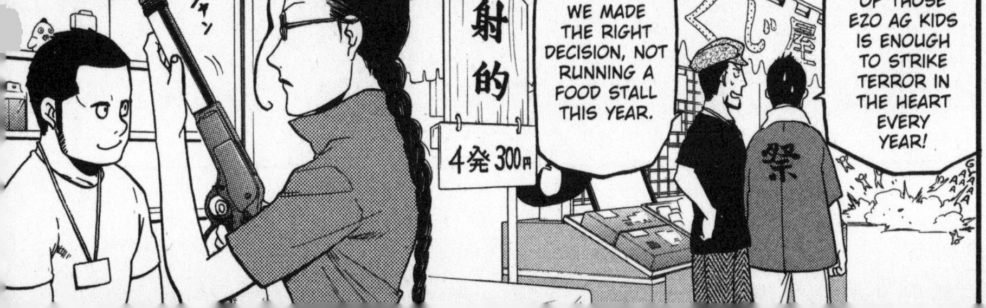
YUP...THE FIERCENESS OF THOSE EZO AG KIDS IS ENOUGH TO STRIKE TERROR IN THE HEART EVERY YEAR!
GYAAAAA
WE MADE THE RIGHT DECISION, NOT RUNNING A FOOD STALL THIS YEAR.
4発 300円
GASHAN (KCHAK)

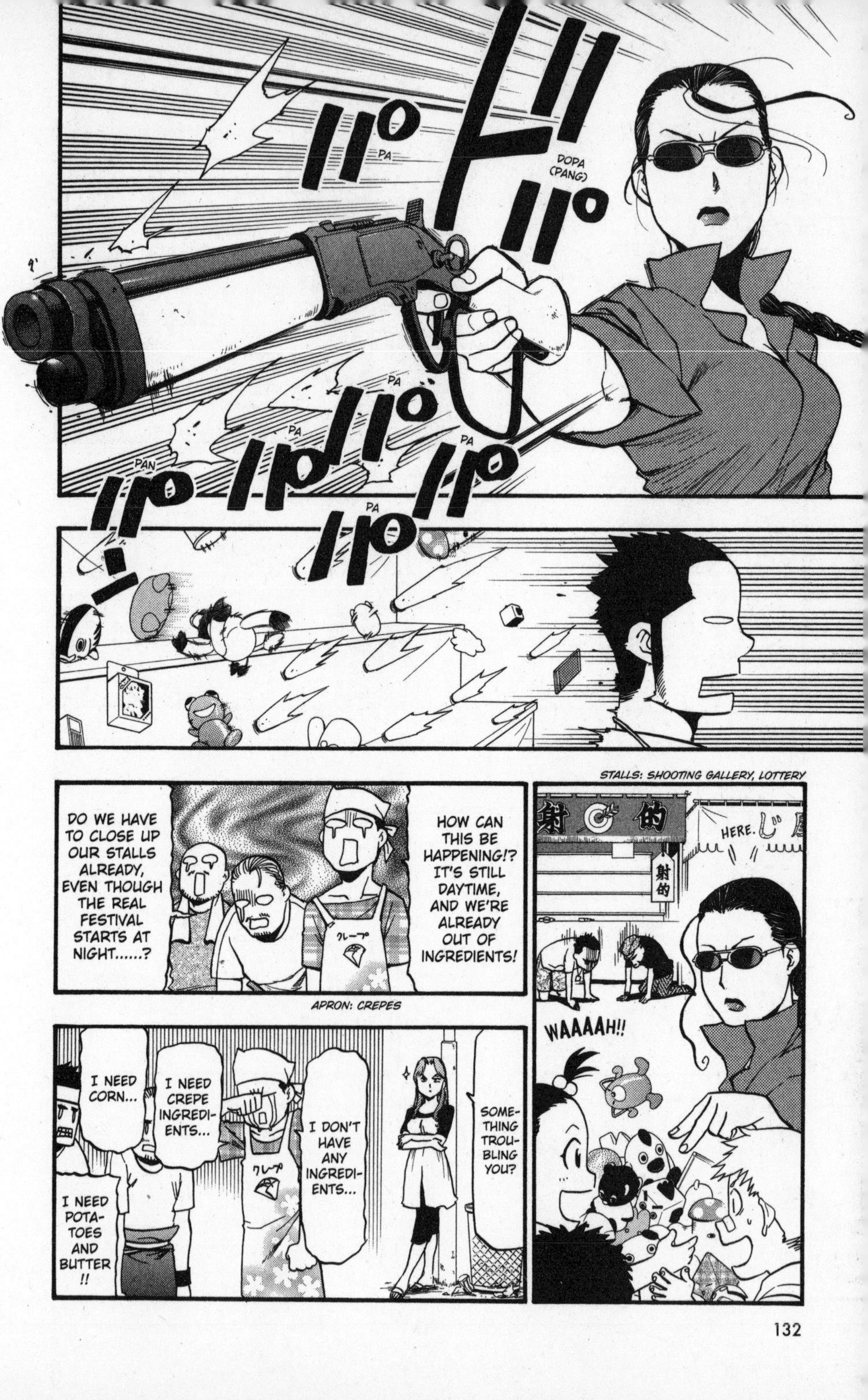
DOPA (PANG)
PA
PA
PA
PA
PAN
PA
STALLS: SHOOTING GALLERY, LOTTERY
HERE.
WAAAAH!!
HOW CAN THIS BE HAPPENING!? IT'S STILL DAYTIME, AND WE'RE ALREADY OUT OF INGREDIENTS!
DO WE HAVE TO CLOSE UP OUR STALLS ALREADY, EVEN THOUGH THE REAL FESTIVAL STARTS AT NIGHT......?
APRON: CREPES
SOMETHING TROUBLING YOU?
I DON'T HAVE ANY INGREDIENTS...
I NEED CREPE INGREDIENTS...
I NEED CORN...
I NEED POTATOES AND BUTTER!!

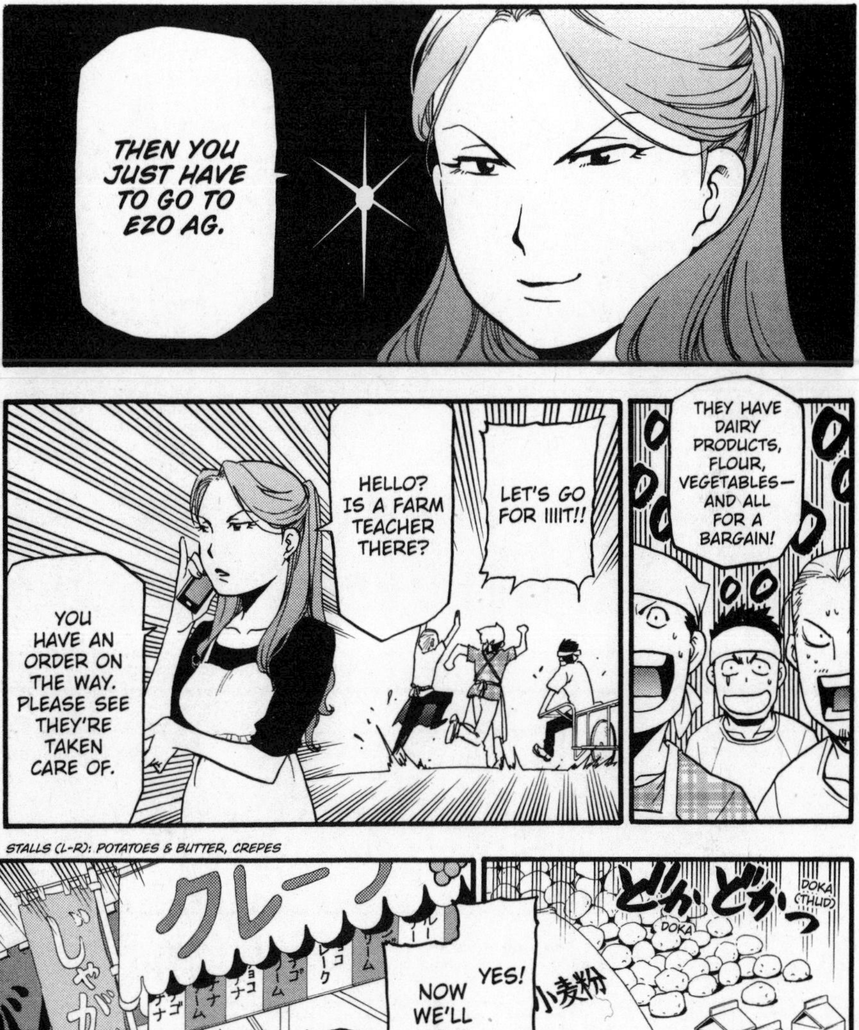
THEN YOU JUST HAVE TO GO TO EZO AG.
THEY HAVE DAIRY PRODUCTS, FLOUR, VEGETABLES— AND ALL FOR A BARGAIN!
LET'S GO FOR IIIIT!!
HELLO? IS A FARM TEACHER THERE?
YOU HAVE AN ORDER ON THE WAY. PLEASE SEE THEY'RE TAKEN CARE OF.

STALLS (L-R): POTATOES & BUTTER, CREPES

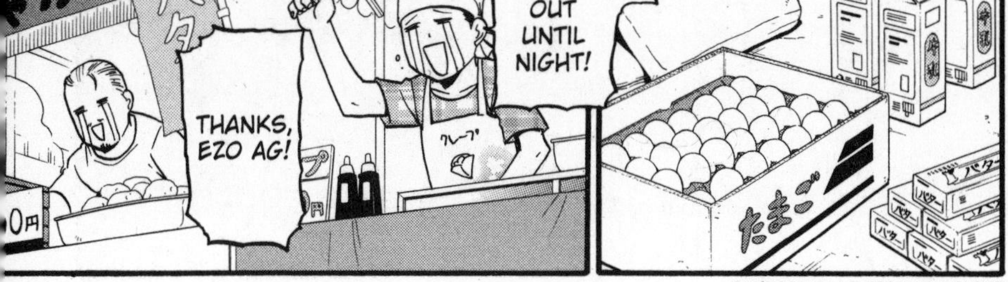
どかどかっ
DOKA DOKA (THUD)
小麦粉
たまご
YES! NOW WE'LL HOLD OUT UNTIL NIGHT!
THANKS, EZO AG!
クレープ
じゃがバタ

PACKAGES: FLOUR, EGGS, MILK, BUTTER

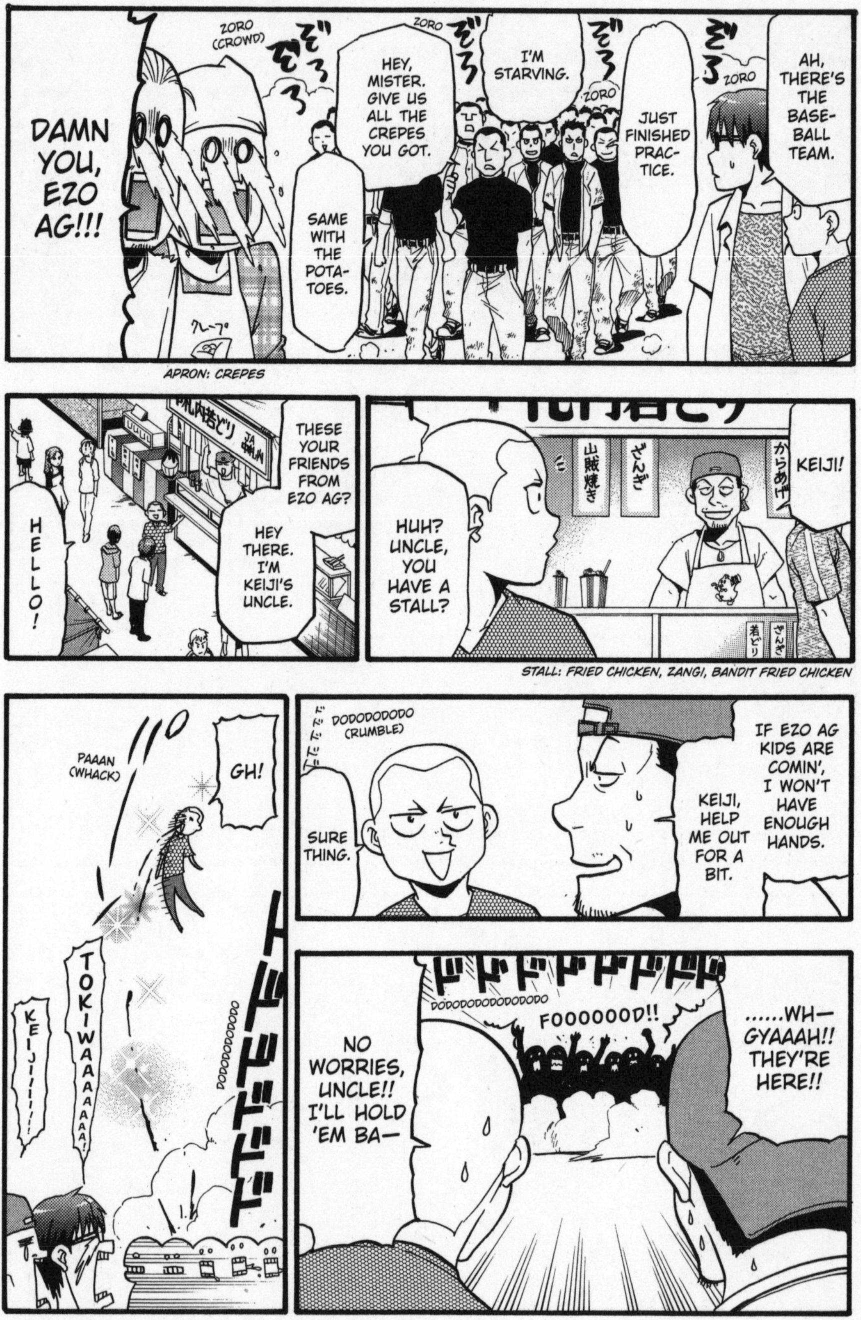
ZORO
AH, THERE'S THE BASE-BALL TEAM.
ZORO
JUST FINISHED PRAC-TICE.
ZORO
I'M STARVING.
ZORO
HEY, MISTER. GIVE US ALL THE CREPES YOU GOT.
SAME WITH THE POTA-TOES.
ZORO (CROWD)
DAMN YOU, EZO AG!!!
APRON: CREPES
KEIJI!
HUH? UNCLE, YOU HAVE A STALL?
STALL: FRIED CHICKEN, ZANGI, BANDIT FRIED CHICKEN
THESE YOUR FRIENDS FROM EZO AG?
HEY THERE. I'M KEIJI'S UNCLE.
HELLO!
IF EZO AG KIDS ARE COMIN', I WON'T HAVE ENOUGH HANDS.
KEIJI, HELP ME OUT FOR A BIT.
DODODODODO (RUMBLE)
SURE THING.
DODODODODODODODO
FOOOOOOD!!
......WH— GYAAAH!! THEY'RE HERE!!
NO WORRIES, UNCLE!! I'LL HOLD 'EM BA—
GH!
PAAAN (WHACK)
TOKIWAAAAAAA!
KEIJI!!!!!!
DODODODODODO

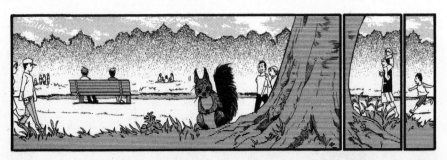

HOW CAN THEY ALL EAT SO MUCH?
YEAH, THERE'S STILL DINNER WHEN WE GO BACK TO THE DORM.
DELICIOUS!
FEEL BETTER ?
HUH?
YOU'VE BEEN DOWN FOR A WHILE NOW.
I THOUGHT SOME GOOD FOOD MIGHT CHEER YOU UP.
AH...

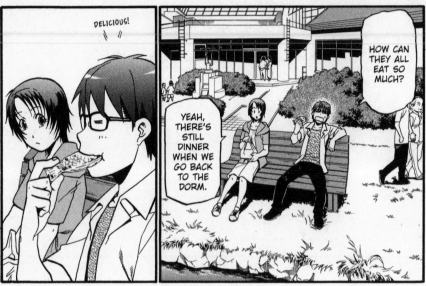

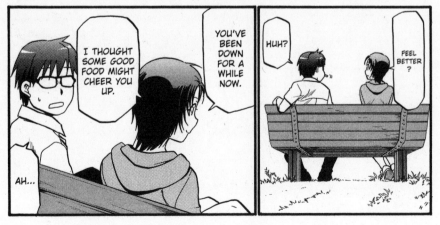

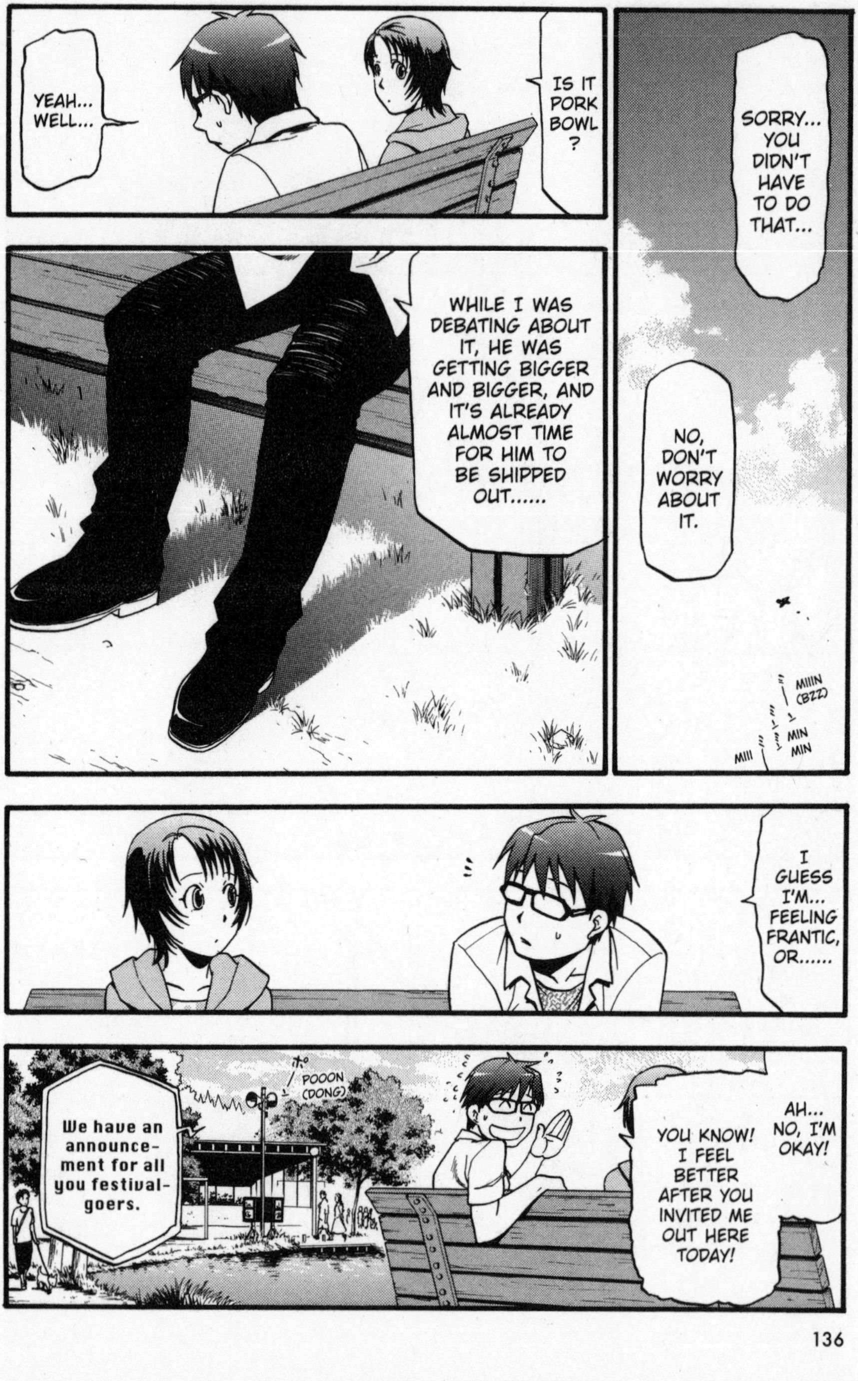
SORRY... YOU DIDN'T HAVE TO DO THAT...
NO, DON'T WORRY ABOUT IT.
MIIIN (BZZ)
MIN MIN
MIII
IS IT PORK BOWL?
YEAH... WELL...
WHILE I WAS DEBATING ABOUT IT, HE WAS GETTING BIGGER AND BIGGER, AND IT'S ALREADY ALMOST TIME FOR HIM TO BE SHIPPED OUT......
I GUESS I'M... FEELING FRANTIC, OR......
AH... NO, I'M OKAY!
YOU KNOW! I FEEL BETTER AFTER YOU INVITED ME OUT HERE TODAY!
POOON (DONG)
We have an announcement for all you festival-goers.

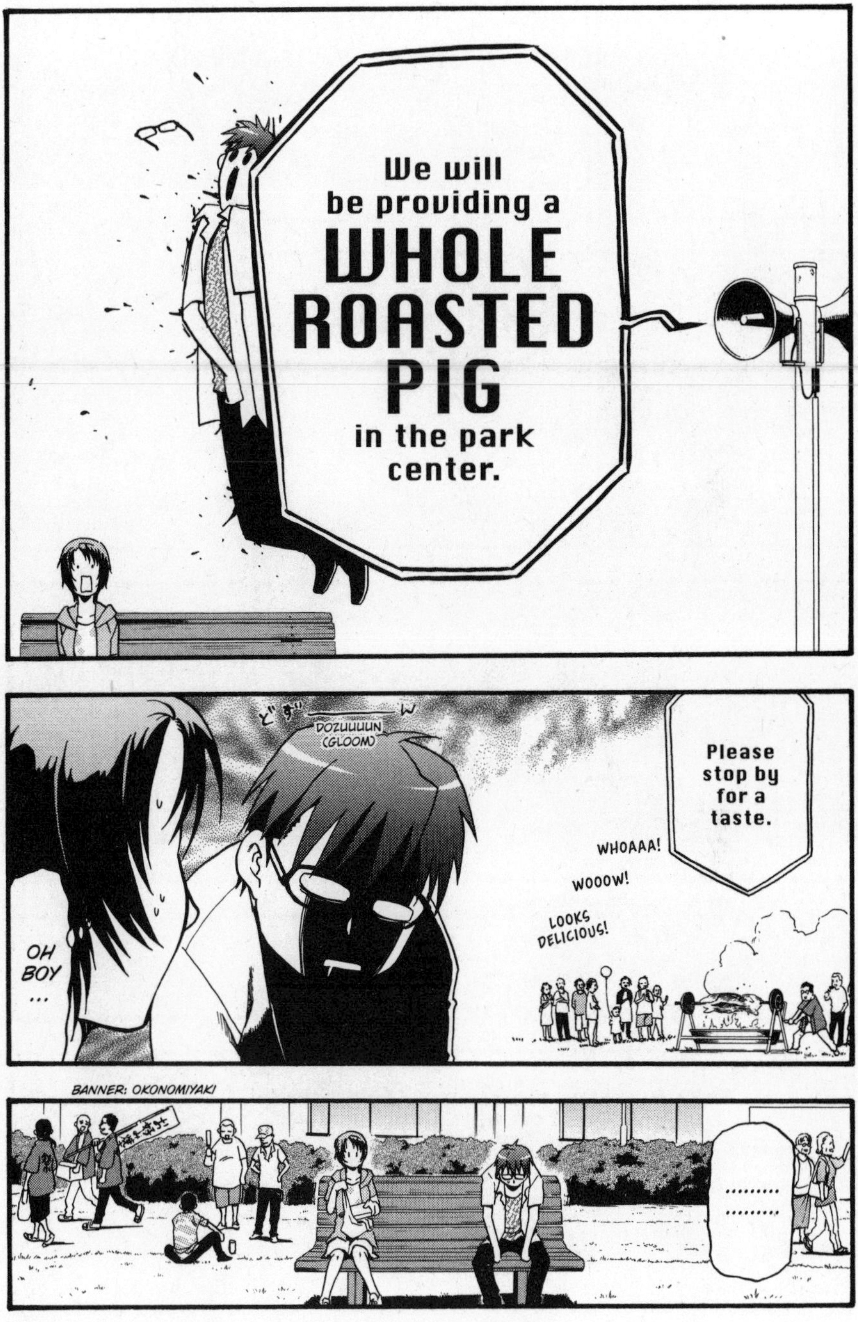
We will be providing a WHOLE ROASTED PIG in the park center.
Please stop by for a taste.
WHOAAA!
WOOOW!
LOOKS DELICIOUS!
DOZUUUUN (GLOOM)
OH BOY ...
BANNER: OKONOMIYAKI
....
....

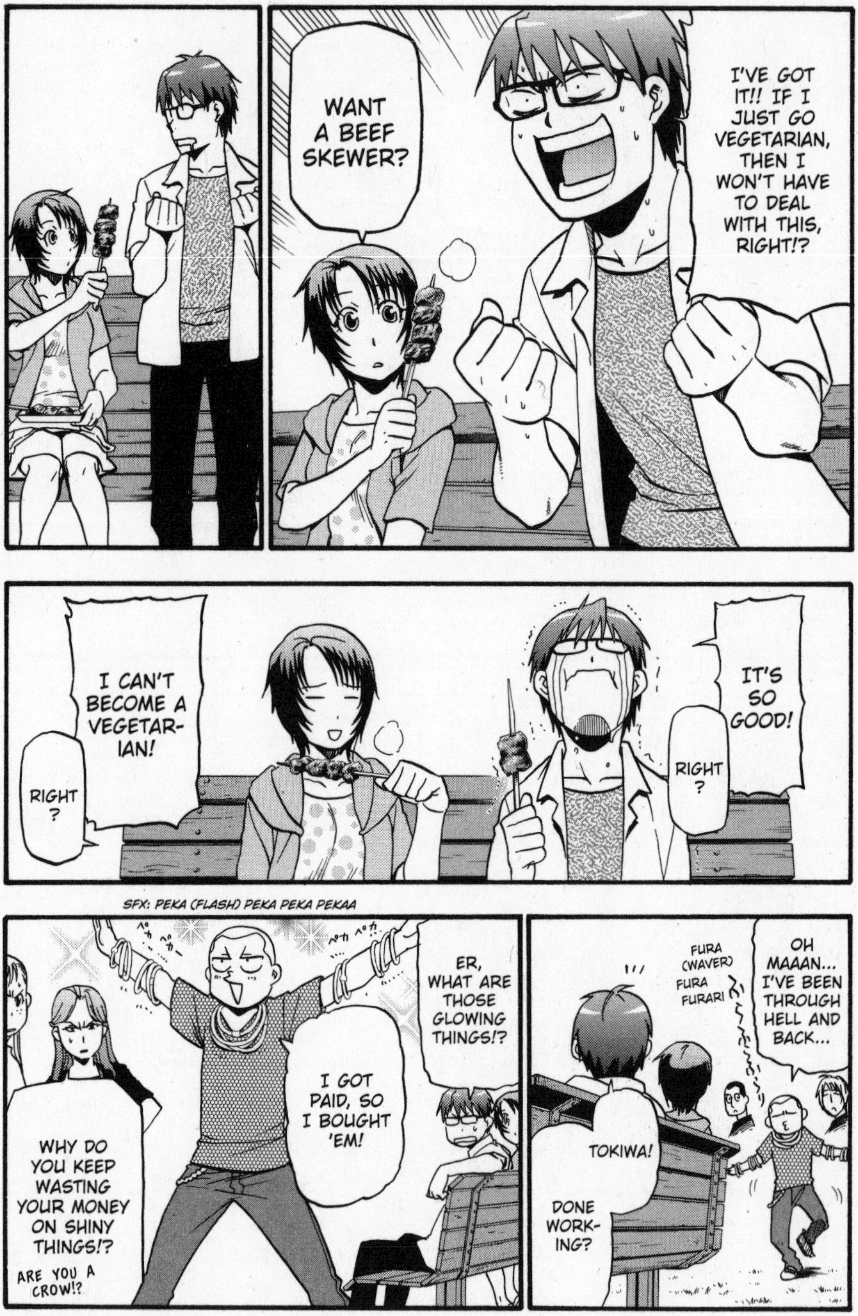

I'VE GOT IT!! IF I JUST GO VEGETARIAN, THEN I WON'T HAVE TO DEAL WITH THIS, RIGHT!?
WANT A BEEF SKEWER?
IT'S SO GOOD!
RIGHT?
I CAN'T BECOME A VEGETARIAN!
RIGHT?
OH MAAAN... I'VE BEEN THROUGH HELL AND BACK...
FURA (WAVER) FURA FURARI
TOKIWA!
DONE WORKING?
SFX: PEKA (FLASH) PEKA PEKA PEKAA
ER, WHAT ARE THOSE GLOWING THINGS!?
I GOT PAID, SO I BOUGHT 'EM!
WHY DO YOU KEEP WASTING YOUR MONEY ON SHINY THINGS!?
ARE YOU A CROW!?

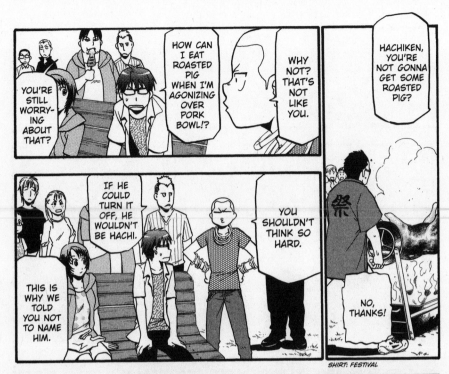

HACHIKEN, YOU'RE NOT GONNA GET SOME ROASTED PIG?
NO, THANKS!
WHY NOT? THAT'S NOT LIKE YOU.
HOW CAN I EAT ROASTED PIG WHEN I'M AGONIZING OVER PORK BOWL!?
YOU'RE STILL WORRYING ABOUT THAT?
YOU SHOULDN'T THINK SO HARD.
IF HE COULD TURN IT OFF, HE WOULDN'T BE HACHI.
THIS IS WHY WE TOLD YOU NOT TO NAME HIM.
SHIRT: FESTIVAL
ARGH, WHAT AM I GONNA DOOO?
WE CAN'T FIGURE IT OUT FOR YOU...
YOU'RE THE SMARTEST PERSON HERE. DON'T ASK US!
GO VEGE-TARIAN?
BUT YOU KNOW, I NAMED COWS WHEN I WAS LITTLE TOO.
I DID IT TOO! THEN I CRIED WHEN THEY GOT TAKEN AWAY TO BE SOLD.
BEEF IS SO DELICIOUS.
WAI (CLAMOR) わい
WAI わい
PORK IS BEST.
YOU GOTTA GET OVER IT.
WARA (CROWD)
WARA わら
わら
WAI わい
WAI わい

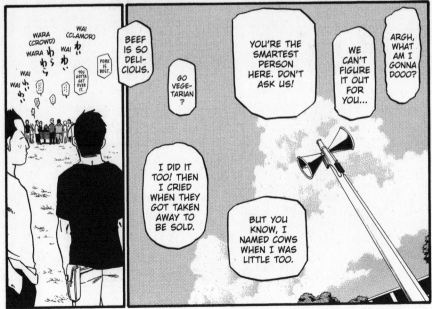

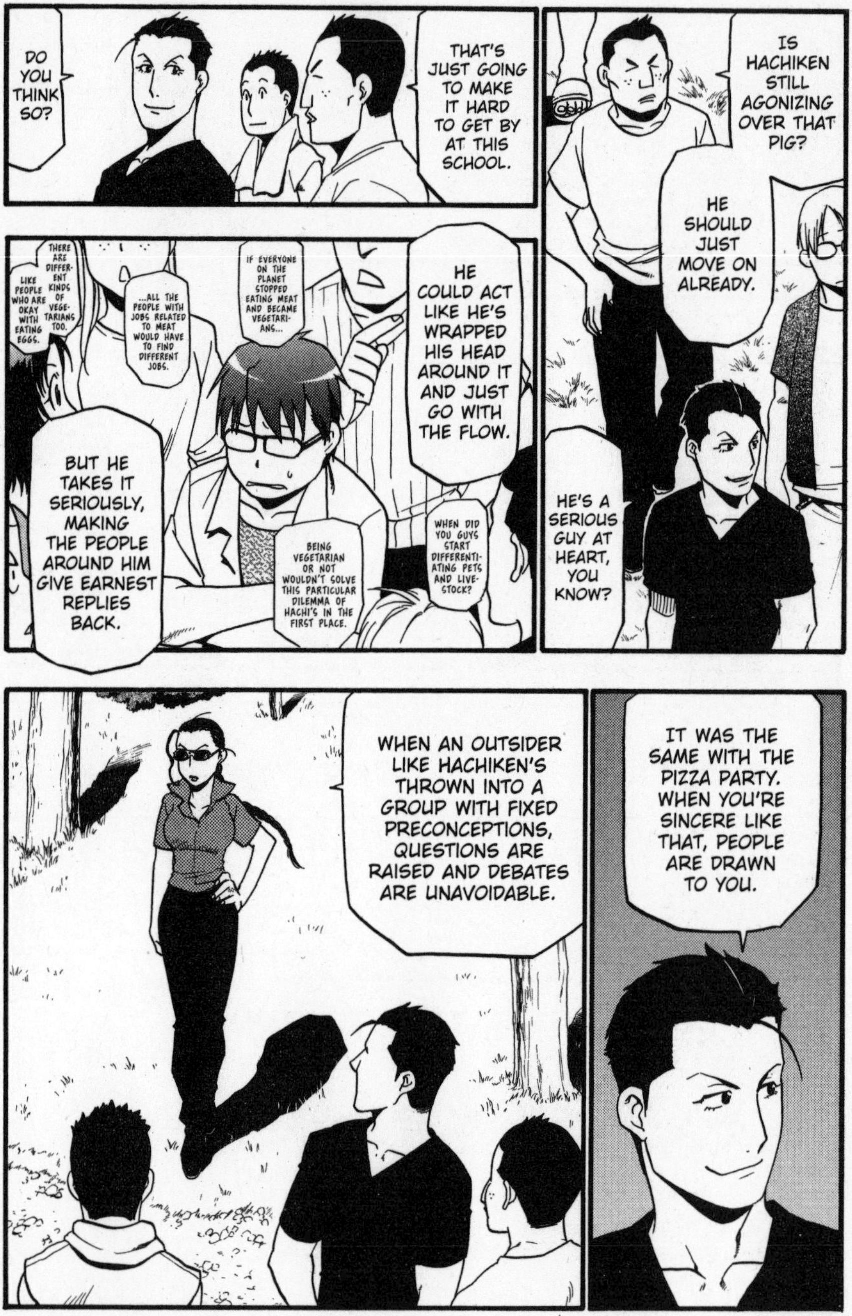
IS HACHIKEN STILL AGONIZING OVER THAT PIG?
HE SHOULD JUST MOVE ON ALREADY.
HE'S A SERIOUS GUY AT HEART, YOU KNOW?
THAT'S JUST GOING TO MAKE IT HARD TO GET BY AT THIS SCHOOL.
DO YOU THINK SO?
HE COULD ACT LIKE HE'S WRAPPED HIS HEAD AROUND IT AND JUST GO WITH THE FLOW.
IF EVERYONE ON THE PLANET STOPPED EATING MEAT AND BECAME VEGETARIANS...
...ALL THE PEOPLE WITH JOBS RELATED TO MEAT WOULD HAVE TO FIND DIFFERENT JOBS.
THERE ARE DIFFERENT KINDS OF VEGETARIANS TOO.
LIKE PEOPLE WHO ARE OKAY WITH EATING EGGS.
WHEN DID YOU GUYS START DIFFERENTIATING PETS AND LIVESTOCK?
BEING VEGETARIAN OR NOT WOULDN'T SOLVE THIS PARTICULAR DILEMMA OF HACHI'S IN THE FIRST PLACE.
BUT HE TAKES IT SERIOUSLY, MAKING THE PEOPLE AROUND HIM GIVE EARNEST REPLIES BACK.
IT WAS THE SAME WITH THE PIZZA PARTY. WHEN YOU'RE SINCERE LIKE THAT, PEOPLE ARE DRAWN TO YOU.
WHEN AN OUTSIDER LIKE HACHIKEN'S THROWN INTO A GROUP WITH FIXED PRECONCEPTIONS, QUESTIONS ARE RAISED AND DEBATES ARE UNAVOIDABLE.

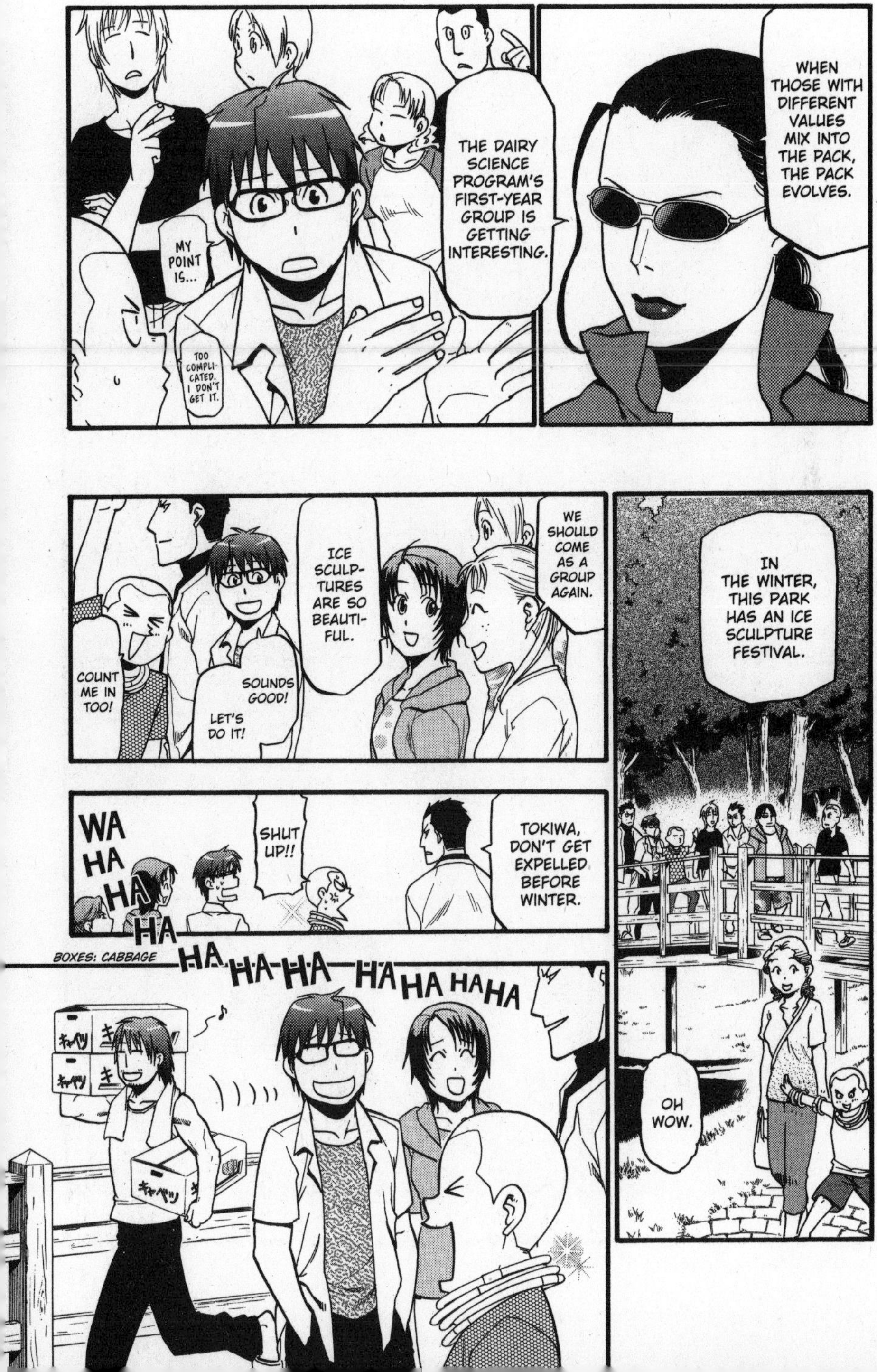
WHEN THOSE WITH DIFFERENT VALUES MIX INTO THE PACK, THE PACK EVOLVES.
THE DAIRY SCIENCE PROGRAM'S FIRST-YEAR GROUP IS GETTING INTERESTING.
MY POINT IS...
TOO COMPLICATED. I DON'T GET IT.
IN THE WINTER, THIS PARK HAS AN ICE SCULPTURE FESTIVAL.
OH WOW.
WE SHOULD COME AS A GROUP AGAIN.
ICE SCULPTURES ARE SO BEAUTIFUL.
SOUNDS GOOD!
LET'S DO IT!
COUNT ME IN TOO!
TOKIWA, DON'T GET EXPELLED BEFORE WINTER.
SHUT UP!!
WA HA HA HA
BOXES: CABBAGE
HA HA HA HA HA HA HA HA

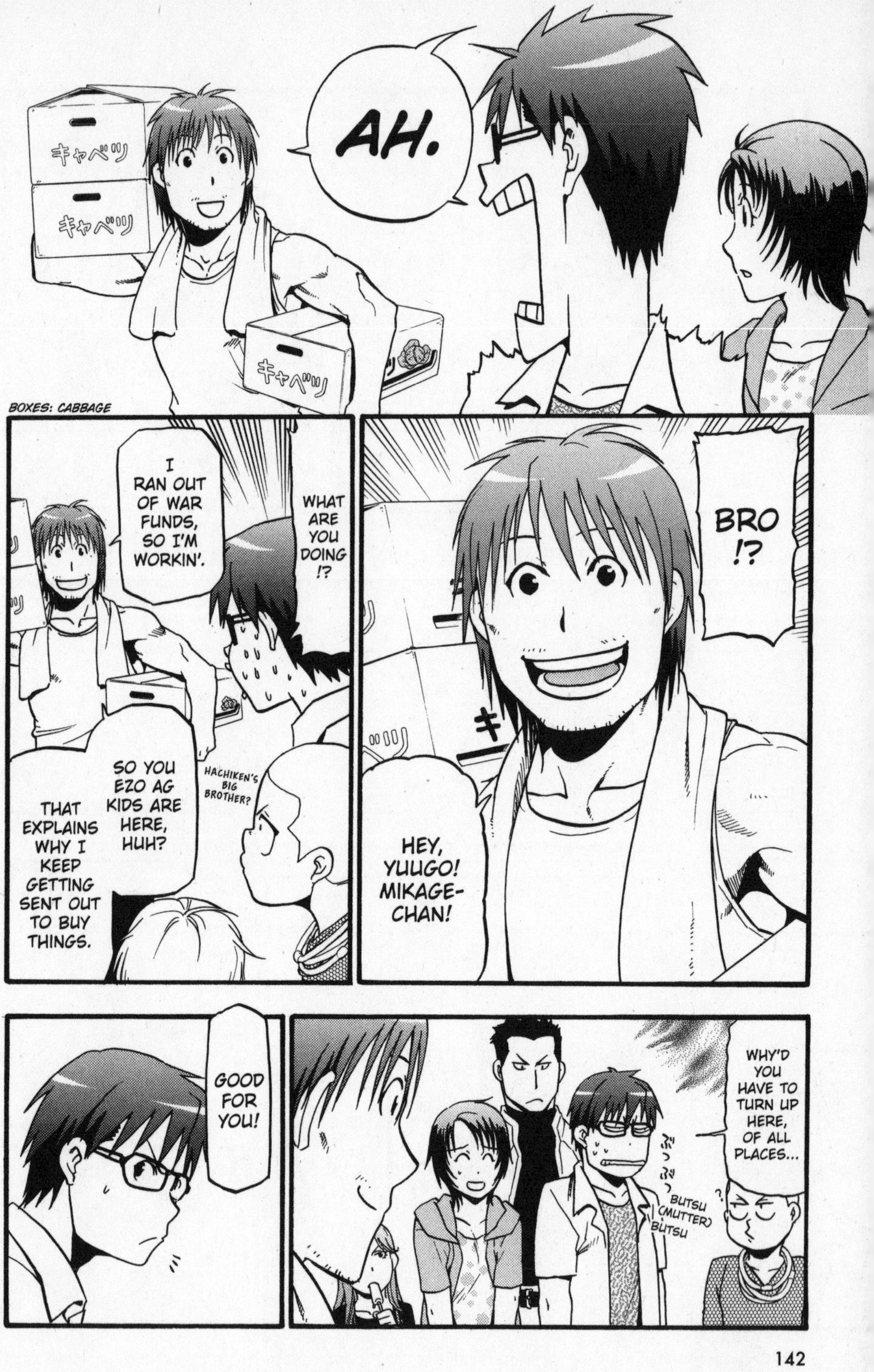
AH.
キャベツ
キャベツ
キャベツ
BOXES: CABBAGE
BRO!?
HEY, YUUGO! MIKAGE-CHAN!
WHAT ARE YOU DOING!?
I RAN OUT OF WAR FUNDS, SO I'M WORKIN'.
HACHIKEN'S BIG BROTHER?
SO YOU EZO AG KIDS ARE HERE, HUH?
THAT EXPLAINS WHY I KEEP GETTING SENT OUT TO BUY THINGS.
WHY'D YOU HAVE TO TURN UP HERE, OF ALL PLACES...
ぶつぶつ
BUTSU (MUTTER) BUTSU
GOOD FOR YOU!

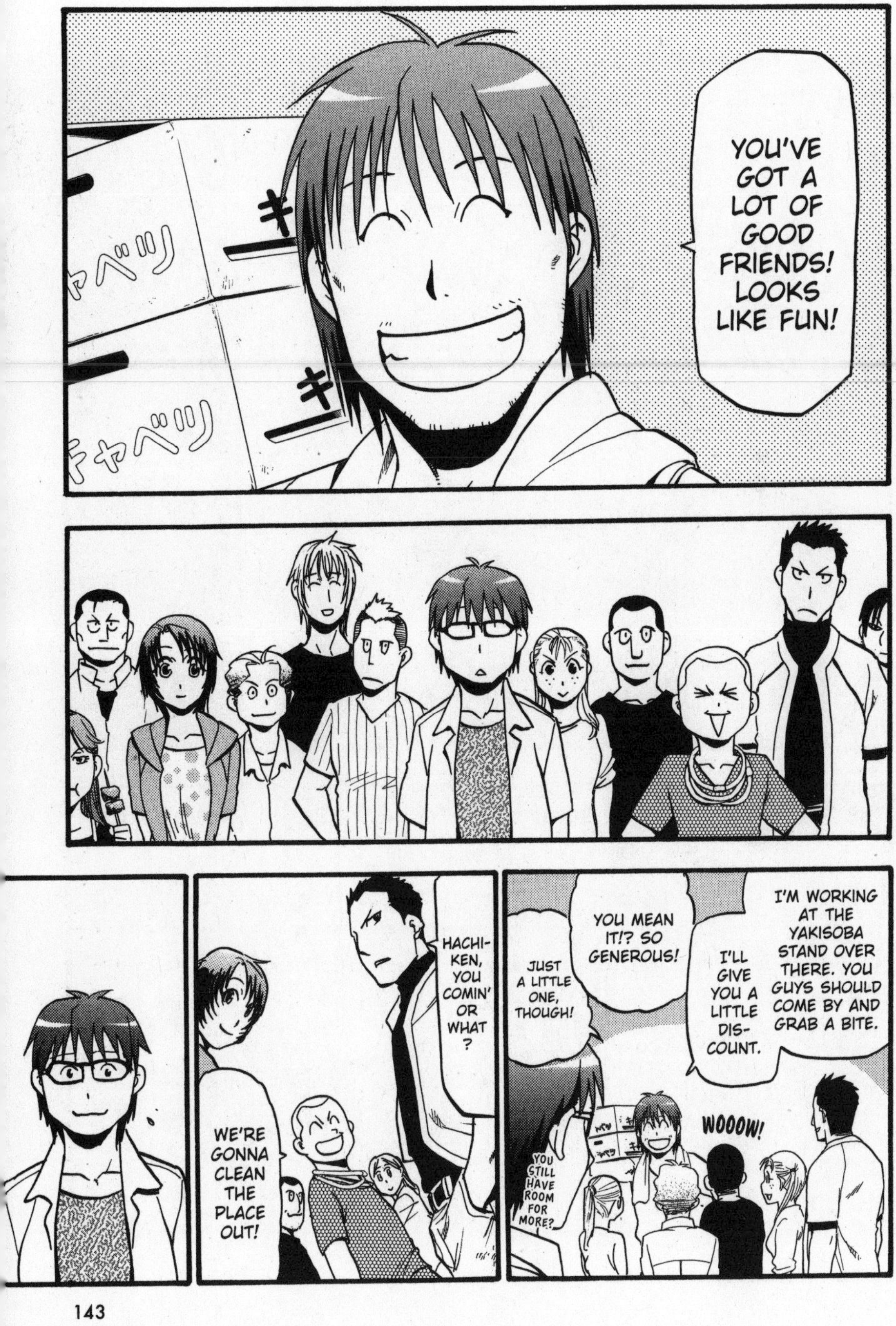
YOU'VE GOT A LOT OF GOOD FRIENDS! LOOKS LIKE FUN!
キャベツ
I'M WORKING AT THE YAKISOBA STAND OVER THERE. YOU GUYS SHOULD COME BY AND GRAB A BITE.
I'LL GIVE YOU A LITTLE DIS-COUNT.
YOU MEAN IT!? SO GENEROUS!
JUST A LITTLE ONE, THOUGH!
WOOOW!
YOU STILL HAVE ROOM FOR MORE?
HACHI-KEN, YOU COMIN' OR WHAT?
WE'RE GONNA CLEAN THE PLACE OUT!

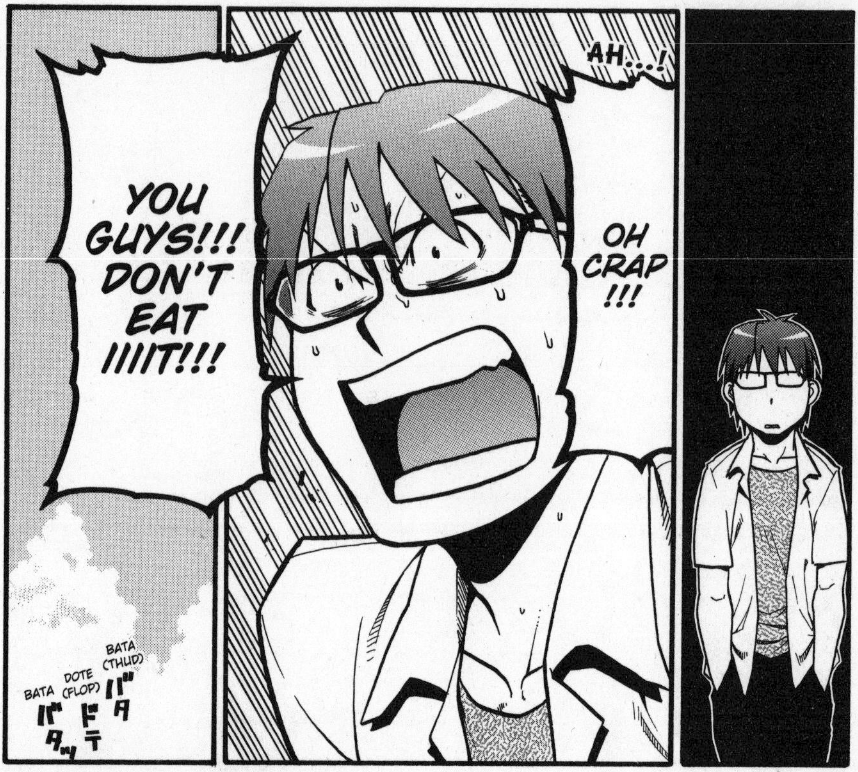
AH...!
OH CRAP!!!
YOU GUYS!!! DON'T EAT IIIIIT!!!
BATA (THUD)
DOTE (FLOP)
BATA

STALL: YAKISOBA / YAKISOBA ¥300, SUPER-SIZED ¥500

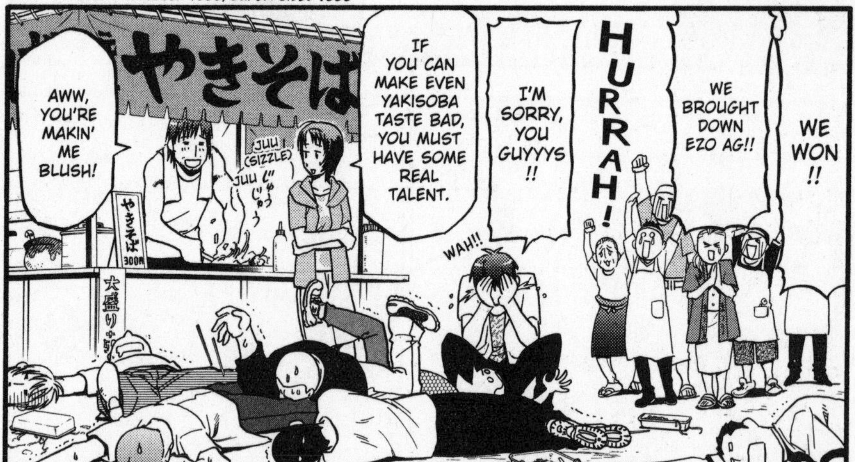
WE WON!!
WE BROUGHT DOWN EZO AG!!
HURRAH!
I'M SORRY, YOU GUYYYS!!
WAH!!
IF YOU CAN MAKE EVEN YAKISOBA TASTE BAD, YOU MUST HAVE SOME REAL TALENT.
JUU (SIZZLE) JUU
AWW, YOU'RE MAKIN' ME BLUSH!
やきそば
やきそば 300円

Chapter 25: Tale of Summer ⑮

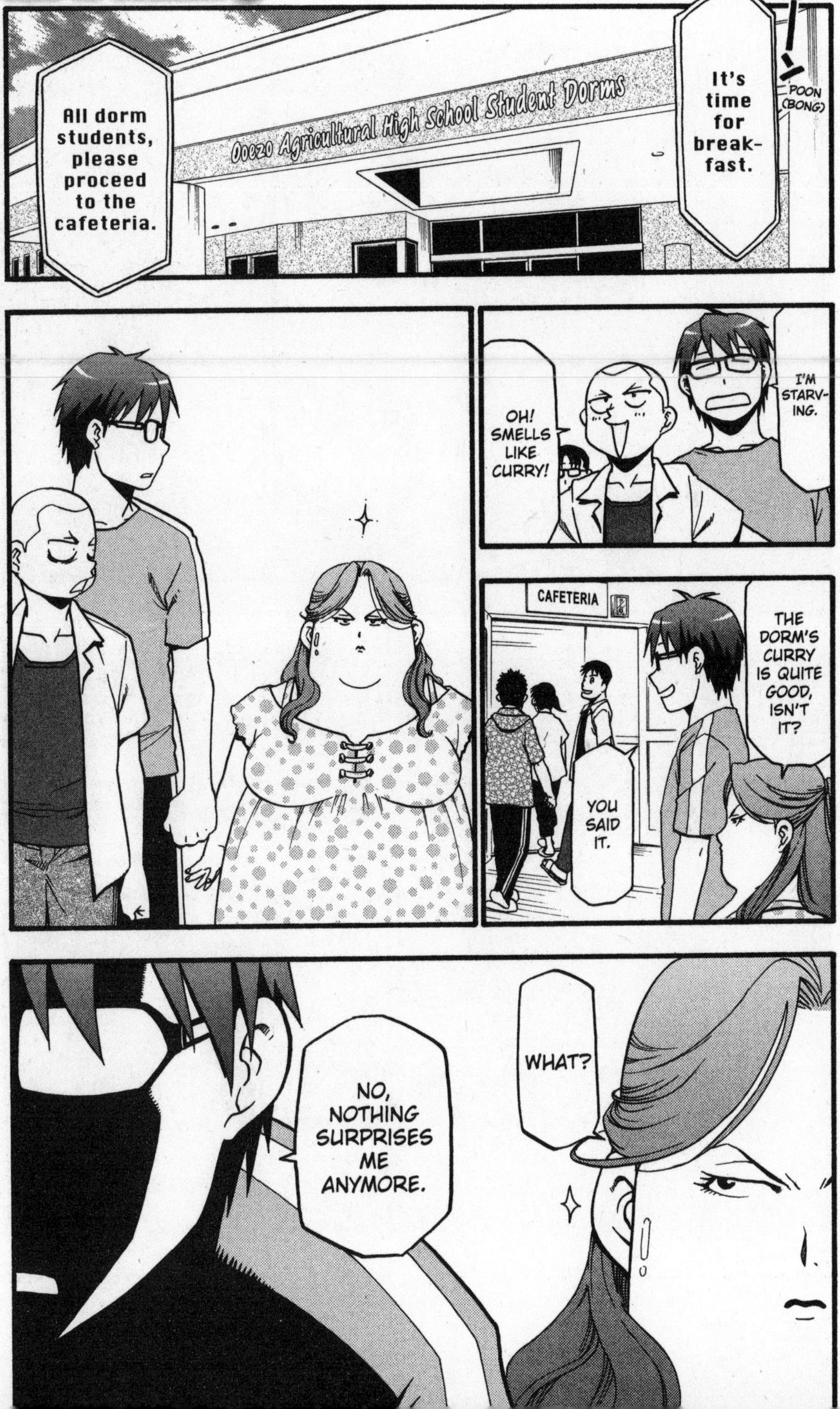
ポーン
POON (BONG)
It's time for breakfast.
Ooezo Agricultural High School Student Dorms
All dorm students, please proceed to the cafeteria.
I'M STARVING.
OH! SMELLS LIKE CURRY!
CAFETERIA
THE DORM'S CURRY IS QUITE GOOD, ISN'T IT?
YOU SAID IT.
WHAT?
NO, NOTHING SURPRISES ME ANYMORE.

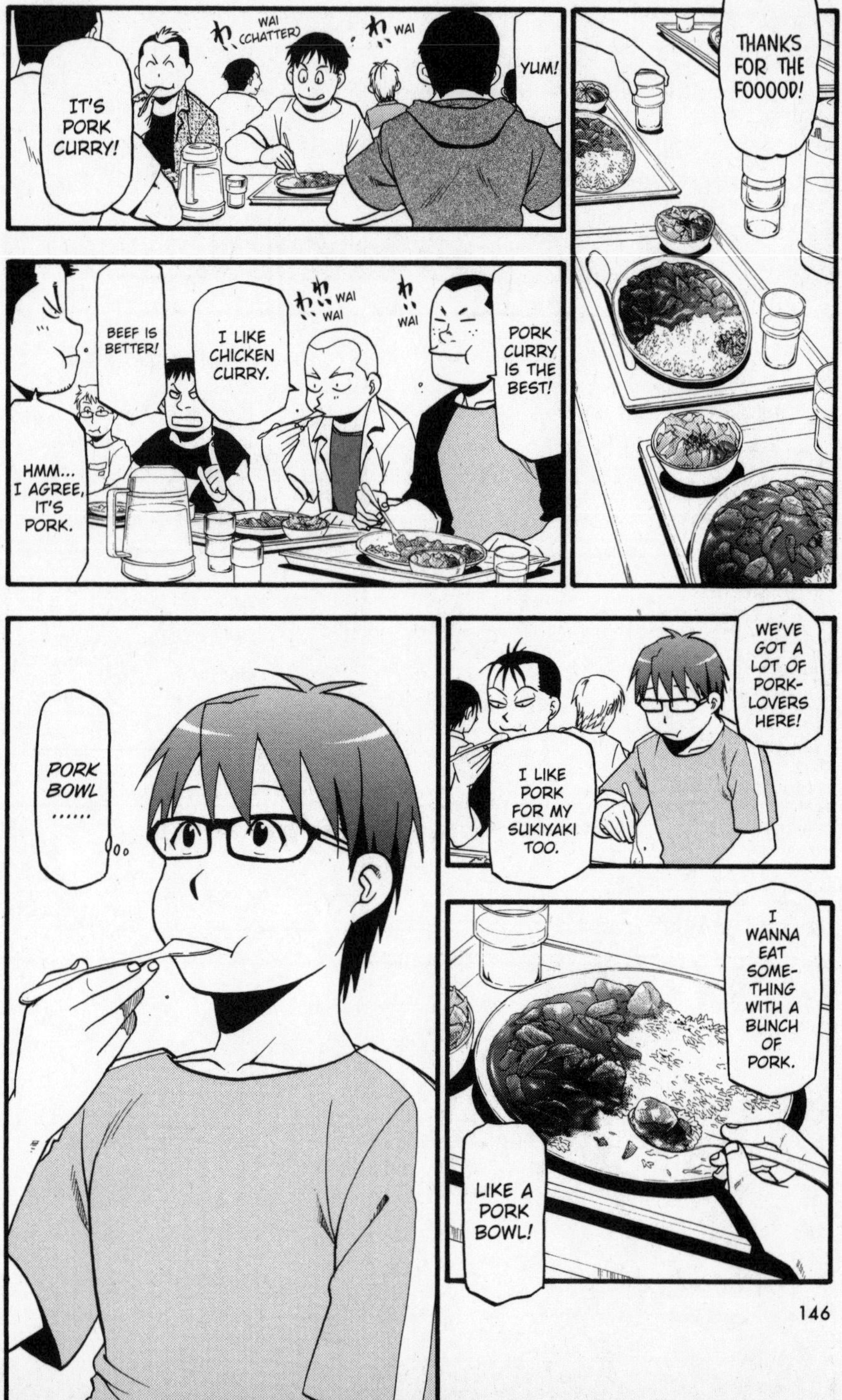
THANKS FOR THE FOOOOD!
YUM!
WAI
WAI (CHATTER)
IT'S PORK CURRY!
PORK CURRY IS THE BEST!
WAI
I LIKE CHICKEN CURRY.
WAI WAI
BEEF IS BETTER!
HMM... I AGREE, IT'S PORK.
WE'VE GOT A LOT OF PORK-LOVERS HERE!
I LIKE PORK FOR MY SUKIYAKI TOO.
I WANNA EAT SOME-THING WITH A BUNCH OF PORK.
LIKE A PORK BOWL!
PORK BOWL ......

ざわ ZAWA
ざわ ZAWA ZAWA

....
....

GEEE PORK'S THE BEST, RIGHT??

NO, BEEF IS.

SO GOOD.

ざわ ざわ ZAWA
ZAWA (CHATTER)

STAFF ROOM

When Spending Nights Away

When You Return to the Dorm

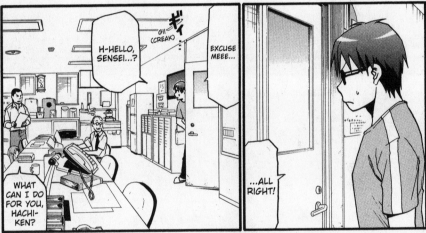

H-HELLO, SENSEI...?

GII (CREAK)

EXCUSE MEEE...

WHAT CAN I DO FOR YOU, HACHI-KEN?

...ALL RIGHT!

I WANTED TO ASK YOU ABOUT SOME-THING...

Chapter 25: Tale of Summer ⑮

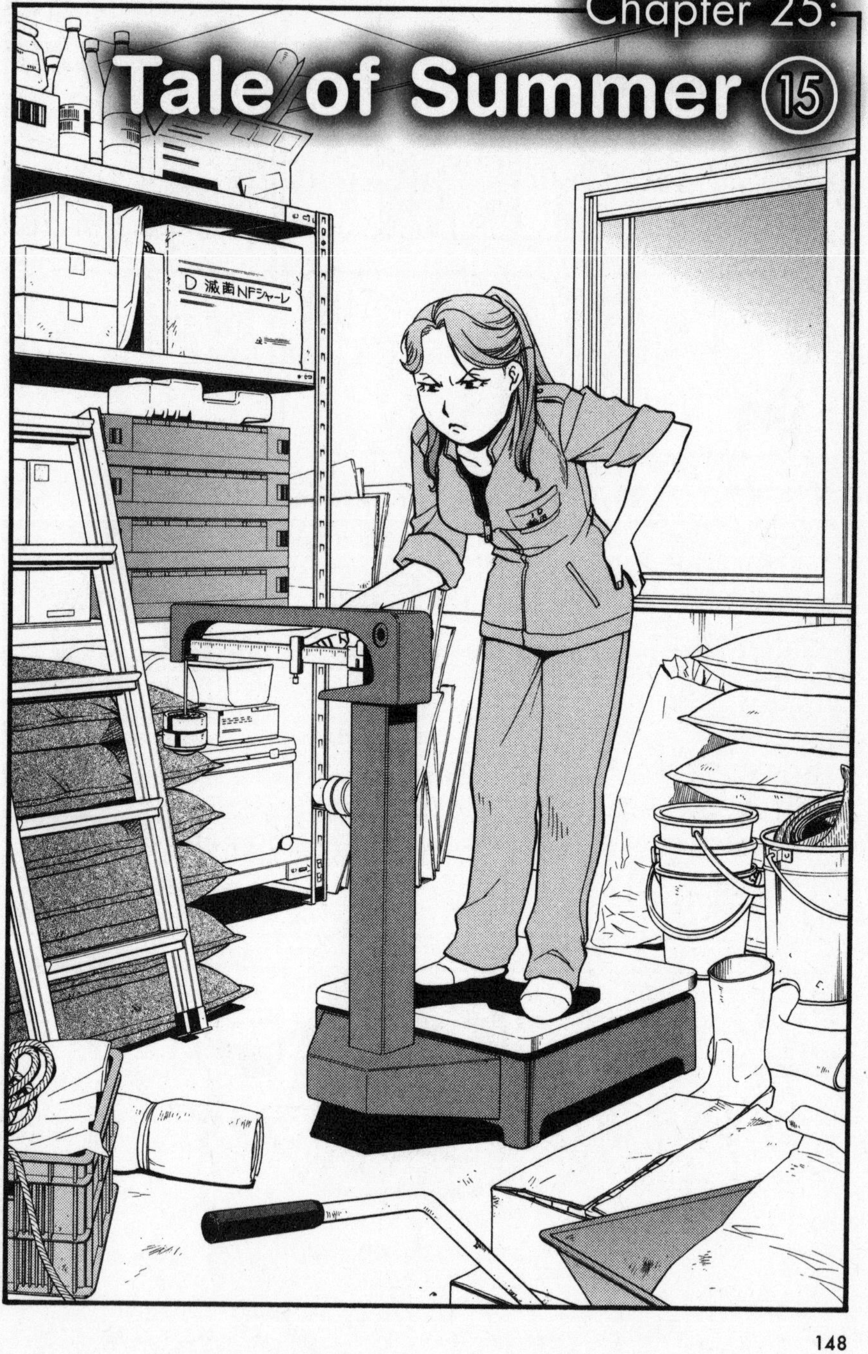
D 滅菌NFシャーレ

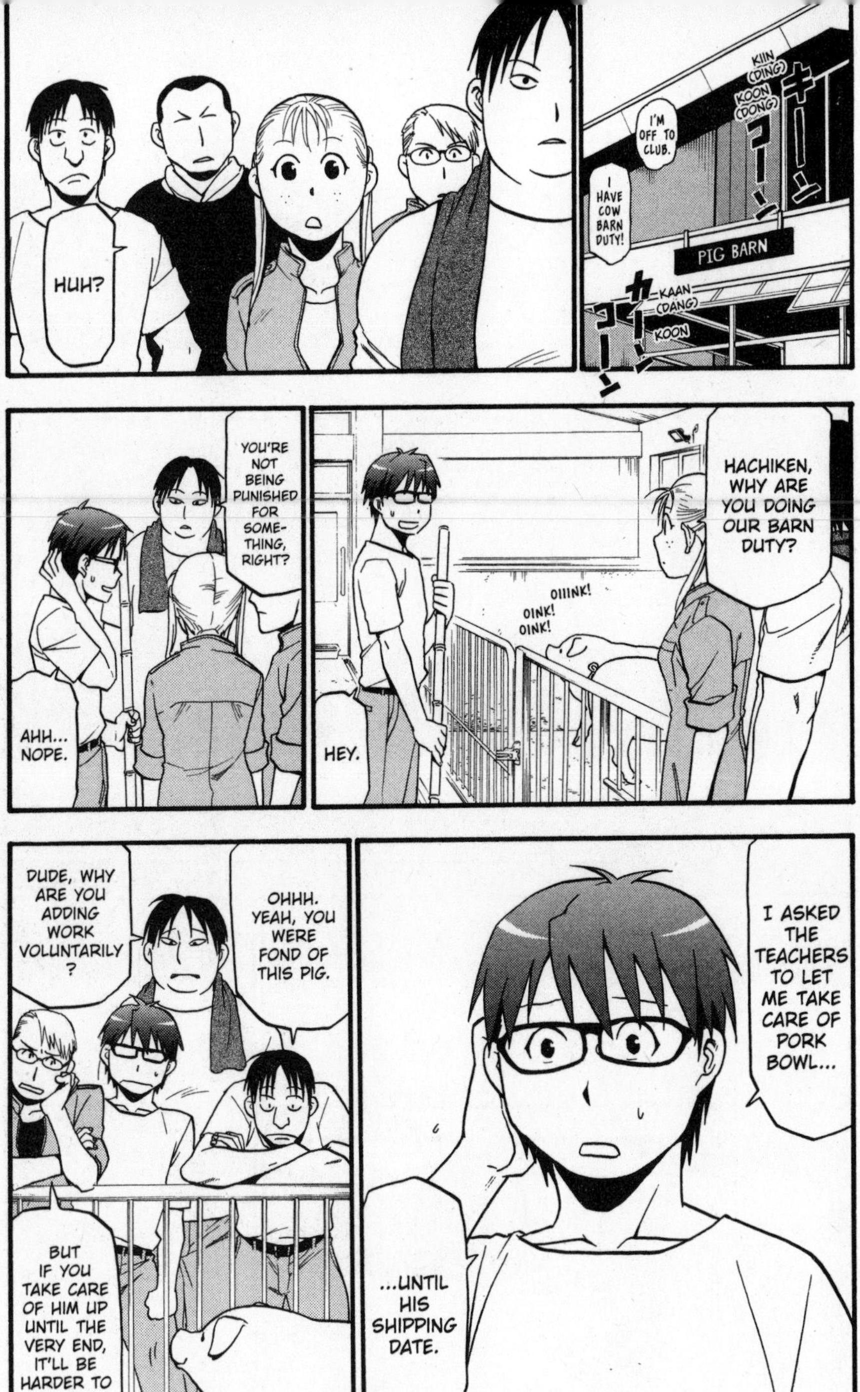
KIIN (DING)
KOON (DONG)
I'M OFF TO CLUB.
I HAVE COW BARN DUTY!
PIG BARN
KAAN (DANG)
KOON
HUH?
HACHIKEN, WHY ARE YOU DOING OUR BARN DUTY?
OIIINK!
OINK! OINK!
HEY.
YOU'RE NOT BEING PUNISHED FOR SOMETHING, RIGHT?
AHH... NOPE.
I ASKED THE TEACHERS TO LET ME TAKE CARE OF PORK BOWL...
...UNTIL HIS SHIPPING DATE.
OHHH. YEAH, YOU WERE FOND OF THIS PIG.
DUDE, WHY ARE YOU ADDING WORK VOLUNTARILY?
BUT IF YOU TAKE CARE OF HIM UP UNTIL THE VERY END, IT'LL BE HARDER TO SAY BYE.

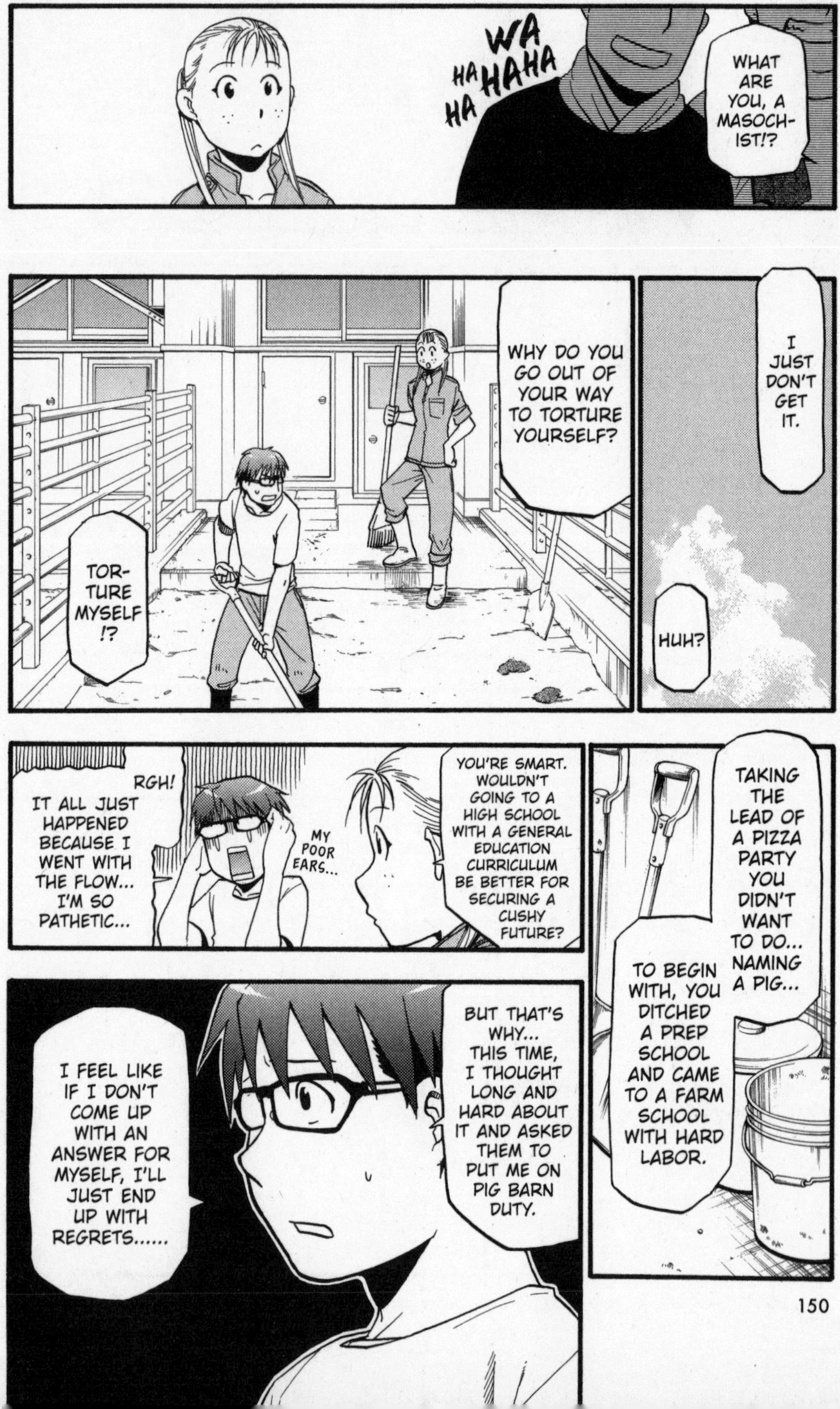
WHAT ARE YOU, A MASOCHIST!?
WA HAHAHA HA HA
I JUST DON'T GET IT.
HUH?
WHY DO YOU GO OUT OF YOUR WAY TO TORTURE YOURSELF?
TORTURE MYSELF!?
TAKING THE LEAD OF A PIZZA PARTY YOU DIDN'T WANT TO DO... NAMING A PIG...
TO BEGIN WITH, YOU DITCHED A PREP SCHOOL AND CAME TO A FARM SCHOOL WITH HARD LABOR.
YOU'RE SMART. WOULDN'T GOING TO A HIGH SCHOOL WITH A GENERAL EDUCATION CURRICULUM BE BETTER FOR SECURING A CUSHY FUTURE?
MY POOR EARS...
RGH!
IT ALL JUST HAPPENED BECAUSE I WENT WITH THE FLOW... I'M SO PATHETIC...
BUT THAT'S WHY... THIS TIME, I THOUGHT LONG AND HARD ABOUT IT AND ASKED THEM TO PUT ME ON PIG BARN DUTY.
I FEEL LIKE IF I DON'T COME UP WITH AN ANSWER FOR MYSELF, I'LL JUST END UP WITH REGRETS......

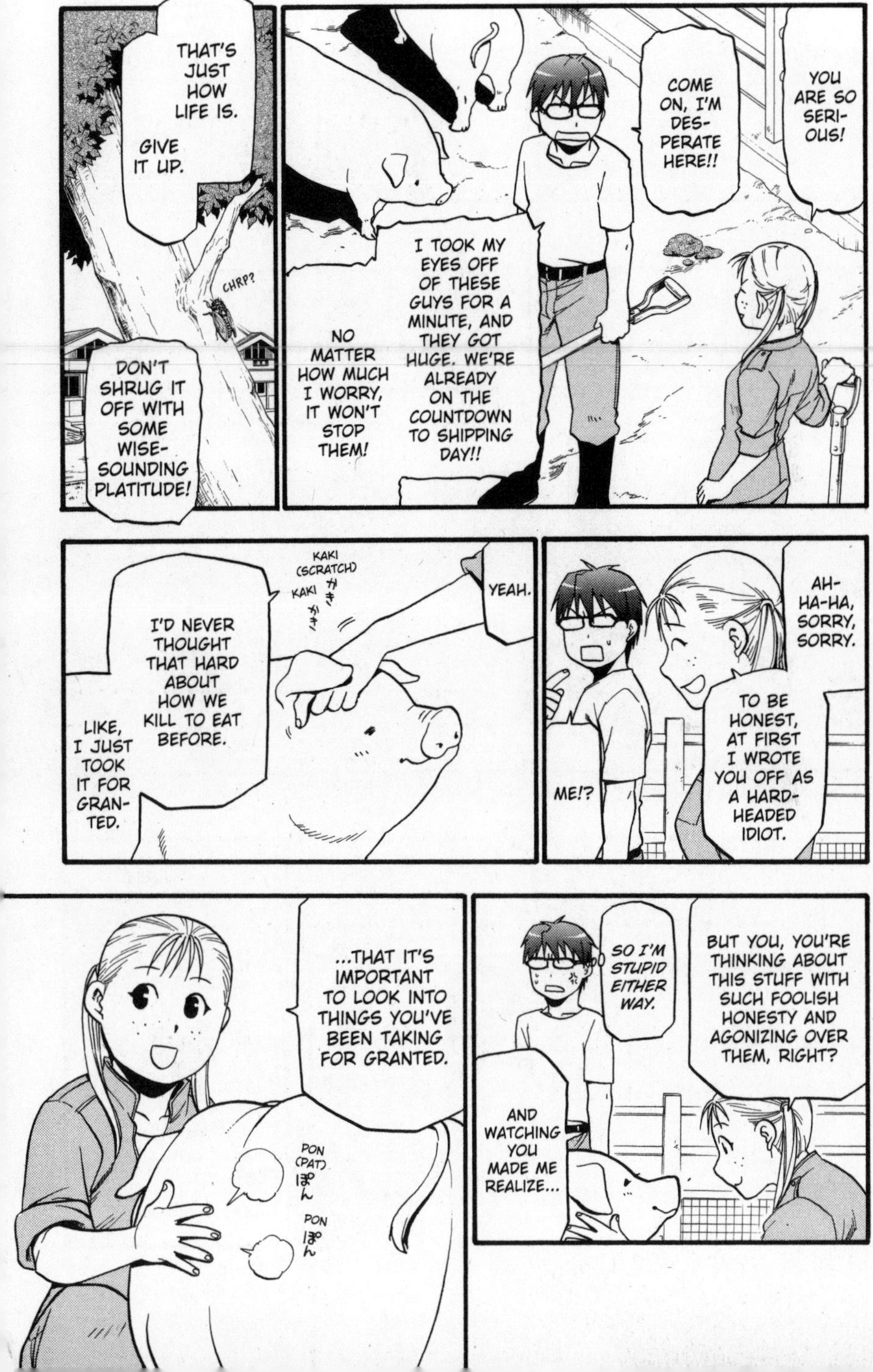
YOU ARE SO SERI-OUS!
COME ON, I'M DES-PERATE HERE!!
I TOOK MY EYES OFF OF THESE GUYS FOR A MINUTE, AND THEY GOT HUGE. WE'RE ALREADY ON THE COUNTDOWN TO SHIPPING DAY!!
NO MATTER HOW MUCH I WORRY, IT WON'T STOP THEM!
THAT'S JUST HOW LIFE IS.
GIVE IT UP.
CHRP?
DON'T SHRUG IT OFF WITH SOME WISE-SOUNDING PLATITUDE!
AH-HA-HA, SORRY, SORRY.
TO BE HONEST, AT FIRST I WROTE YOU OFF AS A HARD-HEADED IDIOT.
ME!?
YEAH.
KAKI (SCRATCH) かき
KAKI かき
I'D NEVER THOUGHT THAT HARD ABOUT HOW WE KILL TO EAT BEFORE.
LIKE, I JUST TOOK IT FOR GRAN-TED.
BUT YOU, YOU'RE THINKING ABOUT THIS STUFF WITH SUCH FOOLISH HONESTY AND AGONIZING OVER THEM, RIGHT?
SO I'M STUPID EITHER WAY.
AND WATCHING YOU MADE ME REALIZE...
...THAT IT'S IMPORTANT TO LOOK INTO THINGS YOU'VE BEEN TAKING FOR GRANTED.
PON (PAT) ぽん
PON ぽん

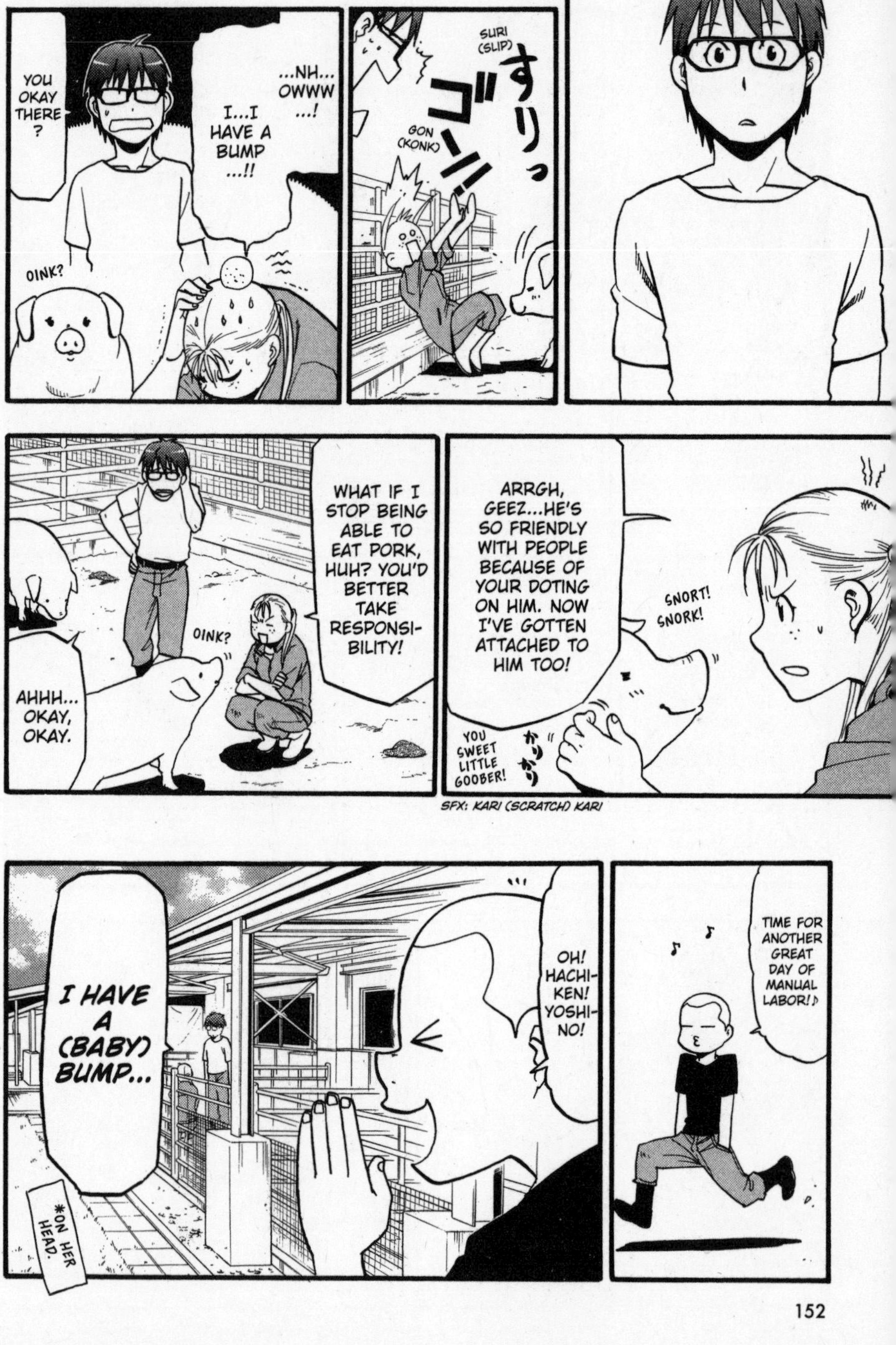
SURI (SLIP)
すりっ
GON (KONK)
ゴン!!
...NH... OWWW ...!
I...I HAVE A BUMP ...!!
YOU OKAY THERE ?
OINK?
ARRGH, GEEZ...HE'S SO FRIENDLY WITH PEOPLE BECAUSE OF YOUR DOTING ON HIM. NOW I'VE GOTTEN ATTACHED TO HIM TOO!
SNORT! SNORK!
YOU SWEET LITTLE GOOBER!
かりかり
WHAT IF I STOP BEING ABLE TO EAT PORK, HUH? YOU'D BETTER TAKE RESPONSI-BILITY!
OINK?
AHHH... OKAY, OKAY.
SFX: KARI (SCRATCH) KARI
TIME FOR ANOTHER GREAT DAY OF MANUAL LABOR!♪
OH! HACHI-KEN! YOSHI-NO!
I HAVE A (BABY) BUMP...
*ON HER HEAD.

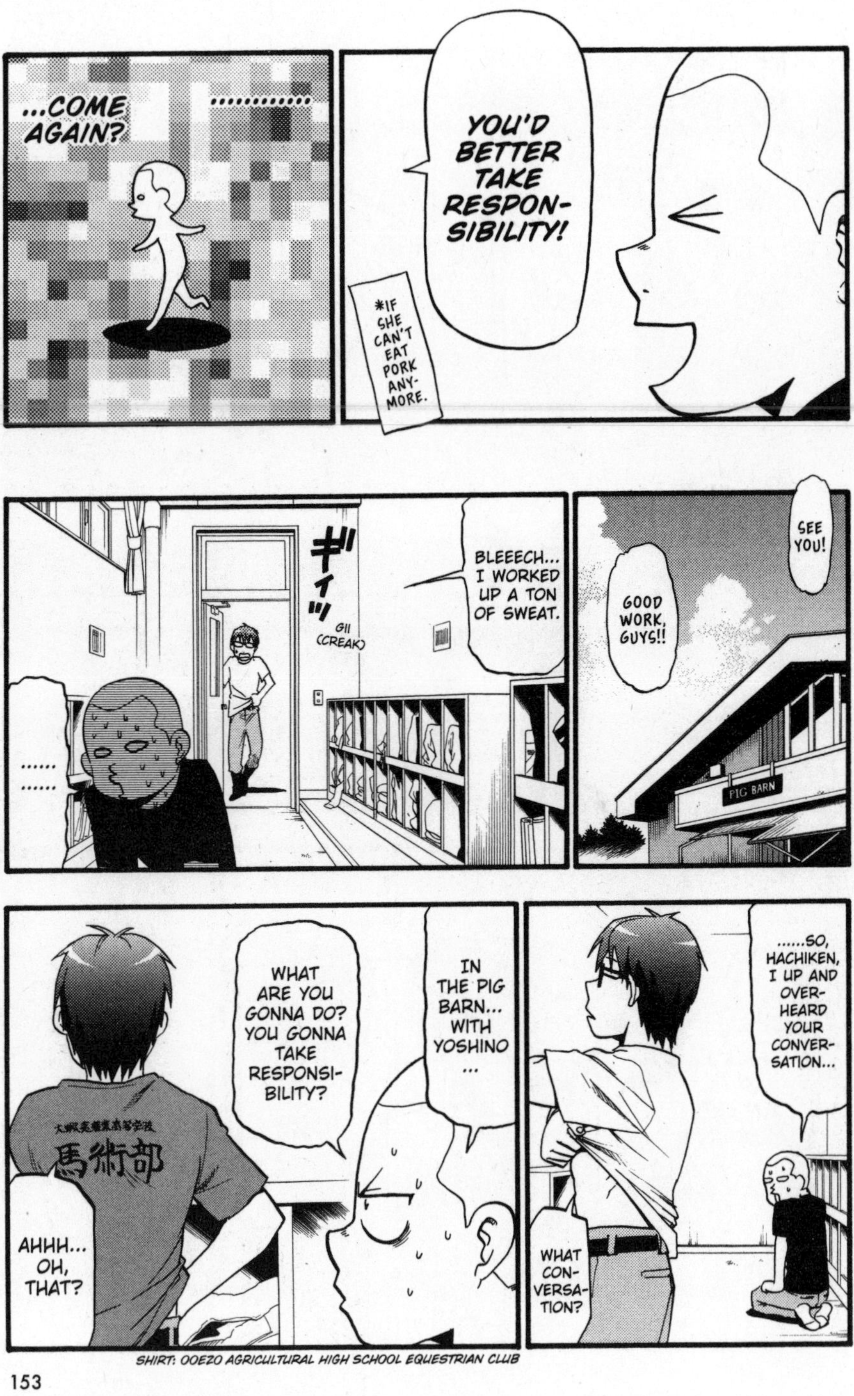
YOU'D BETTER TAKE RESPON-SIBILITY!
*IF SHE CAN'T EAT PORK ANY-MORE.
...COME AGAIN?
....
SEE YOU!
GOOD WORK, GUYS!!
PIG BARN
BLEEECH... I WORKED UP A TON OF SWEAT.
ギイッ
GII (CREAK)
......
......
......SO, HACHIKEN, I UP AND OVER-HEARD YOUR CONVER-SATION...
WHAT CON-VERSA-TION?
IN THE PIG BARN... WITH YOSHINO ...
WHAT ARE YOU GONNA DO? YOU GONNA TAKE RESPONSI-BILITY?
馬術部
AHHH... OH, THAT?
SHIRT: OOEZO AGRICULTURAL HIGH SCHOOL EQUESTRIAN CLUB

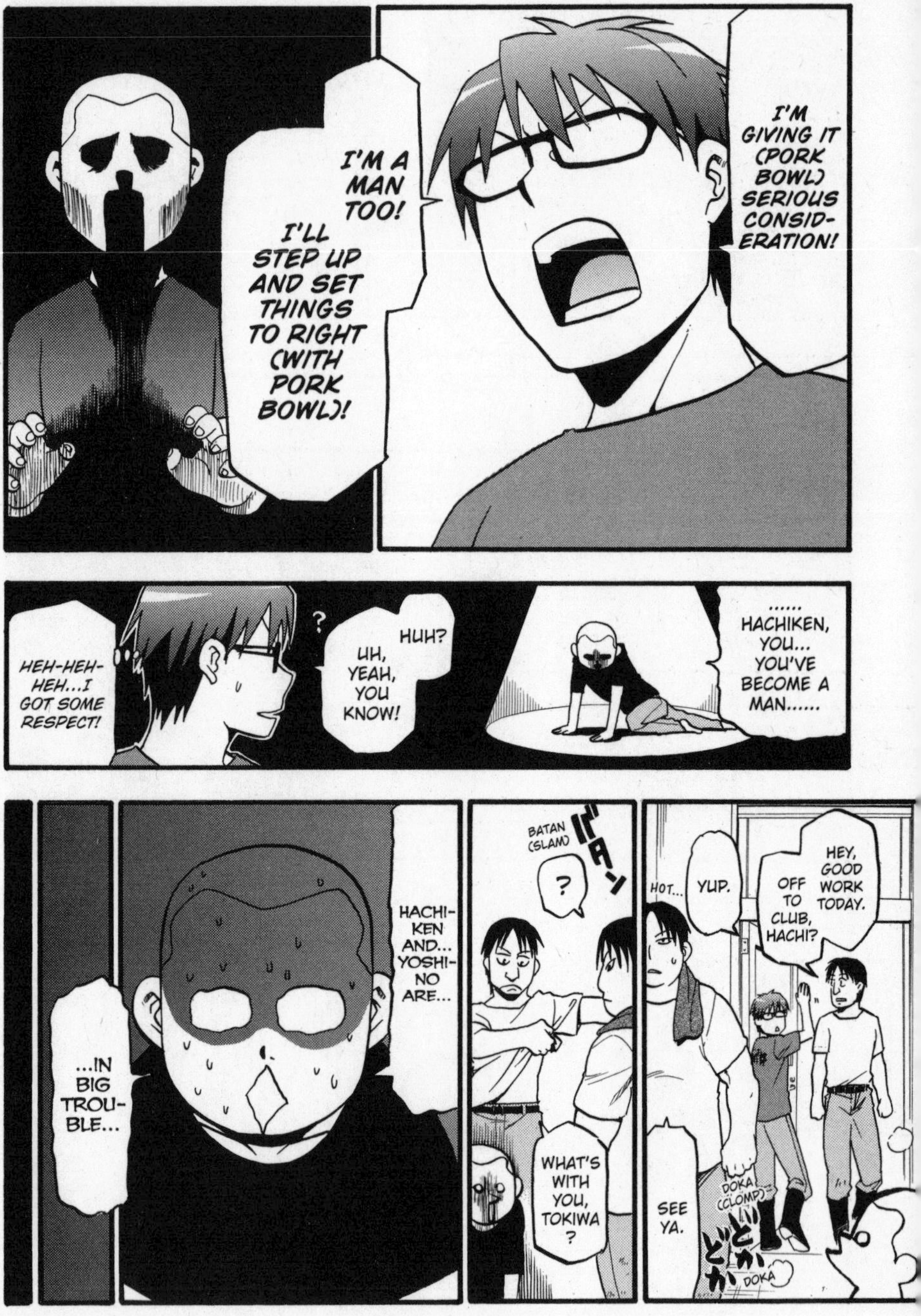
I'M GIVING IT (PORK BOWL) SERIOUS CONSID-ERATION!
I'M A MAN TOO!
I'LL STEP UP AND SET THINGS TO RIGHT (WITH PORK BOWL)!
......HACHIKEN, YOU... YOU'VE BECOME A MAN......
HUH?
UH, YEAH, YOU KNOW!
?
HEH-HEH-HEH...I GOT SOME RESPECT!
HEY, GOOD WORK TODAY.
OFF TO CLUB, HACHI?
YUP.
HOT...
SEE YA.
DOKA (CLOMP)
DOKA
BATAN (SLAM)
?
WHAT'S WITH YOU, TOKIWA?
HACHI-KEN AND... YOSHI-NO ARE...
...IN BIG TROU-BLE...

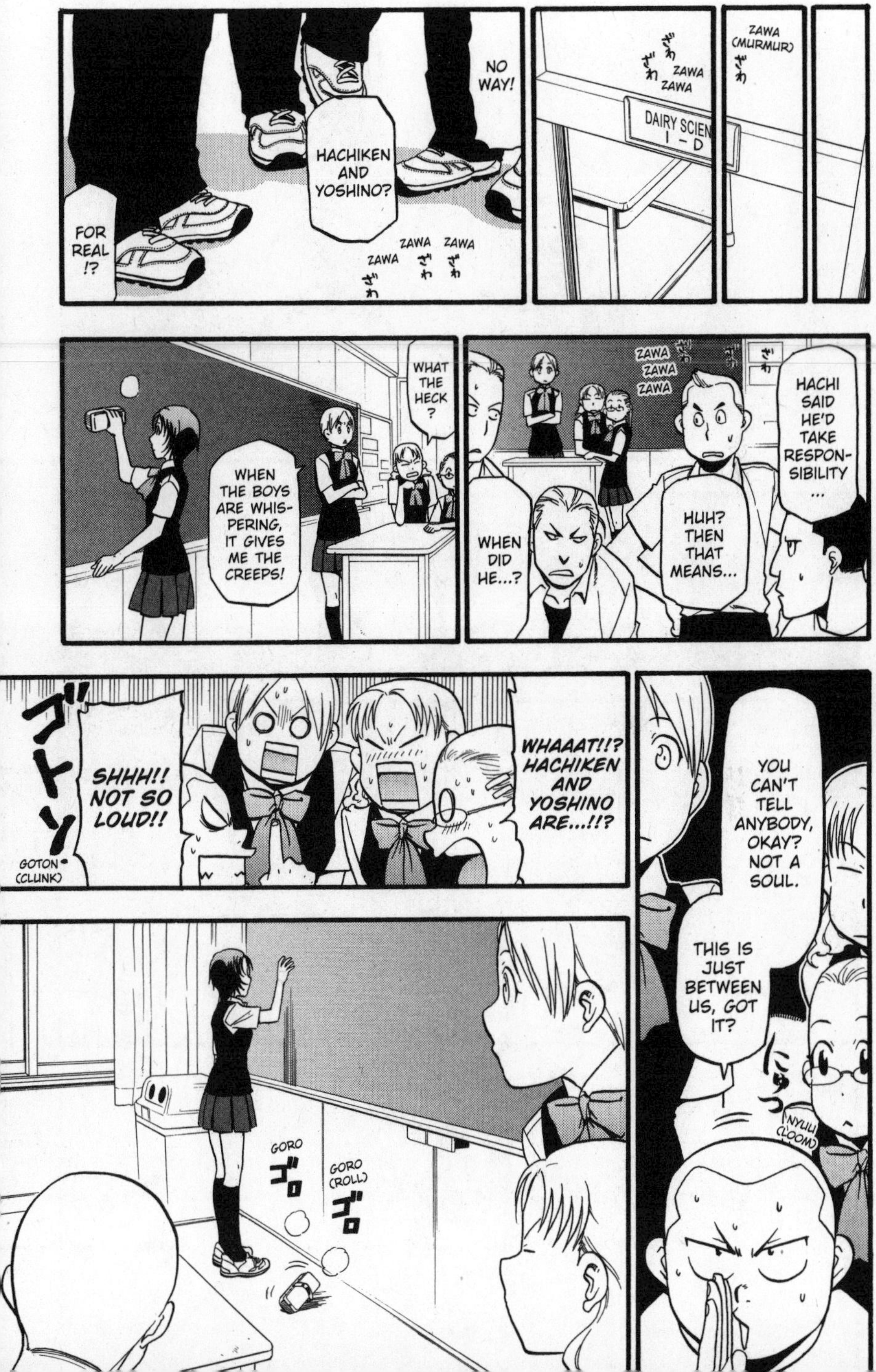
ZAWA (MURMUR)
ZAWA ZAWA
DAIRY SCIEN I – D
NO WAY!
HACHIKEN AND YOSHINO?
FOR REAL!?
ZAWA ZAWA ZAWA
ZAWA ZAWA ZAWA
HACHI SAID HE'D TAKE RESPONSIBILITY...
HUH? THEN THAT MEANS...
WHEN DID HE...?
WHAT THE HECK?
WHEN THE BOYS ARE WHISPERING, IT GIVES ME THE CREEPS!
YOU CAN'T TELL ANYBODY, OKAY? NOT A SOUL.
THIS IS JUST BETWEEN US, GOT IT?
NYUU (LOOM)
WHAAAT!!? HACHIKEN AND YOSHINO ARE...!!?
SHHH!! NOT SO LOUD!!
GOTON (CLUNK)
GORO GORO (ROLL)

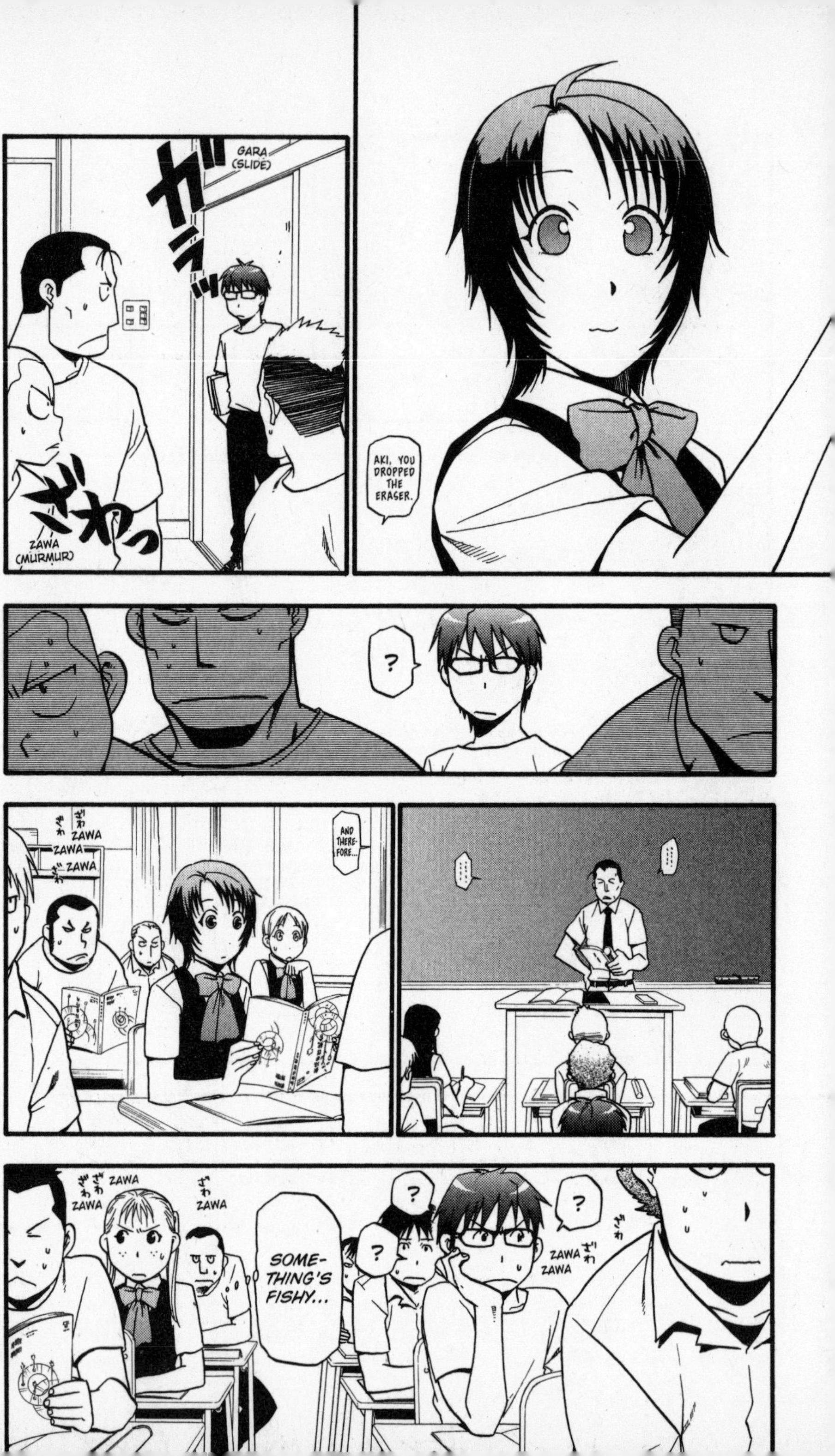
AKI, YOU DROPPED THE ERASER.
GARA (SLIDE)
ZAWA (MURMUR)
?
AND THEREFORE...
ZAWA ZAWA ZAWA
?
?
SOME-THING'S FISHY...
?
ZAWA ZAWA
ZAWA
ZAWA ZAWA

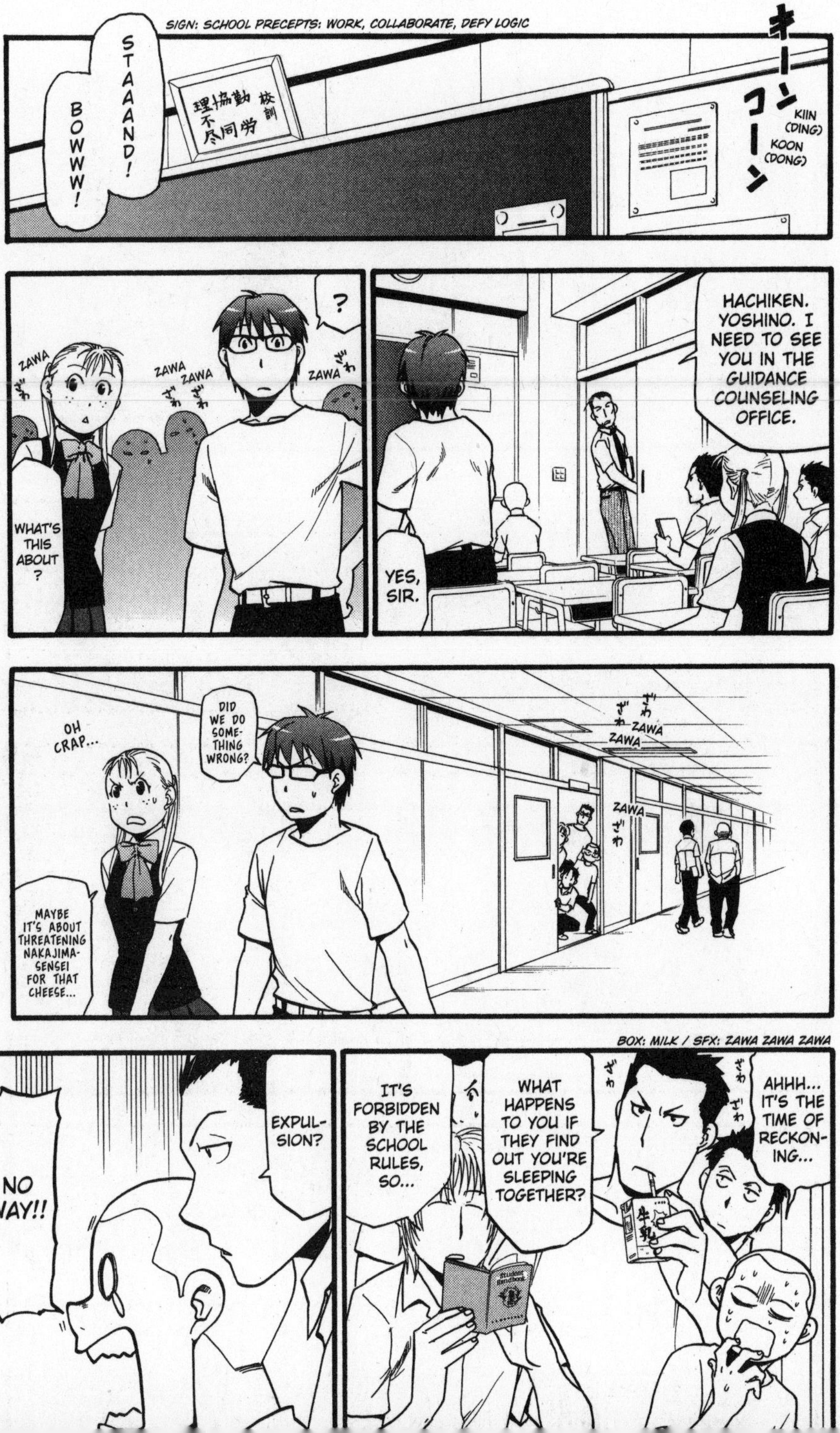
SIGN: SCHOOL PRECEPTS: WORK, COLLABORATE, DEFY LOGIC
KIIN (DING)
KOON (DONG)
STAAAND!
BOWWW!
HACHIKEN. YOSHINO. I NEED TO SEE YOU IN THE GUIDANCE COUNSELING OFFICE.
YES, SIR.
?
ZAWA ZAWA ZAWA ZAWA
WHAT'S THIS ABOUT?
ZAWA ZAWA ZAWA
DID WE DO SOME-THING WRONG?
OH CRAP...
MAYBE IT'S ABOUT THREATENING NAKAJIMA-SENSEI FOR THAT CHEESE...
BOX: MILK / SFX: ZAWA ZAWA ZAWA
AHHH... IT'S THE TIME OF RECKON-ING...
WHAT HAPPENS TO YOU IF THEY FIND OUT YOU'RE SLEEPING TOGETHER?
IT'S FORBIDDEN BY THE SCHOOL RULES, SO...
EXPUL-SION?
NO WAY!!

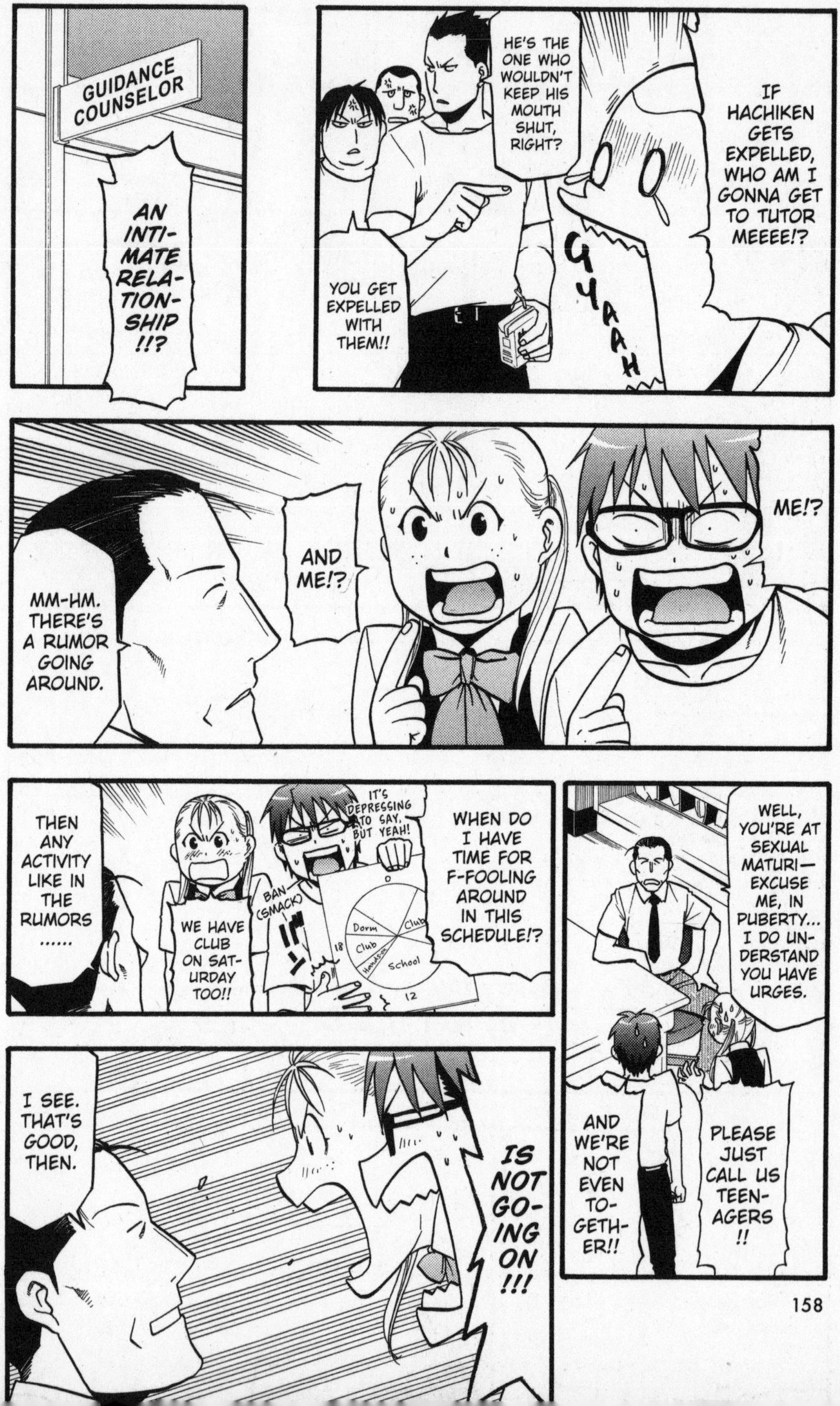
IF HACHIKEN GETS EXPELLED, WHO AM I GONNA GET TO TUTOR MEEEE!?
GYAAH
HE'S THE ONE WHO WOULDN'T KEEP HIS MOUTH SHUT, RIGHT?
YOU GET EXPELLED WITH THEM!!
GUIDANCE COUNSELOR
AN INTI-MATE RELA-TION-SHIP!!?
ME!?
AND ME!?
MM-HM. THERE'S A RUMOR GOING AROUND.
WELL, YOU'RE AT SEXUAL MATURI— EXCUSE ME, IN PUBERTY... I DO UN-DERSTAND YOU HAVE URGES.
PLEASE JUST CALL US TEEN-AGERS!!
AND WE'RE NOT EVEN TO-GETH-ER!!
WHEN DO I HAVE TIME FOR F-FOOLING AROUND IN THIS SCHEDULE!?
IT'S DEPRESSING TO SAY, BUT YEAH!
0
Club
School
12
Club
Dorm
18
BAN (SMACK)
WE HAVE CLUB ON SAT-URDAY TOO!!
THEN ANY ACTIVITY LIKE IN THE RUMORS ......
IS NOT GO-ING ON!!!
I SEE. THAT'S GOOD, THEN.

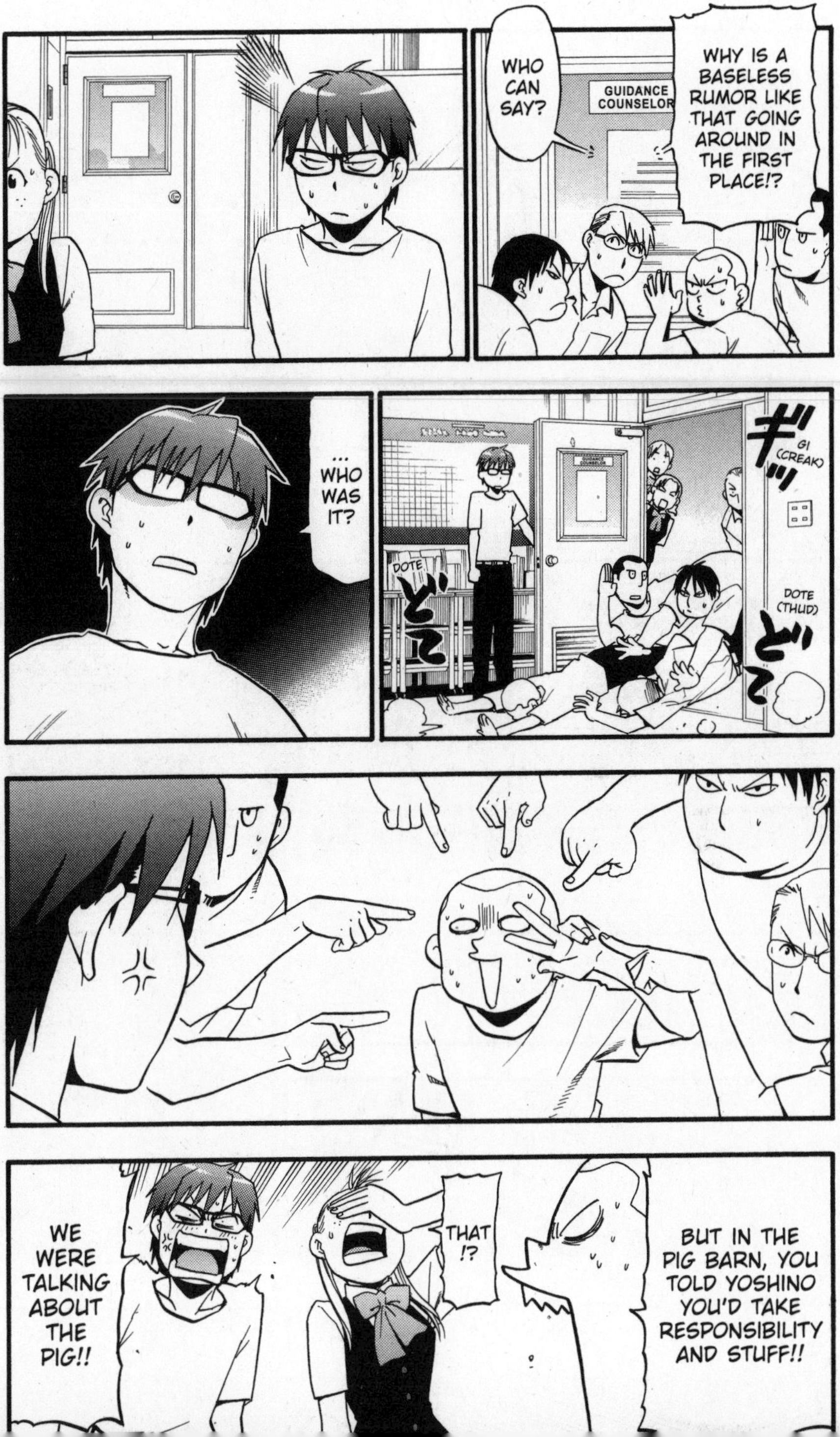
WHY IS A BASELESS RUMOR LIKE THAT GOING AROUND IN THE FIRST PLACE!?
GUIDANCE COUNSELOR
WHO CAN SAY?
ギ
ツ
GI (CREAK)
DOTE (THUD)
どて
DOTE
どて
...WHO WAS IT?
BUT IN THE PIG BARN, YOU TOLD YOSHINO YOU'D TAKE RESPONSIBILITY AND STUFF!!
THAT!?
WE WERE TALKING ABOUT THE PIG!!

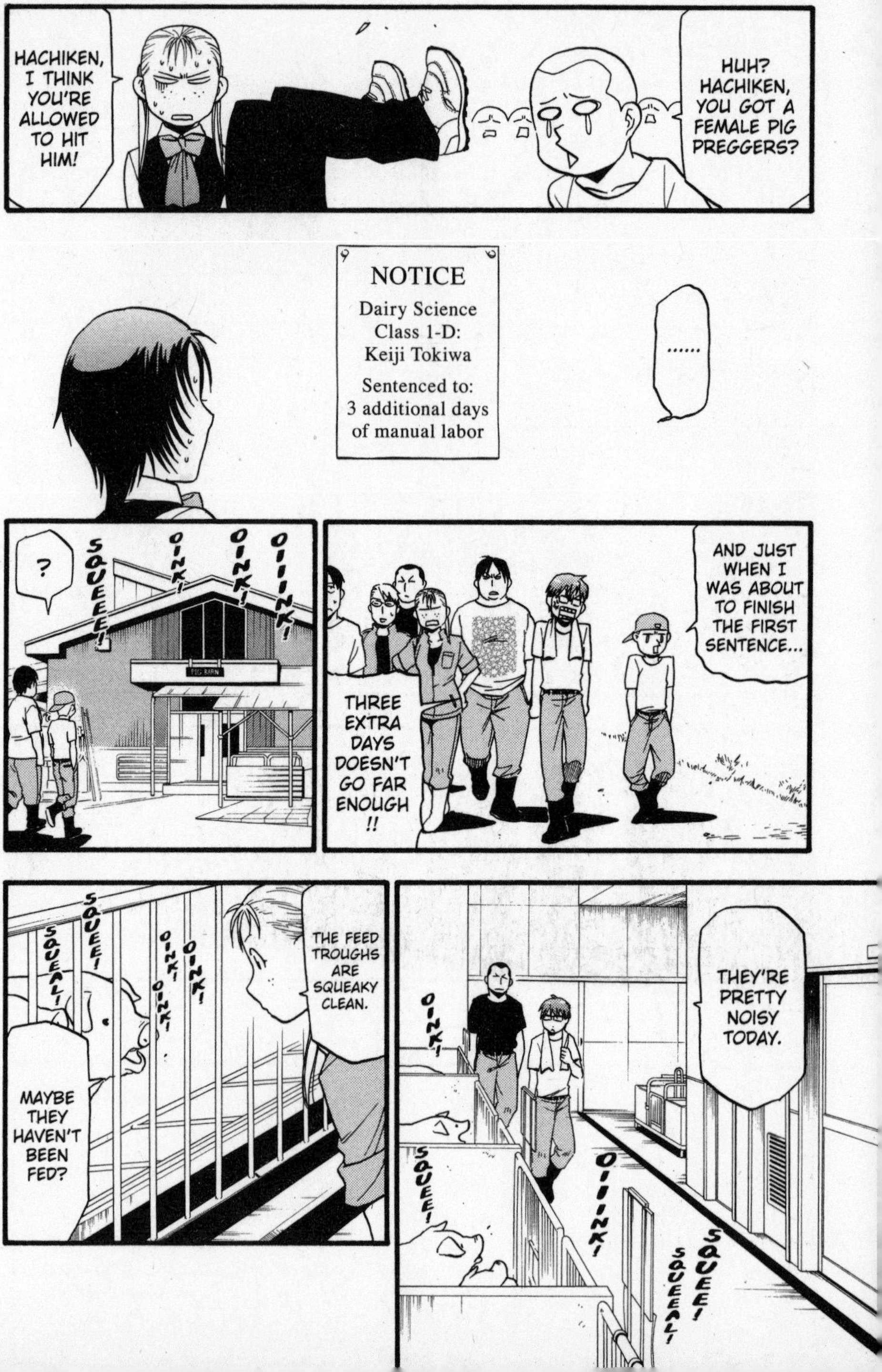
HUH? HACHIKEN, YOU GOT A FEMALE PIG PREGGERS?
HACHIKEN, I THINK YOU'RE ALLOWED TO HIT HIM!
......
NOTICE
Dairy Science Class 1-D: Keiji Tokiwa
Sentenced to: 3 additional days of manual labor
AND JUST WHEN I WAS ABOUT TO FINISH THE FIRST SENTENCE...
THREE EXTRA DAYS DOESN'T GO FAR ENOUGH !!
OIIINK!
OINK!
OINK!
SQUEEEE!
?
PIG BARN
THEY'RE PRETTY NOISY TODAY.
OINK!
OIIINK!
SQUEE!
SQUEE!
SQUEEAL!
THE FEED TROUGHS ARE SQUEAKY CLEAN.
OINK!
OINK!
OINK!
SQUEE!
SQUEAL!
MAYBE THEY HAVEN'T BEEN FED?

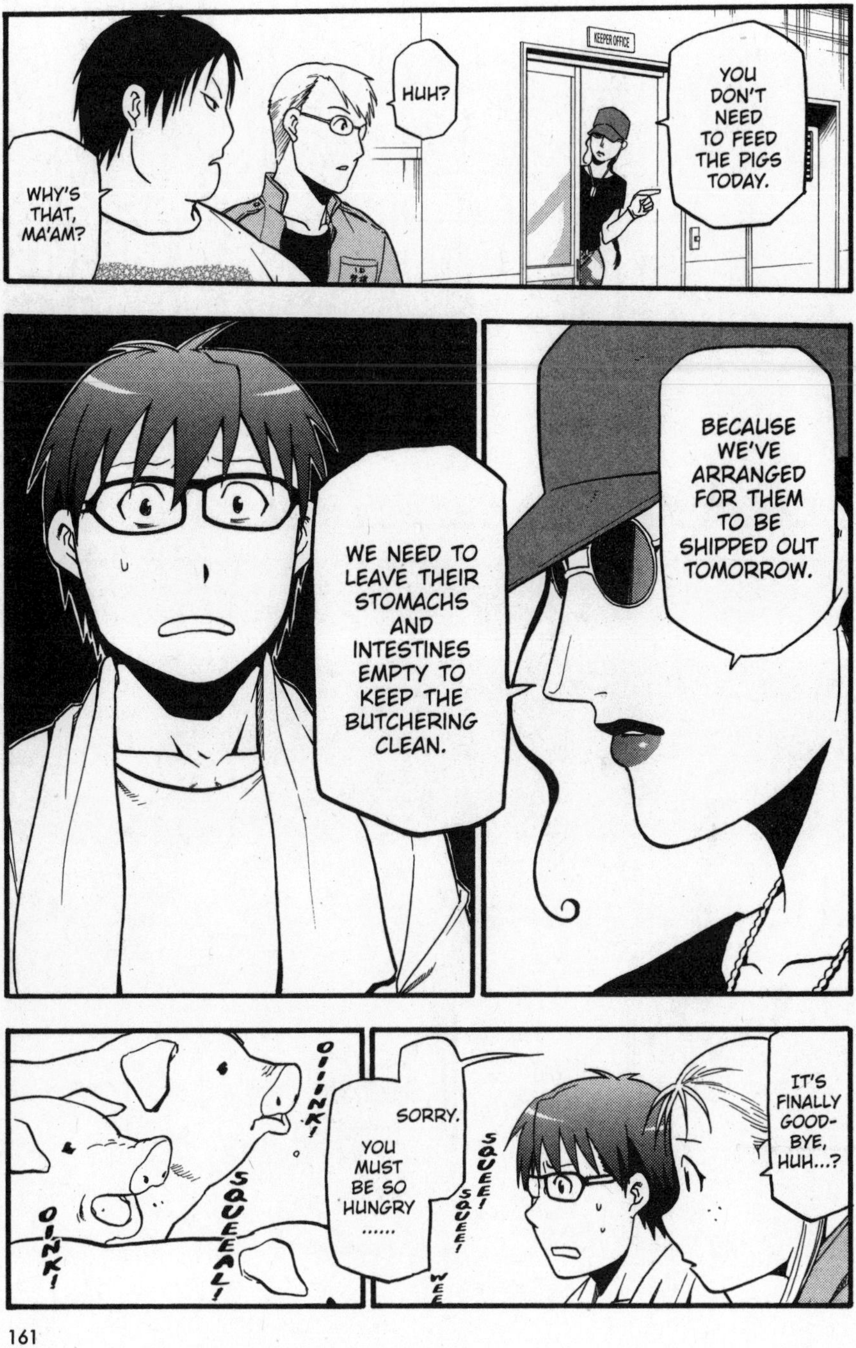
KEEPER OFFICE
YOU DON'T NEED TO FEED THE PIGS TODAY.
HUH?
WHY'S THAT, MA'AM?
BECAUSE WE'VE ARRANGED FOR THEM TO BE SHIPPED OUT TOMORROW.
WE NEED TO LEAVE THEIR STOMACHS AND INTESTINES EMPTY TO KEEP THE BUTCHERING CLEAN.
IT'S FINALLY GOOD-BYE, HUH...?
SQUEE!
SQUEE!
WEE
SORRY.
YOU MUST BE SO HUNGRY ......
OIIINK!
SQUEEEAL!
OINK!

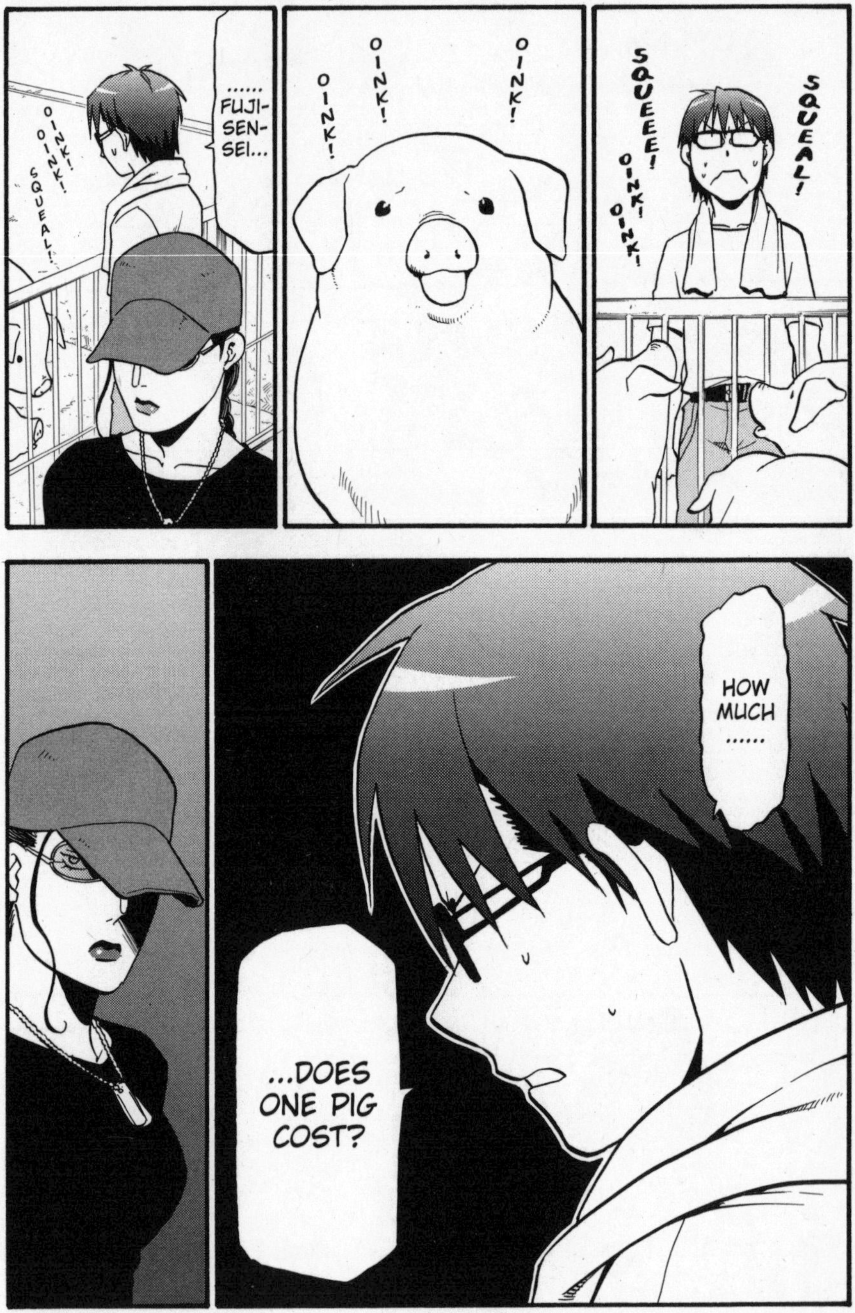
SQUEAL!
SQUEEEE!
OINK! OINK!
OINK!
OINK!
OINK!
......FUJI-SENSEI...
OINK! OINK!
SQUEAL!
HOW MUCH ......
...DOES ONE PIG COST?

Silver Spoon

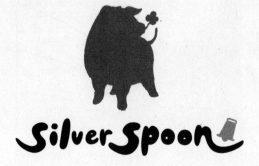

AKI MIKAGE

SHIMIZU FIRST
MIDDLE SCHOOL

EQUESTRIAN CLUB

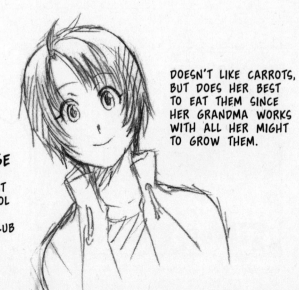

DOESN'T LIKE CARROTS,
BUT DOES HER BEST
TO EAT THEM SINCE
HER GRANDMA WORKS
WITH ALL HER MIGHT
TO GROW THEM.

Chapter 26:

Tale of Summer ⑯

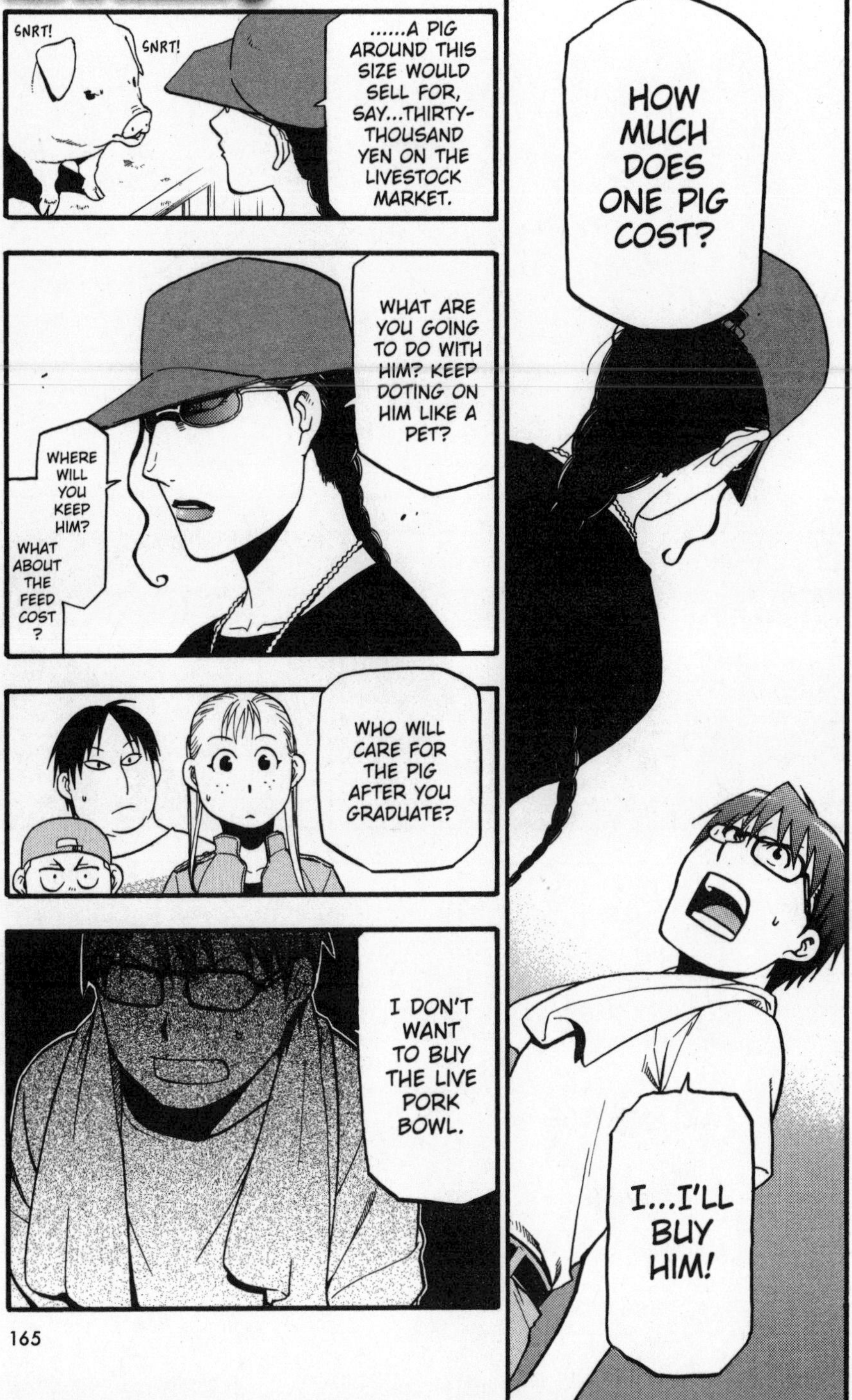

HOW MUCH DOES ONE PIG COST?
I...I'LL BUY HIM!
......A PIG AROUND THIS SIZE WOULD SELL FOR, SAY...THIRTY-THOUSAND YEN ON THE LIVESTOCK MARKET.
SNRT!
SNRT!
WHAT ARE YOU GOING TO DO WITH HIM? KEEP DOTING ON HIM LIKE A PET?
WHERE WILL YOU KEEP HIM? WHAT ABOUT THE FEED COST?
WHO WILL CARE FOR THE PIG AFTER YOU GRADUATE?
I DON'T WANT TO BUY THE LIVE PORK BOWL.

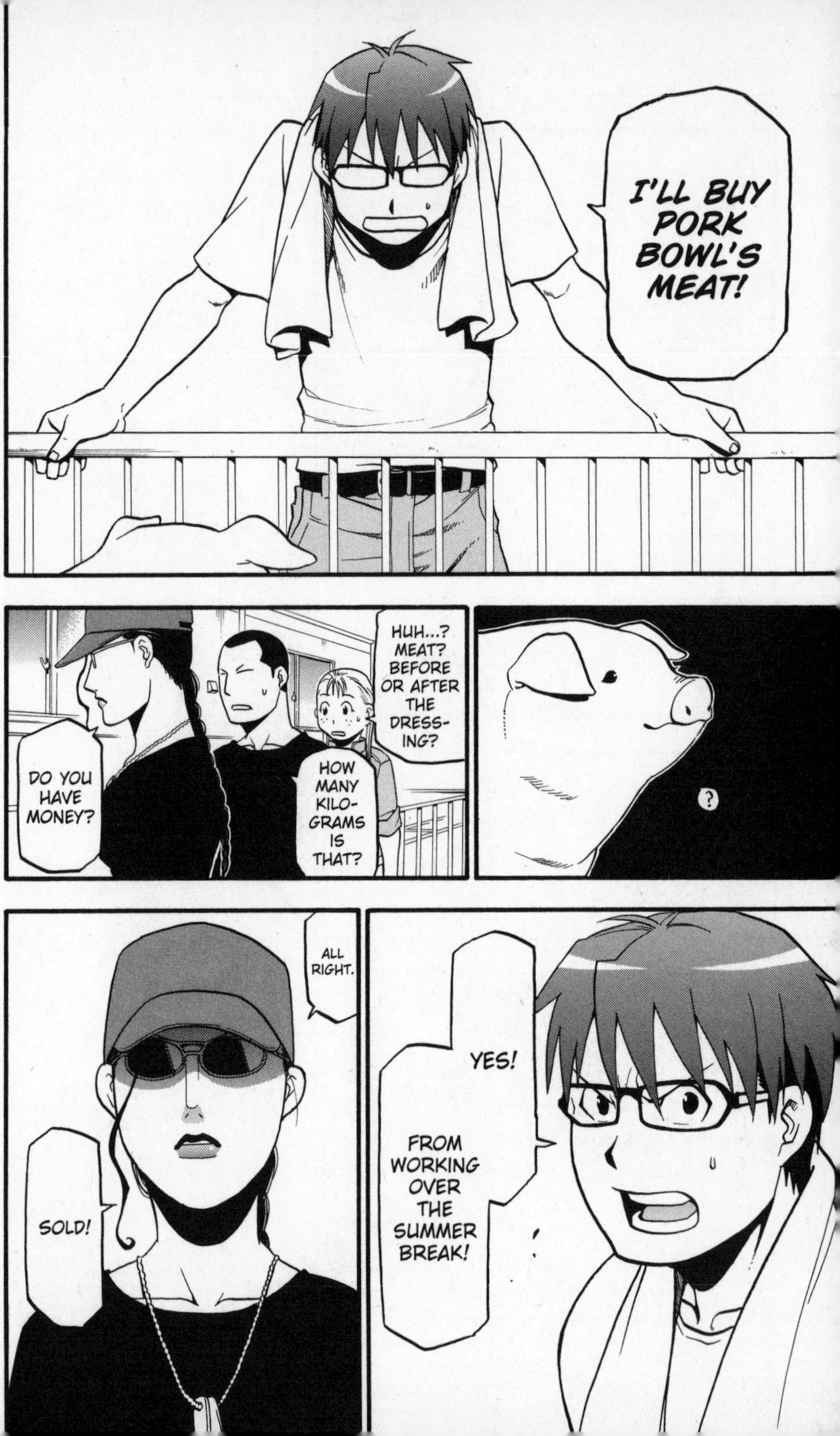
I'LL BUY PORK BOWL'S MEAT!
?
HUH...? MEAT? BEFORE OR AFTER THE DRESSING?
HOW MANY KILOGRAMS IS THAT?
DO YOU HAVE MONEY?
YES!
FROM WORKING OVER THE SUMMER BREAK!
ALL RIGHT.
SOLD!

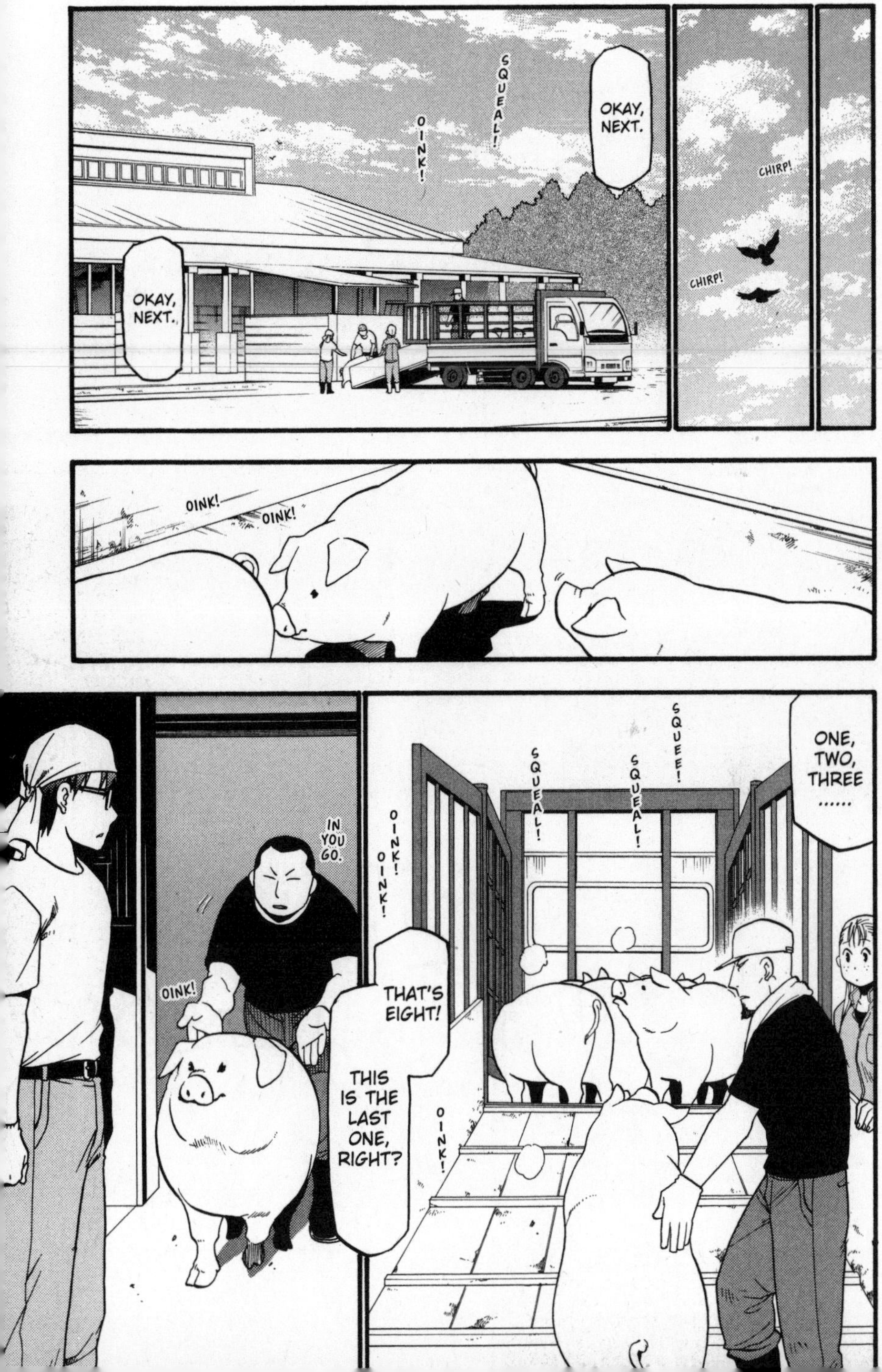
CHIRP!
CHIRP!
OKAY, NEXT.
SQUEAL!
OINK!
OKAY, NEXT.
OINK!
OINK!
ONE, TWO, THREE ......
SQUEE!
SQUEAL!
SQUEAL!
OINK!
IN YOU GO.
OINK!
OINK!
OINK!
THAT'S EIGHT!
THIS IS THE LAST ONE, RIGHT?

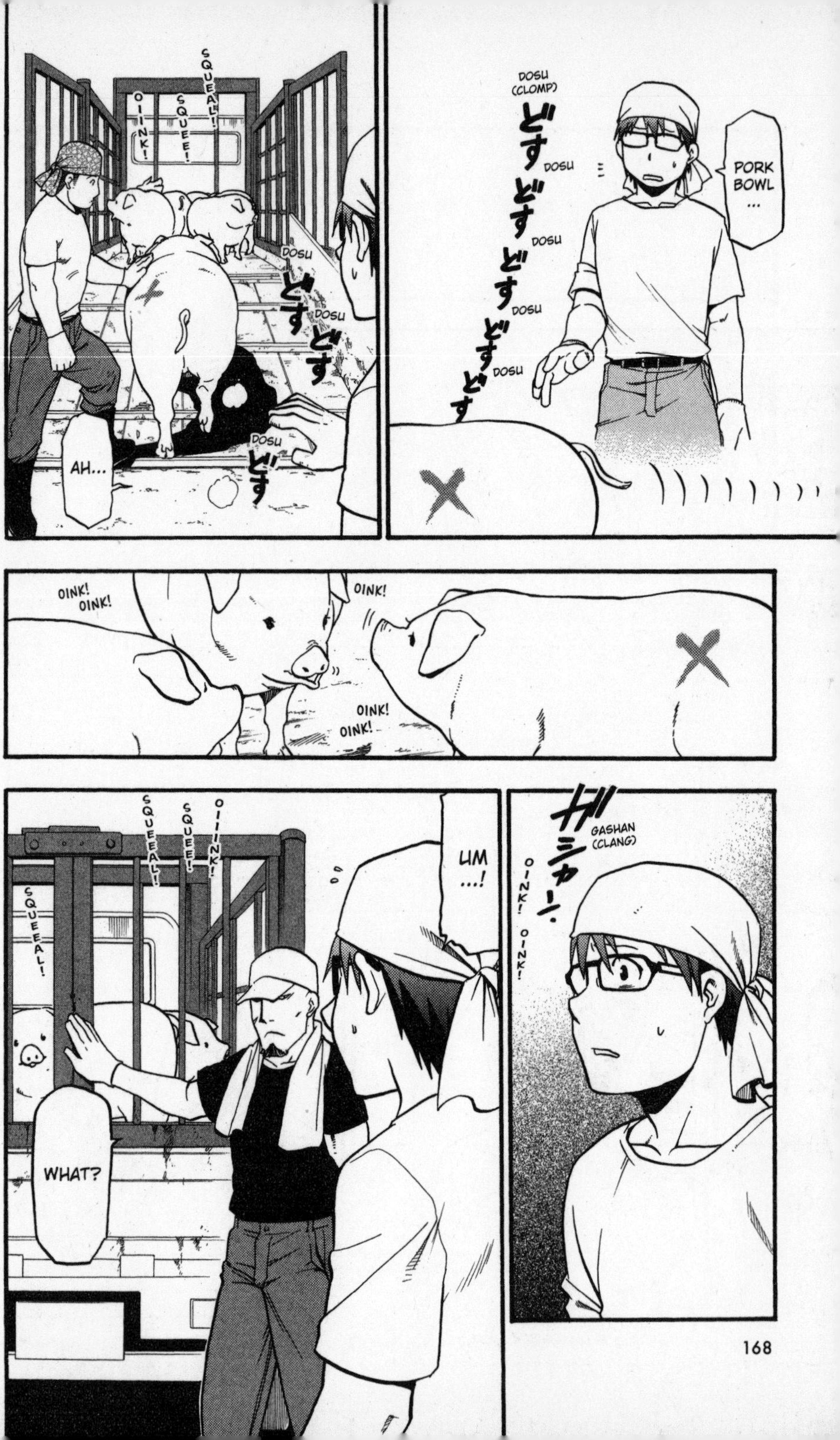
DOSU (CLOMP)
どす
DOSU
どす
DOSU
どす
DOSU
どす
DOSU
どす
PORK BOWL ...
SQUEAL!
SQUEEE!
OIIINK!
DOSU
どす
DOSU
どす
DOSU
どす
AH...
OINK! OINK!
OINK!
OINK! OINK!
GASHAN (CLANG)
ガシャン
OINK! OINK!
UM ...!
SQUEEAL!
SQUEEE!
OIIINK!
SQUEEEAL!
WHAT?

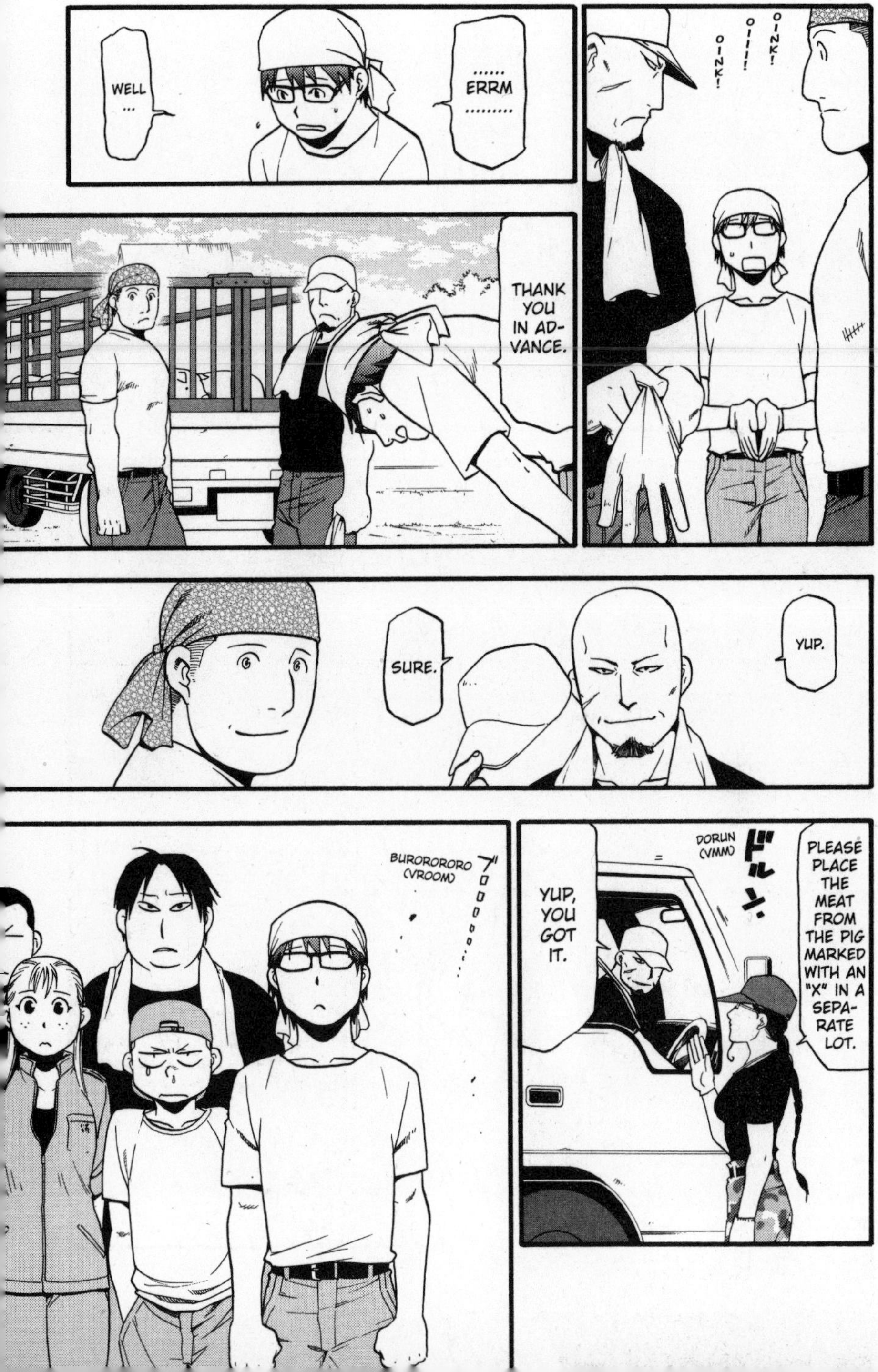
OINK! OINK! OIIII!
......ERRM.........
WELL...
THANK YOU IN ADVANCE.
YUP.
SURE.
PLEASE PLACE THE MEAT FROM THE PIG MARKED WITH AN "X" IN A SEPARATE LOT.
DORUN (VMM)
YUP, YOU GOT IT.
BURORORORO (VROOM)

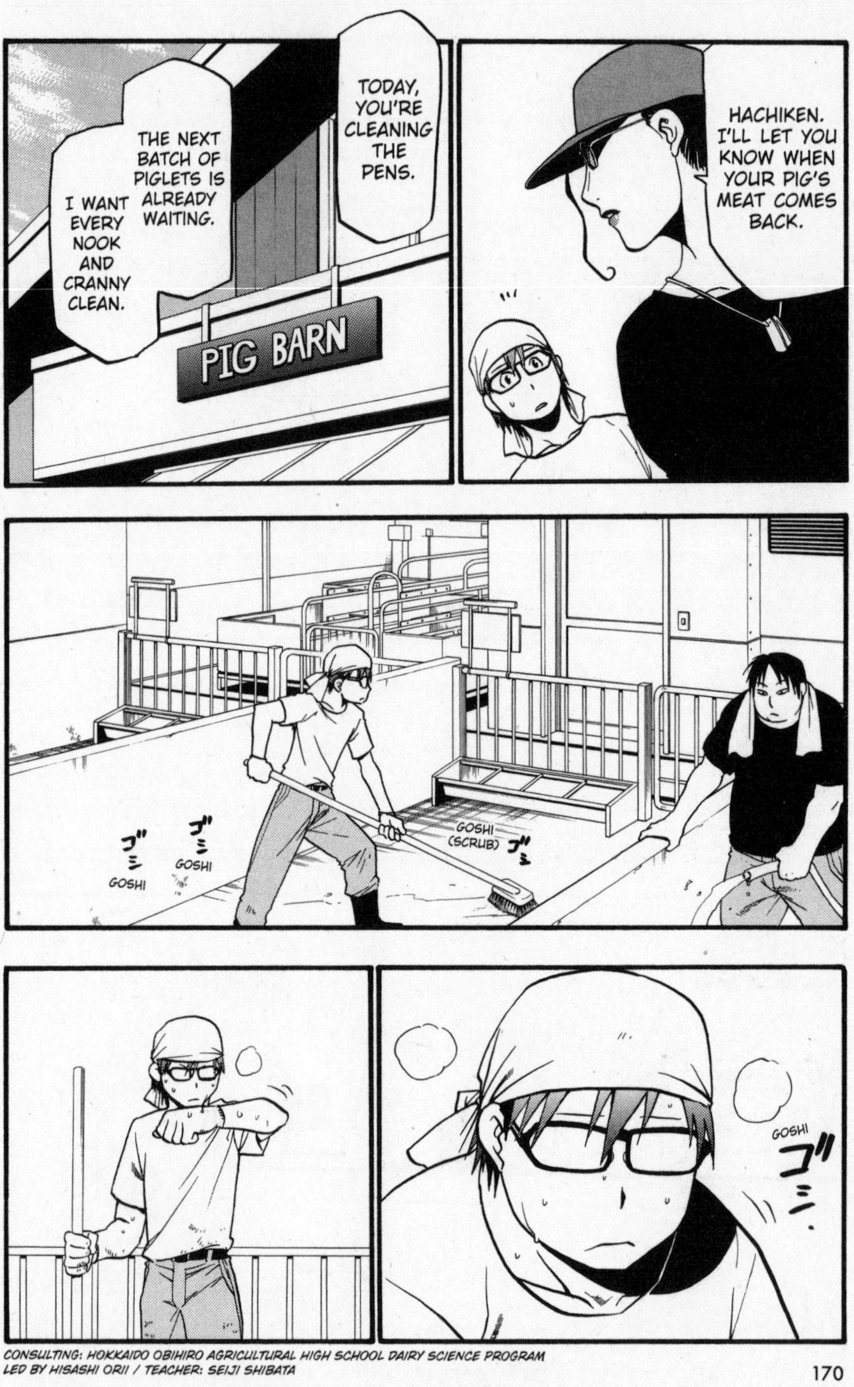
HACHIKEN. I'LL LET YOU KNOW WHEN YOUR PIG'S MEAT COMES BACK.
TODAY, YOU'RE CLEANING THE PENS.
THE NEXT BATCH OF PIGLETS IS ALREADY WAITING.
I WANT EVERY NOOK AND CRANNY CLEAN.
PIG BARN
ゴシ GOSHI (SCRUB)
ゴシ GOSHI
ゴシ GOSHI
ゴシ GOSHI

CONSULTING: HOKKAIDO OBIHIRO AGRICULTURAL HIGH SCHOOL DAIRY SCIENCE PROGRAM
LED BY HISASHI ORII / TEACHER: SEIJI SHIBATA

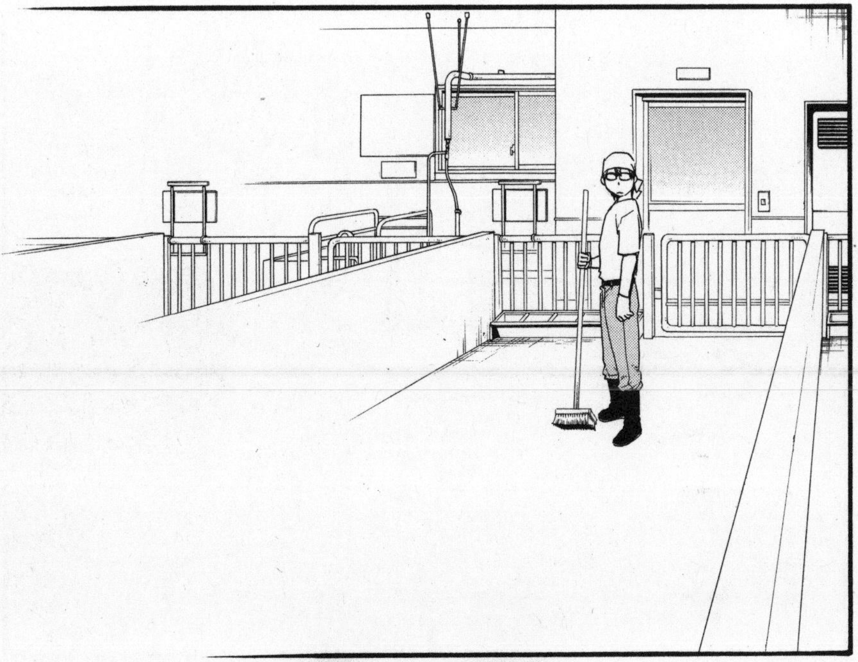

Chapter 26:
Tale of Summer ⑯

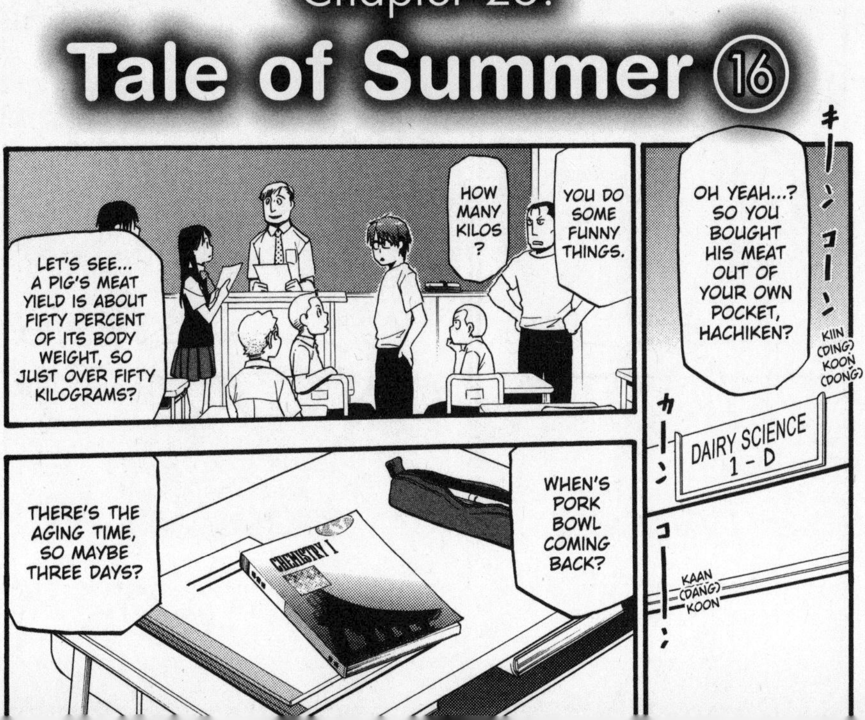
キーンコーン
KIIN (DING) KOON (DONG)
OH YEAH...? SO YOU BOUGHT HIS MEAT OUT OF YOUR OWN POCKET, HACHIKEN?
DAIRY SCIENCE 1 - D
カーンコーン
KAAN (DANG) KOON
YOU DO SOME FUNNY THINGS.
HOW MANY KILOS?
LET'S SEE... A PIG'S MEAT YIELD IS ABOUT FIFTY PERCENT OF ITS BODY WEIGHT, SO JUST OVER FIFTY KILOGRAMS?
WHEN'S PORK BOWL COMING BACK?
THERE'S THE AGING TIME, SO MAYBE THREE DAYS?
CHEMISTRY I

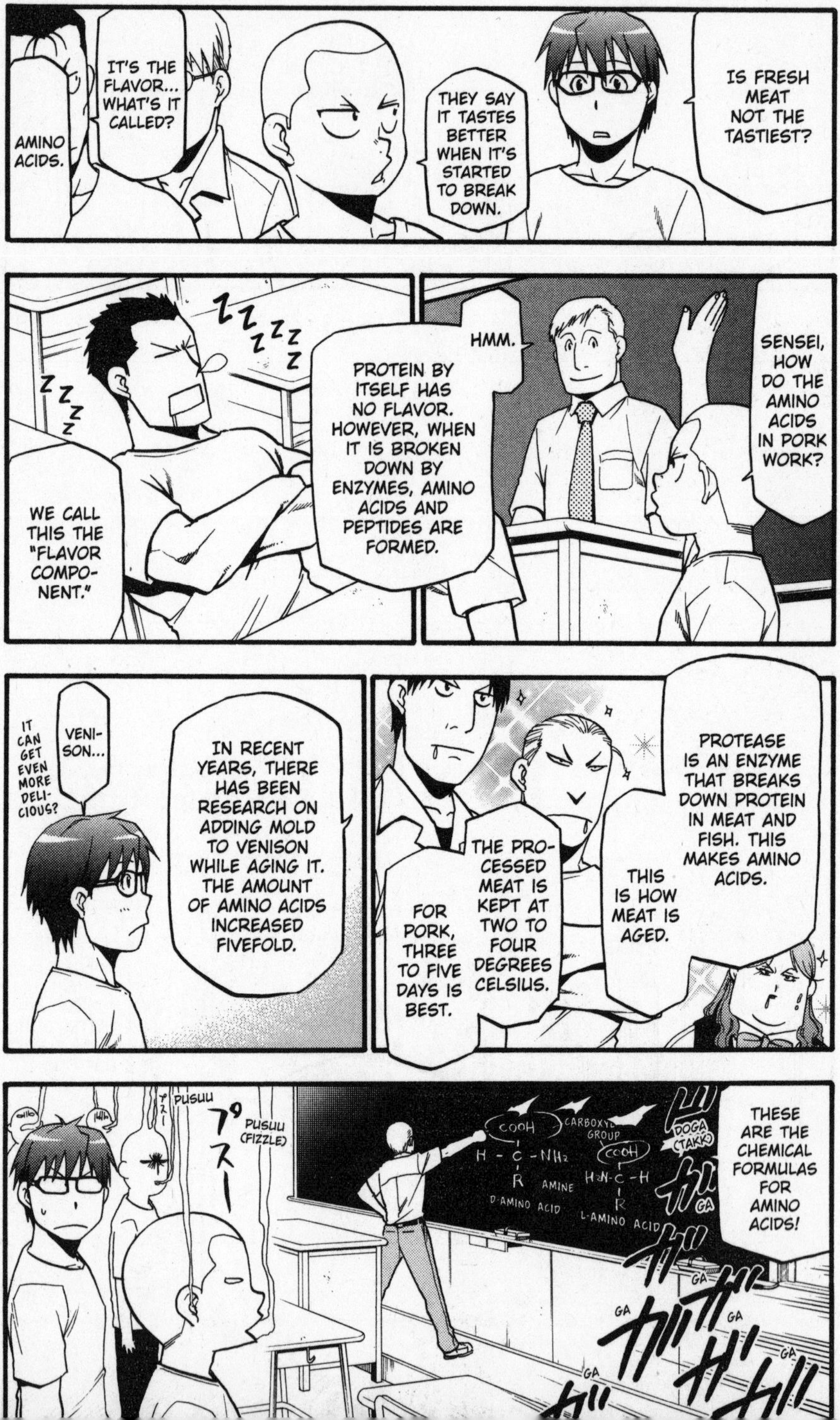
IS FRESH MEAT NOT THE TASTIEST?
THEY SAY IT TASTES BETTER WHEN IT'S STARTED TO BREAK DOWN.
IT'S THE FLAVOR... WHAT'S IT CALLED?
AMINO ACIDS.
SENSEI, HOW DO THE AMINO ACIDS IN PORK WORK?
HMM.
PROTEIN BY ITSELF HAS NO FLAVOR. HOWEVER, WHEN IT IS BROKEN DOWN BY ENZYMES, AMINO ACIDS AND PEPTIDES ARE FORMED.
Z Z Z Z Z Z
WE CALL THIS THE "FLAVOR COMPONENT."
Z Z Z Z
PROTEASE IS AN ENZYME THAT BREAKS DOWN PROTEIN IN MEAT AND FISH. THIS MAKES AMINO ACIDS.
THIS IS HOW MEAT IS AGED.
THE PROCESSED MEAT IS KEPT AT TWO TO FOUR DEGREES CELSIUS.
FOR PORK, THREE TO FIVE DAYS IS BEST.
IN RECENT YEARS, THERE HAS BEEN RESEARCH ON ADDING MOLD TO VENISON WHILE AGING IT. THE AMOUNT OF AMINO ACIDS INCREASED FIVEFOLD.
VENI-SON...
IT CAN GET EVEN MORE DELICIOUS?
THESE ARE THE CHEMICAL FORMULAS FOR AMINO ACIDS!
DOGA (TAKK)
GA
GA
GA
GA
GA
COOH
CARBOXYL GROUP
H - C - NH2
R
AMINE
D-AMINO ACID
COOH
H2N - C - H
R
L-AMINO ACID
PUSUU (FIZZLE)
PUSUU

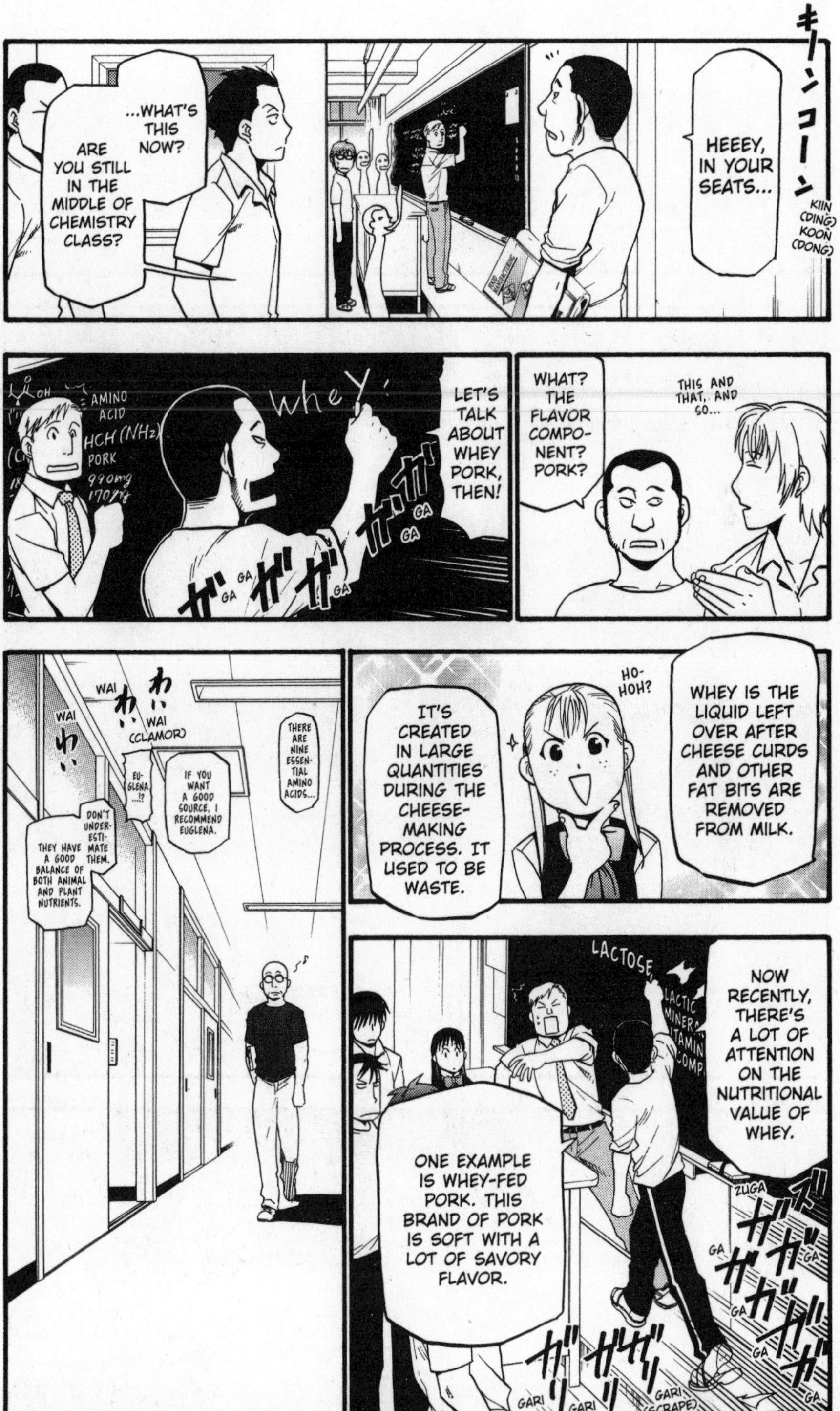
KIIN (DING) KOON (DONG)
HEEEY, IN YOUR SEATS...
...WHAT'S THIS NOW?
ARE YOU STILL IN THE MIDDLE OF CHEMISTRY CLASS?
WHAT? THE FLAVOR COMPONENT? PORK?
THIS AND THAT, AND SO...
LET'S TALK ABOUT WHEY PORK, THEN!
whey
AMINO ACID
HCH (NH2)
PORK
990mg
170mg
GA GA GA GA GA GA
WHEY IS THE LIQUID LEFT OVER AFTER CHEESE CURDS AND OTHER FAT BITS ARE REMOVED FROM MILK.
HO-HOH?
IT'S CREATED IN LARGE QUANTITIES DURING THE CHEESE-MAKING PROCESS. IT USED TO BE WASTE.
NOW RECENTLY, THERE'S A LOT OF ATTENTION ON THE NUTRITIONAL VALUE OF WHEY.
LACTOSE
LACTIC
MINERA
TAMIN
COMP.
ONE EXAMPLE IS WHEY-FED PORK. THIS BRAND OF PORK IS SOFT WITH A LOT OF SAVORY FLAVOR.
ZUGA
GA GA GA GA
GARI GARI GARI (SCRAPE)
WAI WAI WAI (CLAMOR)
There are nine essential amino acids...
If you want a good source, I recommend euglena.
Euglena...!?
Don't underestimate them.
They have a good balance of both animal and plant nutrients.

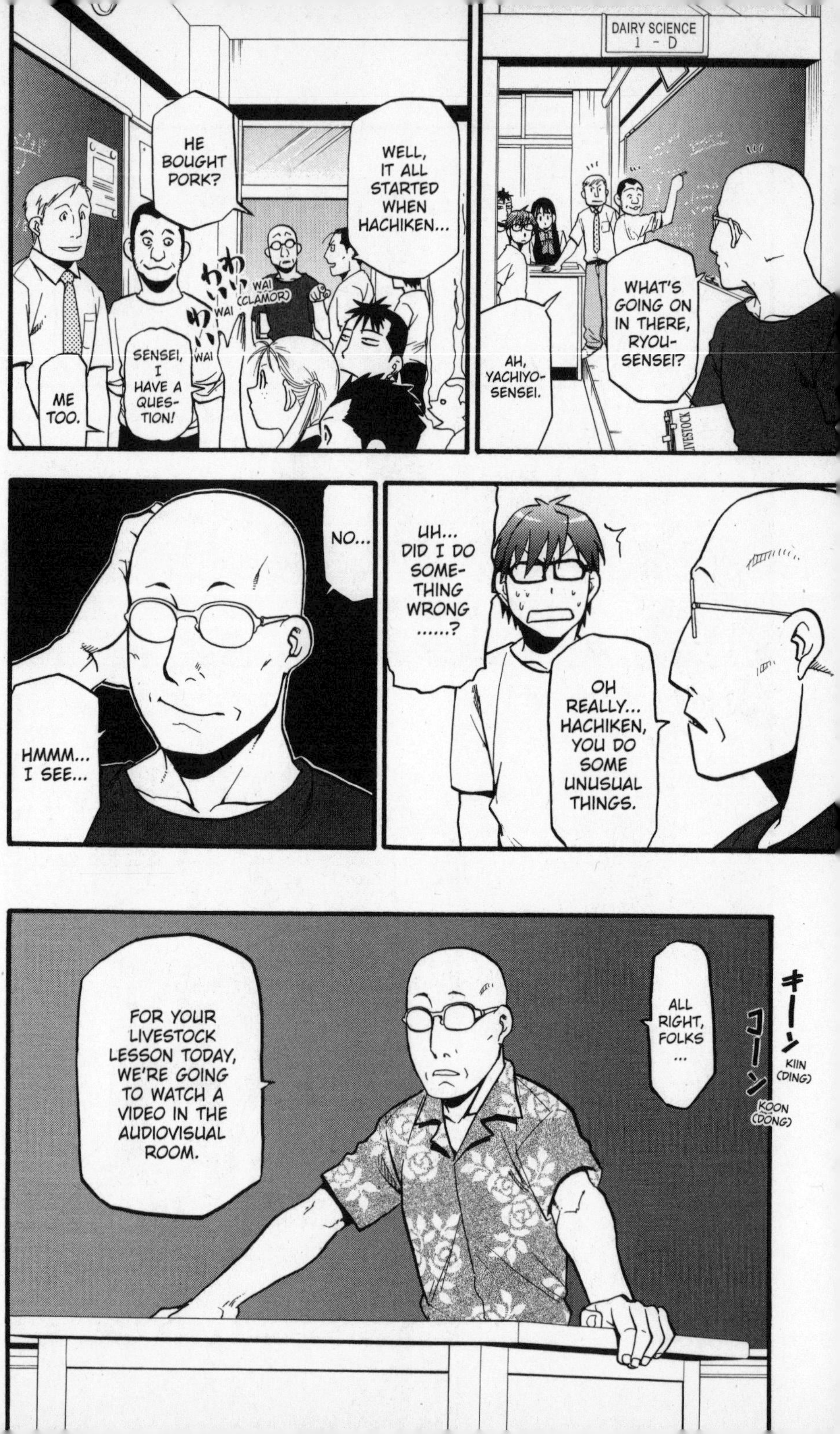

DAIRY SCIENCE 1 - D
WHAT'S GOING ON IN THERE, RYOU-SENSEI?
AH, YACHIYO-SENSEI.
LIVESTOCK
WELL, IT ALL STARTED WHEN HACHIKEN...
HE BOUGHT PORK?
WAI (CLAMOR)
WAI
WAI
SENSEI, I HAVE A QUESTION!
ME TOO.
UH... DID I DO SOMETHING WRONG ......?
OH REALLY... HACHIKEN, YOU DO SOME UNUSUAL THINGS.
NO...
HMMM... I SEE...
KIIN (DING)
KOON (DONG)
ALL RIGHT, FOLKS ...
FOR YOUR LIVESTOCK LESSON TODAY, WE'RE GOING TO WATCH A VIDEO IN THE AUDIOVISUAL ROOM.

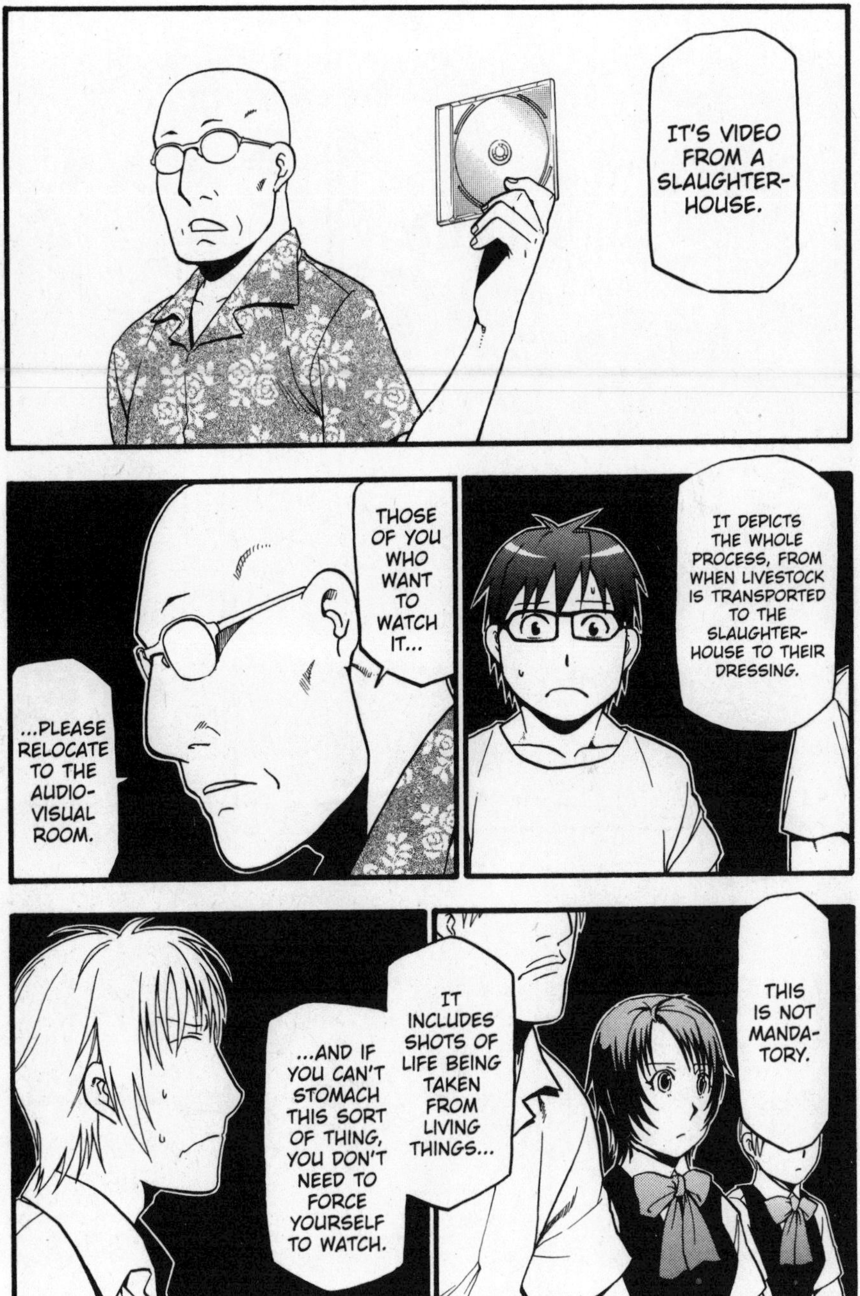
IT'S VIDEO FROM A SLAUGHTER-HOUSE.
IT DEPICTS THE WHOLE PROCESS, FROM WHEN LIVESTOCK IS TRANSPORTED TO THE SLAUGHTER-HOUSE TO THEIR DRESSING.
THOSE OF YOU WHO WANT TO WATCH IT...
...PLEASE RELOCATE TO THE AUDIO-VISUAL ROOM.
THIS IS NOT MANDA-TORY.
IT INCLUDES SHOTS OF LIFE BEING TAKEN FROM LIVING THINGS...
...AND IF YOU CAN'T STOMACH THIS SORT OF THING, YOU DON'T NEED TO FORCE YOURSELF TO WATCH.

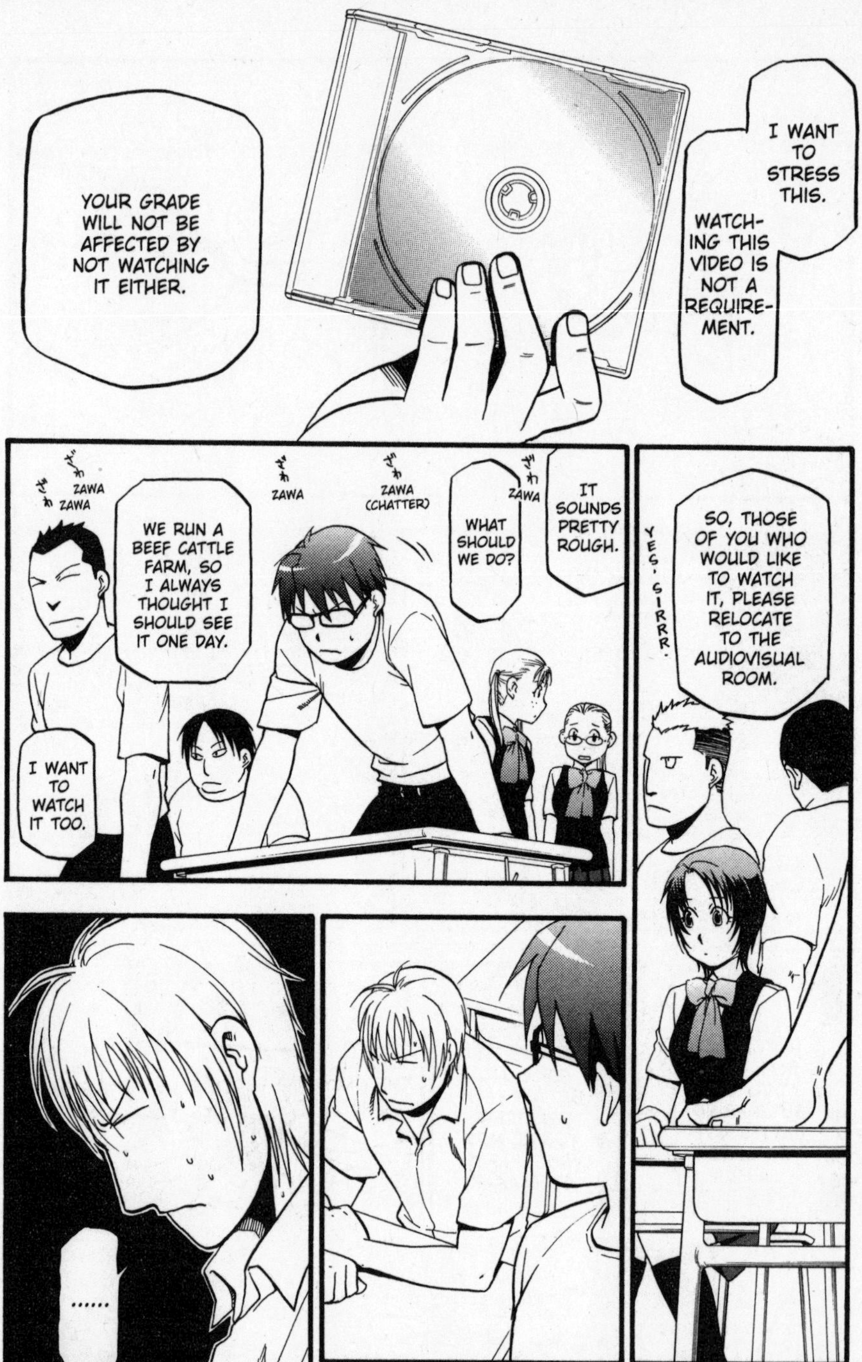
I WANT TO STRESS THIS.
WATCHING THIS VIDEO IS NOT A REQUIREMENT.
YOUR GRADE WILL NOT BE AFFECTED BY NOT WATCHING IT EITHER.
SO, THOSE OF YOU WHO WOULD LIKE TO WATCH IT, PLEASE RELOCATE TO THE AUDIOVISUAL ROOM.
YES, SIRRR.
ZAWA
IT SOUNDS PRETTY ROUGH.
WHAT SHOULD WE DO?
ZAWA (CHATTER)
ZAWA
WE RUN A BEEF CATTLE FARM, SO I ALWAYS THOUGHT I SHOULD SEE IT ONE DAY.
ZAWA ZAWA
I WANT TO WATCH IT TOO.
......

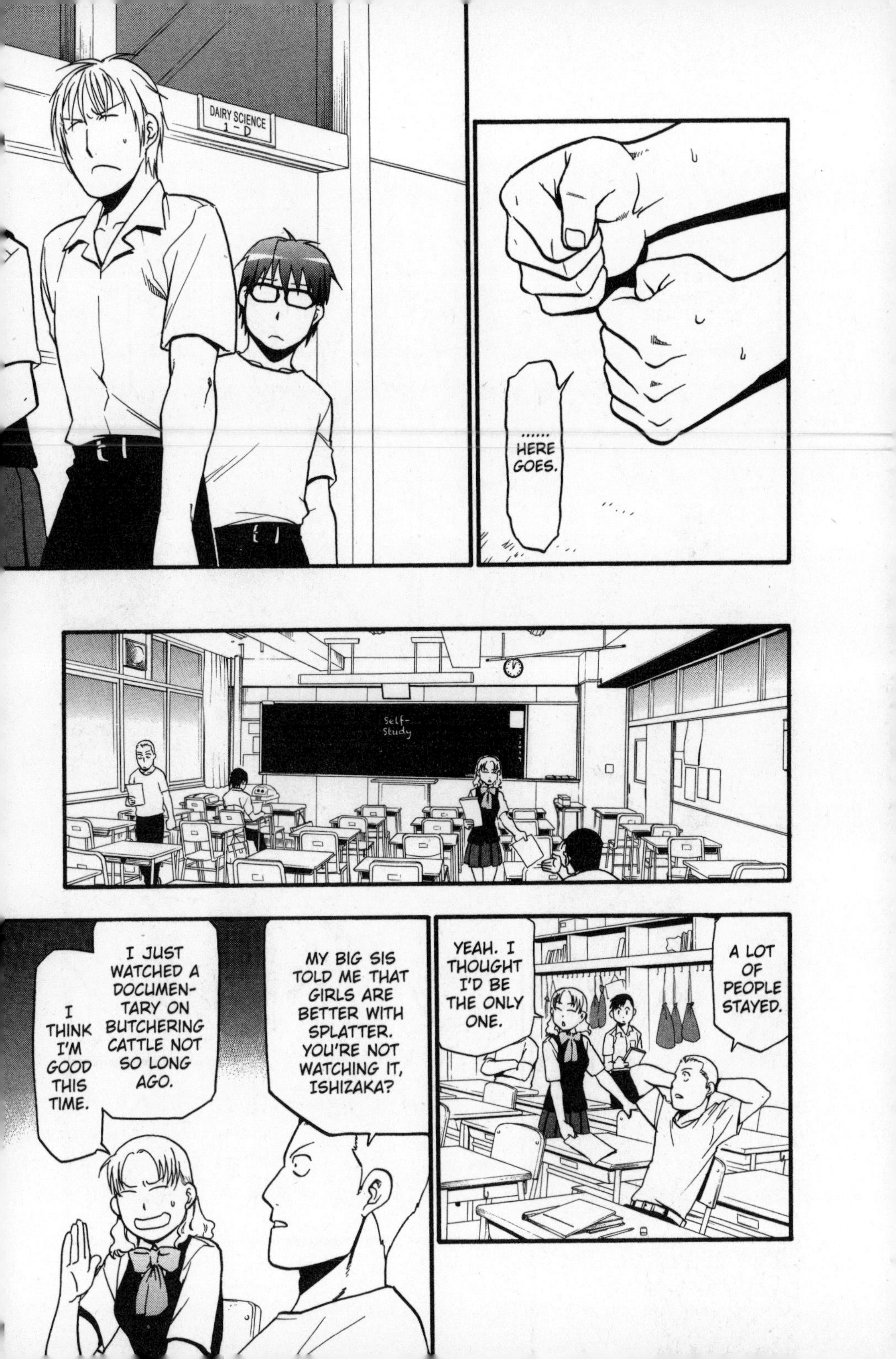
......HERE GOES.
DAIRY SCIENCE 1-D
Self-Study
A LOT OF PEOPLE STAYED.
YEAH. I THOUGHT I'D BE THE ONLY ONE.
MY BIG SIS TOLD ME THAT GIRLS ARE BETTER WITH SPLATTER. YOU'RE NOT WATCHING IT, ISHIZAKA?
I THINK I'M GOOD THIS TIME. I JUST WATCHED A DOCUMENTARY ON BUTCHERING CATTLE NOT SO LONG AGO.

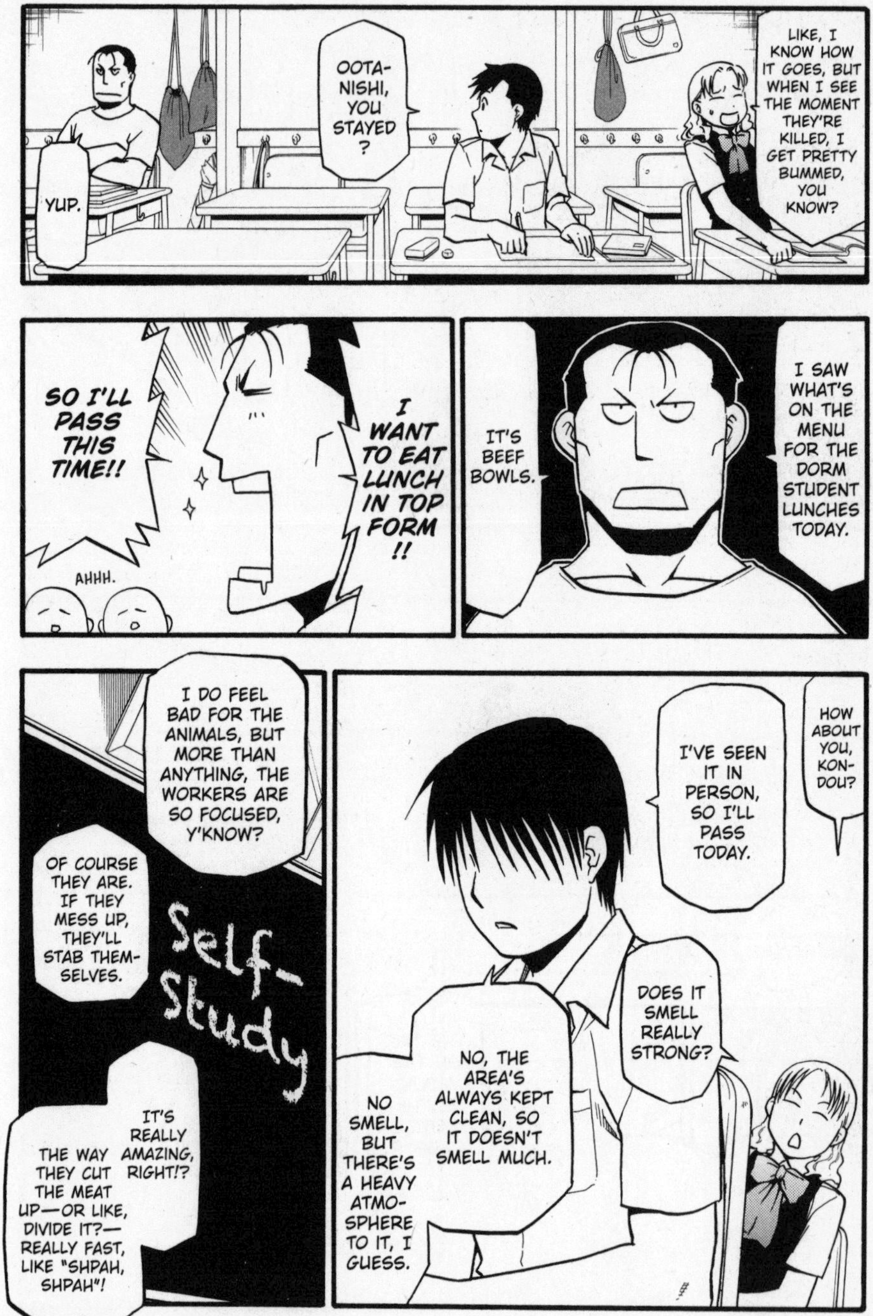
LIKE, I KNOW HOW IT GOES, BUT WHEN I SEE THE MOMENT THEY'RE KILLED, I GET PRETTY BUMMED, YOU KNOW?
OOTA-NISHI, YOU STAYED?
YUP.
I SAW WHAT'S ON THE MENU FOR THE DORM STUDENT LUNCHES TODAY.
IT'S BEEF BOWLS.
I WANT TO EAT LUNCH IN TOP FORM!!
SO I'LL PASS THIS TIME!!
AHHH.
HOW ABOUT YOU, KON-DOU?
I'VE SEEN IT IN PERSON, SO I'LL PASS TODAY.
DOES IT SMELL REALLY STRONG?
NO, THE AREA'S ALWAYS KEPT CLEAN, SO IT DOESN'T SMELL MUCH.
NO SMELL, BUT THERE'S A HEAVY ATMO-SPHERE TO IT, I GUESS.
I DO FEEL BAD FOR THE ANIMALS, BUT MORE THAN ANYTHING, THE WORKERS ARE SO FOCUSED, Y'KNOW?
OF COURSE THEY ARE. IF THEY MESS UP, THEY'LL STAB THEM-SELVES.
Self-Study
IT'S REALLY AMAZING, RIGHT!?
THE WAY THEY CUT THE MEAT UP—OR LIKE, DIVIDE IT?—REALLY FAST, LIKE "SHPAH, SHPAH"!

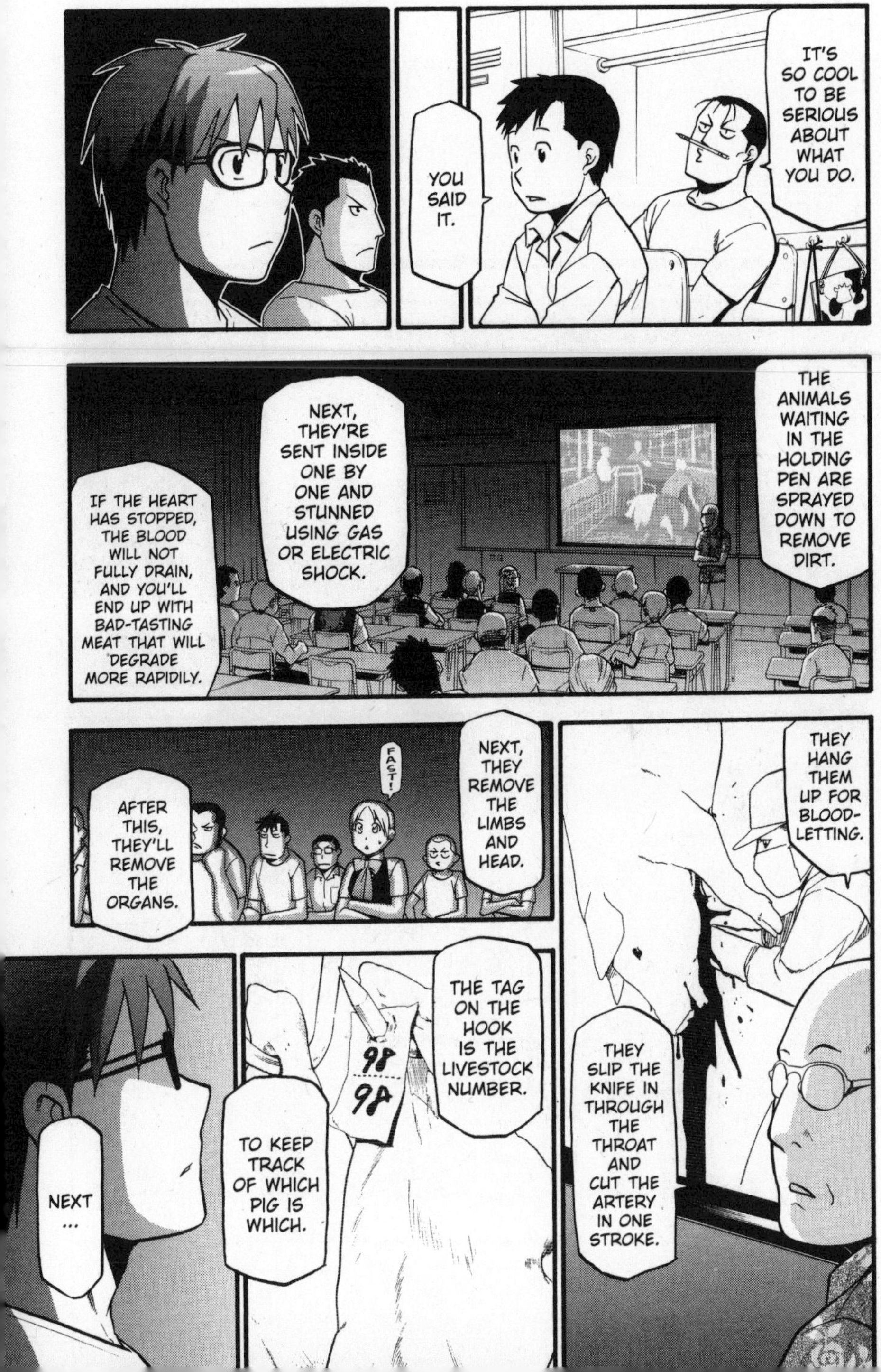
IT'S SO COOL TO BE SERIOUS ABOUT WHAT YOU DO.
YOU SAID IT.
THE ANIMALS WAITING IN THE HOLDING PEN ARE SPRAYED DOWN TO REMOVE DIRT.
NEXT, THEY'RE SENT INSIDE ONE BY ONE AND STUNNED USING GAS OR ELECTRIC SHOCK.
IF THE HEART HAS STOPPED, THE BLOOD WILL NOT FULLY DRAIN, AND YOU'LL END UP WITH BAD-TASTING MEAT THAT WILL DEGRADE MORE RAPIDILY.
THEY HANG THEM UP FOR BLOOD-LETTING.
THEY SLIP THE KNIFE IN THROUGH THE THROAT AND CUT THE ARTERY IN ONE STROKE.
NEXT, THEY REMOVE THE LIMBS AND HEAD.
FAST!
AFTER THIS, THEY'LL REMOVE THE ORGANS.
THE TAG ON THE HOOK IS THE LIVESTOCK NUMBER.
98
98
TO KEEP TRACK OF WHICH PIG IS WHICH.
NEXT ...

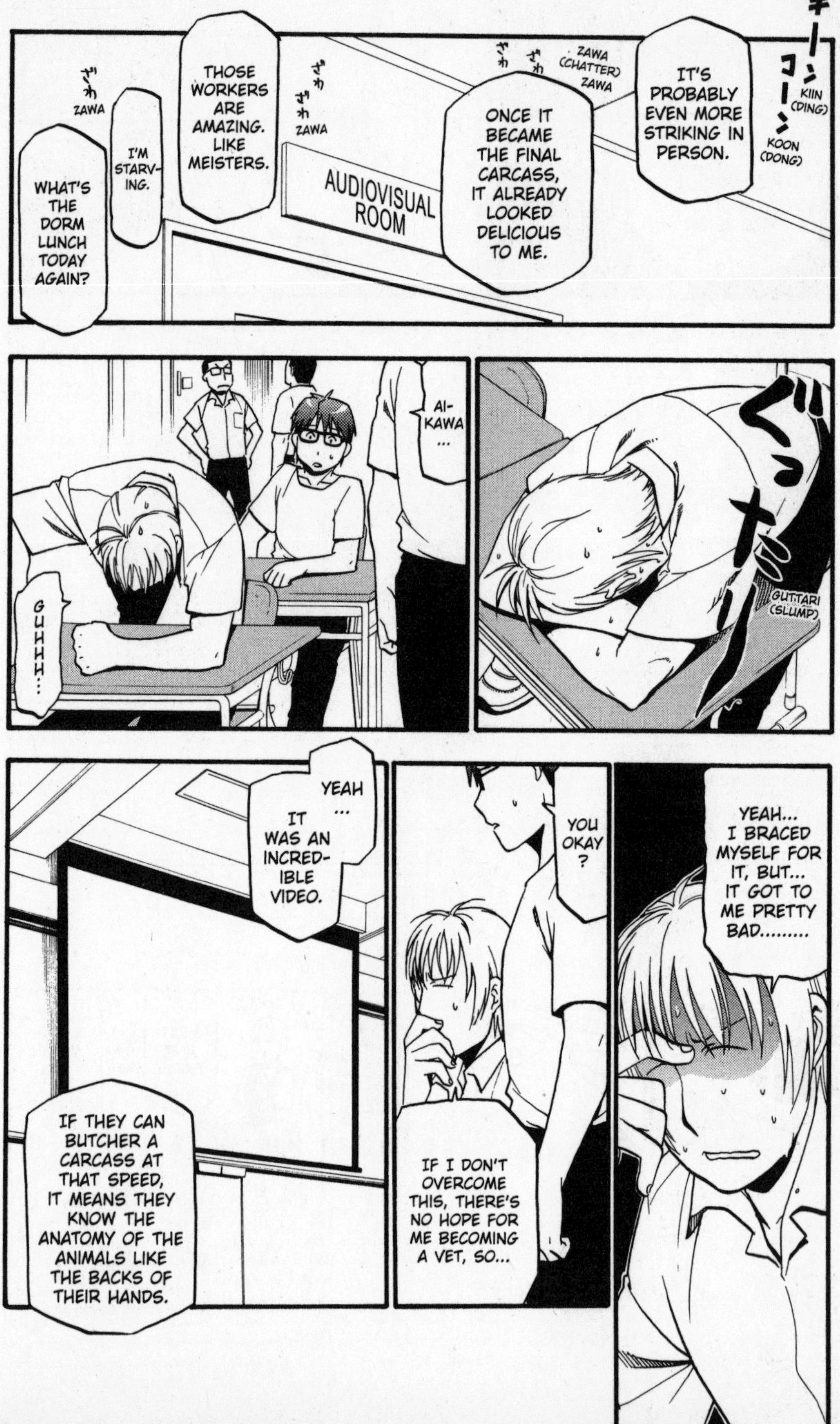
KIIN (DING)
KOON (DONG)
IT'S PROBABLY EVEN MORE STRIKING IN PERSON.
ZAWA (CHATTER) ZAWA
ONCE IT BECAME THE FINAL CARCASS, IT ALREADY LOOKED DELICIOUS TO ME.
AUDIOVISUAL ROOM
ZAWA
THOSE WORKERS ARE AMAZING. LIKE MEISTERS.
ZAWA
I'M STARV-ING.
WHAT'S THE DORM LUNCH TODAY AGAIN?
GUTTARI (SLUMP)
AI-KAWA...
GUHHH...
YEAH... I BRACED MYSELF FOR IT, BUT... IT GOT TO ME PRETTY BAD.........
YOU OKAY?
IF I DON'T OVERCOME THIS, THERE'S NO HOPE FOR ME BECOMING A VET, SO...
YEAH... IT WAS AN INCRED-IBLE VIDEO.
IF THEY CAN BUTCHER A CARCASS AT THAT SPEED, IT MEANS THEY KNOW THE ANATOMY OF THE ANIMALS LIKE THE BACKS OF THEIR HANDS.

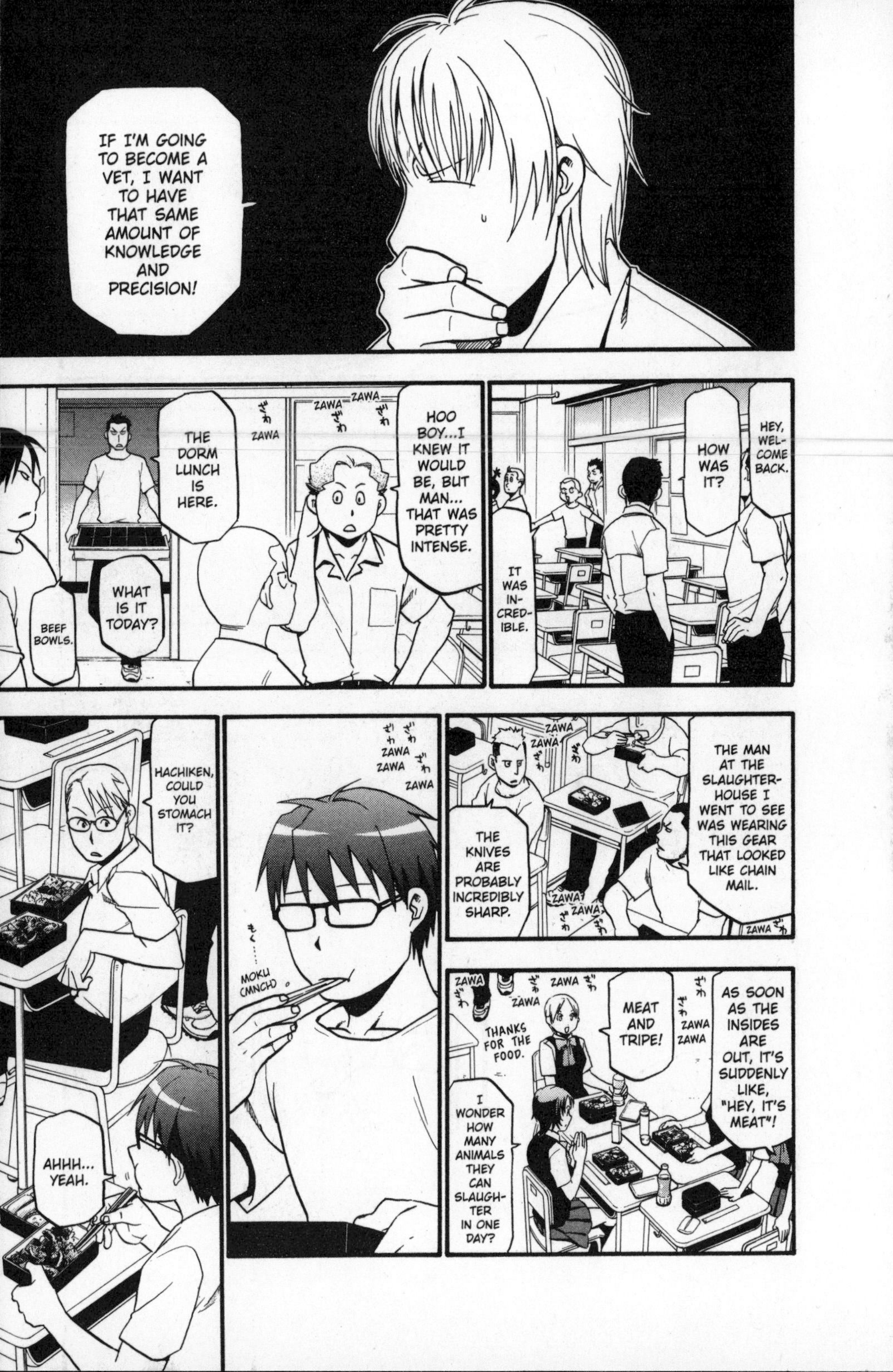

IF I'M GOING TO BECOME A VET, I WANT TO HAVE THAT SAME AMOUNT OF KNOWLEDGE AND PRECISION!
HEY, WELCOME BACK.
HOW WAS IT?
IT WAS INCREDIBLE.
ZAWA ZAWA ZAWA
HOO BOY...I KNEW IT WOULD BE, BUT MAN... THAT WAS PRETTY INTENSE.
THE DORM LUNCH IS HERE.
WHAT IS IT TODAY?
BEEF BOWLS.
THE MAN AT THE SLAUGHTER-HOUSE I WENT TO SEE WAS WEARING THIS GEAR THAT LOOKED LIKE CHAIN MAIL.
THE KNIVES ARE PROBABLY INCREDIBLY SHARP.
ZAWA ZAWA ZAWA ZAWA
AS SOON AS THE INSIDES ARE OUT, IT'S SUDDENLY LIKE, "HEY, IT'S MEAT"!
MEAT AND TRIPE!
ZAWA ZAWA ZAWA ZAWA ZAWA
THANKS FOR THE FOOD.
I WONDER HOW MANY ANIMALS THEY CAN SLAUGHTER IN ONE DAY?
ZAWA ZAWA ZAWA
MOKU CMNCH
HACHIKEN, COULD YOU STOMACH IT?
AHHH... YEAH.

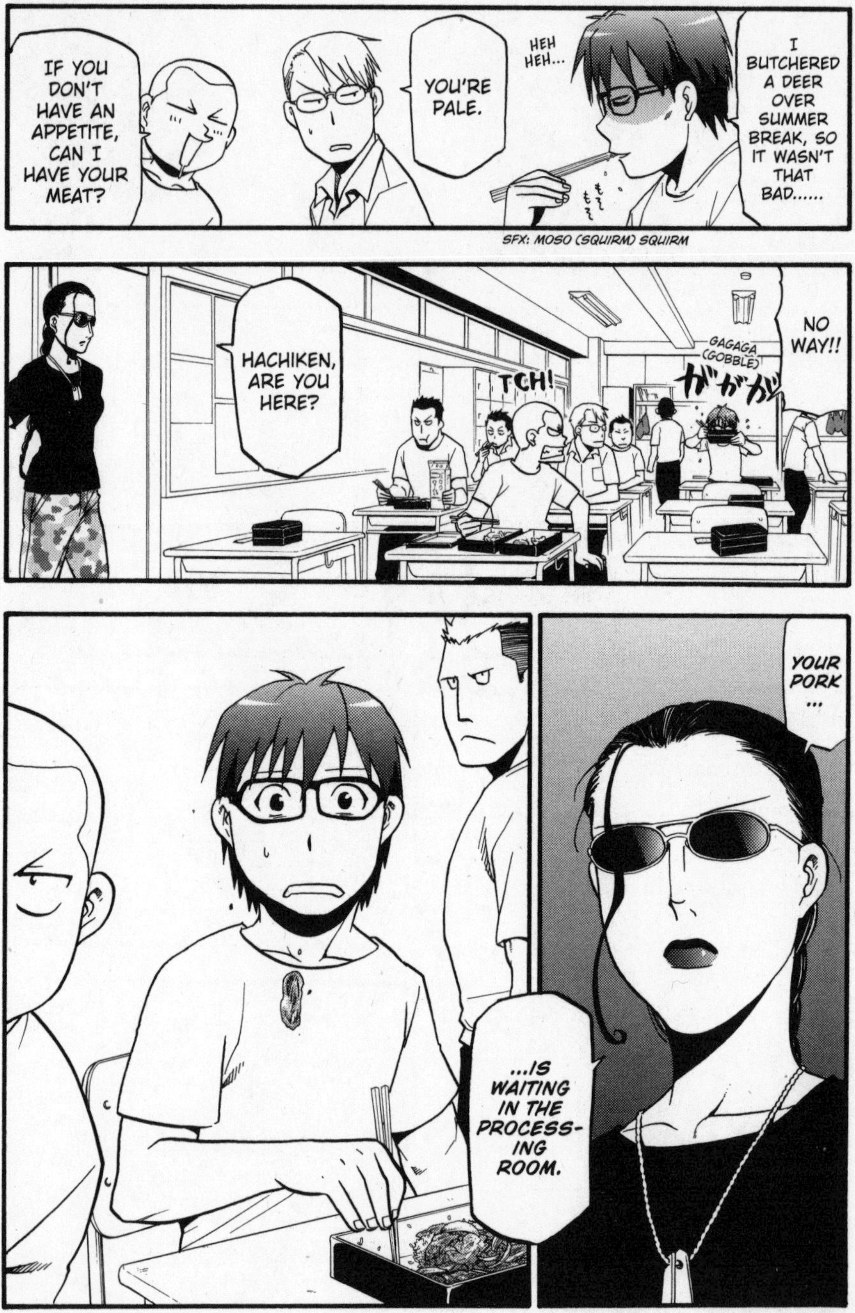
I BUTCHERED A DEER OVER SUMMER BREAK, SO IT WASN'T THAT BAD......
HEH HEH...
YOU'RE PALE.
IF YOU DON'T HAVE AN APPETITE, CAN I HAVE YOUR MEAT?
SFX: MOSO (SQUIRM) SQUIRM
NO WAY!!
GAGAGA (GOBBLE)
TCH!
HACHIKEN, ARE YOU HERE?
YOUR PORK ...
...IS WAITING IN THE PROCESSING ROOM.

Silver Spoon 3 • END

Silver Spoon

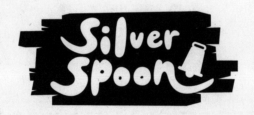

Since I Was Born a Manga Character...

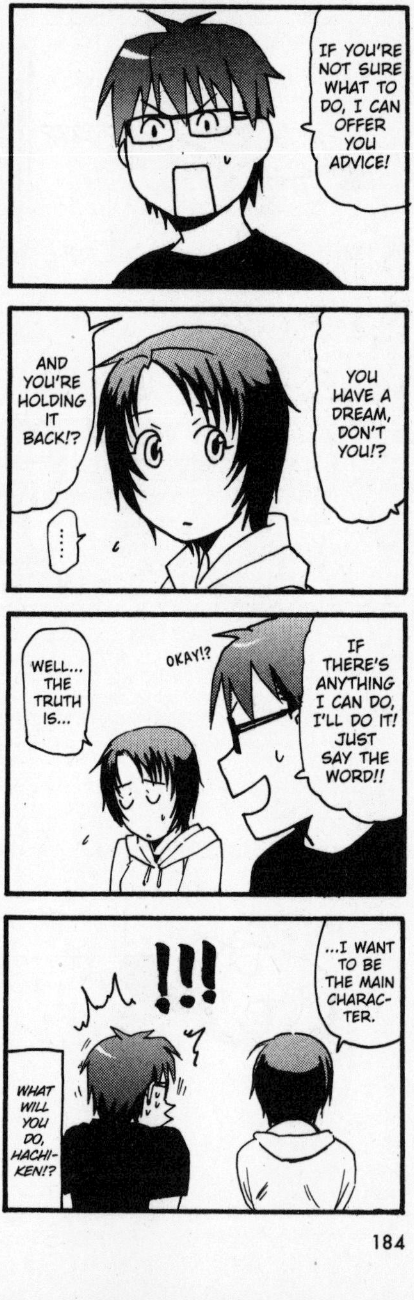
IF YOU'RE NOT SURE WHAT TO DO, I CAN OFFER YOU ADVICE!
YOU HAVE A DREAM, DON'T YOU!?
AND YOU'RE HOLDING IT BACK!?
......
IF THERE'S ANYTHING I CAN DO, I'LL DO IT! JUST SAY THE WORD!!
OKAY!?
WELL... THE TRUTH IS...
...I WANT TO BE THE MAIN CHARACTER.
!!!
WHAT WILL YOU DO, HACHIKEN!?

Secret

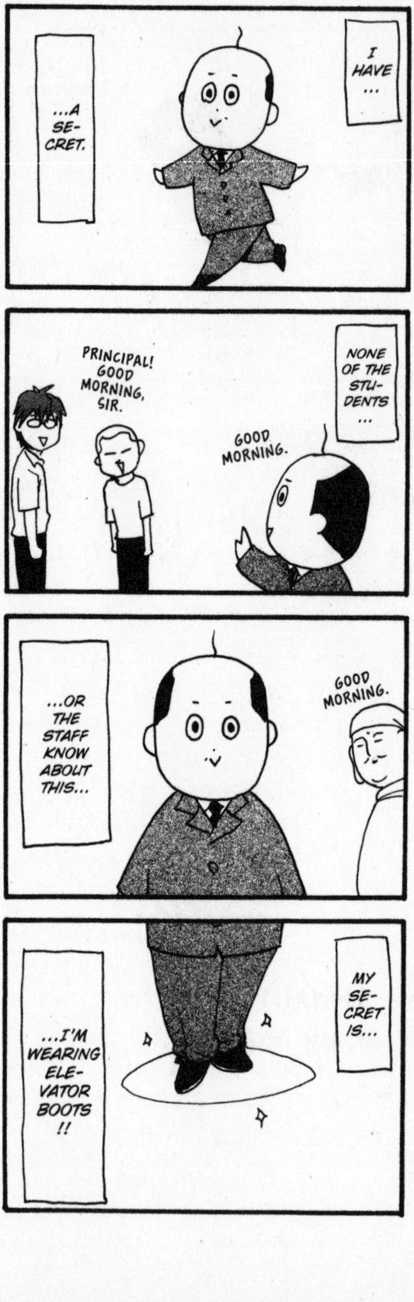
I HAVE...
...A SECRET.
NONE OF THE STUDENTS...
GOOD MORNING.
PRINCIPAL! GOOD MORNING, SIR.
GOOD MORNING.
...OR THE STAFF KNOW ABOUT THIS...
MY SECRET IS...
...I'M WEARING ELEVATOR BOOTS!!

Cow Shed Diaries: Tale of the Special Edition

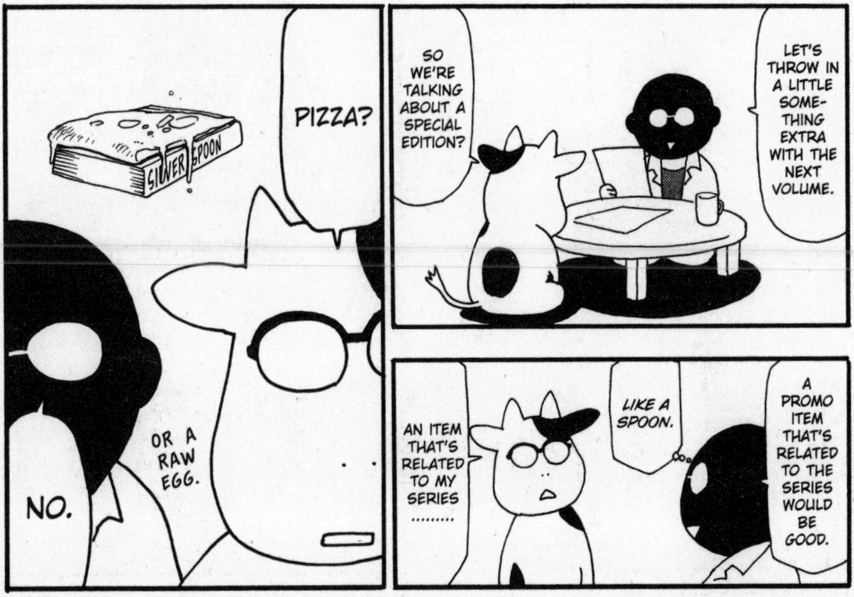
LET'S THROW IN A LITTLE SOME-THING EXTRA WITH THE NEXT VOLUME.
SO WE'RE TALKING ABOUT A SPECIAL EDITION?
A PROMO ITEM THAT'S RELATED TO THE SERIES WOULD BE GOOD.
LIKE A SPOON.
AN ITEM THAT'S RELATED TO MY SERIES ....
PIZZA?
SILVER SPOON
OR A RAW EGG.
NO.

Silver Spoon 3!
Thanks so much for reading. Fall begins in the next volume!
Look forward to it!

あらかわひろむ
Hiromu Arakawa

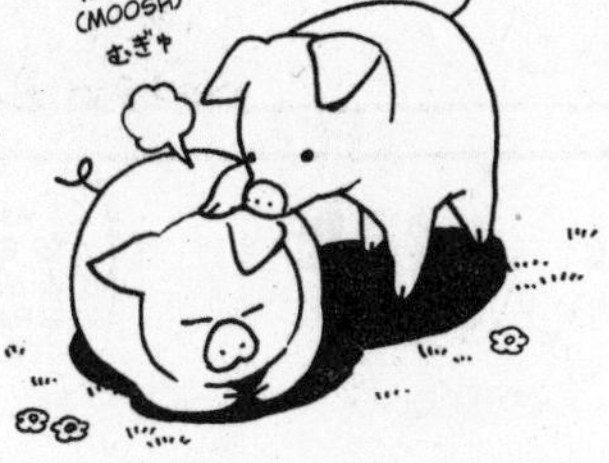
MUGYU (MOOSH)
むぎゅ

~ Special Thanks ~

All of my assistants,
Everyone who helped with collecting material and interviews,
My editor, Takashi Tsubouchi,

AND YOU!!

NEXT......

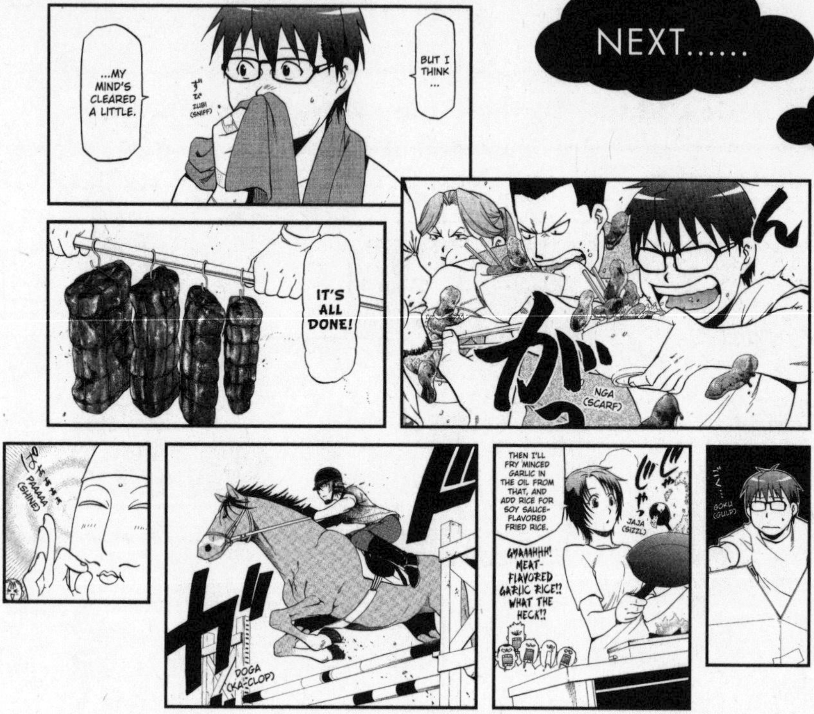
NGA (SCARF)
BUT I THINK ...
...MY MIND'S CLEARED A LITTLE.
ZUBI (SNIFF)
IT'S ALL DONE!
GOKU (GULP)
THEN I'LL FRY MINCED GARLIC IN THE OIL FROM THAT, AND ADD RICE FOR SOY SAUCE-FLAVORED FRIED RICE.
JAJA (SIZZL)
GYAAAHHH! MEAT-FLAVORED GARLIC RICE!? WHAT THE HECK!!
DOGA (KA-CLOP)
PAAAAA (SHINE)

Hachiken eats.
Because he'd loved it...
Because he needs to properly taste it...
Hachiken ponders.
What is the weight of life...?
What can one insignificant boy do...?

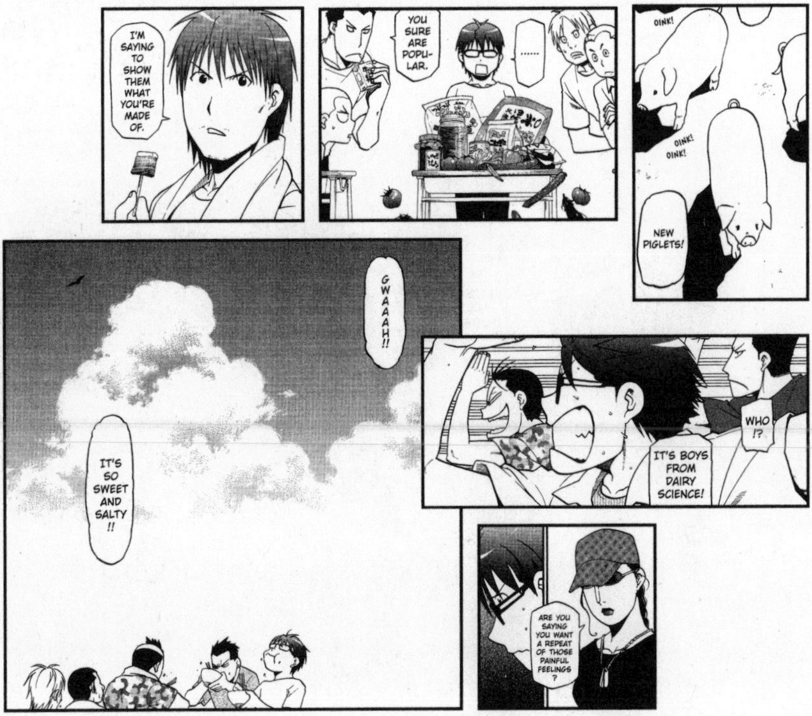
OINK!
OINK! OINK!
NEW PIGLETS!
YOU SURE ARE POPULAR.
......
I'M SAYING TO SHOW THEM WHAT YOU'RE MADE OF.
WHO!?
IT'S BOYS FROM DAIRY SCIENCE!
ARE YOU SAYING YOU WANT A REPEAT OF THOSE PAINFUL FEELINGS?
GWAAAAH!!
IT'S SO SWEET AND SALTY!!

Then Hachiken's first summer comes to a close. And the seasons change to a fall of harvests—

Silver Spoon **Volume 4 coming August 2018!!**

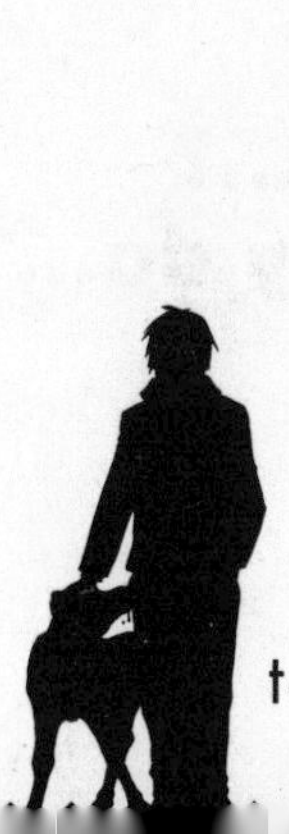

to be continued......

Silver Spoon

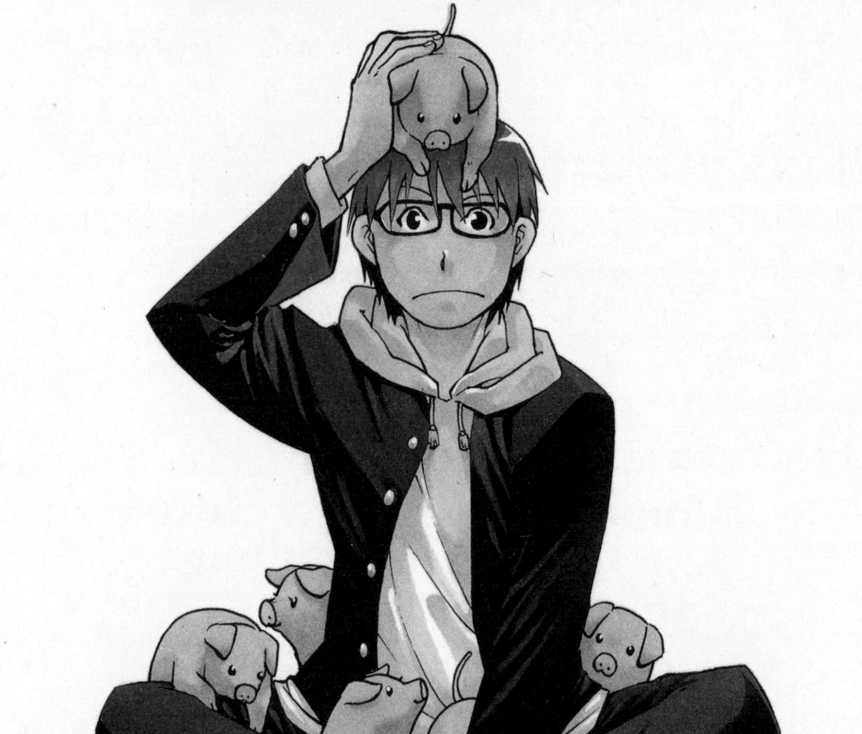

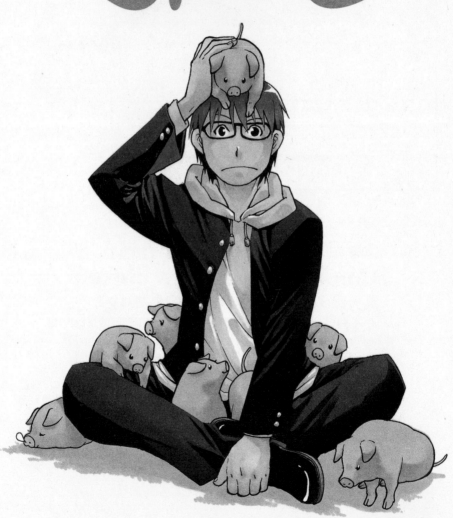

EZO AG'S PRINCIPAL LIVES
BENEATH THE BUTTERBUR LEAVES.

Translation Notes

Common Honorifics
no honorific: Indicates familiarity or closeness; if used without permission or reason, addressing someone in this manner would constitute an insult.
-san: The Japanese equivalent of Mr./Mrs./Miss. If a situation calls for politeness, this is the fail-safe honorific.
-sama: Conveys great respect; may also indicate the social status of the speaker is lower than that of the addressee.
-kun: Used most often when referring to boys, this honorific indicates affection or familiarity. Occasionally used by older men among their peers, but it may also be used by anyone referring to a person of lower standing.
-chan: An affectionate honorific indicating familiarity used mostly in reference to girls; also used in reference to cute persons or animals of either gender.
-sensei: A respectful term for teachers, artists, or high-level professionals.
-niisan, nii-san, aniki, etc.: A term of endearment meaning "big brother" that may be more widely used to address any young man who is like a brother, regardless of whether he is related or not.
-neesan, nee-san, aneki, etc.: The female counterpart of the above, nee-san means "big sister."

Currency Conversion
While conversion rates fluctuate, an easy estimate for Japanese Yen conversion is ¥100 to 1 USD.

Page 12
The cows' names are taken from magazines published by Shogakukan, the Japanese publisher of *Silver Spoon*. *Silver Spoon* appears in the magazine *Weekly Shounen Sunday*; other referenced magazines are *Big Comic (Original)* and *CoroCoro Comic*.

Page 38
The Super Cub is a Honda motorcycle that debuted in 1958.

Page 49
Tokyo U (the University of Tokyo, also known as Todai) is generally considered to be the most prestigious university in Japan.

Page 97
Mukimuki Memorial (or *"Muki ♥ Memo"* for short) is a reference to the classic dating sim series, *Tokimeki Memorial*. The first game was released in 1994. Why *"mukimuki"*? Well, Nishikawa is a potato farmer, and the verb *muku* can mean "to peel."

Page 122
Ramune is a Japanese carbonated soft drink.

Dango are sweet dumplings made from rice flour and often served on a skewer with various sauces or seasonings.

Takoyaki are pan-fried batter balls filled with octopus bits.

Page 124
Yakisoba is a stir-fried noodle dish.

Taiyaki are fish-shaped cakes with filling, most commonly red bean paste.

Ikayaki is grilled squid. At festivals, it's usually grilled tentacle on a stick.

Page 127
Okonomiyaki ("how you want it" grill) is a savory grilled pancake made with flour, eggs, shredded cabbage, and a variety of condiments. In *okonomiyaki* restaurants, you might cook it yourself from the batter and ingredients provided.

Page 134
Bandit fried chicken (*sanzoku-yaki*) is a large teriyaki chicken thigh, deep-fried.

Zangi is Hokkaido-style fried chicken.

Page 146
Sukiyaki is a hot pot dish of thinly sliced meat, vegetables, and other ingredients simmered at the dinner table.

Page 184
In Japanese, "elevator shoes" are called "secret shoes," so not only is the principal trying to appear taller (to no avail), he's also using some cute wordplay as he reveals his secret.

Page 189
It is a running joke that the principal (due to his stature) is a *korpokkur,* a race of tiny people in Ainu folklore that live under butterbur leaves and avoid being seen by humans.

Silver Spoon
HIROMU ARAKAWA

Translation: **Amanda Haley** 🌾 Lettering: **Abigail Blackman**

This book is a work of fiction. Names, characters, places, and incidents are the product
of the author's imagination or are used fictitiously. Any resemblance to actual events,
locales, or persons, living or dead, is coincidental.

GIN NO SAJI SILVER SPOON Vol. 3
by Hiromu ARAKAWA
© 2011 Hiromu ARAKAWA
All rights reserved.
Original Japanese edition published by SHOGAKUKAN.
English translation rights in the United States of America, Canada, the United Kingdom,
Ireland, Australia and New Zealand arranged with SHOGAKUKAN
through Tuttle-Mori Agency, Inc.

English translation © 2018 by Yen Press, LLC

Yen Press
1290 Avenue of the Americas
New York, NY 10104

Visit us at yenpress.com
facebook.com/yenpress
twitter.com/yenpress
yenpress.tumblr.com
instagram.com/yenpress

First Yen Press Edition: June 2018

Yen Press is an imprint of Yen Press, LLC.
The Yen Press name and logo are trademarks of Yen Press, LLC.

The publisher is not responsible for websites (or their
content) that are not owned by the publisher.

Library of Congress Control Number: 2017959207

ISBN: 978-1-9753-2746-0

10 9 8 7 6 5 4 3 2 1

WOR

Printed in the United States of America